ACCOUNTA
FOR
BANKING STUDENTS

by

J. R. Edwards, M.Sc.(Econ.); FCA; ATII
and
H. J. Mellett, B.Sc.(Econ.); FCA

The Institute
of Bankers

10 Lombard Street, London EC3V 9AS

First published: 1983
Reprinted 1984

ISBN: 0 85297 079–X (paperback)

Printed and bound in England by Eyre & Spottiswoode Limited at Grosvenor Press Portsmouth

Preface

Accountancy is a practical subject concerned with the measurement of useful financial information and its communication to interested parties. There are many groups of individuals who use financial information as the basis for resource allocation decisions; these include management, shareholders, bankers, trade suppliers and employees. Because of this common interest in financial information as a basis for decision making, much of the material contained in this book is of equal relevance to each of these groups. Different user groups require financial information for different types of resource allocation decisions however, and this book is primarily written to meet the needs of bankers and, more specifically, to help banking students prepare for and pass the *Accountancy* paper in Stage 2 of The Institute of Bankers examinations.

We have written this text because we believe that, although there are a number of very useful books available, there is no *single* text which entirely meets the needs of students preparing for the IOB *Accountancy* examination. Discussions with accounting teachers and both successful and unsuccessful examination candidates, at conferences and at IOB Local Centre examiners' meetings, have reinforced this view. *Accountancy for Banking Students* is accordingly designed to fill this gap.

The book naturally assumes a basic knowledge of accountancy, particularly the ability to prepare final accounts from either a trial balance or incomplete records, and is organised in such a way as to enable students to proceed from the subject of *Accounts* (at Stage 1 level) to the standard required in the *Accountancy* examination in a series of logical stages. The book contains a full coverage of syllabus topics, and a student who acquires a good understanding of the various matters discussed can be confident of success in the examination.

Chapters 1–3 concentrate on the preparation of company accounts in accordance with the regulations imposed by company law and the professional accounting bodies; they also examine the relationship between the principal financial statements. Chapters

4–6 examine the major departures from single company, historical cost-based financial reports: Chapter 4 deals with the reorganisation of a company's capital structure which usually follows a prolonged period of either successful or disastrous trading results; Chapter 5 deals with the preparation of accounts based on the financial results achieved by a 'group' of related companies; while Chapter 6 examines the effect of inflation on historical cost based accounting reports, and explains the procedures which have been devised to deal with this problem.

Chapters 7–9 cover the use of company accounts as the basis for valuing shares; for assessing a company's past performance and present financial position, and for estimating future prospects. Chapters 10 and 11 examine the financial information and accounting techniques available to management as the basis for reaching resource allocation decisions. Each Chapter is self-contained, and together they comprise a comprehensive treatment of topics at the appropriate level for the *Accountancy* examination. Teachers and students can therefore choose to study topics in whichever order they consider suitable, though we regard as most appropriate the order followed in the text.

Bankers come into contact with the accounting process primarily as users of financial information but we believe that, in order to assess the significance of the information they receive, they must understand both why and how it is prepared. The principal feature of this book is that it combines together an examination of these three major facets of accountancy as a process of communication; namely *why* particular types of financial information are provided, *how* the information is prepared, and the *significance* of the data which are made available. Questions in the *Accountancy* examination reflect this emphasis. The majority of questions contain at least two parts. The first of these calls for the preparation of financial information, while the second part requires the student to explain why it is prepared and/or what the information means.

Accountancy for Banking Students makes extensive use of examples, within each Chapter, both for explanatory purposes and to test the student's understanding of the points discussed. In addition, most Chapters contain a final section which consists of a number of questions which students are expected to work. Many of the examples and most of the questions are taken from past *Accountancy* examination papers; in all cases solutions are provided and, under the heading 'examiner's comments', attention is drawn to aspects of the question which caused candidates particular difficulties. Sometimes the numerical solutions do not represent the only possible arrangement of the figures; also, the comments are not necessarily exhaustive in all cases. This is in the nature of the accounting process; figures mean different things to different people and, as examiners, we look for logical argument rather than conformity to a prescribed model. *Students are strongly urged to work questions* before they look at the solutions. Striving to prepare answers is an essential part of the learning process, and little is gained by simply comparing the question with the solution provided, rather than first working the question.

Some notes on *preparing for the examination* and on *examination technique* are included as an appendix.

Acknowledgments
We wish to thank The Institute of Bankers for permission to reproduce questions from past examination papers, and we acknowledge the help we have received from Don Fiddes, Brian Rawle and John Mortimer, at the Institute, who recognised the need for this book, encouraged us to write it, and provided a great deal of helpful guidance during the course of its preparation. We are also grateful to Howard Burnside of Westpac Banking Corporation for reviewing the original draft and making some useful suggestions for improvement.

Our thanks are also due to Jill Fry and Helen Richards for successfully deciphering and typing successive manuscripts, and to David Whelpton (formerly Deputy Secretary of the Institute) for bringing the book to the point of publication.

Finally we wish to thank Sandie and Penny for their ever-patient support, and we dedicate this book to them and to our children, Ross, Katherine, Ewen, Helen, Catherine and Elizabeth.

J. R. Edwards
H. J. Mellett

University College, Cardiff

Contents

CHAPTER 3   **Valuation of Company Assets
and Liabilities**

CHAPTER 4   **Capital Reduction, Reorganisation
and Reconstruction**

CHAPTER 5 **Group Accounts**

CHAPTER 8 Interpretation of Accounts: Ratio Analysis

CHAPTER 9 Interpretation of Accounts: Funds Flow Analysis

CHAPTER 10   **Internal Accounting Reports**

CHAPTER 11   **Investment Project Appraisal**

List of illustrative examples and questions accompanied by detailed solutions.

Examples and questions taken from past *Accountancy* examination papers of The Institute of Bankers are indicated thus*.

CHAPTER 3   **Valuation of Company Assets and
              Liabilities**

CHAPTER 6 Current Cost Accounting

CHAPTER 7 Share and Business Valuation

CHAPTER 8 Interpretation of Accounts: Ratio Analysis

CHAPTER 9 Interpretation of Accounts: Funds Flow Analysis

CHAPTER 11 Investment Project Appraisal

CHAPTER 1

The Nature and Use of Accounting Statements

1.1 INTRODUCTION

The Institute of Bankers celebrated its centenary in 1979 while the Institute of Chartered Accountants in England and Wales (ICAEW), perhaps the best known British professional accounting body, reached the same historic landmark just one year later. Both accounting and banking have a much longer history, of course, but each recognised the need to establish a formal institute to fulfil a wide range of important functions at about the same time. These functions include, among others, the establishment of educational standards (with examinations leading to universally recognised qualifications); and the provision of a focal point to discuss professional matters. In the case of chartered accountants, the ICAEW has become identified as a single authoritative voice that can speak, on behalf of its practising members, to business, the general public and the government. Both professions have flourished over the last one hundred years, and have made valuable contributions to British economic development. The activities of the banks and the accounting firms complement one another, but there is also some overlap which produces an element of competition, for example, in the field of advice on taxation, and this is healthy and in the customer's interests.

The accountant needs to familiarise himself with certain of the bank's activities, while the banker, who is an important user of financial information, must achieve a thorough knowledge of the nature of the accounting process and the scope and limitations of accounting reports.

It is the purpose of this book to equip the aspiring banker, i.e. the banking student, with some of the tools needed for his chosen profession. The purposes of Chapter 1 are to re-introduce readers to the main accounting reports, which were the subject of their earlier studies in accountancy, and to examine the relationship between these accounting reports.

1.2   THE ACCOUNTING PROCESS

Accounting is essentially concerned with recording, measuring and communicating financial facts to interested parties. The process begins with a transaction, or economic event, such as the delivery of goods, the supply of services, or the receipt or payment of cash. The process ends when this economic event is embodied in a financial statement designed to enable the prospective user to make well-informed decisions, e.g. a bank statement which informs a customer that his bank balance has fallen to a low level might indicate that he should take steps either to reduce the level of his expenditure or to make a formal application for an overdraft facility. The various stages in the accounting process are presented diagrammatically in figure 1.1.

Figure 1.1

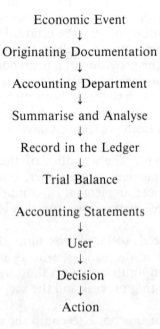

Economic Event
↓
Originating Documentation
↓
Accounting Department
↓
Summarise and Analyse
↓
Record in the Ledger
↓
Trial Balance
↓
Accounting Statements
↓
User
↓
Decision
↓
Action

Originating documents or vouchers are made out as soon as the events occur, and these provide a permanent record of all movements of goods and services or cash into, out of, or within a business. It is important that the document is made out immediately, since any delay increases the risk of an error which can undermine the entire accounting process. The documents and vouchers, recording economic events as they occur, quite naturally originate in many different departments of a company, but copies of all of them are sent to the accounts department where they are summarised, analysed, and then entered in the appropriate ledger account. Periodically, at least once a year, but probably more often, the balances are extracted from the ledger accounts and assembled in a trial balance. There may be some post trial balance adjustments, e.g. an invoice received late from a supplier or an accrual for electricity outstanding but, when these have been made, the final accounts, which consist of a profit and loss account, balance sheet and statement of funds, are prepared. These accounting statements are then made available to both management and a variety of external users to help them reach better informed decisions than would otherwise have been the case. For example, an accounting report which shows management that the menswear department of a retail store is making losses whereas the sporting goods department is prospering may result in floor space being transferred from the former to the latter activity.

If we re-examine the process illustrated and described above, we can see that it contains two basic accounting elements, namely *recording* and *reporting* financial information. In terms of the development of accountancy, the book-keeping function has the far longer history, and evidence exists which shows that accounting records were kept thousands of years ago for control purposes i.e. to provide records of amounts owed, amounts to be collected and properties owned at a particular point in time. In more recent times accounting records have been used increasingly as a basis for preparing accounting reports. Indeed the present day accountant devotes much more of his time to the preparation and interpretation of accounting reports than to book-keeping. Part of the reason for this is that the book-keeping function has been reduced to a fairly routine process, both as the result of increased mechanisation and computerisation, and because of the introduction of more effective systems of internal control. The result is that book-keeping makes few demands on the accountant's professional skill and this leaves him free to devote more time to the reporting function which has grown immensely in importance during the present century.

The emergence of the large scale limited liability company has been the single most important factor stimulating the need for financial reports. In the one-man business there is little need for the development of reporting procedures; the owner/manager retains close contact with all aspects of business activity, and is able to assess progress simply by examining his bank balance and from his direct contact with customers, suppliers, and employees. In this situation, accounting reports provide the owner with little additional information which can help him manage his affairs, and they are prepared only for tax purposes and, in the case of a limited company, to comply with the requirements of the Companies Acts. This changes as businesses increase in size, since it results in the separation of the ownership and managerial functions; it causes top management to become more remote from the shop floor, and it increases companies' reliance on trade credit, the bank and other forms of loan finance. The result is an increase in the demand for accounting information as a basis for investment and credit granting decisions. The various users of accounting reports are considered further in section 1.3.

1.3   USERS OF ACCOUNTING INFORMATION
1.3.1   Internal and External Users
Users of accounting information are conventionally classified as either internal or external to the company. Internal users consist of a single group, namely management, and their access to the company's accounting records is unrestricted. Indeed, it is their responsibility to ensure that the accounting system is suitably designed to make available the range of financial information which management needs as a basis for decision making. If the required information is unavailable, it is fair to say that management has only itself to blame. The position of external users of accounting reports is different. Shareholders are legally entitled to receive a copy of the annual accounts, but that is all. In this context is must be remembered, however, that, in the majority of UK limited companies, the directors hold the majority of the shares and, in those cases, management and ownership coincide. Creditors, on the other hand, will have access to the public information filed with the Registrar of Companies, though they may also be able, in individual cases, to bring pressure on management to disclose more.

It was not so long ago that shareholders and creditors were regarded as the only important external users of accounting reports, but that is no longer the case. In recent years there has developed an increased appreciation of the fact that there exists a large number of groups of individuals who possess a legitimate interest in company performance. In 1975 the accounting profession published a document, called *The Corporate Report*, in an attempt to stimulate discussion concerning the scope and aims of published financial reports in the light of modern needs and conditions. This report lists the following seven user groups who are thought to have a reasonable claim to corporate financial information:

1. The equity investor group including existing and potential shareholders and holders of convertible securities, options or warrants.
2. The loan creditor group including existing and potential holders of debentures and loan stock, and providers of short-term secured and unsecured loans and finance.
3. The employee group including existing, potential and past employees.
4. The analyst-adviser group including financial analysts and journalists, economists, statisticians, researchers, trade unions, stockbrokers and other providers of advisory services such as credit rating agencies.
5. The business contact group including customers, trade creditors and suppliers and in a different sense competitors, business rivals, and those interested in mergers, amalgamations and takeovers.
6. The government including tax authorities, departments and agencies concerned with the supervision of commerce and industry, and local authorities.
7. The public including taxpayers, ratepayers, consumers and other community and special interest groups such as political parties, consumer and environmental protection societies and regional pressure groups.

Each of the above groups has a common interest in company accounts, but they will use the financial information available to them as the basis for often quite different decisions. For instance, the equity investor group, i.e. shareholders, will want help in reaching share trading decisions: whether to retain their present investment, whether to increase it, or whether to dispose of their shareholding. Employees, on the other hand, require financial information to help assess employment prospects and also for the purpose of collective bargaining. There are significant variations :

the quantity of financial information made available to each of these groups, and this is caused by differential legal requirements, voluntary decisions by management to make financial information available to particular users, and the ability of certain individuals to succeed in demanding additional disclosure.

1.3.2 Bankers as Users of Accounting Information The bank is not listed as a separate user group, in *The Corporate Report*, but it clearly falls into the 'loan creditor group' category. The bank is an extremely important source of corporate finance, particularly in recent years when profits have been low and companies have been unable to finance as much activity from internally generated funds. In 1981, for instance, net advances to limited companies amounted to £4,445m, which was 42% of the total additional finance made available from external sources including share issues (Central Statistical Office, *Financial Statistics*). It must also be remembered that banks provide a vast amount of financial support for unincorporated enterprises, namely sole traders and partnerships.

Bankers are therefore substantial users of accounting information, both to help them reach an initial loan decision and also to monitor progress after the advance has been made. In the past, finance provided by the clearing banks invariably took the form of an overdraft or short-term loan, though in practice these facilities were in many cases effectively transformed into long-term finance as the result of periodic renewal. Nevertheless, the advances remained technically subject to repayment on call or at short notice. In recent years, however, the banks have become more willing to make a longer-term commitment, both in recognition of the changing nature of companies' financial requirements, and as a result of increased competition from other financial institutions. Whether the advance is short-term, medium-term or long-term, the banker will want to satisfy himself on the following points, namely that:

1. the company will be able to meet the interest payments accruing during the period of the loan;
2. the company will be able to repay the capital sum at the end of the loan period;
3. the company is able to offer adequate security, e.g. the assets owned by the company are expected to remain sufficient to cover the amount of the loan after first meeting all prior claims;

4. the loan does not contravene any restrictive covenants contained in the company's articles of association, e.g. these may provide that loans are not to exceed a certain percentage of the shareholders' equity.

Although the above features are common to all loan appraisals, the banker is likely to emphasize different aspects of his investigation depending on the expected duration of the loan. For a short-term loan, the banker will be interested in estimates of the net cash flow over the next few months, whereas for a longer term advance the banker will need to be convinced that the company is financially stable and that adequate profits will be earned throughout the foreseeable future. The ability of a borrower to repay both the interest and capital sum will be the banker's prime consideration, and if forecasts indicate that these conditions cannot be met the advance will not be made. However, even the best laid plans may be thwarted by unexpected events, and adequate security should be obtained. Prospective borrowers will be expected to meet this latter condition, irrespective of whether the loan is short- or long-term, but the degree of risk increases with the duration of the loan, and this will be in the banker's mind when assessing whether the security offered is acceptable (i.e. an asset which might be expected to retain its value in the short-term only would not be acceptable as security for a long-term advance).

The bank manager will normally expect to receive a copy of the company's most recent annual accounts in order to help him to reach a loan decision. In general, however, the annual accounts will only satisfy the banker's information requirements to a limited extent. This is because:

1. they will be out of date. If the accounts are prepared on a calendar year basis, they are unlikely to be available until March or April of the following year. These will be of limited use to a banker who is asked for money in April and even less useful when the loan request is made later in the year. For instance, the accounts may list an asset which would be considered ideal security, but this information is of no use to the bank if the asset has since been sold;

2. the annual accounts are past history, whereas the banker wants to know what is likely to happen to the company in the future. Last year's accounts may show a good profit and a steady financial position, but trading conditions are subject to constant change, and a series of setbacks may result in

heavy losses and a rapid deterioration in the company's financial structure.

Both these criticisms point to the need for additional, more relevant, accounting information. Fortunately the bank is usually in a good position to ensure that appropriate data is provided, since failure or refusal to make available the required information will result in rejection of the request for finance. The banker will require special-purpose reports which enable him to appraise the future prospects of the company, including its ability to make the necessary interest and loan repayments. These reports will probably consist of an up-to-date statement of the company's financial position, and forecast accounts which set out estimates of future cash flows and profitability. The period covered by these forecasts should coincide with the expected duration of the loan so that the banker can make a rational assessment of the company's ability to meet the conditions imposed for repayment.

Much of the accounting information which the banker requires will often be readily available. For example, where finance is required for a new project, the kind of estimates referred to above should already have been prepared in order to enable management to decide whether the proposed course of action is worthwhile. This will not always be the case, however, particularly where the customer is a small business which does not operate a formal management accounting system. In this latter situation, relevant financial estimates must nevertheless be obtained from the businessman, although he may receive some professional advice either from an accountant or from the banker himself in order to comply with this requirement. The banker must however guard against making unnecessary demands for information, since compliance might prove unduly costly and cause the potential customer to look towards alternative sources of finance. This is not to suggest that the banker should 'make do' where inadequate financial details are supplied, but it does point to the need for him to make a realistic assessment of his requirements in the light of the customer's request. In all cases the bank manager should be on the lookout for any display of excessive optimism on the part of management, and must consider the likely effect of actual results falling signficantly below expectations. In this context, particular attention will be paid to the accuracy of any past forecasts prepared by management, and to the banker's assessment of his customer's personality. Many of the management accounting techniques which are used to assess future prospects, and are therefore of interest to bankers, are considered in Chapters 9–11.

After the advance has been made, it is important to ensure that progress is properly monitored. Again the annual accounts will not normally satisfy the banker's information requirements; he should also insist that the borrower prepares and submits regular, perhaps quarterly, accounts which show profit earned to date and the developing financial condition of the company. Quite possibly the accounts will show that results are coming up to expectations, or at least that they are sufficiently favourable to enable the borrower to meet the conditions of the loan. In either case repayment will take the expected course. Alternatively, trading conditions may prove unfavourable with the result that the accounts show large losses and a rapidly deteriorating financial condition. Whether the loan can be 'called in' depends on the terms and conditions of the advance, but wherever possible the banker should take prompt action to obtain repayment before the company's assets are reduced even further by continuing losses.

1.4 REVISION OF PRINCIPAL ACCOUNTING STATEMENTS

Readers will be familiar with the nature of the profit and loss account and balance sheet from their earlier studies, and they should also have had a great deal of practice in preparing these two accounting statements. Final accounts questions, at The Institute of Bankers Stage 1 level, typically involve either one of the following two possibilities depending on whether the firm operates a formal system for recording business transactions:

1. Candidates are given a trial balance, together with a list of necessary adjustments, and are required to prepare final accounts.
2. Candidates are given lists of assets and liabilities at the beginning and end of an accounting period, together with details of *cash* transactions during the year, and asked to prepare final accounts.

Example 1.1 (see below), taken from a past Stage 1 examination paper, falls into the former category. Readers are strongly urged to work this question and to compare their answer with the solution provided. They should also work questions 1.1 and 1.2, contained in section 7 of this chapter, in order to make sure that they possess the basic accounting skills required by candidates *beginning* a Stage 2 course leading to the *Accountancy* exam.

Example 1.1

The following trial balance was extracted from the books of Lingford Ltd. as at 31 December, 19X1:

	£	£
Share capital		50,000
Share premium		8,000
Motor vans at cost	40,000	
Provision for depreciation at 1 January, 19X1		14,800
Purchases	129,938	
Sales		179,422
Rent and rates	2,500	
General expenses	5,842	
Wages	19,876	
Bad debts	542	
Provision for doubtful debts at 1 January, 19X1		684
Directors' salaries	16,000	
Trade debtors and trade creditors	16,941	11,171
Stock at 1 January, 19X1	28,572	
Bank balance	24,921	
Profit and loss account as at 1 January, 19X1		21,055
	£285,132	£285,132

You are given the following additional information:
  (i)   the authorised and issued share capital is 50,000 ordinary shares of £1 each;
  (ii) wages due but unpaid at 31 December, 19X1 amounted to £264;
  (iii) the provision for doubtful debts is to be increased by £102;
  (iv) stock at 31 December, 19X1 was £38,292;
  (v)   rent and rates amounting to £300 were paid in advance at 31 December, 19X1;
  (vi) depreciation on motor vans is to be charged at the rate of 20 per cent per annum on cost;
  (vii) it is proposed to pay a dividend of £5,000 for the year 19X1.

REQUIRED: A trading and profit and loss account for the year 19X1, not necessarily in a form for publication, and a balance sheet as at 31 December, 19X1.
NOTE: Ignore taxation

Solution

Workings

The journal entries given below may be used to incorporate the effect of the adjustments required by the additional information (ii)–(vii). Students may alternatively prefer to omit journal entries and make the adjustments directly to the relevant totals given in the trial balance.

Journal entries (narrative omitted)	£	£
(ii) Wages	264	
Accrued expense		264
(iii) Bad debts	102	
Provision for doubtful debts		102
(iv) Stock	38,292	
Cost of goods sold		38,292
(v) Prepaid expense	300	
Rent and rates		300
(vi) Depreciation	8,000	
Provision for depreciation		8,000
(vii) Dividend	5,000	
Proposed dividend		5,000

Trading and Profit and Loss Account of Lingford Ltd. for 19X1	£	£
Sales		179,422
Less: Stock at 1 January, 19X1	28,572	
Purchases	129,938	
Stock at 31 December, 19X1	(38,292)	
Cost of goods sold		120,218
Gross profit		59,204
Less: Depreciation	8,000	
Rent and rates (2,500–300)	2,200	
General expenses	5,842	
Wages (19,876 + 264)	20,140	
Bad debts (542 + 102)	644	
Directors' salaries	16,000	52,826
Net profit		6,378
Add: Profit and loss account at 1 January, 19X1		21,055
		27,433
Less: Dividend		5,000
Retained profit		22,433

Balance Sheet of Lingford Ltd. as at 31 December, 19X1
Fixed Assets

	£	£
Motor vans at cost		40,000
Less: Provision for depreciation		22,800
		17,200

Current assets

Stock	38,292	
Trade debtors, less provision for doubtful debts (16,941–786)	16,155	
Prepaid expense	300	
Bank balance	24,921	
	79,668	

Less: Current Liabilities

Creditors and accruals (11,171 + 264)	11,435	
Proposed dividend	5,000	
	16,435	
Working Capital		63,233
		80,433

Financed by:

Authorised and issued ordinary share capital (£1 shares)		50,000
Share premium account		8,000
Retained profit		22,433
		£80,433

The above accounts are presented in the vertical format which is popular with companies today.

The preparation of final accounts is a topic which we will return to and develop at various stages in this book. Chapters 2 and 3 are concerned with the preparation of final accounts in accordance with the requirements of the Companies Acts and the regulations imposed by the professional accounting bodies. Chapter 5 deals with the preparation of consolidated accounts for a group of companies; Chapter 6 examines the effect of inflation accounting procedures on final accounts, while Chapters 9 and 10 include discussion of the preparation and use of forecast final accounts.

1.5   DIFFERENT MEASURES OF BUSINESS ACTIVITY

The balance sheet and the profit and loss account are quite different accounting statements, both in terms of the form which they take and the information which they are designed to communicate. The balance sheet is a summary of the assets belonging to a company and the various ways in which these assets are financed, i.e. it is a document which might be regarded as setting out the financial 'state of play' as at a *particular date*. It has been described as an instantaneous photograph of the business, and this is an apt metaphor, but like all photographs it does not tell the whole story, merely the situation at a particular point in time. A day later, or a day earlier, the financial photograph might look quite different. For example, a medium-term loan raised on the last day of an accounting period might immediately transform the short-term financial position of a company from weak to healthy. Fraudulent manipulation of accounting information is unusual, but 'window-dressing' is more common and users of accounts should keep an eye open for procedures which improve the apparent profitability or financial condition of a company.

The profit and loss account, on the other hand, is intended to supply information concerning events which have occurred *during* an accounting period. The relationship between the two statements is indicated by figure 1.2.

Figure 1.2

The company is formed on 1 January, 19X1 and the first year's annual accounts deal with the year to 31 December, 19X1. These will consist of a profit and loss account covering the period from formation to December 31, and a balance sheet which sets out the financial position at the year end. Balance sheets will subsequently be prepared at twelve monthly intervals during the life of the company, and profit and loss accounts will be based on transactions which have occurred between the date of the previous balance sheet and the date of the current balance sheet.

The drawback of the profit and loss account is that, although it provides certain useful information concerning progress made during a particular accounting period, it does not tell us all that we want to know, e.g. it does not tell us how much the company has spent on fixed assets during the year. To provide a comprehensive view of financial progress, three financial statements must be prepared based on the transactions that have occurred during an accounting period. These are:

1. The profit and loss account.
2. The statement of source and application of working capital.
3. The cash statement.

The preparation of these three 'flow' statements is illustrated in example 1.2.

Example 1.2

The following information is provided in respect of Sprouse Ltd.:

Summarised profit and Loss Account for 19X1

	£000	£000
Sales		2,200
Less: Stock at 1 January, 19X1	500	
Purchases	1,500	
Stock at 31 December, 19X1	(600)	
Cost of goods sold		1,400
Gross Profit		800
Less: Depreciation	350	
Other expenses	170	
		520
Net Profit		280

Balance Sheet as at 31 December, 19X1

19X0 £000		£000	£000
2,200	Fixed assets at cost		3,400
350	Less: Provision for depreciation		700
1,850			2,700
	Current Assets		
500	Stock	600	
300	Trade debtors	360	
250	Bank balance	140	
1,050		1,100	
	Less: Current Liabilities		
500	Trade creditors	520	
550	Working capital		580
2,400			3,280
	Financed by:		
1,400	Share capital		2,000
1,000	Retained profit		1,280
2,400			£3,280

'Other expenses' are paid for in cash immediately. The company issued 600,000 £1 shares at par during the year and purchased fixed assets costing £1,200,000.

REQUIRED

The following financial statements for 19X1:

  (i) The profit and loss account
  (ii) The statement of source and application of working capital
  (iii) The cash statement

Solution

It is first necessary to calculate receipts and payments for inclusion in the cash statement.

	Receipts £000	Payments £000
Sales and purchases	2,200	1,500
Add: Opening debtors and creditors	300	500
Less: Closing debtors and creditors	(360)	(520)
	2,140	1,480

Financial Statements for 19X1	Profit Flows £000	Working Capital Flows £000	Cash Flows £000
Revenue flows:			
In Sales	2,200	2,200	
Receipts from customers			2,140
Out Purchases	(1,500)	(1,500)	
Increase in stock	100	100	
Cost of goods sold	(1,400)	(1,400)	
Payments to suppliers			(1,480)
Depreciation	(350)		
Other expenses	(170)	(170)	(170)
	(1,920)	(1,570)	(1,650)
Internally generated flows	280	630	490
Capital flows:			
In Share capital		600	600
Out Fixed assets		(1,200)	(1,200)
Net flow	280	30	(110)

Each of the above accounting statements is based on the transactions undertaken by Sprouse Ltd. *during* 19X1, but they contain different information and report widely divergent *net* 'flows'. The differences can be explained numerically by means of a series of reconciliations:

1. Net profit reconciled with the increase in working capital.

		£000
Profit earned		280
Add: Depreciation		350
Working capital generated from operations		630
Less: Capital outflows minus capital inflows		600
Increase in working capital		30

Depreciation must be added back to profit because it is a 'book entry' and does not represent an outflow of working capital (see Chapter 9, section 2.1). An issue of shares and the purchase of fixed assets, on the other hand, are capital transactions which do not affect profit but respectively increase and diminish working capital.

2. Increase in working capital reconciled with the reduction in cash.

	£000	£00
Increase in working capital		30
Add: Increase in trade creditors		20
		50
Less: Increase in stock	100	
Increase in debtors	60	
		160
Reduction in bank balance		110

The items appearing in the above reconciliation occur because the working capital statement is based on movements of *goods* (when a credit purchase takes place creditors and stock increase, while a credit sale causes stock to diminish and debtors to increase), whereas the cash statement reports the flow of money into and out of the business. During 19X1, Sprouse made purchases totalling £1,500,000, but payments to suppliers amounted only to £1,480,000, and so the difference of £20,000 is a temporary source of finance. Conversely, the extra investment of £160,000 in stock and debtors is a drain on the company's cash resources.

3. Net profit reconciled with the reduction in cash

	£000	£000
Profit earned		280
Add: Depreciation		350
Increase in trade creditors		20
		650
Less: Increase in stock	100	
Increase in debtors	60	
		160
Cash generated from operations		490
Less: Capital outflows minus capital inflows		600
Reduction in bank balance		110

It will be noticed that the above calculation comprises a combination of the items included in both the previous reconciliations. This is because the cash statement takes no account of the accruals concept, which forms the basis for calculating figures for inclusion in the profit and loss account, while the profit and loss account ignores capital inflows and outflows which are included in the cash statement.

The financial totals contained in each of the above three statements differ, but this is because each document is designed to focus attention on contrasting aspects of the company's progress. These objectives are examined below, and illustrated by reference to example 1.2.

1.5.1 The Profit and Loss Account The three functions of this document are:

1. to show how much profit has been earned. The importance traditionally attached to the profit and loss account (the term is used here to cover the manufacturing account, trading account, general profit and loss account and appropriation account) is attributable to the fact that the wellbeing of a company substantially depends on whether sufficient profits are generated for the following two purposes:

   (a) Dividends. A company must be able to pay shareholders a reasonable return on their investment. Alternatively, in the case of an unincorporated enterprise, profits must be sufficient to cover the owners' drawings.

   (b) Expansion. Management will normally wish to expand the level of business activities and, although some of the finance required is likely to be raised externally, the remainder must be provided out of retained profit.

2. to explain how the reported balance of profit was computed. Users will want to assess the adequacy of reported profit, and for this reason the calculation of profit, by matching expenditure with revenue, is given 'above the line' in the manufacturing account, trading account and general profit and loss account. This will, for instance, enable the user to compare profit with sales and also calculate the gross profit mark-up. Additional information, such as the balance sheet figure for net assets and the results achieved by other firms, will of course be needed in order to make a more comprehensive assessment of the company's performance;

3. to show the disposition of reported profit. The allocation of profit between retention and distribution, is shown 'below the line' in the profit and loss appropriation account.

1.5.2 The Statement of Source and Application of Working Capital Readers will be familiar with the basic calculations involved in preparing the Statement of Source and Application of

Working Capital from their earlier work on the Statement of Funds. There is, however, a difference between the two documents which needs to be pointed out. The title of the former document describes exactly what it does; it lists transactions which cause *working capital* to increase and to decrease. The statement of funds provides this information, but it *also* includes a statement which analyses the net change in working capital into increases and decreases in individual current assets and current liability balances. The additional data thus provided is identical to that contained in reconciliation 2, above, though the presentation is a little different. The statement of funds is discussed further in Chapter 9.

The statement of source and application of working capital is a similar type of document to the profit and loss account: each measures the flow of resources through the firm, but the statement focusses attention on a quite different financial magnitude—working capital rather than profit. The importance of profit is discussed above, but an adequate balance of working capital is just as crucial to a firm's wellbeing, otherwise it will be unable to pay its debts as they fall due. The situation where a businessman has failed to attach due significance to both profit and working capital is, however, familiar to the experienced bank manager. The normal sequence is for the entrepreneur to identify a promising new project, to embark upon the project, to discover that it is under-capitalised, and then to approach the bank manager for a loan or an overdraft facility. The bank manager is unlikely to provide the finance requested unless a thorough appraisal of the financial implications of the project is first undertaken. This exercise should have taken place before the project was begun, and the belated analysis may well show that management's initial optimism was unfounded, in which case the finance will be refused and the company may fail. This emphasises the need for plans to be prepared, in advance, which assess both the profitability and the financial implications of a proposed project.

The statement is primarily designed to focus attention on developments in the company's financial structure, but it is worth noting that the figure for 'working capital from operations' is sometimes used to assess trading performance. This is because both profit and working capital from operations are measures of internally generated flows of resources, but the latter is less easily manipulated than the former. More specifically, the extent of the charge for depreciation, debited to the profit and loss account, depends on managerial estimates of the useful life and scrap value of the company's fixed assets. It also depends a great deal on the depreciation method employed. Cases have been known where management has taken an excessively optimistic view regarding say the life of the asset, and this has resulted in the charge being reduced and profit being artificially inflated. The auditor will of course try to guard against this happening, but it is nevertheless worthwhile to compare different years' figures for working capital generated from operations to see whether they show the same trend as reported profits. Any marked difference should be investigated.

The numerical difference between profit and the net change in working capital, over a twelve month period, is presented succinctly in reconciliation 1, above, based on the information contained in example 1.2. This shows that the working capital *generated from operations* is arrived at by adding back to profit any expenses which do not involve an outflow of funds, while the overall net change in working capital also takes account of inflows and outflows of capital. The figure for working capital generated from operations will therefore always exceed profit (if there is a loss, working capital will decline by a lesser amount and may even show an increase), but the net change in working capital will be either higher or lower than profit depending on the size and direction of the capital flows. In example 1.2 capital outflows, in the form of expenditure on fixed assets, exceed inflows from the share issue by £600,000, and the overall effect is a net increase in working capital of only £30,000, whereas reported profit amounted to £280,000.

1.5.3 The Cash Statement Cash has been described as the 'life blood' of a business, and it is fair to say that a company will only survive and prosper, in the long run, if it is able to generate sufficient cash inflows to cover cash outflows. It does not necessarily follow, of course, that cash inflows must match cash outflows in any individual accounting period, and, moreover, it is quite possible for a company to report a substantial profit for a year during which the cash balance has fallen, and vice versa. For example, Sprouse (example 1.2) earned a satisfactory profit during 19X1, and the working capital also increased, but cash went down by £110,000, mainly as the result of heavy expenditure on fixed assets. This may not turn out to be a cause for concern, but it is an important financial development and its significance must be carefully assessed. The purposes of the cash statement are, therefore, to report the net change in the cash balance and to help explain how the surplus or deficit arose by listing the cash inflows and cash outflows which occurred during the accounting period.

An important virtue of the cash statement, by comparison with the other two flow statements is that it is based on 'hard facts'. The profit and loss account is prepared in accordance with the accruals concept which translates receipts and payments into revenues and expenditures for reporting purposes. This is done so that the resulting figure for profit can be used to assess trading performance, but it obliges management and the accountant to exercise a great deal of subjective judgement which considerably increases the scope for error and bias. The statement of source and application of working capital is less susceptible to error because those charges made in the profit and loss account which involve a great deal of subjective judgement, e.g. depreciation, are not deducted when calculating working capital generated from operations. However, sales revenue and the items of expenditure which are listed in the statement of source and application of working capital are subject to the accruals concept, and some scope for error and bias therefore remains. To summarise: calculation of the increase or decrease in working capital depends for its accuracy on estimates of doubtful debts and the valuation of closing stock, while the net profit figure is also subject to any errors made when computing the depreciation charge. None of these uncertainties arise when preparing the cash statement.

The purpose of the above discussion is to show that each of the three flow statements have different rather than conflicting objectives. None of the three documents should be considered inherently superior, and they should be used to complement each other when an attempt is made to assess financial developments. Until about twenty years ago, British companies' published accounts supplemented the balance sheet only with a profit and loss account, though the other two flow documents were often prepared for internal use. The need for additional accounting information was gradually recognised, however, and the voluntary publication of a statement of funds became fairly common practice during the 1960s. In 1975 the accounting profession made publication compulsory for most companies. Little interest has been shown in an historical statement of cash flows, probably because much of the relevant information appears at the foot of the statement of funds, but there is a much stronger demand for the publication of cash forecasts which company directors have, in the main, resisted.

Readers should test their understanding of the calculations and concepts discussed so far by working example 1.3 taken from The Institute of Bankers April 1982 *Accountancy* examination.

Example 1.3

The following financial information is provided in respect of the affairs of Pontcanna plc.

Balances at:	1 January 1981 £000	31 December 1981 £000
Stock and work in progress	876	921
Trade debtors less provision for doubtful debts	534	617
Trade creditors	261	309
Plant at cost	1,300	1,500
Debenture interest outstanding	—	18

Transactions during 1981 included:	£000
Receipts from customers	2,160
Purchases	1,245
Administration and other expenses paid in cash	702
Purchase of plant, 1 January 1981	200
Issue of 12% debentures for cash 1 January 1981	300

Plant is depreciated at the rate of 10% per annum on cost. The provision for doubtful debts at 31 December 1981 has been increased by £54,000.

Required:

(a) The following financial statements for 1981:

(i) Profit and loss account.

(ii) Source and application of working capital.

(iii) Receipts and payments of cash.

The statements should be presented in the following form:

	Profit & Loss Account £000	Source and Application of Working Capital £000	Receipts and Payments of Cash £000
Inflows:			
Less Outflows:			
Purchases			
Payments			
Administration and other expenses			
Etc.			
Net inflow (outflow)			

[16]

(b) The following reconciliations based on the figures calculated in your answers to (a).

(i) Net profit or loss with net increase or decrease in working capital.

(ii) Net increase or decrease in working capital with net increase or decrease in cash. [8]

(c) An explanation of the various ways in which financial information contained in the profit and loss account and the statement of source and application of working capital may be used to assess corporate progress.

[6]

Note:

It is essential that candidates show how they arrive at each of the figures in their answer to this question.

[Total marks for question—30]

Solution

(a) *Workings:*

	£000			£000
(i) Sales:		(ii)	Payments to suppliers:	
Receipts from customers	2,160		Purchases	1,245
Add: Increase in debtors less provision for doubtful debts	83		*Less:* Increase in creditors	48
Increase in provision for doubtful debts	54			
	2,297			1,197

	£000
(iii) Debenture interest charge:	
Debenture interest paid	18
Debenture interest outstanding	18
	36

		Profit & Loss Account £000	Source and Application of Working Capital £000	Receipts and Payments of Cash £000
Inflows:	Sales	2,297	2,297	
	Receipts			2,160
	Debentures		300	300
		2,297	2,597	2,460
Outflows:	Purchases	1,245	1,245	
	Increase in stock and work in progress	(45)	(45)	
	Cost of sales	1,200	1,200	
	Payments to suppliers			1,197
	Administration and other expenses	702	702	702
	Provision for doubtful debts	54	54	
	Depreciation	150		
	Debenture interest	36	36	18
	Purchase of plant		200	200
		2,142	2,192	2,117
Net inflow		155	405	343

			£000	£000
(b)	(i)	Net profit		155
		Add: Depreciation		150
		Working capital generated from operations		305
		Add: Debenture issued	300	
		Less: Purchase of plant	200	
			—	100
		Increase in working capital		405
	(ii)	Increase in working capital		405
		Add: Debenture interest outstanding		18
		Increase in creditors		48
				471
		Less: Increase in stock and work in progress	45	
		Increase in debtors	83	
			—	128
		Increase in cash		343

(c) The profit and loss account identifies the increase, or decrease, in shareholders' wealth during a particular accounting period; it also provides a measure of the effectiveness with which management has utilised the resources available to it. Because the profit and loss account contains details of the various items of income and expenditure, it helps to explain why the company has made a profit or incurred a loss during the year. The profit and loss account does not comprise a full record of transactions affecting the financial position of the company. The account lists only revenue and expenditure; capital transactions are entirely excluded.

The purpose of the statement of source and application of working capital is to provide a full record of the financial transactions undertaken during an accounting period. It is intended to provide an insight into the financial policy pursued by management during the year and the effect of that policy on the financial structure and stability of the concern.

Examiner's comments: Most common errors:
1. Failure to allocate capital flows to the appropriate accounting statements, i.e. the statements of source and application of working capital and receipts and payments of cash.
2. Failure to apply the accruals concept to the appropriate accounting statements, i.e. the statement of source and application of working capital and the profit and loss account.
3. Reconciliations called for under (b) often not attempted.

1.6 PROFIT, WORKING CAPITAL AND CASH:
Some popular misconceptions and errors

It should be clear from the discussion in section 5 of this Chapter that there is not necessarily a close correspondence between profit and the net increase or decrease in working capital or cash. Indeed, it is possible to think up examples of business transactions which affect just one of the balances, any two of them, all three, or none at all. Questions are sometimes asked (e.g. question 5 on the September 1982 paper, reproduced as Question 1.4 in section 7 of this Chapter) which test the candidate's understanding of the effect of a number of proposed transactions and adjustments on various financial magnitudes. Some of the common misconceptions revealed and errors made when answering this type of question are discussed below.

1.6.1 Bonus Issue of Shares Profits earned and retained within a business remain legally available for distribution, though in practice this will not normally be possible as reinvestment in business assets is likely to have taken place, i.e. the resources will have been used to finance expansion. A bonus issue (sometimes called a capitalisation issue or scrip issue) recognises this fact and is accounted for by making an appropriate transfer from reserves to the share capital account.

Example 1.4

Balance Sheet Extract

	£
Authorised Share Capital. £1,000,000 divided into ordinary shares of £1 each	
Issued Share Capital. 300,000 ordinary shares of £1 each fully paid ..	300,000
Reserves	650,000
	950,000

Show the revised balance sheet extract, assuming the company makes a bonus issue of two for one, thereby capitalising £600,000 of the balance on reserves.

Revised Balance Sheet Extract

	£
Authorised Share Capital. £1,000,000, divided into ordinary shares of £1 each	
Issued Share Capital. 900,000 ordinary shares of £1 each fully paid ..	900,000
Reserves	50,000
	950,000

The term 'bonus issue' is something of a misnomer since no one receives any tangible benefit, neither the company nor the shareholders. In the company's books an entry is made to record the transfer from reserves to share capital, but that is all. As far as the shareholders are concerned, they have three times as many shares, but the book value of their equity interest remains unchanged at £950,000 and the market value of each share will fall to approximately one third of the former price. The issue therefore affects neither profit, nor working capital, nor cash. (Bonus issues are examined in detail in Chapter 4).

1.6.2 Varying the Depreciation Charge A popular misconception is that the quantity of funds available to a business can be altered by varying the depreciation charge, and that a company's cash difficulties can therefore be solved by increasing the amount deducted in the profit and loss account. It seems likely that the reason for this misunderstanding is the conventional presentation of data in the Statement of Source and Application of Funds.

Example 1.5

Extract from a Statement of Source and Application of Funds

SOURCE	£
Net profit	325,000
Add: Depreciation	200,000
Funds generated from operations	525,000

Show the revised extract assuming the depreciation charge is increased to £300,000.

Revised Extract from a Statement of Source and Application of Funds

SOURCE	£
Net profit	225,000
Add: Depreciation	300,000
Funds generated from operations	525,000

The above format shows depreciation as a source of funds, and it might seem reasonable to assume that available funds can therefore be increased by raising the amount of the charge, but this would be wrong. Depreciation is a deduction in the profit and loss account and, if the charge is increased to £300,000, profit is reduced to £225,000 but funds generated internally remain unchanged at £525,000. The important point which the student should therefore grasp is that the funds available are increased as the result of profitable trading activity: the depreciation charge earmarks a proportion of those funds for retention in the business, but it cannot affect their volume.

1.6.3 Revaluation of Fixed Assets Fixed assets are reported in a company's balance sheet at their original cost less accumulated depreciation to date. As time goes by it is possible that a large discrepancy will arise between the original cost of a fixed asset and its present-day value. Management might therefore decide to remove the undervaluation, perhaps because it intends to raise a loan and wishes to show the assets available as security at their true value. Freeholds are the most likely subject for this type of adjustment, partly because they are ideal security for a loan and partly because the excess of current value over book value is likely to be much greater than for other fixed assets.

Example 1.6

Balance Sheet Extract

	£
Freehold property at cost	500,000
Less: Accumulated depreciation	100,000
	400,000

Show the revised balance sheet extracts assuming the freehold property is revalued professionally at £1,000,000.

The freehold will be reported at £1,000,000, and the revaluation surplus of £600,000 is credited to 'Revaluation reserve' which appears immediately after share capital in the company's balance sheet.

Revised Balance Sheet Extract

	£
Freehold property at professional revaluation	1,000,000
Share Capital	xxxxxxx
Revaluation reserve	600,000

We can see that once again the adjustment is merely a book entry, and in this case affects neither reported profit, nor working capital nor cash.

1.6.4 Change in Credit Periods Allowed or Received The period of credit allowed to customers may be increased as part of a strategy designed to improve the attractiveness of a company's products. Alternatively, or in addition, a company may pay its trade creditors more quickly in order to obtain discounts for prompt settlement. Changing the period of credit allowed or received will have direct implications for cash flow, but will affect neither working capital nor profit unless discounts are involved.

Example 1.7

Balance Sheet Extracts

	£
Current Assets:	
Stock	90,000
Trade debtors	60,000
Bank balance	70,000
	220,000
Less Current Liabilities:	
Trade creditors	40,000
Working capital	180,000

Produce the revised balance sheet extracts assuming that twice the period of credit had been allowed customers, so that the year end balance for trade debtors becomes £120,000 i.e. it is assumed for simplicity that the level of sales is not affected by the new policy.

The extra credit allowed to customers results in a reduction of £60,000 in the amount of cash collected:

Revised Balance Sheet Extracts

	£
Current Assets:	
Stock	90,000
Trade debtors	120,000
Bank balance	10,000
	220,000
Less: Current Liabilities:	
Trade creditors	40,000
Working capital	180,000

Note: Working capital and profit remain unchanged.

1.6.5   Change of Accounting Policy   Students will be familiar with the fact that a number of different methods exist for valuing business assets. Fixed assets may be depreciated on the straight line basis, reducing balance basis, or in accordance with usage, while stock may be valued on the marginal cost or total cost basis, and purchases may be matched with sales using the last in first out (LIFO) or first in first out (FIFO) cost flow assumption. This is not an exhaustive list of the alternatives available, even for fixed assets and stocks, but it demonstrates the fact that a wide range of options exist, and it is management's job to choose between them. Sometimes management changes its mind and decides to adopt a new method of valuation, e.g. it may decide to change from the marginal cost to the total cost method of stock valuation. This will result in closing stock being revalued upwards, by, say, £100,000, but the important point for students to grasp is that the whole of this increase is *not* reported as profit arising during the current accounting period. There will have been stocks on hand at the beginning of the accounting period, and these must also be restated at a total cost valuation and the increase recorded as profit arising in prior accounting periods.

Example 1.8

Trading Account for 19X1

	£000	£000
Sales		1,400
Less: Opening stock valued at marginal cost	200	
Cost of goods manufactured during 19X1	900	
Less: Closing stock valued at marginal cost	(280)	
Cost of goods sold		820
Gross Profit		580

Produce the revised trading account for 19X1 assuming that stock is to be accounted for on the total cost basis and the following valuations are obtained:

At 1 January, 19X1	£250,000
At 31 December, 19X1	£360,000

Revised Trading Account for 19X1

	£000	£000
Sales		1,400
Less: Opening stock valued at total cost	250	
Cost of goods manufactured during 19X1	900	
Less: Closing stock valued at total cost	(360)	
Cost of goods sold		790
Gross Profit		610

Notes:
1. Closing stock has been revalued upwards by £80,000 (£360,000–£280,000), of which £50,000 (the difference between the opening figure of stock on the two valuation bases) is attributable to prior accounting periods and should be added to profit brought forward. The remaining £30,000 is reported as additional profit for the current accounting period, and increases gross profit from £580,000 to £610,000.
2. Stocks are included in the balance sheet at £380,000 and the reported value of working capital therefore increases by £80,000.
3. Cash is not affected by changing the method of stock valuation.

1.6.6 Reserves Where an examination question shows a company in financial difficulties and under pressure from its creditors, students often suggest that the company can solve its cash problems by using the reserves to pay outstanding liabilities. This is, of course, quite wrong, and reveals a total misunderstanding of the relationship which exists between sources of finance and assets as exhibited in a company's balance sheet.

Example 1.9

Summarised Balance Sheet as at 31 December 19X1

SOURCES OF FINANCE	£	ASSETS	£
Share capital......................	200,000	Fixed assets at net book value	210,000
Reserves............................	135,000		
	335,000		
Current liabilities.................	75,000	Stock	100,000
		Debtors	90,000
		Cash	10,000*
	410,000		410,000

*this amount is needed to meet day to day operating requirements.

From the above balance sheet it appears that the company has been successful and has built up substantial reserves as a result of generating and retaining profits over the years. It is also clear that these reserves have been reinvested in fixed assets, stock and debtors, and no cash which is surplus to operating requirements now remains. It is therefore a company's assets which must be examined to discover whether there are liquid resources available to meet an existing or future liability, and not the sources of finance which merely list the book value of the various claims against those assets.

1.7   QUESTIONS AND SOLUTIONS

Questions 1.1 and 1.2 are taken from earlier Stage 1 exams. and indicate the level of knowledge of final accounts preparation expected from students commencing their studies for the *Accountancy* examination. Students should work these questions. If they produce satisfactory solutions they should proceed with their studies; if not, they should undertake further revision of final accounts preparation using a suitable text such as C. C. Magee, *Framework of Accountancy*. Question 1.3 tests students' understanding of the relationship between profit, working capital and cash; while question 1.4 examines the effect of a range of proposed transactions and adjustments on various financial magnitudes.

Question 1.1

The following information is extracted from the books of Denston, a trader, at December 31, 19X1:

Total bank account for 19X1:

	£		£
Opening balance	821	Cash paid to suppliers	18,624
Cash received from customers	24,264	Salaries	2,249
Closing balance	1,030	Rent and rates	824
		Lighting and heating	168
		General expenses	1,781
		Drawings	2,469
	£26,115		£26,115

	31 Dec. 19X0	31 Dec. 19X1
	£	£
Stock in trade	2,141	2,648
Debtors	3,219	3,388
Creditors for:		
purchases	1,842	1,891
lighting and heating	31	42
Rent and rates paid in advance	100	120
Fixed assets	2,200	see note

2 200
— 220
1980

REQUIRED:

(i) Denston's balance sheet at 31 December, 19X0.

(ii) Denston's trading and profit and loss account for 19X1 and his balance sheet at December 31, 19X1.

Note: Depreciation, for 19X1, is to be charged on fixed assets at the rate of 10 per cent per annum on the opening balance.

Solution

(i)   *Balance Sheet, 31 December, 19X0*

	£	£
Fixed assets at book value		2,200
Current Assets:		
Stock in trade	2,141	
Debtors	3,219	
Prepaid expense	100	
Bank balance	821	
	6,281	
Less: Current Liabilities:		
Trade creditors	1,842	
Accrued expense	31	
	1,873	
Working capital		4,408
		6,608
Financed by: Capital (balancing figure)		6,608

(ii) *Workings:*

The following items of revenue and expenditure must first be calculated:

Sales:	£	Purchases:	£
Cash received from customers...	24,264	Cash paid to suppliers	18,624
Add: Debtors at 31 December, 19X1	3,388	*Add:* Creditors at 31 December, 19X1	1,891
Less: Debtors at 31 December, 19X0	(3,219)	*Less:* Creditors at 31 December, 19X0	(1,842)
	24,433		18,673

Rent and rates:		Lighting and heating:	
Cash paid	824	Cash paid	168
Add: Prepaid at 31 December, 19X0	100	*Add:* Accrued at 31 December, 19X1	42
Less: Prepaid at 31 December, 19X1	(120)	*Less:* Accrued at 31 December, 19X0	(31)
	804		179

Trading and Profit and Loss Account for 19X1

	£	£
Sales		24,433
Less: Stock in trade at 31 December, 19X0	2,141	
Purchases	18,673	
Stock in trade at 31 December, 19X1	(2,648)	
Cost of goods sold		18,166
Gross profit		6,267
Less: Salaries	2,249	
Rent and rates	804	
Lighting and heating	179	
General expenses	1,781	
Depreciation	220	
		5,233
Net profit		1,034

Balance Sheet at 31 December, 19X1

	£	£
Fixed Assets at book value, £2,200 – £220 =		1,980
Current Assets:		
Stock in trade	2,648	
Debtors	3,388	
Prepaid expense	120	
	6,156	
Less: Current Liabilities:		
Trade creditors	1,891	
Accrued expense	42	
Bank overdraft	1,030	
	2,963	
Working Capital		3,193
		5,173
Financed by:		
Capital at 31 December, 19X0		6,608
Add: Net profit		1,034
Less: Drawings		(2,469)
		5,173

Question 1.2

Paxton and Lark are in partnership sharing profits in the ratio 3:2 and the following trial balance was extracted from their books at 31 December, 19X1.

	£	£
Capital: Paxton		23,348
Lark		19,294
Debtors and creditors	11,131	7,283
Stock in trade: 1 January, 19X1	14,169	
Freehold premises at cost	25,000	
Motor vans at cost	12,000	
Sales		128,488
Purchases	89,952	
Rent and rates	2,460	
Lighting and heating	841	
Salaries and wages	14,865	
General expenses	1,861	
Bad debts	622	
Provision for doubtful debts at 1 January, 19X1		862
Provision for depreciation of motor vans at 1 January, 19X1		6,400
Motor Expenses	1,326	
Drawings: Paxton	4,162	
Lark	2,984	
Bank balance	4,302	
	£185,675	£185,675

You are given the following additional information:
 (i) Stock in trade 31 December, 19X1: £15,022.
 (ii) Rates paid in advance 31 December, 19X1: £160.
 (iii) Lighting and heating due at 31 December, 19X1: £191.
 (iv) Provision for doubtful debts to be increased to £981.
 (v) Depreciation has been and is to be charged on the vans at the annual rate of 20 per cent of cost.
 (vi) Lark ordered goods for his own use at a cost of £122 and this amount was paid by the firm and debited to purchases.
 (vii) After the above trial balance was prepared an advice was received from the firm's bank stating that £56 charges had been debited to the current account.

REQUIRED: A trading profit and loss account for 19X1 and a balance sheet at 31 December, 19X1.

Solution

The adjustments required to incorporate the effect of the additional information are made on the face of the final accounts (i.e. journal entries omitted).

Trading and Profit and Loss Account 19X1

	£	£	£
Sales			128,488
Less: Stock in trade at 1 January, 19X1		14,169	
Purchases	89,952		
Less: Partner's drawings	122		
		89,830	
Stock in trade at 31 December, 19X1		(15,022)	
Cost of goods sold			88,977
Gross profit			39,511
Less: Rent and rates, £2,460 – £160 prepaid		2,300	
Lighting and heating, £841 + £191 accrued		1,032	
Salaries and wages		14,865	
General expenses, £1,861 + £56 bank charges		1,917	
Bad debts, £622 + £119 increase in provision		741	
Motor expenses		1,326	
Depreciation		2,400	
			24,581
Net profit			14,930
Paxton		8,958	
Lark		5,972	
			14,930

Balance Sheet as at 31 December, 19X1

	£	£
Fixed Assets:		
Freehold premises at cost		25,000
Motor vans at cost..	12,000	
Less: Accumulated depreciation	8,800	
		3,200
		28,200
Current Assets:		
Stock in trade...	15,022	
Debtors less provision for doubtful debts, £11,131 – £981	10,150	
Prepaid expense	160	
Bank balance, £4,302 – £56 charges	4,246	
	29,578	
Current Liabilities:		
Creditors	7,283	
Accrued expense..	191	
	7,474	
Working Capital..		22,104
		50,304

Financed by:	Paxton	Lark	£
Capital at 1 January, 19X1	23,348	19,294	
Add: Net profit...	8,958	5,972	
Less: Drawings—cash	4,162	2,984	
—goods		122	
	(4,162)	(3,106)	
	28,144	22,160	50,304

Question 1.3   (Taken from the April 1979 *Accountancy* paper)

The following information is provided in respect of the affairs of Bute Ltd. for 1978 :

At 1 January 1978 :	£
Stock..	86,500
Trade debtors	63,200
Trade creditors	47,500
Plant at cost	110,000
Transactions during 1978 :	
Sales	246,800
Payments to suppliers	186,900
Administration, selling & distribution expenses	47,500
Research & development expenditure	13,800
Purchase of plant, 1 January 1978	10,000
At 31 December 1978 :	
Stock..	96,600
Trade debtors	71,000
Trade creditors	42,500

Plant is depreciated at the rate of 10% per annum on cost. The research and development expenditure comprises £4,800 in respect of basic research, which is to be written off against the income of 1978, and £9,000 development expenditure which is to be capitalised and classified as a current asset in the balance sheet at 31 December 1978.

Required:

(a) Statements of profit and loss, sources and applications of working capital and cash receipts and payments conforming to the following general format.

	Profit & Loss £	Working Capital £	Cash £
Inflows			
Less : Outflows			
Net Inflow (Outflow)			

NOTE: Each item comprising total outflows should be separately specified in the above statements.

(*b*) Reconciliations, based on the figures calculated under (*a*), of (i) the net profit or loss with the net movement in working capital and (ii) the net movement in working capital with the net increase or decrease in cash.

(*c*) Brief comments on the purposes and limitations of the three concepts, namely profit, working capital and cash, for the purpose of assessing business activity.

NOTE: *It is essential that candidates show how they arrive at the figures in the answer to this question.*

Solution [30]

(a)

INFLOWS	Profit & Loss £	Working Capital £	Cash £
Sales	246,800	246,800	239,000W1
OUTFLOWS			
Purchases	181,900W2	181,900	186,900
Stock adjustment	(10,000)	(10,100)	
Cost of Sales	171,800	171,800	
Administration, selling and distribution expenses	47,500	47,500	47,500
Research & development expenditure	4,800	4,800	13,800
Depreciation	12,000		
Plant purchased		10,000	10,000
	236,100	234,100	258,200
NET INFLOW (OUTFLOW)	10,700	12,700	(19,200)

Workings:
1. Cash received = 246,800 (sales) + 63,200 (opening debtors) − 71,000 (closing debtors) = 239,000
2. Purchases = 186,900 (cash paid) + 42,500 (closing creditors) − 47,500 (opening creditors) = 181,900

		£	£
(b) (i)	Net profit		10,700
	Add: Depreciation		12,000
	Less: Plant purchased		(10,000)
	Net increase in working capital		12,700
(ii)	Net increase in working capital		12,700
	Less Increased investment in stock	10,100	
	debtors	7,800	
	development costs	9,000	
	Reduced finance from creditors	5,000	
			31,900
	Net reduction in cash		(19,200)

(c) Comments should cover the following matters:
Profit measures the performance of management and the extent to which a firm achieves the objective of maximising shareholders' wealth. Although used as a basis for decision-making concerning the allocation of resources, a major drawback is the fact that the data relates primarily to past events. A further limitation is the subjective nature of the calculation which provides scope for error and fraud.

Working Capital is a measure of the financial strength of the concern and provides some indication of the firm's ability to meet debts as they fall due. The measurement procedures are less subjective than profit calculation, due to the exclusion of charges designed to amortise fixed assets over their expected useful life. Nevertheless estimation errors which can occur when valuing current assets and liabilities may affect the usefulness of this yardstick of financial performance.

Cash In common with working capital movements, historical statements of net cash flow possess limited predictive quality due to the inclusion of capital account changes. Nevertheless it possesses the virtue of being an entirely objective measure of financial performance, and it may forewarn users of accounting information concerning emerging liquidity problems when, as in the case of Bute Ltd., healthy increases in profit and working capital balances are accompanied by a significant decline in cash.

Examiners comments: Most common errors: Same as for Pontcanna plc, see example 1.3.

Question 1.4 (Taken from the September 1982 *Accountancy* paper).

The accountant of Wiley Ltd. has prepared the following estimated balance sheet as at 31 December 1982 for the company's directors.

ESTIMATED BALANCE SHEET AS AT 31 DECEMBER 1982

	£	£		£	£
Ordinary share capital					
(£1 shares)		500,000	Freehold property at cost		600,000
			Less: Depreciation		100,000
Reserves at 1 January					500,000
1982	250,000		Stock valued at marginal		
Add: Net profit for			cost		590,000
1982	50,000		Trade debtors		160,000
		300,000			
		800,000			
Loan repayable 1985		250,000			
Trade creditors		140,000			
Bank overdraft		60,000			
		£1,250,000			£1,250,000

The directors are disappointed with the estimated net profit for 1982 and the estimated financial position as at 31 December 1982 displayed in the balance sheet shown above. The following suggestions are made for consideration by the company's accountant.

(i) A bonus (capitalisation) issue of shares to existing shareholders on the basis of one additional £1 share for every two shares held at present.

(ii) Increase the depreciation charged on the freehold buildings from £20,000 to £30,000.

(iii) Arrange for a loan of £100,000, also repayable in 1985, to be made to the company on 31 December 1982.

(iv) Value stock at total cost, £680,000, for the purpose of the accounts. The 1981 accounts included stock at marginal cost of £400,000 and the corresponding figure for total cost at that date was £470,000.

(v) Offer cash discounts for prompt payment in respect of future sales. If this course is followed it is estimated that sales will be unaffected, but discounts of £3,000 will be allowed during the period October–December 1982 and trade debtors at the year end will amount to £120,000.

Required:

Taking each course of action *separately,* a statement showing the following:

(a) net profit for 1982;

[5]

(b) bank overdraft (or balance) at 31 December 1982;

[5]

(c) working capital at 31 December 1982; and

[5]

(d) liquidity ratio, defined as the ratio of trade debtors + bank balance (if any) to current liabilities at 31 December 1982.

[5]

Consider each course of action *separately* and present your answer in a table, as shown below:

Course of action	Net profit £	Bank overdraft (or balance) £	Working capital £	Liquidity ratio
(i)				
(ii)				
(iii)				
(iv)				
(v)				

NOTES: Ignore taxation.

Assume that no course of action will alter the amount of bank interest payable.

[Total marks for question: 20]

Solution

Course of action	Net profit £	Bank overdraft (or balance) £	Working Capital £	Liquidity ratio
(i)	50,000	60,000	550,000	0.8:1
(ii)	40,000	60,000	550,000	0.8:1
(iii)	50,000	(40,000)	650,000	1.4:1
(iv)	70,000	60,000	640,000	0.8:1
(v)	47,000	23,000	547,000	0.7:1

Workings:
The original forecasts had produced an estimated trading profit of £50,000, a bank overdraft of £60,000, working capital of £550,000 and a liquidity ratio of 0.8:1. The effects of each of the five proposals are as follows:
1. The proposed bonus issue changes none of the estimates.
2. If the depreciation charge is increased to £30,000, net profit falls to £40,000 but none of the other estimates are affected.
3. The loan will cause the bank overdraft to be converted into a bank balance of £40,000, working capital will increase to £650,000 and the liquidity ratio becomes 1.4:1.
4. Valuing stock at total cost causes cost of sales to fall by £20,000 (*both* opening and closing stock must be restated at total cost) and reported profit becomes £70,000. Working capital increases to £640,000 as the result of using the higher closing stock valuation.
5. The policy of allowing cash discounts will reduce closing debtors by £40,000, but it will cost the company £3,000 and the balance of £37,000 will be received in cash. The estimated profit therefore falls to £47,000, the bank overdraft becomes £23,000, working capital becomes £547,000 and the liquidity ratio falls to 0.7:1, i.e. £120,000: (£140,000 + £23,000).

Examiner's comments: Most common errors: The fifth proposal caused greatest difficulty. Elsewhere the answers were generally good with the most common errors occurring under proposal 1, where the bonus issue was thought to produce a cash inflow of £250,000, and under proposal 4, where the revaluation of stock was thought to increase reported profit by the full £90,000 (the increase in the closing stock valuation) to £140,000.

CHAPTER 2

Form and Content of Company Accounts

2.1 SOURCES OF DISCLOSURE REQUIREMENTS

Under the Companies Act 1948, the directors have a legal responsibility for the preparation and publication of accounting information which gives a 'true and fair view' of their company's financial affairs. The contents of the balance sheet, profit and loss account and directors' report are each subject to disclosure requirements prescribed by the following: the government, the accounting profession and, in the case of quoted companies, the London Stock Exchange. The disclosure requirements currently in force have been built up gradually over the years.

The Companies Act 1900 introduced the requirement for an annual audit but continued to allow the directors a free hand regarding the content of the accounts. Many company directors acted responsibly and published accounts which were adequate, but others made use of numerous devices to minimise their informative value. For instance, one popular procedure was to disclose a single figure for fixed assets, so that it was impossible to discover either what proportion of the total represented intangible assets, or whether any depreciation had been charged on the tangible fixed assets. The legislature's response was the introduction of a small number of disclosure requirements in the Companies Act 1928, and these have since been added to by successive Companies Acts. The legal requirements currently in force regarding disclosure are contained in the Companies Act 1948 as subsequently amended by the Companies Acts 1967, 1980 and 1981. These are the statutes referred to in the remainder of this Chapter.

Professional accounting bodies were established throughout Britain, during the second half of the nineteenth century, but it was some time before these bodies assumed a measure of direct responsibility for the form and content of company accounts. In

1942, following press criticism of accounting practices, the Institute of Chartered Accountants in England and Wales formed a committee whose job it was to identify best accounting practices and make recommendations encouraging their widespread adoption. These *Recommendations on Accounting Principles* successfully raised overall reporting standards and a number of their provisions were incorporated in the Companies Act 1948. A great deal of diversity in accounting practice nevertheless persisted, and this became the subject of further criticism in the late 1960s. In order to avert the threat of detailed legal regulation of company accounts, the profession took steps to 'put its own house in order'. The Accounting Standards Committee, formed in 1970, is responsible for preparing *Statements of Standard Accounting Practice* (SSAPs), which are issued after approval by the Councils of each of the six major professional accounting bodies. To date (June 1983), twenty SSAPs have been issued.

An important difference between the Recommendations and the SSAPs is that, whereas compliance with the former is merely considered desirable, conformity with the latter is normally regarded as essential. The government has not, however, accepted responsibility for enforcing accounting standards; instead the job is left to the accounting profession. For instance, where a company fails to comply with the requirements of an SSAP, the auditor will usually be expected to 'qualify' his audit report. Failure to qualify a report will render the auditor liable to disciplinary measures, although there has been some criticism of the professional accounting bodies on the grounds that they do not take a firm enough line with offenders. A number of accounting requirements, initially contained in SSAPs, have since been incorporated in the Companies Act 1981, and now receive the force of law. The Standards affected have not been withdrawn, however, and remain relevant because it is necessary to refer to these more detailed documents to interpret the brief instructions contained in the Act.

Companies whose shares are listed (quoted) on the London Stock Exchange must also comply with the regulations imposed by that institution. The Stock Exchange has traditionally obliged quoted companies to disclose extra information in their accounts, although many of the requirements which the Stock Exchange first introduced have since been extended to all limited companies by either the accounting profession or the legislature. For example, the Stock Exchange introduced a requirement for holding companies to publish a consolidated balance sheet in 1939, and this was repeated in *Recommendation 7* in 1944 and the Companies Act 1948. Regulations which apply only to quoted companies are published in *The Stock Exchange Listing Agreement*, but these are outside the scope of the *Accountancy* examination syllabus.

2.2 CONTENT OF THE ANNUAL REPORT

Directors are legally required to prepare, at least once a year, final accounts setting out the financial results achieved by the company. These accounts must be laid before the company at the annual general meeting, and they must be circulated beforehand to all shareholders, debenture-holders and any other persons entitled to attend the meeting. In addition, the directors must file a copy of the company's accounts (see section 7 of this Chapter) with the Registrar of Companies, where they are available for public inspection. The accounts are normally included in a document called 'the annual report' which contains a wide range of other financial and general information. For a large company, it is an extensive document; to take an example, the 1981 annual report of The Shell Transport and Trading Company plc. covers 56 pages. A typical annual report prepared for a large public company contains the following main items:

1. The Chairman's Review. This review invariably appears as the first item in the annual report, and it is one area which is not subject to any regulations regarding content. The chairman is free to say exactly what he wishes, but his comments will generally cover the following broad areas:

(a) An assessment of the year's results.
(b) An examination of factors influencing those results, e.g. the economic and political climate or the effect of strikes.
(c) A reference to major developments e.g. takeovers or new products.
(d) Capital expenditure plans.
(e) An assessment of future prospects.

The Chairman's message will usually convey a fair amount of optimism even if the financial facts published later in the report make depressing reading. A strong point in favour of the chairman's review is that it is readable and readily comprehensible to the layman. A major drawback is that, with regard to future prospects, it must be based on opinion rather than fact, but it is useful background material when attempting to assess progress by an interpretation of the financial information contained in the accounts.

2. *The Auditors' Report.* This report covers the information contained in the three principal financial statements: the profit and loss account; the balance sheet; and the statement of funds. In preparing their report, the auditors are also required to consider whether the information contained in the directors' report is consistent with the accounts and, if it is not, they are required to say so. They are not required to report on the chairman's review, but an auditor would be unlikely to sign an unqualified report where the review contained an erroneous factual statement, e.g. where the entire loss for the year is blamed on a strike by the workforce, whereas it was actually caused by falling demand. The auditors are appointed by, and responsible to, the members of the company and must report to them on the accounts prepared by the directors. A typical report might contain the following wording:

Report of the Auditors to the members of Minster plc;
We have audited the accounts set out on pages 20 to 40 in accordance with approved Auditing Standards.

In our opinion the accounts on pages 20 to 40 give a true and fair view of the state of affairs of the company at 31 December, 1981 and of the profit and source and application of funds for the year then ended and comply with the Companies Acts 1948–81.
Cardiff 30 June, 1983.   Edwards, Mellett & Co.,
                                                             Chartered Accountants.

The first sentence informs shareholders of the scope of the audit i.e. that work done complies with the instructions issued by the professional accounting bodies for the guidance of auditors. The second sentence sets out the auditors' findings. You will notice that it does not *certify the accuracy* of the accounts, but instead expresses the opinion that the accounts show a *true and fair* view. The auditor of a limited company must be professionally qualified, however, and would be expected to exercise appropriate skill and judgement in reaching his conclusions. If the auditor has any reservations regarding the truth and fairness of the accounts, e.g. perhaps he believes that the provision for bad debts is inadequate, he must refer to this fact in his report. Details of the qualification will, in these circumstances, normally appear at the beginning of the second sentence. Readers may have noticed that the specimen audit report does not state that the accounts comply with relevant

SSAPs, but it is reasonable to assume that there has been compliance unless there is a statement to the contrary.

A qualified audit report is today more common than used to be the case; a random survey of accounts filed at Companies House, recently carried out by the newsletter *Audit Report*, showed 24% to have been qualified. Not all of these qualifications are necessarily of major importance to bankers and other users of accounting reports. For instance, the failure of a company to depreciate its freehold property contravenes SSAP12 and will, quite properly, result in a qualified audit report. However, this qualificaion is unlikely to be of very great concern to a banker, interested in the asset primarily as security for a loan which has been made, when he knows that the property could easily be sold for a figure significantly in excess of its original cost.

One quarter of the qualifications, referred to in the previous paragraph, arose because of shortcomings in the systems of internal control operated within small companies (the 'small business qualification'). Many of the 'checks and balances' which are needed in a large company are neither practical, appropriate nor necessary in a small enterprise. The most effective form of security for many of these small organisations is the close involvement of the directors in all aspects of business activity, but this may produce auditing problems. For example, a company may operate primarily on a cash basis but, because cash transactions are handled entirely by the directors, complete security is virtually assured. However, in the absence of independently verifiable evidence to support these transactions, it will not be possible for the auditor to confirm the complete reliability of the company's records and the following qualification will be made:

> In common with many businesses of similar size and organisation the company's system of control is dependent upon the close involvement of the directors (who are major shareholders). Where independent confirmation of the completeness of the accounting records was therefore not available we have accepted assurances from the directors that all the company's transactions have been reflected in the records.

This type of qualification will be noted by a company's bank, but it will not necessarily be a cause for great concern, because the banker is able to assess its significance on the basis of his personal knowledge of the directors involved.

3. The Balance Sheet. Its form and content are examined in section 3 of this Chapter.

4. The Profit and Loss Account. Its form and content are examined in sections 3 and 4.1 of this Chapter.

5. Notes on the Accounts. These are examined in sections 4.2 and 5 of this Chapter.

6. The Directors' Report. Its content is examined in section 6 of this Chapter.

7. The Statement of Funds. Its form and content are examined in Chapter 9.

8. Supplementary Current Cost Accounts. These are examined in Chapter 6.

In the case of small companies, which includes most private companies, neither the Chairman's Review nor the Supplementary Current Cost Accounts (items 1 and 8) are likely to be provided.

2.3   STANDARDISED FORMATS

2.3.1   Rules for Presentation   The major source of new company law in Great Britain today is the series of Directives drafted by the European Commission. The Companies Act 1981 implements proposals contained in the Fourth Directive on Company Law, which is designed to harmonise corporate financial reporting procedures throughout the EEC. *The new rules apply for accounting periods beginning on or after 15 June, 1982.* The result is that a company which prepares accounts on a calendar year basis will *first* have to comply with the requirements of the Act in its accounts for the calendar year 1983, and these will be published in the spring or early summer of 1984.

The current legal regulations relating to the form and content of company accounts are set out in Schedule 1 of the 1981 Act, which combines the new rules with those previously in existence. Companies may choose from two balance sheet formats and four profit and loss account formats. Both balance sheets contain the same headings and the only difference is the method of presentation— format 1 uses a vertical layout and format 2 a horizontal layout. The profit and loss accounts offer a choice between two alternative approaches, each of which may be presented in a vertical or horizontal format. The essential difference between these two approaches is in the method used to classify items of expenditure. Formats 1 (vertical) and 3 (horizontal) analyse expenses by function, and therefore disclose figures for cost of sales, distribution costs and administrative expenses. Formats 2 (vertical) and 4 (horizontal) analyse expenses by type, and therefore show figures for raw materials, staff costs and depreciation.

The vertical format has become popular in industry in recent years, and it is likely that balance sheets and profit and loss accounts prepared in compliance with the 1981 Act will be presented in this manner, i.e. companies are likely to use balance sheet format 1 and profit and loss account format 1 or 2. It is more difficult to forecast which of the profit and loss account approaches will prove more popular, and both methods may well be used widely. It has been decided that, for the purpose of the *Accountancy* examination, format 1 should be used where students are required to present a profit and loss account and/or a balance sheet in accordance with the requirements of the Companies Acts. The items to be disclosed in order to comply with format 1 are:

Profit and Loss Account (1)

1. Turnover
2. Cost of sales (2)
3. Gross profit or loss
4. Distribution costs (2)
5. Administrative expenses (2)
6. Other operating income
7. Income from shares in group companies
8. Income from shares in related companies
9. Income from other fixed asset investments (3)
10. Other interest receivable and similar income (3)
11. Amounts written off investments
12. Interest payable and similar charges (3)
13. Tax on profit or loss on ordinary activities
14. Profit or loss on ordinary activities after taxation
15. Extraordinary income
16. Extraordinary charges
17. Extraordinary profit or loss
18. Tax on extraordinary profit or loss
19. Other taxes not shown under the above items
20. Profit or loss for the financial year.

Notes:
1. The following additional items do not appear in the standardised format, but the Act requires them to be disclosed:
   (a) Profit or loss on ordinary activities before tax.
   (b) Transfers to or from reserves.
   (c) The aggregate amount of dividends paid or proposed.
2. These items must include any provisions for depreciation which have been made.
3. Amounts receivable from and payable to group companies are to be shown separately.

Example 2.2. (see section 4.1 of this Chapter) illustrates the way in which the above information will be presented in practice.

Balance Sheet

A. Called up share capital not paid (1)
B. Fixed assets
   I.   Intangible assets
      1. Development costs
      2. Concessions, patents, licences, trade marks and similar rights and assets
      3. Goodwill
      4. Payments on account
   II. Tangible Assets
      1. Land and buildings
      2. Plant and machinery
      3. Fixtures, fittings, tools and equipment
      4. Payments on account and assets in course of construction
   III. Investments
      1. Shares in group companies
      2. Loans to group companies
      3. Shares in related companies
      4. Loans to related companies
      5. Other investments other than loans
      6. Other loans
      7. Own shares (4)
C. Current assets
   I.   Stocks
      1. Raw materials and consumables
      2. Work in progress
      3. Finished goods and goods for resale
      4. Payments on account
   II. Debtors (5)
      1. Trade debtors
      2. Amounts owed by group companies
      3. Amounts owed by related companies
      4. Other debtors
      5. Called up share capital not paid (1)
      6. Prepayments and accrued income (2)
   III. Investments
      1. Shares in group companies
      2. Own shares (4)
      3. Other investments
   IV. Cash at bank and in hand
D. Prepayments and accrued income (2)

E. Creditors: amounts falling due within one year
    1. Debenture loans (6)
    2. Bank loans and overdrafts
    3. Payments received on account
    4. Trade creditors
    5. Bills of exchange payable
    6. Amounts owed to group companies
    7. Amounts owed to related companies
    8. Other creditors including taxation and social security
    9. Accruals and deferred income (3)
F. Net current assets (liabilities)
G. Total assets less current liabilities
H. Creditors: amounts falling due after more than one year
    1. Debenture loans (6)
    2. Bank loans and overdrafts
    3. Payments received on account
    4. Trade creditors
    5. Bills of exchange payable
    6. Amounts owed to group companies
    7. Amounts owed to related companies
    8. Other creditors including taxation and social security
    9. Accruals and deferred income (3)
I. Provisions for liabilities and charges
    1. Pensions and similar obligations
    2. Taxation, including deferred taxation
    3. Other provisions
J. Accruals and deferred income (3)
K. Capital and reserves
    I.   Called up share capital (7)
    II. Share premium account
    III. Revaluation reserve
    IV. Other reserves
        1. Capital redemption reserve
        2. Reserve for own shares
        3. Reserves provided for by the articles of association
        4. Other reserves
    V. Profit and loss account

Notes:
1.–3. Each of these items may be shown in any of the positions given for them.
4. The nominal value of the shares held shall be shown separately.
5 The amount, if any, falling due after one year shall be shown for each item. For instance, a company may receive payment by instalments, for goods supplied, in which case any instalments receivable more than one year after the balance sheet date should be shown separately.
6. The amount of any convertible loans must be shown separately.
7. Both the nominal value of the issued share capital and the amount paid up must be given.

Example 2.5 (see section 5 of this Chapter) illustrates the way in which the above information will be presented in practice.

The Act includes the following instructions and advice for companies using the standardised formats:

1. Once a particular format has been chosen, it must be followed each year unless there are special reasons for a change which must be fully disclosed.
2. The letters (A–K), Roman numerals (I, II, III, etc.) and Arabic numerals (1, 2, 3, etc.) need not be reproduced in the accounts.
3. The order of the balances, indicated by Arabic numerals, may be changed.
4. Balances indicated by Arabic numerals may be combined in the balance sheet and profit and loss account and the breakdown given by way of note. It is likely that, in practice, companies' balance sheets will give only the main headings and sub-headings, e.g. current assets and the total figure for stock will be given, but the break-down of stock into raw materials, work in progress, finished goods and payments on account will be shown in a note to the accounts.
5. Any balance indicated by an Arabic numeral may be included with another if the amount is immaterial, e.g. if trade creditors are £526,000 and payments received on account amount to only £2,000, the latter heading can be omitted and trade creditors shown as £528,000. No statutory guidance is provided for assessing materiality and judgement must be exercised.
6. Corresponding amounts for the preceding financial year must be given for balances appearing in the accounts and in the notes to the accounts.
7. Directors *may* give more information than appears in the standard format. That is, additional items may be added (e.g. rents paid could be disclosed in the profit and loss account) and existing items may be sub-analysed (e.g. separate figures may be given for bank loans and bank overdrafts—see balance sheet heading E2).
8. Headings must not be abbreviated, e.g. 'Bank loans and overdrafts' should not be abbreviated to 'Bank overdrafts' *even if the company has no bank loans.*
9. Items may be omitted if there are nil balances for both the current year and the preceding year.

2.3.2 The True and Fair View Although alternative layouts are permitted, the Companies Act 1981 prescribes a fairly rigid framework for the final accounts. Standardised reporting procedures have existed in France and Germany for some time, and the EEC Fourth Directive on Company Law substantially followed German practice, but for the other Common Market countries, including Britain, significant changes had to be made to the prevailing legal requirements. In Britain, prior to the 1981 Act, statutory reporting requirements were based on the concept of minimum disclosure. This approach obliged directors to disclose sufficient information to account properly for the resources entrusted to them, but it allowed them ample scope to disclose more should they wish to do so. Furthermore, the directors could employ whatever method of presentation they considered most likely to communicate effectively the facts to be reported.

Concern has been expressed, in certain quarters, that standard formats are inflexible, and will both prevent innovation and hinder the preparation of accounts in a form most suitable for a particular company. Only time will show whether these anxieties are well-founded, but the Act attempts to reduce the potential risks by emphasising the *over-riding requirement* that the accounts should show a *true and fair view*. Directors are therefore *required* to:

(a) provide additional information, not required by the standard disclosure requirements, where failure to do so would result in the publication of accounts which do not give a true and fair view. (It was noted, in section 3.1 of this Chapter, that additional information *may* always be given. The difference here is that additional information *must* be given if the accounts would otherwise not show a true and fair view.)

(b) Depart from the standard format disclosure requirements where compliance would prevent a true and fair view from being given. Where this happens, the directors must give details of the departure, reasons for it, and its effect, by way of note.

2.4 THE PROFIT AND LOSS ACCOUNT

2.4.1 Non-Recurring Profits and Losses The profits earned and losses suffered by a business either arise from normal operating activities or accrue as a result of non-recurrent transactions or events outside the normal scope of a company's trading activities.

The problem is how to account for these non-recurrent transactions, e.g. a loss arising on the closure of a particular branch. In the absence of detailed regulations, one option would be to include non-recurrent items in the profit and loss account, whereas an alternative option would be to show them in the 'Statement of Retained Profits' which many companies publish (see example 2.2). The case for excluding non-recurrent transactions from the profit and loss account is based on the idea that their inclusion distorts the true trend of operating results and therefore causes wrong conclusions to be drawn regarding a company's past performance and likely future prospects.

Example 2.1

The following information is provided in respect of the affairs of Parlock plc which made a non-recurring gain of £1,500,000 in 19X3.

Annual profits for:	Including non-recurring gain £000	Excluding non-recurring gain £000
19X1	2,400	2,400
19X2	2,600	2,600
19X3	3,500	2,000
19X4	1,400	1,400

Inclusion of the non-recurring gain might cause individuals examining the accounts for 19X3 to assume that annual profits are still rising, whereas in reality operating profits have begun to fall.

On the other hand, there are strong arguments for including non-recurring transactions in the profit and loss account. These are:

1. Non-recurring transactions have exactly the same effect on the financial position of a business as normal operating transactions, and for this reason they should be given equal prominence.

2. Allocation of individual transactions either to the profit and loss account or directly to reserves is a matter of judgement, and this provides scope for both error and the manipulation of financial information. In either case the result may be that the wrong conclusions will be drawn regarding a company's performance.

3. Exclusion could cause users to overlook the effect of a non-recurrent transaction when assessing corporate performance.

4. It is the directors' job to manage all aspects of business activity, whether they give rise to recurrent or non-recurrent profits and losses, and the reported profit figure should therefore measure management's overall performance.

The compromise solution, incorporated in SSAP6 entitled 'Extraordinary Items and Prior Year Adjustments' requires almost all non-recurrent profits and losses to be reported in the profit and loss account *with full disclosure of their effect*. This ensures that readers do not overlook the financial effect of important transactions, but, at the same time, it enables them to identify recurring profits which might be considered more relevant when attempting to predict likely future results. SSAP6 distinguishes four categories of non-recurring profits and losses, and the accounting treatment of a particular item depends on the category into which it falls:

(i) *Exceptional items.* These are items which are abnormal as regards their size but which result from the ordinary activities of the business. Examples include:
   (a) abnormal charges for bad debts, write-offs of obsolete stock and work in progress and abortive research and development expenditure;
   (b) abnormal provisions for losses on long term contracts;
   (c) under or over-provisions of tax in respect of previous years.
These items relate to ordinary operating activities and should therefore appear 'above the line', i.e. they should be taken into account in calculating post-tax reported profit for the year. Exceptional items must be separately disclosed, either on the face of the profit and loss account or by way of a note (see example 2.2).

(ii) *Extraordinary items.* These arise as the result of events outside normal trading activities; they are material in amount and are not expected to recur frequently. Examples include:
   (a) the discontinuance of a significant part of a company's business;
   (b) the sale of a fixed asset or investment not acquired with the intention of resale;
   (c) writing off intangibles, including goodwill, because of unusual developments during the year;
   (d) the expropriation of assets.
These items are not associated with normal operations, and they are therefore brought into the profit and loss account (less attribu-

table taxation) *after* post-tax profits arising from ordinary activities have been computed (see example 2.2).

(iii) *Prior year adjustments.* These consist of only:

(a) Material adjustments applicable to prior years arising from changes in accounting policies, e.g. where a company changes from the marginal cost to the total cost basis for stock valuation.

(b) The correction of fundamental errors made when preparing earlier years' accounts, e.g. where the directors forget to count the stocks in one of the warehouses and, as a result, materially understate profit.

Prior year items (net of any related tax) are adjusted against retained profits brought forward from previous years (see example 2.2). SSAP6 makes it clear that any adjustments to *incorrect estimates*, made in earlier years, must not be accounted for as prior year items and must be shown on the face of the profit and loss account. For example, a major customer may go into liquidation, owing £1,000,000, and the company may make a bad debt provision of £600,000 in anticipation of an ultimate payment of 40p in the £ to unsecured creditors. This optimism may prove unfounded, in which case the remaining balance of £400,000 will have to be written off in the following year. When this happens, the additional write-off is not accounted for as a prior year item, despite the fact that it was caused by a liquidation which occurred in a previous year. Instead, it must be accounted for as an exceptional item provided the amount is material. Similarly, adjustments to wrongly estimated extraordinary items must be accounted for as extraordinary items when the correction is made.

(iv) *Special cases.* The main ones are:

(a) An unrealised profit arising on the revaluation of fixed assets, which must be credited directly to revaluation reserve.

(b) The use of a share premium account to write off:
Preliminary expenses.
Expenses or commission paid or discount allowed on an issue of shares or debentures.
Any premiums payable on the redemption of preference shares or debentures.

The Companies Act 1981 made the disclosure of exceptional and extraordinary items a legal requirement, but it is still necessary to refer to SSAP6 for the definition of these items and detailed instructions regarding their disclosure.

Example 2.2 (which includes one example each of the treatment of an exceptional item, an extraordinary item, and a prior year adjustment)

The following balances relating to 19X1 have been extracted from the books of Rockingham plc:

	£000
Turnover	11,170
Cost of sales	7,721
Profit on the sale of investments	500
Administration expenses	621
Distribution costs	133
Interest payable	26
Interim dividend paid	250
Retained profit at 1 January, 19X1	3,875

The following additional information is provided:

1. Shares in Postbridge Ltd. were sold during the year. These shares were purchased ten years ago and were the only investments owned by the company. It is estimated that attributable tax payable will be £150,000.
2. The company's cost of sales includes a £200,000 write-off of uninsured stocks damaged by fire.
3. After the above balances were extracted, the directors decided to adopt the policy of depreciating the company's freehold building which has been owned for some years. This decision will require the opening book value of the building to be reduced to £700,000, and a charge for 19X1, of £114,000 must be added to cost of sales.
4. Corporation tax on profits from normal trading operations is estimated at £1,200,000.
5. The directors propose to pay a final dividend of £600,000.

REQUIRED:

The profit and loss account and statement of retained profits of Rockingham plc for 19X1 in a form suitable for publication so far as the information permits.

Solution:

Workings (not for publication):	£000
Cost of sales	7,721
Add: Additional depreciation	114
Adjusted cost of sales	7,835

Profit and Loss Account of Rockingham plc for 19X1

	£000	£000
Turnover		11,170
Less: Cost of sales (note 1)		7,835
Gross Profit		3,335
Less: Distribution costs	133	
Administrative expenses	621	
	—	754
Operating Profit		2,581
Less: Interest payable		26
Profit before taxation		2,555
Tax on profit from ordinary activities		1,200
Profit after tax and before extraordinary item		1,355
Profit on extraordinary item, less tax (note 2)		350
Profit for the year attributable to the shareholders		1,705
Less: Dividends paid and proposed		850
Retained profits for the year		855

Statement of Retained Profits of Rockingham plc for 19X1

	£000
Retained profit at 1 January, 19X1	3,875
Prior year adjustment arising from change of accounting policy (note 3)	(700)
	3,175
Retained profit for the year	855
Retained profit at 31 December, 19X1	4,030

Notes:
1. *Exceptional Item.*
   Cost of sales includes a £200,000 write off of uninsured stock damaged by fire. This amount requires disclosure as an exceptional item in view of its abnormal size.
2. *Extraordinary Item.*
   During the year the company realised a profit of £500,000, less tax of £150,000, on the sale of its shareholding in Postbridge Ltd. purchased some years ago.
3. *Prior Year Adjustment.*
   The directors have decided to depreciate the company's freehold building, purchased some years ago, in order to give a fairer presentation of the results and financial position of the company.

2.4.2 Notes to the Profit and Loss Account

The information listed below must be given either on the face of the profit and loss account or, as is more usual, by way of notes in order to comply with the Companies Acts. The list is not fully comprehensive but it indicates the level of knowledge expected from candidates taking the *Accountancy* examination. (The same comment applies to the balance sheet notes given in section 5 of this Chapter).

Revenue

1. Turnover and pre-tax profit. The following analysis must be given:
   (a) Separate figures for turnover and pre-tax profit in respect of each class of business carried on by the company.
   (b) The amount of turnover attributable to each geographical market supplied by the company.

The above information may be omitted, however, if the directors believe that disclosure would be seriously prejudicial to the company's interest.

2. Income from listed investments arising under profit and loss account headings 9 and 10 of prescribed format 1 (see page 49). The Act does not contain explicit requirements for companies to disclose unlisted investment income, but the remaining income arising under profit and loss account headings 9 and 10 must take the form of income from unlisted investments, and most companies will voluntarily disclose the amount involved.

3. Rentals arising from the ownership of land and buildings, net of outgoings, must be given where they constitute a substantial part of the company's revenue.

Expenditure

1. The interest charge must be analysed between amounts payable on:
   (a) Bank loans and overdrafts, and other loans wholly repayable within five years.
   (b) All other loans.
2. Hire charges in respect of plant and machinery.
3. Auditors' remuneration, including expenses.
4. Depreciation.
5. Directors' remuneration:
   (a) Remuneration for services to the company or its subsidiaries, distinguishing fees, other emoluments, pensions, and compensation for loss of office.
   (b) Figures for the chairman's emoluments, the emoluments of the highest paid director, if more than the chairman, and the number of directors in each ascending £5,000 band of emoluments. The requirements of this paragraph do not apply to duties discharged mainly outside the UK.
   (c) The number of directors who have waived emoluments and the aggregate amount waived.

Example 2.3

Easington plc has six directors, two of whom are non-executive directors, and each received an annual fee of £2,500 for 19X1. In addition, the chairman, who is also non-executive, received a fee of £5,000. The managing director received a salary of £16,000 and the other executive directors each received salaries of £12,000. In addition, the company made payments to a pension scheme, on behalf of the executive directors, of 20% of their salaries. A pension of £3,000 per annum was paid to a former director.

REQUIRED:

The information relating to directors' emoluments, to be included in the notes to the accounts.

Solution:

Directors' Emoluments:

Emoluments of directors, including pension contributions

	£
Directors' fees	20,000 W1
Other emoluments	62,400 W2
	82,400
Pension paid to a former director	3,000
	85,400
Emoluments of chairman	5,000
Emoluments of highest paid director	21,700

Number of directors (excluding those above) whose emoluments were within the ranges:

	Number
£0–5,000	2
£15,001–£20,000	3

W1. (6 × £2,500) + £5,000.

W2. £16,000 + (3 × £12,000) + 20% of [£16,000 + (3 × £12,000)].

6. Employees:
   (a) The weekly average number of persons employed by the company during the year, both in total and analysed into categories defined by the directors.
   (b) Separate figures for amounts paid to employees in respect of (i) wages and salaries (ii) social security costs (iii) other pension costs.
   (c) The number of employees (other than directors) in each ascending band of £5,000, beginning with emoluments in the range £20,001–£25,000.
7. Taxation:
   (a) The basis for computing U.K. corporation tax and the total charge for the year, distinguishing between tax on profit arising from ordinary activities and tax on extraordinary items (see section 4.1 of this Chapter) and transfers between the profit and loss account and the deferred tax account (see Chapter 3, section 8.2).
   (b) Details must be given of any special circumstances which significantly affect the amount of the tax charge for the current or future years, for example, capital allowances.
8. Amounts set aside for the redemption of share capital and loans.
9. Separate figures for dividends paid and dividends recommended on each class of share.

Example 2.4

The following balances relating to 19X1 have been extracted from the books of Cadnam plc.

	£
Turnover	2,860,000
Dividends received from temporary investments:	
listed	70,000
unlisted	30,000
Cost of sales	1,700,000
Distribution expenses	200,000
Administration expenses:	
Chairman's fee	2,500
Directors' emoluments	22,000
Motor vehicle expenses	10,000
Depreciation of office buildings and vehicles	46,000
Printing and stationery	7,000
Lighting and heating	23,000
Rates	18,000
Auditors' remuneration	20,000
Auditors' expenses	4,000
Office salaries and general expenses	155,000
Total administration expenses	307,500
Dividends paid: Ordinary shares	25,000
Preference shares	10,000
Bank overdraft interest	16,000
Interest paid and accrued on debentures redeemable 19X8	15,000

The following additional information is provided:

1. The directors' emoluments consist of annual fees paid to the company's two executive directors, of £2,000 each, and a salary of £18,000 paid to the director responsible for administration and distribution activities.
2. Cost of sales includes:
   (i) Material costs £620,000.
   (ii) The salary of the managing director, who is responsible for manufacturing operations, £25,000.
   (iii) Depreciation of plant and machinery £152,000.
3. The corporation tax charge for the year, calculated at the rate of 52% on taxable profits, is £350,000.
4. The company's issued share capital consists of £250,000 8% preference shares and 500,000 ordinary shares of £1 each. The directors intend to recommend to the general meeting a final dividend of 10p per share on the ordinary shares.
5. It is the directors' policy to make an annual transfer of £10,000 to a debenture redemption reserve.

REQUIRED:

The profit and loss account of Cadnam plc for 19X1 together with relevant notes, complying with the *minimum* requirements of the Companies Act 1981, so far as the information permits.

Note: Ignore advance corporation tax.

Solution:

Profit and Loss Account of Cadnam plc for 19X1

	Note	£	£
Turnover			2,860,000
Less: Cost of sales			1,700,000
Gross Profit			1,160,000
Less: Distribution costs		200,000	
Administrative expenses		307,500	
			507,500
Operating Profit	1		652,500
Add: Investment income	2		100,000
			752,500
Less: Interest payable	3		31,000
Profit before tax			721,500
Corporation tax	4		350,000
Profit after tax			371,500
Less: Dividends paid and proposed	5	95,000	
Transfer to debenture redemption reserve		10,000	
			105,000
Retained profit for the year			266,500

Notes:

1. Operating profit is stated after charging:

	£
Directors' emoluments, including chairman's fee	49,500
Depreciation of tangible assets	198,000
Auditors' remuneration and expenses	24,000

2. Investment income includes income from listed investments of 70,000

3. Interest payable on: bank overdraft 16,000
   loan repayable after 5 years 15,000

4. Corporation tax is based on taxable profit for the year at the rate of 52%
5. Dividends, preference—4% paid 10,000
   —4% proposed 10,000
   ordinary—5p per share paid 25,000
   10p per share recommended 50,000

6. Directors' remuneration: fees 6,500
   other emoluments 43,000

Emoluments of chairman 2,500
Emoluments of highest paid director 27,000
Number of directors (excluding the above) whose emoluments are in the range:

	Number
£15,001–£20,000	1

2.5   NOTES TO THE BALANCE SHEET

The following information must be given on the face of the balance sheet or, as is more usual, by way of notes in order to comply with the Companies Acts.

Sources of Finance

1. Share Capital:
   (a) Authorised share capital.
   (b) Issued share capital, giving both number and aggregate value of shares for each class.
   (c) For redeemable shares, the earliest and latest date of redemption, whether redemption is mandatory or at the company's option, and any premium payable on redemption.
   (d) Details of any shares issued during the year, including the reason for the issue.
   (e) Details of any option to subscribe for unissued shares e.g. conversion rights attaching to loans outstanding.
   (f) Details of any arrears of cumulative dividends.
2. Debentures:
   (a) Details of any debentures issued during the year, including the reason for the issue.
   (b) Details of redeemed debentures which the company has power to reissue.
3. Reserves and provisions for liabilities and charges:
   For each heading shown in the balance sheet, a reconciliation of the opening and closing balances must be given and transfers to and from the reserve or provision explained.
4. Creditors:
   (a) For each item shown under creditors, debts payable in more than five years time must be shown, distinguishing between debts repayable by instalments and other debts. In the case of the former, the company must also disclose the total amount of the debt. For example, if the company has a bank loan of £60,000 repayable by six equal instalments commencing one year after the balance sheet date, the company's acounts will have to show that there is a total debt repayable by instalments of £60,000, of which £10,000 falls due for repayment in more than five years time.
   (b) Details of any amounts secured, including an indication of the nature of the security provided.
   (c) In respect of items E8 and H8 of prescribed format 1 (see pages 50–51), separate figures must be given for:
      (i) proposed dividends
      (ii) social security costs
      (iii) taxation (for this purpose tax due on profit earned is treated as a liability rather than a provision).

Assets

1. Fixed Assets:
   (a) For each category of fixed asset appearing in the balance sheet, the opening and closing balances for cost (or revalued amount) and accumulated depreciation, and details of all movements during the year, i.e. revaluations, additions, disposals and depreciation.

(b) For assets revalued during the year, the names or qualifications of the valuers, the basis of valuation and the amount. For assets revalued in earlier years, only the year of the valuation and the amount need be given.

(c) Land and buildings must be analysed into freeholds, long leaseholds (i.e. leaseholds with an unexpired term of at least 50 years) and short leaseholds.

2. Intangible Assets:

(a) For goodwill, other than goodwill arising on consolidation (see Chapter 5, section 4.1), the period over which it is being written off should be given together with the reasons for choosing that period.

(b) For development costs it is necessary to disclose the reasons for capitalisation and the period over which the amount capitalised is being, or is to be, written off (see Chapter 3, section 6).

3. Investments:

The following information must be provided whether investments are classified as fixed assets (normally trade investments) or current assets (i.e. investments representing the temporary employment of surplus funds):

(a) Listed investments must be analysed into those quoted on the London Stock Exchange and those quoted on other reputable stock exchanges.

(b) The market value of listed investments where different from book value.

(c) Where a company holds, in another company, either (i) more than 10% of any class of equity share or (ii) share capital having a book value which exceeds 10% of its own assets, it must disclose

   (i) the company's name
   (ii) its country of incorporation and
   (iii) the proportion of shares held in each class together with appropriate descriptions

4. Loans to employees, directors and other officers:

(a) The amount of financial assistance provided to enable employees to purchase shares in the company or its holding company.

(b) Loans to directors. These are not normally allowed, but where they do occur companies (other than banks) must provide details of the amount outstanding at the beginning and end of the year and the maximum amount outstanding during the year.

(c) The number of other officers, defined as decision makers rather than persons who mainly implement the decisions of others, who owe money to the company and the total amount outstanding.

5. Stocks:

Any material differences between book value and replacement cost must be given for each balance sheet item.

Guarantees and financial commitments

1. Details of any charge on the assets of the company to secure the liabilities of any other person, including the amount secured.

2. For contingent liabilities, e.g. under a bill of exchange receivable discounted with a bank, the amount of the potential liability and the nature of any security provided.

3. Future capital expenditure, distinguishing the amount authorised by the board, the amount contracted but not provided for in the accounts, and the amount for which orders have not yet been placed.

4. Pension commitments provided for and not provided for, giving separate figures for commitments to pay pensions to past directors.

Example 2.5

The following balances relating to 19X1 have been extracted from the books of Downham plc.

	£000
Issued share capital:	
1,500,000 £1 ordinary shares fully paid	1,500
£500,000 12% debenture loan redeemable 19X8	500
Retained profit at 1 January, 19X1	370
Profit after tax for 19X1	290
Freehold and leasehold properties at cost	600
Plant and machinery at cost	2,600
Accumulated depreciation at 31 December, 19X1:	
Freehold properties	100
Leasehold properties	120
Plant and machinery	465
Bank overdraft	106
Trade creditors	308
Corporation tax due 30 September, 19X2	280
Social security payments outstanding	7
Debenture redemption reserve	150
Investments at cost	175
Stocks	530
Trade debtors	296
Prepaid expenses	20
Cash in hand	5
Interest due on debentures	30

The following additional information is provided:
1. Authorised share capital is £2,000,000.
2. A transfer of £50,000 is to be made to the debenture redemption reserve in anticipation of the redemption of the debentures in 19X8.
3. The directors propose to recommend a dividend of 10p per ordinary share to the annual general meeting.
4. The company's freehold properties cost £400,000 and four years remains on the lease of the other properties.
5. Additions to plant and machinery during 19X1 totalled £600,000. There were no sales of fixed assets during the year.
6. Depreciation charged in the profit and loss account was:

	£000
Freehold properties	25
Leasehold properties	20
Plant and machinery	110

7. The following information is provided relating to the company's investments:

	Jig plc	Saw plc
Cost of shares	£125,000	£50,000
Number of shares held	100,000	10,000
Type of share	Ordinary	Ordinary
Number of shares issued and fully paid	500,000	200,000
Market value per share on the London Stock Exchange	£1.20	£6.00

Jig supplies Downham with raw materials and the shares were purchased some years ago. The shares in Saw represent a temporary investment of surplus funds.
8. The debentures carry a charge on the freehold properties of Downham and the bank overdraft is secured against the leasehold properties.

REQUIRED:
The balance sheet of Downham plc at 31 December, 19X1, together with relevant notes complying with the minimum requirements of the Companies Acts 1948–81 so far as the information permits.
Note: Ignore advance corporation tax.

Solution:

Calculation of retained profit for inclusion in published balance sheet	£000	£000
Profit after tax		290
Less: Dividends	150	
Transfer to debenture redemption reserve	50	
		200
Retained profit for the year		90
Retained profit at 1 January, 19X1		370
Retained profit at 31 December, 19X1		460

Balance Sheet as at 31 December, 19X1

	Note	£000	£000	£000
Fixed Assets				
Tangible assets: Land and buildings				380
Plant and machinery				2,135
	1			2,515
Investments	2			125
Current Assets				
Stocks			530	
Debtors: Trade debtors		296		
Prepayments and accrued income		20		
			316	
Investments	2		50	
Cash at bank and in hand			5	
			901	
Creditors: amounts falling due within one year				
Bank loans and overdrafts	3		106	
Trade creditors			308	
Other creditors including social security and deferred income	4		467	
			881	
Net current assets				20
Total assets less current liabilities				2,660
Creditors: amounts falling due after more than one year				
Debenture loans	5			500
				2,160
Capital and Reserves				
Called up share capital	6			1,500
Debenture redemption reserve	7			200
Profit and loss account				460
				2,160

Notes:

1. Tangible fixed assets

	Land and Buildings			
	Freeholds	*Short Leaseholds*	*Plant and Machinery*	*Total*
	£000	£000	£000	£000
Cost:				
At 1 January, 19X1	400	200	2,000	2,600
Additions	—	—	600	600
At 31 December, 19X1	400	200	2,600	3,200

Land and Buildings .

	Freeholds	Short Leaseholds	Plant and Machinery	Total
	£000	£000	£000	£000
Accumulated depreciation:				
At 1 January, 19X1	75	100	355	530
Charge for year	25	20	110	155
At 31 December, 19X1	100	120	465	685
Net book value	300	80	2,135	2,515

2. Investments

	Book Value	Market Value
	£000	£000
Fixed asset investments listed on the Stock Exchange	125	120
Other investments listed on the Stock Exchange	50	60

The fixed asset investment comprises 20% of the ordinary issued share capital of Jig plc.

3. Bank loans and overdrafts
The bank overdraft is secured on the company's leasehold properties.

4. Other creditors including taxation and social security
The balance is made up as follows:

	£000
Dividend payable	150
Social security	7
Corporation tax due 30 September, 19X2	280
Other creditors	30
	467

5. Debenture loan
The company's debenture loan is redeemable in 19X8 and is secured on the company's freehold properties.

6. Called up share capital

	£000
Authorised	2,000
Issued 1,500,000 ordinary shares, fully paid	1,500

7. Debenture redemption reserves

	£000
At 1 January, 19X1	150
Transfer from profit and loss account	50
At 31 December, 19X1	200

2.6 CONTENT OF THE DIRECTORS' REPORT

The legal requirement to publish a directors' report, as part of the annual accounts, was first introduced in 1928. The Companies Act 1967, in particular, made significant additions to the statutory disclosure requirements. The disclosures required by the provisions currently in force are summarised below:

1. A review of business developments during the year and of the position at the end of the year.
2. Details of the principal business activities and of any changes in those activities during the year.
3. Recommended dividends, if any.
4. Transfers to reserves, if any.
5. Significant changes in fixed assets during the year, if any.
6. Any substantial differences between the book value and market value of land and buildings, where the directors consider this information to be of significance to members and debenture holders.
7. Separate figures for political and charitable contributions where in total they exceed £200. The amount of each political contribution over £200 together with the name of the recipient.
8. Details of the company's policy (where the number of employees exceeds 250) with regard to the employment of disabled persons, including those who become disabled while working for the company.
9. Names of persons who were directors at any time during the year.
10. The interest of the directors (including the interests of any spouse or infant children) at the year end in the shares and debentures of the company:
    (a) at the beginning of the year or date of appointment, if later;
    (b) at the year end.
11. Particulars of any important post balance sheet events.
12. An indication of:
    (a) likely future developments in the business of the company;
    (b) activities, if any, in the field of research and development.

13. Where a company has acquired an interest in its own shares during the year, either directly or through a nominee, full details of the transaction.

Example 2.6

The following financial information and facts are provided relating to the affairs of Bransgore plc for 19X1.
(i) Authorised share capital, £10,000,000.
(ii) Manufacturing wages, £7,300,000.
(iii) Throughout the year the directors of the company were E. Phillips and J. Phillips.
(iv) Recommended final dividend on ordinary shares, £700,000.
(v) Bills of exchange payable, £60,000.
(vi) Interest payable and similar charges, £136,000.
(vii) The directors have authorised capital expenditure of £2,000,000. No orders have yet been placed.
(viii) Contributions: Charitable £2,000
                Political   150

(ix) Hire charges in respect of plant and machinery, £36,000.
(x) Share premium account, £1,500,000.

REQUIRED:
Indicate which of the following sections of the annual report, if any, would contain each of the above items:
(a) The profit and loss account.
(b) The balance sheet.
(c) Notes to the profit and loss account and balance sheet.
(d) The directors' report.
Your answer should be presented in the following form:

Item	Section of annual report, if any
(i)	(a) or (b) or (c) or (d) or 'not published'
(ii)	
etc.	

Solution:

Item	Section
(i)	(c)
(ii)	not published
(iii)	(d)
(iv)	(c) and (d)
(v)	(b)
(vi)	(a)
(vii)	(c)
(viii)	(d)
(ix)	(c)
(x)	(b)

2.7 MODIFIED ACCOUNTS

All companies, irrespective of their size, must present their shareholders, debenture-holders, and other persons entitled to attend the annual general meeting, with accounts which comply, in full, with the requirements set out in sections 2 to 6 of this Chapter. Companies must also file accounts with the Registrar of Companies but, in the case of 'small' and 'medium sized' companies, these may be abridged versions of the accounts presented to the annual general meeting. The identification of small and medium sized companies is based on the following criteria:

Limits:	Small	Medium
1. Turnover	£1,400,000	£5,750,000
2. Balance sheet total*	£700,000	£2,800,000
3. Average number of employees.........	50	250

*defined as gross assets (headings A + B + C + D in prescribed format 1, see section 3.1 of this chapter).

To qualify as a small or medium sized company, *for exemption purposes*, the following conditions must be met:

(a) At least two of the limits must not be exceeded in either the current year or the preceding year;

(b) The company must be a private company engaged in neither banking, nor insurance, nor shipping, and not normally a member of a group.

The 'modified accounts', filed by small and medium sized companies, benefit from a number of exemptions which may be summarised as follows:

Small companies

(a) Neither a profit and loss account nor a directors' report need be filed.

(b) The modified balance sheet need only include the headings preceded by letters and Roman numerals, except that aggregate debtors falling due after more than one year must also be given.

(c) The amount of information given by way of notes is significantly reduced.

Medium companies

(a) Profit and loss accounts, prepared in accordance with prescribed format 1 (see section 3.1 of this chapter), may combine into a single item, headed 'gross profit or loss', items 1, 2, 3 and 6.

(b) Neither disclosure of turnover nor analysis of turnover and profit need be given by way of note.

The reason for the above concessions is that medium and small private companies are often essentially family concerns which, it is thought, should not be subjected to the close public scrutiny considered desirable in the case of larger companies. Not everyone agrees with this view, and continued opposition to the exemptions granted is based on the argument that it is reasonable to demand full disclosure, from all companies, in exchange for the privilege of limited liability. It must be remembered, however, that small and medium sized companies have to prepare full accounts for shareholders, and others, so the price of confidentiality is the extra cost of preparing the modified accounts. For this reason, the directors of many companies may ignore the exemptions offered and instead file full accounts with the Registrar. The banker should be aware of the limitations of modified accounts, but he will normally be in a position to insist on seeing the full accounts, and will often require management to supply further financial information before deciding whether to make an advance.

2.8   QUESTIONS AND SOLUTIONS

The following comprehensive questions are principally designed to test the student's ability to prepare accounts complying with the minimum requirements of the Companies Acts 1948–81.

Question 2.1

The following trial balance was extracted from the books of Ringwood Ltd. as at 31 December, 19X1.

Trial Balance as at 31 December, 19X1

	£	£
Authorised and issued ordinary share capital (£1 shares)		200,000
Retained profit at 1 January, 19X1		280,540
Accruals		7,500
Trade creditors		26,250
Bank overdraft		19,400
Stock and work in progress	236,500	
Trade debtors	107,300	
Turnover		1,052,000
Cost of goods sold, excluding depreciation	736,600	
Distribution costs	29,100	
Salaries and staff bonuses	106,800	
Directors' emoluments	22,000	
Rent and rates	3,700	
Telephone, postage and stationery	4,890	
Travel and entertainment expenses	1,200	
Audit fee	5,000	
Bad debts	2,500	
Office cleaning	1,700	
Subscriptions and donations	400	
Investments at cost	26,000	
Plant and machinery at cost	410,000	
Provision for depreciation 1 January, 19X1		108,000
Interest on bank overdraft	2,000	
Goodwill at 1 January, 19X1	10,000	
Bills of exchange payable		12,000
	1,705,690	1,705,690

The following information is provided:

1. The balance of stock and work in progress is made up as follows:

	£
Raw materials	57,000
Work in progress	26,800
Finished goods	152,700
	236,500

2. The company purchased plant costing £18,000 on 30 June, 19X1, paying £6,000 in cash and issuing the supplier with two bills of exchange, each for £6,000, maturing on 30 June, 19X2 and 30 June, 19X3. During the year the company also scrapped plant which cost £10,000 some years ago, and possessed a book value of £2,500 at the date of disposal. The latter transaction has not yet been recorded in the books.

3. A provision for depreciation of plant and machinery of £37,000 is to be made for 19X1.
4. Goodwill of £16,000 arose as the result of purchasing the business assets of a former supplier some years ago. The cost is being written off over eight years.
5. A provision for taxation of £50,000 is to be made in the profit and loss account.
6. The investment consists of shares in a supplier which were valued on the Stock Exchange at £27,500 at 31 December, 19X1.
7. The company is solely engaged in manufacturing and supplying aluminium plated gnomes to hardware shops.
8. The directors propose to recommend a dividend of 10p per share to the annual general meeting.

REQUIRED:
The profit and loss account of Ringwood Ltd. for 19X1 and balance sheet at 31 December, 19X1 together with relevant notes attached thereto. The accounts should comply with the minimum requirements of the Companies Acts 1948–81 so far as the information permits.
Note: Ignore advance corporation tax.

Solution:

Workings (not for publication):

	£
1. Cost of sales: As per trial balance	736,600
Add: Depreciation of plant	37,000
Loss on disposal of plant scrapped	2,500
Amortisation of goodwill	2,000
	778,100

2. Administration expenses: Salaries and staff bonuses	106,800
Directors' emoluments	22,000
Rent and rates	3,700
Telephone, postage and stationery	4,890
Travel and entertainment	1,200
Audit fee	5,000
Bad debts	2,500
Office cleaning	1,700
Subscriptions and donations	400
	148,190

Profit and Loss Account of Ringwood Ltd. for 19X1

	Note	£	£
Turnover			1,052,000
Less: Cost of sales			778,100
Gross profit			273,900
Less: Distribution costs		29,100	
Administrative expenses		148,190	
			177,290
Operating profit	1		96,610
Less: Interest payable	2		2,000
Profit before tax			94,610
Corporation tax			50,000
Profit after tax			44,610
Less: Dividends proposed	3		20,000
Retained profit for the year			24,610
Retained profit at 1 January, 19X1			280,540
Retained profit at 31 December, 19X1			305,150

Balance Sheet of Ringwood Ltd. as at 31 December, 19X1

	Note	£	£
Fixed Assets			
Intangible assets: Goodwill...	4		8,000
Tangible assets: Plant and machinery	4		262,500
Investments..	5		26,000
			296,500
Current Assets			
Stocks:			
Raw materials and consumables		57,000	
Work in progress		26,800	
Finished goods and goods for resale.............................		152,700	
		236,500	
Debtors:			
Trade debtors..		107,300	
		343,800	
Creditors: amounts falling due within one year			
Bank loans and overdrafts		19,400	
Trade creditors		26,250	
Bills of exchange payable..		6,000	
Other creditors including taxation and social security............	6	70,000	
Accruals and deferred income...		7,500	
		129,150	
Net current assets..			214,650
Total assets less current liabilities			511,150
Creditors: amounts falling due after more than one year			
Bills of exchange payable...			6,000
			505,150
Capital and Reserves			
Called up share capital...	7		200,000
Profit and loss account...			305,150
			505,150

Notes:

	£
1. Operating profit is stated after charging:	
Directors' emoluments	22,000
Auditors' remuneration and expenses...............................	5,000
Depreciation of tangible assets.......................................	37,000
Amortisation of intangible assets....................................	2,000
2. Interest payable: Bank overdraft	2,000
3. Dividends: Ordinary shares, 10p per share recommended	20,000

4. Fixed Assets:

	Tangible: Plant and Machinery £	Intangible: Goodwill £
Cost:		
At 1 January, 19X1	392,000	16,000
Additions	18,000	—
Disposals	(10,000)	—
At 31 December, 19X1	400,000	16,000
Accumulated depreciation:		
At 1 January, 19X1	108,000	6,000
Charge for year	37,000	2,000
Disposals	(7,500)	—
At 31 December, 19X1	137,500	8,000
Net book value	262,500	8,000

5. Balance consists of listed investments: at cost £26,000
   at market value......... £27,500

6. Other creditors including taxation and social security. The balance is made up as follows:

	£
Corporation tax due 30 September, 19X2	50,000
Dividends payable	20,000
	70,000

7. Called up share capital:

Authorised	200,000
Issued 200,000 ordinary shares, fully paid	200,000

Question 2.2

The following trial balance has been prepared for Boscombe plc whose principal activities are the manufacture and sale of gardening equipment and building materials.

Trial Balance as at 31 December, 19X1

	£000	£000
Ordinary share capital (£1 shares)		1,000
Retained profit at 1 January, 19X1		503
12% debentures, redeemable 19X10		500
Trade creditors		260
Turnover: Gardening equipment		3,630
Building materials		1,975
Bank balance	32	
Freehold properties at cost	500	
Plant and machinery at cost	2,400	
Provision for depreciation of plant and machinery at 31 December, 19X1		800
Stocks	750	
Trade debtors	670	
Cost of sales: Gardening equipment	2,520	
Building materials	1,180	
Administration expenses	482	
Distribution costs	174	
Interim dividend paid	100	
Interest on debentures	60	
Proceeds from sale of freehold property		200
	8,868	8,868

You are given the following additional information:

1. The administration expenses, distribution costs and interest charge relate 75% to the gardening equipment business and 25% to building materials.
2. During July, 19X1 a major customer went into liquidation owing the company £120,000. A dividend of 20p in the £ was received from the liquidator in December, 19X1 and the bad debt incurred of £96,000 is included in administration expenses.
3. In December, 19X1, the company sold one of the freehold properties, which had cost £120,000 some years ago, for £200,000. It is estimated that the corporation tax liability arising in respect of this capital gain will be £24,000. T. Mathias & Co., a firm of chartered surveyors, has valued the remaining properties at £600,000 and the directors have decided to write the new valuation into the books.
4. The £500,000 debenture was issued on 1 January, 19X1 in order to enable the company's overdraft to be repaid. The directors plan to make annual transfers of £50,000 to a debenture redemption reserve in anticipation of repayment in 19X10.
5. A provision for taxation of £500,000 is to be made in the profit and loss account.

6. The directors propose to pay a final dividend of 2p per share.
7. Since the balance sheet date, the company has disposed of its building materials division at a large profit.

REQUIRED:

The profit and loss account of Boscombe plc for 19X1 and balance sheet at 31 December, 19X1 together with relevant notes attached thereto. The account should comply with the minimum requirements of the Companies Acts 1948–1981 and SSAP6 so far as the information permits.

Note: Ignore advance corporation tax and depreciation of freehold properties.

Solution:

Workings (not for publication):

		Gardening £000	Building £000	Total £000
Turnover		3,630	1,975	5,605
Less: Cost of sales		2,520	1,180	3,700
Gross profit		1,110	795	1,905
Less: Administration expenses	482			
Distribution costs	174			
Interest charge	60			
Apportioned 75 : 25	716	537	179	716
Pre-tax profit		573	616	1,189

P+M 2400
–(800
——————
      1600

Profit and Loss Account of Boscombe plc for 19X1

	Note	£000	£000
Turnover	1		5,605
Less: Cost of sales			3,700
Gross profit			1,905
Less: Distribution costs		174	
Administrative expenses		482	
		—	656
Operating profit	2		1,249
Less: Interest payable	3		60
Profit from ordinary activities			1,189
Tax on profit from ordinary activities			500
Profit on ordinary activities after tax			689
Profit on extraordinary item, less tax	4		56
Profit for the year attributable to shareholders			745
Less: Dividends paid and proposed	5	120	
Transfer to debenture redemption reserve		50	
		—	170
Retained profit for the year			575
Retained profit 1 January, 19X1			503
Retained profit 31 December, 19X1			1,078

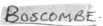

Balance Sheet as at 31 December, 19X1

Fixed Assets	Note	£000	£000
Tangible fixed assets			
Land and buildings...			600
Plant and machinery......................................			1,600
	6		2,200
Current Assets			
Stocks..		750	
Debtors:			
Trade debtors...		670	
Cash at bank and in hand...............................		32	
		1,452	
Creditors: amounts falling due within one year			
Trade creditors...		260	
Other creditors including taxation and social security.................	7	544	
		804	
Net current assets..			648
Total assets less current liabilities			2,848
Creditors: amounts falling due after more than one year			
Debenture loans..	8		500
			2,348
Capital and Reserves			
Called up share capital.......................................	9		1,000
Revaluation reserve..	10		220
Other reserves			
Debenture redemption reserve.............................	10		50
Profit and loss account......................................			1,078
			2,348

Notes:
  1. Turnover
     The contributions of the various activities of the group to turnover and profit before tax are as follows:

	Turnover £000	Profit before tax £000
Gardening equipment.........	3,630	573
Buildings materials............	1,975	616
	5,605	1,189

  2. Operating profit is stated after charging an exceptional loss of £96,000 arising from the liquidation of a major customer.
  3. Interest payable: Loans repayable after five years, £60,000.
  4. Extraordinary item: During the year the company realised a profit of £80,000, less tax £24,000, on the sale of a freehold property.

£

5. Dividends: Ordinary shares, 10p per share paid 100,000

2p per share recommended. 20,000

6. Tangible Fixed Assets:

	Freehold Land and Buildings £000	Plant and Machinery £000	Total £000
Cost at 1 January	500		
Disposal..	(120)		
Revaluation	220		
Cost or valuation (see below) at 31 December, 19X1......................	600	2,400	3,000
Accumulated depreciation at 31 December, 19X1......................	—	800	800
Net book value..................................	600	1,600	2,200

The company's remaining freehold properties were revalued at £600,000 by T. Mathias & Co., chartered surveyors, in December, 19X1.

7. Other creditors including taxation and social security. The balance is made up as follows:

£

Corporation tax due 30 September, 19X2 524,000

Dividends payable... 20,000

544,000

8. Debenture loan: The company's debenture loan is repayable in 19X10.
9. Called up share capital:

Issued 1,000,000 ordinary shares, fully paid............ £1,000,000

10. Movement on reserves:

	Revaluation reserve £	Debenture redemption reserve £
At 1 January, 19X1......................	—	—
Revaluation during the year	220,000	—
Transfer from profit....................	—	50,000
At 31 December, 19X1.................	220,000	50,000

Question 2.3

Using the information given in question 2.2, prepare a list of the items which the Companies Acts require the directors of Boscombe plc to disclose in their report to shareholders.

Solution:

Directors' report extracts

1. Principal activities

The company's principal activities are the manufacture and sale of gardening equipment and building materials.

2. Dividends
   The directors have paid and recommended the following dividends for the year 19X1.

		£
Ordinary dividends:	Interim of 10p per share paid	100,000
	Final of 2p per share proposed.........	20,000
		120,000

3. Transfer to reserves
   (a) The directors propose to transfer £50,000 profit to debenture redemption reserve and carry the balance forward as retained profit.
   (b) The surplus of £220,000 arising on the revaluation of the company's freehold building has been carried to revaluation reserve.

4. Post balance sheet event
   Since the balance sheet date the company has disposed of its building materials division at a large profit.

5. Changes in fixed assets
   The company sold one of its freehold buildings during the year. Full details of this transaction are given in notes 4 and 6 to the accounts.

CHAPTER 3

Valuation of Company Assets and Liabilities

3.1 THE ACCOUNTING STANDARDS COMMITTEE

In the mid-1960s, the British accountant's ability to prepare for publication entirely reliable factual statements of a company's financial position was unquestioned. The popular view was that the accounting process was time-consuming, painstaking, meticulous, and even boring, but that it was all worthwhile because the result of the accountant's labours was an absolutely accurate statement of a company's financial position. The accountant no longer enjoys immunity from public criticism and the quality of his work is constantly being challenged, as are the standards prevailing in many of the other established professions.

In accountancy, the more critical attitude stems from a series of events in the late 1960s, among which the GEC/AEI takeover is perhaps the best known. In October 1967, GEC (The General Electric Company) made a takeover bid for the shares of AEI (Associated Electrical Industries). Often the directors of a company which is the subject of a takeover bid wish to resist the move, and this was the case on this occasion. One of the defensive tactics, employed by the directors of AEI, was to circulate its shareholders with a document explaining the advantages of retaining their present investment, and informing them that the company's forecast profit for 1967 was £10m. In the event, the takeover bid was successful and the accounts of AEI for 1967 were eventually published in April 1968, but instead of reporting a profit of £10m they revealed a *loss* of £4½m. An obvious explanation for this massive discrepancy might have been that substantial errors were made when preparing the forecast, but an investigation showed that this was not the case. The 'forecast' for 1967 was prepared late in the year (October) so that only a small element of estimating was required, and this function was efficiently performed. The investigation instead revealed that the discrepancy was mainly caused by the new management team taking a different (less optimistic) view regarding the value of AEI's assets.

The general public was shocked to discover that accountancy was not the precise science they had believed it to be, and that the level of reported profit was substantially a matter of opinion rather than objective fact. For instance, it was widely recognised, for the first time, that the amount of the depreciation charge, and therefore the balance sheet value of fixed assets, could differ enormously depending on such matters as estimates of the asset's useful life and the depreciation method considered appropriate. Prompt action was required to prevent any further erosion of the accountant's reputation, and the profession's response was to establish The Accounting Standards Committee (ASC), in 1970, whose job is to reduce the variety in accounting methods by publishing authoritative Statements of Standard Accounting Practice (SSAPs) which identify appropriate accounting procedures for companies to follow.

The standard-setting process can be described briefly as follows: The ASC identifies a topic requiring consideration as the possible subject for a future SSAP. Usually, one or more research studies are undertaken, and their findings are frequently published. A preliminary draft is then circulated to committees of the various professional accounting bodies, for comment, and it is also the subject of discussion in meetings between the ASC and organisations particularly affected by the topic under consideration. Next, an 'Exposure Draft' is circulated widely for further comment and, because it is generally expected that the SSAP will not differ significantly from the Exposure Draft, the proposals receive a great deal of attention at this stage. An SSAP is then prepared, in the light of views received, and circulated to the Councils of the major accounting bodies for approval and publication. To date (June 1983), the ASC has published twenty SSAPs which deal with both the valuation of certain assets and liabilities and the way in which the information relating to those items should be disclosed in the accounts. The SSAPs included in the *Accountancy* syllabus are listed below, together with an indication of where they are dealt with in this book.

SSAP	*Title*	*Chapter*
1	Accounting for the results of associated companies	5
2	Disclosure of accounting policies	3
6	Extraordinary items and prior year adjustments	2
8	The treatment of taxation under the imputation system in the accounts of companies	3
9	Stocks and work in progress	3
10	Statements of source and application of funds	9
12	Accounting for depreciation	3
13	Accounting for research and development	3
14	Group accounts	5
15	Accounting for deferred taxation	3
16	Current cost accounting	6

3.2 SSAP2: DISCLOSURE OF ACCOUNTING POLICIES

The aim of this statement is to ensure that:

(i) Companies prepare their accounts in accordance with certain 'fundamental accounting concepts' specified in the statement (any deviation from these concepts must be disclosed).

(ii) Companies report which 'accounting policies' they have chosen from the 'accounting bases' available for the purpose of valuing the assets and liabilities which appear in their accounts. The statement does not establish accounting standards for individual assets and liabilities; this job is done in other SSAPs issued by the ASC, e.g. SSAP9 which deals with the valuation of stocks and work in progress (Standards have not yet been issued for all assets and liabilities, e.g. goodwill remains at the Exposure Draft stage—June 1983).

The terms 'fundamental accounting concepts', 'accounting policies' and 'accounting bases' are given the following interpretation in SSAP2:

Fundamental accounting concepts. Company accounts are based on the following four broad assumptions:

(a) The going concern concept. This assumes that the company will continue in business for the foreseeable future. The main effect of this assumption is that the liquidation value of fixed assets, which may be significantly different from book value, can be ignored because there is no intention to discontinue business activity.

(b) The accruals concept. This requires:

    (i) revenues to be matched with related expenses when measuring profit;

    (ii) revenues and expenses to be included in the profit and loss account as they are earned and incurred rather than when they are received and paid.

(c) The consistency concept. This requires a company to employ the same accounting policy for valuing similar assets both within an accounting period and during consecutive accounting periods. For instance, if a company depreciates certain items of plant on the straight line basis, similar items of plant must also be depreciated on the straight line basis and the straight line method must also be used in the next accounting period.

(d) The concept of prudence. This prevents companies from anticipating profits (e.g. profit must not be recognised until an item of stock is actually sold), but requires them to provide for all foreseeable losses (e.g. if it seems likely that a debt will prove to be bad, it must be provided for despite the fact that collection remains a possibility).

Accounting bases. Alternative accounting bases have been developed for the purpose of valuing a wide variety of assets and liabilities, including

(a) stock and work in progress—see section 3

(b) long-term contracts—see section 4

(c) tangible fixed assets—see section 5

(d) research and development expenditure—see section 6

(e) goodwill—see section 7

(f) deferred taxation—see section 8.2.

For example, the alternative bases available for accounting for the decline in value of tangible fixed assets include straight line, reducing balance, usage and the annuity method. Each of these bases are acceptable for the purpose of valuing fixed assets for inclusion in company accounts, since they all broadly comply with the four fundamental concepts i.e. they are in accordance with:

(a) The going concern concept, since they assume that the company will remain in business long enough to allow the original cost to be recovered, and therefore do not require assets to be restated at their liquidation values;

(b) The accruals concept, since the cost is spread over the life of the asset as benefit is received, rather than written off when the payment is made;

(c) The consistency concept, provided the selected method is applied to similar assets each year;

(d) The concept of prudence, since provision is made for the loss which will be realised when the asset is scrapped at the end of its useful life.

However, each depreciation method will normally produce a significantly different charge, and this can have an enormous effect on the level of reported profit, for instance, see example 3.7.

Accounting policies. This is the term used to describe the accounting bases chosen by a particular company for the purpose of valuing assets and liabilities. The following extracts from the 1982 accounts of the Beecham Group are typical examples of how companies disclose the accounting policies used for valuing stocks and for calculating depreciation:

Stocks
Stocks are stated at the lower of cost and net realisable value generally using the first in first out method of valuation. The cost of finished and partly processed goods comprises raw materials, direct labour and expenses, and related production overheads.

Depreciation
The cost of fixed assets, except freehold land, is written off in equal annual instalments over the estimated useful lives of the assets. The average lives for each major asset category are:

Freehold buildings............................	50 years
Leasehold land and buildings................	Term of lease
Plant and equipment..........................	10/15 years
Vehicles—motor cars	5 years
—lorries and other vehicles.........	7 years

The main provisions of SSAP2 were incorporated in the Companies Act 1981, though reference must still be made to the statement for definitions and other background details.

The valuation of assets and liabilities for inclusion in company accounts is examined in sections 3 to 8 of this Chapter. The relevant valuation rules contained in the Companies Act 1981 and in SSAPs 8, 9, 12, 13 and 15 are referred to, as appropriate, and identified by typesetting in italics. The regulations are reproduced in sufficient depth for the *Accountancy* examination, but reference should be made to the Act and individual Standards if the exact wording is required.

3.3   STOCK AND WORKS IN PROGRESS

The way in which stocks and, indeed, all other assets are valued has direct implications for the level of reported profit. If assets are over-valued, profits will be overstated whereas, if they are under-valued, profits will be understated. In either case, users of the accounts will be provided with misleading financial information, and decisions which lead to an optimum allocation of resources are less likely to be taken. It must, of course, be recognised that valuation errors cancel out over time. For instance, the closing stock of one accounting period is the opening stock of the next and so, if over valuation occurs, reported profits will be too high in period 1 and too low in period 2 but, in neither accounting period, does reported profit give a fair reflection of the company's actual performance.

The quantity of resources tied up in stock will depend on factors such as delivery periods, the length of the production cycle, and production policy, i.e. whether the level of production is matched closely with sales, or whether output is maintained at a steady level so that stock is built up during quiet periods to meet demand in the busier periods ahead. Nevertheless, for most companies stock comprises a significant proportion of gross assets and, for this reason, the level of reported profit can vary a great deal depending on the valuation method used. For example, assume that, at the end of its first year in business, a company's accounts show gross assets of £2m, including stock of £600,000 and reported profits amount to £200,000. An alternative valuation method might result in a stock figure of £450,000. If the alternative is adopted, the values of stock and gross assets will be reduced respectively by 25% and 7.5%, while reported profit will fall by 75% to £50,000.

Both SSAP9 and the Companies Act 1981 require companies to value stock at cost, except where this exceeds net realisable value (i.e. market price less all further costs to completion and less all costs to be incurred in marketing, selling and distributing the item), in which case the latter figure should be used. To ensure that full provision is made for foreseeable losses, SSAP9 requires the comparison between cost and net realisable value to be based on individual items of stock, with the proviso that groups of similar items may be compared where the comparison of individual items is impracticable. The 'lower of cost and net realisable value' rule is therefore consistent with the fundamental accounting concepts discussed in section 2 of this Chapter, particularly the concept of prudence which requires companies not to anticipate profits but to provide for all foreseeable losses.

Example 3.1

The following information is provided in respect of Banbury Ltd:

Item of Stock	Cost	Net Realisable Value
	£	£
A	500	580
B	300	370
C	250	330
D	760	600

[handwritten: 500 / 300 / 250 / 600 / 1650 ✓ P 29/10/85]

REQUIRED

Calculations of the total value of Banbury's stock, based on the lower of cost and net realisable value rule, assuming that cost is compared with net realisable value.

(a) on an individual item basis
(b) on a total basis

Solution

(a) Individual item basis:

Item of Stock	Cost	NRV	Lower of Cost and NRV: Individual Item Basis
	£	£	£
A	500	580	500
B	300	370	300
C	250	330	250
D	760	600 <160	600 *P 29/10/85*
			1,650

(b) Total cost basis:

Item of Stock	Cost	NRV	Lower of Cost and NRV: Total Basis
	£	£	£
A + B + C + D	1,810	1,880	1,810

Comparing cost with the NRV of individual items results in a lower stock value (£1,650 as compared with £1,810) and therefore a lower profit figure. This is because the comparison of total figures for cost and NRV results in a foreseeable loss of £160 on item D (£760 cost—£600 NRV) being offset by total unrealised gains of £230 on items A–C (£1,280 NRV–£1,050 cost).

The principal situations in which NRV is likely to be below cost are where there has been:

1. A major increase in costs or fall in selling price.
2. Physical deterioration of stocks.
3. Obsolescence of products.
4. A decision, as part of a company's marketing strategy, to manufacture and sell particular products at a loss.

5. Errors in production or purchasing.

In practice, any of the above circumstances are unlikely to apply to more than a small proportion of the company's stock. For the remainder, NRV will exceed cost and can be ignored when valuing stock for inclusion in the accounts. However, there will still remain the problem of deciding how to compute cost; there are two basic areas of difficulty:

(a) Whether to value stock on the marginal cost or the total cost basis.

(b) How to identify purchases with issues to production and to match finished goods with sales, i.e. a choice has to be made between, for instance, FIFO and LIFO.

These matters are examined in the following two sub-sections:

3.3.1 Marginal Cost or Total Cost   The main difference between these two methods is their treatment of fixed factory costs, and it is therefore a problem that is primarily confined to manufacturing companies. The marginal cost basis includes only the variable costs associated with producing a single extra unit of output, whereas the total (or absorption) cost basis also includes a proportion of fixed factory costs. The main arguments for and against the total cost basis, which are the reverse of the arguments for and against the marginal cost basis are as follows:

For total cost:

(a) Each unit manufactured benefits from the provision of facilities which result in fixed costs being incurred, and a proportion of their cost should therefore be included in the value of stock.

(b) The accruals concept requires costs to be matched with related revenues, and the *total* cost of stock unsold at the balance sheet date should therefore be carried forward and matched against revenue arising during the following accounting period.

Against total cost:

(c) Fixed costs are a function of time rather than production, and should not therefore be carried forward but should be charged against the revenue arising during the period when they are incurred.

(d) The valuation of stock will depend on the level of production, rather than the materials and work involved, since the quantity manufactured determines the amount of fixed cost attributed to each item, i.e. a low level of output will cause each unit to be charged with a high element of fixed cost.

(e) Fixed costs cannot be directly related to particular items of stock and are therefore apportioned on an arbitrary basis.

SSAP9 favours the use of the total cost basis for external reporting purposes, and the statement defines the costs to be included in stock as those incurred 'in bringing the product or service to its present location and condition'. This will normally mean that the valuation should include a share of factory overheads, but not distribution costs or administrative expenses. The problem, referred to under (d) above, is avoided by the requirement that the calculation of the overhead element should be based on the 'normal level of activity, taking one year with another'.

Example 3.2 tests students' understanding of the difference between the marginal cost and total cost bases of stock valuation. It should be worked by students *before* examining the solution provided.

Example 3.2 (Taken from the April, 1982 *Accountancy* paper).

At the beginning of 1981 Deer Ltd. was incorporated and manufactures a single product. At the end of the first year's operations the company's accountant prepared a draft profit and loss account which contained the following financial information:

PROFIT AND LOSS ACCOUNT OF DEER LTD FOR 1981

	£	£
Sales (200,000 units)		600,000
Less: Prime cost of units manufactured during 1981		
(500,000 units)	800,000	
Deduct closing stock	480,000	
	———	
Prime cost of goods sold	320,000	
Fixed Costs:		
Factory expenses	200,000	
General expenses	100,000	620,000
	———	———
Net loss		£20,000
		═══

Additional finance is required, and the directors are worried that the company's bank manager is unlikely to regard the financial facts shown above as a satisfactory basis for a further advance. The company's accountant made the following observation and suggestion:

'The cause of the poor result for 1981 was the decision to value closing stock on the prime cost basis. An acceptable alternative practice would involve charging factory expenses to the total number of units produced and carrying forward an appropriate proportion of those expenses as part of the closing stock value.'

Required:

(a) A revised profit and loss account, for presentation to the company's bank, valuing closing stock on the total (absorption) cost basis suggested by the company's accountant.

[8]

(b) Assuming that, in 1982, the company again produces 500,000 units but sells 700,000 units, calculate the expected profit using each of the two stock valuation bases. Assume also that, in 1982, sales price per unit and costs incurred will be the same as for 1981.

[6]

(c) Comment briefly on the accountant's suggestion and its likely effect on the bank manager's response to the request for additional finance.

[6]

[Total marks for question—20]

Solution:

(a)

Profit and Loss Account for 1981—total cost basis

	£000	£000
Sales...		600
Less: Prime costs...........................	800	
Factory expenses.....................	200	
Total cost of manufacture.........	1,000	
Deduct closing stock...............	600 W1	
Cost of goods sold..................	400	
General expenses.....................	100	
		500
Net profit..............................		100

W1. The company produced 500,000 units but sold only 200,000 units, and so it had 300,000 units in stock. The total cost basis therefore results in a stock valuation of $(300,000 \div 500,000) \times £1,000,000 = £600,000$.

$STOCK \div PROD \times COST$

(b)   *Forecast Profit and Loss Accounts for 1982*

		Prime Cost		Total Cost
		£000		£000
Sales		2,100		2,100
Less: Opening stock.............	480		600	
Prime costs	800		800	
Factory expenses	—		200	
	1,280		1,600	
Deduct closing stock	160 W2		200 W2	
	1,120		1,400	
Factory expenses	200		—	
General expenses	100		100	
		1,420		1,500
Net profit		680		600

W2. The opening stock is 300,000 units and 500,000 units are expected to be manufactured during 1982. Assuming 700,000 units are sold, 100,000 units will remain in stock at the end of 1982. The closing stock valuations are therefore:
Prime cost basis: $(100,000 \div 500,000) \times £800,000 = £160,000$
Total cost basis: $(100,000 \div 500,000) \times £1,000,000 = £200,000$

(c) Total cost is an acceptable basis for valuing stock; indeed it is the method favoured for external reporting purposes by SSAP9. Provided the resulting valuation does not exceed net realisable value there is no reason why it should not be used.

The use of different valuation bases does not, of course, alter the underlying financial facts, but it can affect the allocation of profit between consecutive accounting periods. Use of the total cost basis, which relates indirect manufacturing costs to output rather than time, will produce higher profits than the marginal (prime) cost basis when production exceeds sales. Three-fifths of the fixed factory costs $(£200,000 \times \frac{3}{5} = £120,000)$ are added to the value of closing stock for the purpose of preparing the revised profit and loss account for 1981, and this converts a reported loss of £20,000 into a reported profit of £100,000. The situation is reversed when sales exceed production. (See forecast results for 1982 above).

The company's bank manager no doubt will be aware of the effect of different accounting policies on reported profit and he should not be significantly influenced by a change of method which gives an improved appearance to the underlying facts. Nevertheless, use of the marginal cost approach, when output exceeds sales, will unduly deflate profits where there is a ready market for the goods manufactured. In such circumstances, use of the total cost basis is fully justified.

Examiner's comments:
Main student errors: Many answers to requirement (a) included a proportion of the fixed general expenses as well as the fixed factory expenses in the closing value of stock. Answers to requirement (b) often omitted the opening stock, and few candidates grasped the point that the absorption cost basis increases reported profit when the volume of production exceeds sales, but reduces profit in the opposite circumstances.

3.3.2   FIFO or LIFO   The price at which goods are purchased will normally increase during the year and, consequently, items in stock at the year end will have been purchased at a variety of different prices. In theory, the accruals concept requires the cost of items sold to be matched individually against their sales proceeds,

but this is usually impracticable because of the large number of items bought and sold during an accounting period. To simplify the process, assumptions are made concerning the flow of goods through the firm. The main alternative assumptions are 'first in first out' (FIFO), 'last in first out' (LIFO) and 'weighted average cost' (AVCO). The effect of different cost flow assumptions on reported profit and the balance sheet value of stock is illustrated by comparing and contrasting FIFO and LIFO (AVCO produces results which fall somewhere between these two extremes):

FIFO: This assumes that the items which have been longest in stock are used first, and stock on hand represents the latest purchases or production. The effect is that, during a period of rising prices, cost of sales is reported at a low figure, reported profit is maximised and the balance sheet figure for stock represents most recent purchase prices.

LIFO: This assumes that the items purchased or produced most recently are used first, and the quantities of stock on hand represent earliest purchases or production. The result is that cost of sales is higher than under the FIFO assumption, and reported profit is correspondingly lower. In the balance sheet, stocks are valued at a relatively low figure, representing prices ruling weeks, months or even years earlier.

Both FIFO and LIFO have their advocates. Some argue that FIFO is superior because it is more likely to approximate the actual flow of goods through the company. Supporters of LIFO argue that their method works better during a period of inflation, because it produces a more realistic measure of profit.

Example 3.3

Glenusk Ltd. bought an item of stock for £100 on 1st January, 19X1, and a second item for £103 on the morning of 10th January. On the afternoon of 10th January, one of the items was sold for £110. Using FIFO and LIFO for identifying purchases with sales produces the following alternative results:

	FIFO £	LIFO £
Sales	110	110
Cost of goods sold.....................	100	103
Gross profit..............................	10	7
Balance sheet value of stocks.........	103	100

Between 1st January and 10th January the cost of Glenusk's stock increased from £100 to £103. It is therefore argued, in certain quarters, that £3 represents a gain arising from holding stock during a period of rising prices and only the remaining £7 should be reported as normal profit arising from business operations (holding gains are examined more fully in Chapter 6, section 2). Looked at another way, in the absence of inflation the item would have sold for £107, but the customer had to pay £3 extra to compensate Glenusk for the higher purchase price which it must pay to replace the item sold. The drawback of LIFO is that stock is reported at a low figure in the balance sheet. This is not particularly noticeable in example 3.3, but a company which uses LIFO for a number of years will report stock, in the balance sheet, at only a fraction of its current cost.

The Companies Act 1981 approves FIFO, LIFO and AVCO, whereas SSAP9 rejects LIFO on the grounds that it fails to produce a balance sheet figure for stock which bears a reasonable relationship to actual cost. The conflict between these two regulations has not yet been resolved, but it seems possible that the Companies Act 1981 will give a new lease of life to LIFO. *An additional requirement introduced by the 1981 Act, which will be particularly relevant where LIFO is used, is for companies to disclose by way of note any material difference between the balance sheet value of stocks and replacement cost.*

3.4   LONG TERM CONTRACT WORK IN PROGRESS

Companies in the manufacturing and construction industries sometimes undertake contracts which extend over a number of accounting periods. A strict application of the prudence concept would require companies which engage in long term contracts to defer recognition of profit until the contract is complete. This would produce unsatisfactory results, with reported profits fluctuating a great deal depending on how many jobs happened to be completed during a particular accounting period. An alternative practice, which is thought to provide a better measure of corporate performance, is to recognise profit as work proceeds.

The valuation and disclosure of information relating to long term contract work in progress is dealt with in SSAP9, which states that profit should only be recognised on long term work in progress (defined as work which extends beyond a twelve month period) when the work is well advanced and the outcome can be assessed with reasonable certainty. SSAP9 gives no guidance to help decide whether these conditions are met, and each case must be considered on its merits. As a general rule, a contract which is less than 25% complete is unlikely to be sufficiently well advanced, and the information provided in examination questions will make it possible to judge whether the outcome can be assessed with reasonable certainty. *Long-term work in progress must be reported in the accounts at cost plus attributable profit (based on work carried out to date), less any foreseeable losses and progress payments received and receivable. If, however, anticipated losses on individual contracts exceed costs incurred less progress payments received and receivable, the deficit should be shown separately, in the balance sheet, as a provision.*

The matters which students should consider, when dealing with questions on contract valuation, and the procedures involved are illustrated in example 3.4.

Example 3.4

(a) Ashwell p.l.c. entered into a contract to build a bridge for £1,350,000 on 1st January, 19X1. At 31st December, 19X1 architects certified that the work was 70% complete, and the following additional information is provided:

	£
Costs incurred to date	600,000
Estimated further costs to completion	350,000
Progress payments received and receivable	300,000

Steps:
1. Consider whether it is a long term contract. The answer is 'yes' because it extends over a period in excess of twelve months.
2. Consider whether the contract is sufficiently advanced for the outcome to be assessed with reasonable certainty. Again, the answer is 'yes', because work is 70% complete.
3. Estimate total contract profit:

	£	£
Contract price		1,350,000
Less: Costs to date	600,000	
Estimated further costs	350,000	
		950,000
Estimated total profit		400,000

4. Compute attributable profit on the basis of work carried out to date, i.e. 70% of £400,000 = £280,000.

On the grounds of prudence, it is sometimes suggested that the attributable profit should be reduced by an arbitrary fraction, e.g. 2/3rds, or by cash received as a proportion of the value of work done. SSAP9 does not require this adjustment to be made.

$400 \div 100 = 4 \times 70 = £280.000 \quad 70\%$

5. Prepare the balance sheet valuation.

Contract work in progress:	£
Costs to date	600,000
Add: Attributable profit.........................	280,000
	880,000
Less: Progress payments received and receivable.........	300,000
Balance sheet value............................	580,000

(b) Consider the effect on the above calculations if the contract price was £750,000, but all the other facts and estimates were unchanged. In these circumstances the estimated loss on the contract would be £200,000 (contract costs £950,000—contract price £750,000), and this loss would have to be fully provided for in the accounts for 19X1. The balance sheet value would become:

Contract work in progress:	£	£
Costs to date		600,000
Less: Foreseeable loss	200,000	
Progress payments received and receivable..............	300,000	
		500,000
Balance sheet value		100,000

No further loss will result from this contract provided the estimates are fulfilled. The balance sheet value of the contract is £100,000 and the estimated further costs are £350,000. Those two amounts are together exactly covered by the balance still to be invoiced in respect of the contract, i.e. £750,000 (contract price)—£300,000 (progress payments) = £450,000.

Example 3.5 (Taken from the September, 1981 *Accountancy* paper).

Cavour Ltd. is a firm of building contractors. The following information is provided relating to their uncompleted contracts at 31 December, 1980:

Contract	A	B	C	D
Date contract commenced	1.1.80	1.2.80	1.8.80	1.10.80
Expected completion date	30.4.81	31.3.81	31.1.81	31.3.82
	£	£	£	£
Cost of work to 31 December, 1980.	159,000	57,000	15,000	4,000
Estimated further costs to completion	36,000	15,000	2,000	62,000
Value of work certified to 31 December, 1980.	200,000	50,000	18,000	—
Contract price	260,000	65,000	21,000	75,000
Progress payments received and receivable at 31 December, 1980.	175,000	40,000	—	—

Required:

(a) A statement showing your calculations of the separate values to be placed on each contract at 31 December, 1980. The statement should show the profit or loss, if any, included in each of the valuations. You should include in the statement appropriate narratives to explain the treatments chosen.

(b) A statement of the information in respect of the four contracts which would appear in the balance sheet of Cavour Ltd. at 31 December, 1980.

NOTE: *Your calculations should take account of the requirements contained in Statement of Standard Accounting Practice 9.*

[20]

Solution:

(a) *Workings:*

	Contract A		Contract B	
Contract price		260,000		65,000
Less: Costs to date	159,000		57,000	
Estimated future costs	36,000		15,000	
		195,000		72,000
Estimated total profit (foreseeable loss)		65,000		(7,000)

Contract A.   Attributable profit based on the value of work certified to date as a proportion of the contract selling price is $(200,000 \div 260,000) \times £65,000 = £50,000.$
Contract B.   Foreseeable loss, £7,000.
Contract C.   Contract expected to last 6 months, not a long term contract.
Contract D.   Contract insufficiently advanced to allow the final outcome to be assessed with reasonable certainty.

Statement of Contract Values

	A £	B £	C £	D £
Costs to date	159,000	57,000	15,000	4,000
Add: Attributable profit	50,000			
Less: Foreseeable loss		7,000		
	209,000	50,000		
Less: Progress payments	175,000	40,000		
	34,000	10,000	15,000	4,000

(b) Balance Sheet extract:
Current Assets:
Long term contract works in progress at cost plus attributable profit, less foreseeable losses and progress payments received and receivable at 31st December, 1980. 48,000
Other contract 15,000

Examiner's comments:
Main student errors: The most common errors were to provide for only a proportion of the expected loss on contract B, to treat contract C as long-term, and to take credit for a proportion of the profit expected to arise on the completion of contract D.

3.5 DEPRECIATION OF TANGIBLE FIXED ASSETS

Depreciation can be defined as the decline in the value of a fixed asset to a company; it is normally caused by a combination of usage, the passage of time and obsolescence. There are two reasons for charging depreciation in the accounts:

(a) To ensure that the revenue recognised during a particular accounting period bears the full cost of resources used up during the same time period. If depreciation was omitted, profit would be overstated and wrong assessments might be made of a company's performance.

(b) To maintain intact the company's capital base by earmarking, for retention within the business, over a fixed asset's useful life, a quantity of resources equal to its original cost. It is quite likely that these resources will be immediately reinvested in operating assets and will therefore not be available, in the form of cash, to finance replacement when the asset wears out. In these circumstances, it will be management's job to arrange an alternative source of finance when the need arises (this matter is discussed further in Chapter 9, section 7.1).

To compute the annual depreciation charge, the disposal value and expected useful life of the fixed asset must first be estimated. The difference between the cost and the estimated disposal value of the asset, called the depreciable amount, gives the balance to be written off, while the estimated life of the asset determines the period over which the write off is to take place. It is important that estimates of both the asset's disposal value and useful life are accurate, since errors will result in too high or too low a depreciation charge, and the consequent under- or overstatement of reported profit.

In recent years, the high rate of inflation has meant that many fixed assets have been sold for figures well in excess of the original estimates. This is particularly noticeable in the case of assets which remain in good working order, but are sold because a superior version has come on to the market. This has resulted in the development of an active second-hand market in certain items of plant and machinery. For instance, photographic equipment is often sold for large amounts, sometimes even for figures approaching the asset's original cost. Where the high disposal value was not anticipated at the outset, excessive charges will have been made in the accounts, and profit will have been understated. Turning to estimates of an asset's useful life, an over-optimistic assessment, not compensated for by an unexpected rise in the disposal value, results in the overstatement of profit during the asset's life, while reported profits are unduly depressed in the year that the item is sold and the balance remaining is written off.

Example 3.6

Tintern Ltd. was incorporated on 1st January, 19X1 and purchased a single fixed asset for £120,000. It was estimated that the fixed asset would last six years and then possess a negligible disposal value. It was decided to depreciate the asset on the straight line basis, and this resulted in an annual charge of £120,000 ÷ 6 = £20,000. Trading activity was at a steady level and the annual profits before depreciation, for the first four years, were £50,000. At the end of 19X4 it was discovered that the fixed asset was worn out and in need of replacement.

The reported profits for each of the years 19X1–X4 were as follows:

Year	Profit before depreciation £	Depreciation £	Reported profit £
19X1	50,000	20,000	30,000
19X2	50,000	20,000	30,000
19X3	50,000	20,000	30,000
19X4	50,000	60,000 W1	(10,000)

W1. This comprises two elements: the annual depreciation charge of £20,000; plus the loss on disposal of £40,000, being the balance remaining in the books at the end of 19X4 when the asset was scrapped.

We are told that the annual level of trading activity was steady, and this is borne out by the fact that profit before depreciation was £50,000 in each of the years 19X1–19X4. If the fixed asset's useful life had been accurately forecast, the annual depreciation charge would have been £120,000 ÷ 4 = £30,000, and reported profit, after charging depreciation, would also have been steady at £20,000 per annum. The effect of the forecasting error was to over-state reported profit in each of the first three years by £10,000, and to under-state profit by £30,000 in 19X4. The result was that published profit figures were an unreliable measure of Tintern's trading performance, and users of the company's accounts are likely to have been misled.

The straight line method of depreciation is used in example 3.6, but readers will be aware of the fact that there exist many other methods which can be used to spread the depreciable amount (original cost minus scrap value) over the asset's estimated useful life. The main alternatives are the reducing balance basis, the sum of the digits method, the usage basis and the annuity method.

Whichever method is used, the total amount written off will be the same, but the distribution of the depreciable balance over the asset's life will vary a great deal. The straight line basis results in an equal annual charge, the reducing balance basis and sum of the digits method each produce relatively high charges in the early years of an asset's life and relatively low charges in later years, the usage method results in a variable charge depending on the level of production, while the annuity method produces a charge which increases over the asset's life. It is management's job to make a fair allocation of the depreciable amount between accounting periods expected to benefit from using the fixed asset, and they should select the method which is most appropriate bearing in mind the type of asset and the way it is used in the business. The choice of method is important because it will affect the level of reported profit.

Example 3.7 (Taken from the April, 1983 *Accountancy* paper).

Larchmont Ltd. was established on 1 January 1983 to manufacture a single product using a machine which cost £400,000. The machine is expected to last for four years and then have a scrap value of £52,000. The machine will produce a similar number of goods each year and annual profits before depreciation are expected to be in the region of £200,000. The financial controller has suggested that the machine should be depreciated using either the straight line method or the reducing balance method. If the latter method is used, it has been estimated that an annual depreciation rate of 40% would be appropriate.

Required:

(a) Calculations of the annual depreciation charges and the net book values of the fixed asset at the end of 1983, 1984, 1985 and 1986 using:
(i) the straight line method;
(ii) the reducing balance method.

[10]

(b) A discussion of the differing implications of these two methods for the financial information published by Larchmont Ltd. for the years 1983–1986 inclusive. You should also advise management which method you consider more appropriate bearing in mind expected profit levels.

[10]

NOTE: Ignore taxation.   [Total marks for question—20]

Solution:

(a)

$$\frac{400}{52} \div 4 = 87p.a.$$

	Straight line method		Reducing Balance method	
Year	Depreciation charge	Net book value	Depreciation charge	Net book value
	£	£	£	£
1983	87,000	313,000	160,000	240,000
1984	87,000	226,000	96,000	144,000
1985	87,000	139,000	57,600	86,400
1986	87,000	52,000	34,560	51,840
	348,000		348,160	

(b) The discussion should cover the following main points:

The reducing balance method, using a 40% rate of write-off, produces a marginally higher total depreciation charge and a marginally lower net book value at the end of 1986, but the differences are not material. Both methods succeed in reducing the book value of the machine to its expected scrap value by the end of four years.

The allocation of the total depreciation charge between the four years differs significantly under the two methods. In 1983 the reducing balance method produces a charge which is £73,000 *higher* than under the straight line method; the situation is substantially reversed in 1986 when the reducing balance charge is £52,440 *lower*.

The effect of the different rates of asset write-off has significant implications for the level of reported profits and the balance sheet figures for capital employed. If the straight line basis is used, reported profit is expected to be stable at £113,000 (£200,000 – £87,000), while the reducing balance basis will result in a reported profit of £40,000 in 1983, increasing to £165,440 in 1986. In the balance sheet, the book value of fixed assets will initially decline much more quickly under the reducing balance method.

The level of activity is expected to remain unchanged over the four years and so the straight line basis, which produces an equal annual charge, is preferred.

Examiner's comments:

Main student errors:

1. The estimated scrap value was ignored when calculating the depreciation charge on the straight line basis, resulting in an incorrect annual charge of £100,000.
2. The 40% rate of depreciation, specified for the reducing balance method, was applied to the depreciable amount, £348,000 (£400,000 – £52,000), instead of the original cost.

The Companies Act 1981 and SSAP12 contain the following requirements relating to fixed assets and depreciation:

1. *Companies must depreciate all fixed assets, other than freehold land, over their expected useful life* (see example 3.8).

2. *Where fixed assets are revalued, depreciation must be provided on the revalued figure* (see example 3.8).

3. *If it becomes apparent that the balance remaining will not be recovered in full out of future profits, the asset should be immediately written down to the estimated recoverable*

amount which should then be written off over the asset's remaining useful life (see example 3.9).
SSAP12 contains the following additional requirements:

4. *Where there is a revision of an asset's estimated useful life, the remaining balance should be written off over the revised period* (see example 3.9).

5. *When a new depreciation method is adopted, with the objective of providing users with a fairer presentation of the financial results and position of the company, the asset must be written off over its remaining useful life on the new basis.* For example, using the reducing balance basis, an item of plant may have been written down to £30,000 by the end of 19X1. In 19X2, management may decide to change to the straight line basis in order to give a fairer presentation of the results and financial position of the company. Assuming a remaining useful life of 4 years and a disposal value of £2,000, at the end of that period, the annual charge will be (£30,000 − £2,000) ÷ 4 = £7,000. The effect of the change must be disclosed, if material.

6. *The accounts should disclose, for each category of fixed asset, the depreciation methods used and the useful life or depreciation rates used.*

Example 3.8 (To illustrate regulatory requirements 1 and 2)

Gibside Ltd. purchased a freehold property for £600,000, including land £100,000, on 1st January, 19X1. On 1st January, 19X6 the property was revalued by R. Jones & Co., Chartered Surveyors, at £2,000,000, including a figure of £400,000 for land. It is the company's policy to depreciate its buildings on the straight line basis over 25 years. No adjustment to the expected life of the asset was required when the revaluation took place.

REQUIRED:
(a) Calculations of the depreciation charge for each of the years 19X1–19X6.
(b) The balance sheet figures for freehold property at 31st December, 19X5 and 19X6, and the transfer to revaluation reserve arising from the revaluation on 1 January, 19X6.

Solution:
(a) Depreciation charge:
   19X1–19X5: 4% of £500,000 (£600,000 − £100,000) = £20,000
   19X6: 5%* of £1,600,000 (£2,000,000 − £400,000) = £80,000

   *20 years life remains.

(b) Balance sheet figures, freehold property:

		£
19X5: Cost..		600,000
Less: Accumulated depreciation (5 × £20,000)........................		100,000
		500,000
19X6: As revalued by R. Jones & Co., Chartered Surveyors..............		2,000,000
Less: Accumulated depreciation		80,000
		1,920,000
Transfer to revaluation reserve:		
Freehold property revaluation on 1st January, 19X6		2,000,000
Less: Book value of property at 1st January, 19X6..........................		500,000
		1,500,000

Example 3.9 (To illustrate regulatory requirements 3 and 4).

Kinross Ltd., which makes up its accounts on a calendar year basis, purchased plant for £200,000 on 1st January, 19X1, to manufacture goods for export. Management decided to write off the plant on the straight line basis over 10 years, assuming a nil residual value. In December, 19X4 there was a change of government in the main country to which goods were exported, and all imports were banned as from 1st January, 19X5. The directors of Kinross have estimated that plant utilisation will decline to 30% of its previous level. As a result, the plant is worth only £50,000 on 1 January, 19X5, and this amount is to be written off by 31 December, 19X6 when production will cease.

REQUIRED:
  (a) Calculations of the amount of depreciation written off against profit for each of the years 19X1–19X6, based on the above information.
  (b) The balance sheet figures for plant at 31st December, 19X4.

Solution:

(a) Depreciation charge:

	£	£
19X1–19X4: 10% of £200,000		20,000
19X4: additional write off computed as follows:		
Book value of plant: Cost...................................	200,000	
Less: Accumulated depreciation...............	80,000	
	120,000	
Revised figure...	50,000	
		70,000
19X5–19X6: £50,000 ÷ 2...		25,000

(b) Balance sheet extract, 31 December, 19X4

	£
Plant and machinery at cost...................................	200,000
Less: Accumulated depreciation	150,000 W1
	50,000

W1. (4 × £20,000) + £70,000

3.6   RESEARCH AND DEVELOPMENT EXPENDITURE   SSAP 13

Companies incur research and development (R&D) expenditure with the intention of improving profits by increasing the range or quality of products in which they trade. Where the expenditure is expected to produce future benefits, the accruals concept requires the outlay to be carried forward as an asset and charged against revenue when the benefit emerges. However, it is often impossible to forecast either whether R&D expenditure will produce a future benefit or, if a future benefit is expected to materialise, the value of the benefit. For this reason, the prudent solution is to exclude R&D expenditure from the balance sheet by writing it off against revenue as it is incurred. Against this treatment must be weighed the argument that a subjective valuation, based on informed guesswork, is superior to an arbitrary valuation of zero where future benefits are expected to arise.

The difficulty of forecasting and quantifying a future benefit varies depending on the exact nature of the R&D expenditure incurred. SSAP13 identifies four separate categories:

(a) Fixed assets used to provide facilities for R&D activities.

(b) Pure (or basic) research, i.e. original investigation under-taken in order to gain new scientific or technical knowledge and understanding. Basic research is not primarily directed towards any specific practical aim or application. For example, where a pharmaceutical company engages in research into the general nature of a headache.

(c) Applied research, i.e. original investigation undertaken in order to gain new scientific or technical knowledge and directed towards a specific practical aim or objective. For example, where the pharmaceutical company is attempting to discover a means of ameliorating the pain associated with a headache.

(d) Development, i.e. the use of scientific or technical knowledge in order to produce new or substantially improved materials, devices, products, processes, systems or services prior to the commencement of commercial production. For example, where the pharmaceutical company develops a pill to be marketed, based on its findings under (c).

SSAP13 requires R&D expenditure on fixed assets (item a) to be capitalised and written off over their expected useful life in the normal way. Pure and applied research expenditures (items b and

c) should be written off immediately, while development expenditure (item d) may be capitalised where certain stringent conditions are fulfilled. These conditions require management to produce evidence which shows that the development expenditure relates to a clearly defined project that will result in the company providing a new or improved product or service which it can reasonably expect to market at a profit. In such circumstances, development expenditure can be carried forward and written off against revenue over the periods benefiting from the sale of the product. The Companies Act 1981 gives legal support to the main provisions contained in SSAP13.

3.7   GOODWILL

The Companies Act 1981 obliges companies to capitalise goodwill purchased from another company, and then to write it off over a period not exceeding its 'useful economic life'. No guidance is given for estimating 'useful economic life', and the matter is left to the directors. The requirement to write off goodwill does not apply to goodwill arising on consolidation (see question 3.2 for an illustration of the accounting treatment of goodwill, and example 7.4, in Chapter 7, for the calculation of goodwill).

3.8   TAXATION IN COMPANY ACCOUNTS

3.8.1   Mainstream Corporation Tax and Advance Corporation Tax   Mainstream corporation tax (MCT) is levied at 52% on taxable profits of £500,000 or over (38% on taxable profits up to £100,000, with a sliding scale operating from £100,000 to £500,000). For example, taxable profits of £600,000 will result in MCT payable of £600,000 × 52% = £312,000. *SSAP8 requires companies to disclose the amount of the MCT charge, as a separate item, in the profit and loss account, and to give the rate of tax either on the face of the profit and loss account or by way of note.* MCT is due for payment nine months after the end of the accounting period in the case of companies formed since 5th April, 1965; the date when corporation tax was introduced. Prior to that date companies were subject to income tax on their profits, and they paid that tax on 1st January *following* the 5th of April *following* the end of their accounting period. The effect of this was that the period of credit received from the Inland Revenue varied depending on when the

accounting period ended, but it could be significantly in excess of 9 months. These rules are retained for payments of corporation tax made by companies formed before 6th April, 1965.

Example 3.10

	A Ltd.	B Ltd.	C Ltd.
Year of incorporation...........	1966	1960	1958
Accounts made up to............	31 Dec., 1982	31 Dec., 1982	30 June, 1982
Date corporation tax payable .	30 Sept., 1983	1 Jan., 1984	1 Jan., 1984
Period of 'credit'................	9 months	12 months	18 months

One effect of these rules is that companies formed since 5th April, 1965, should show only one year's tax assessment as a liability in the balance sheet, whereas companies formed earlier will often show two years assessments as a liability e.g. A Ltd. will show, in its 1982 accounts, the tax due on 30th September, 1983; while B Ltd. will show the tax assessments for both 1981 and 1982, due respectively for payment on 1st January, 1983 and 1st January, 1984.

Where dividends are paid to shareholders, during an accounting period, the tax rules require companies to make an advance payment of corporation tax to the Inland Revenue. Advance corporation tax (ACT), calculated at 3/7ths of the dividend, is payable to the Inland Revenue on the quarterly date (31 March, 30 June, 30 September, 31 December) following the payment of the dividend, and it may be offset against the MCT assessment for the accounting year in which payment is made.

Example 3.11

The following information is provided for Somerton plc which makes up its accounts on a calendar year basis:

Incorporated in December, 1970

Dividends paid to shareholders during 1982: £

March: final dividend for 1981...	210,000
August: interim dividend for 1982..	70,000
Proposed final dividend for 1982, paid March, 1983......................	245,000

Advance corporation tax paid

31 March, 1982 (3/7ths × £210,000)	90,000
30 September, 1982 (3/7ths × £70,000)...................................	30,000
31 March, 1983 (3/7ths × £245,000)	105,000
Taxable profits for 1982..	600,000

Tax payable to the Inland Revenue on 30th September, 1983 is calculated as follows:

£

Mainstream corporation tax charge for 1982, 52% of 600,000 312,000

Less: Advance corporation tax paid during 1982, £90,000 + £30,000.. 120,000

Tax payable 30 September, 1983... 192,000

Note that the offset against MCT is restricted to ACT paid *during* 1982. The final dividend proposed for 1982 is paid in March, 1983 and the related ACT, £105,000 (3/7ths × £245,000), can be offset only against tax levied on profits arising during that year. The £105,000 must therefore be shown in the 1982 balance sheet as a current liability, and the double entry is completed by recording the same amount as a deferred asset representing ACT recoverable. *SSAP8 requires companies to deduct ACT recoverable from the balance sheet figure for deferred tax; alternatively, if there is no credit balance on the deferred tax account, ACT recoverable should be shown as a current asset.*

From the shareholders' point of view, the dividend is received net of *income tax* at the basic rate. For example, if a shareholder receives a dividend of £70, the company will pay to the Inland Revenue, in respect of that dividend, 3/7ths × £70 = £30 as ACT. As far as the shareholder is concerned, the company has paid a gross dividend of £100 (£70 + £30) and deducted £30 income tax which has been paid to the Inland Revenue. Provided the individual is a basic rate income tax payer, he will incur no further liability in respect of dividend income.

A company which receives a dividend from another U.K. company (called franked investment income) is in a somewhat similar position. The company paying the dividend has already accounted for ACT to the Inland Revenue, and the recipient company is therefore allowed to offset this 'tax credit' against ACT payable in respect of any dividend which it declares.

SSAP8 requires companies to show investment income 'gross' (i.e. the amount received plus related tax credit) in the published profit and loss account, with the amount 'suffered' by deduction at source added to the MCT charge for the year.

Example 3.12

The following information is provided in respect of Wookey Ltd., which was incorporated in 1950 and prepares accounts on a calendar year basis.

	£
Operating profit	1,000,000
Dividends received from U.K. companies in June, 1982, net	14,000
Final dividend for 1981, paid in March, 1982	315,000
Interim dividend for 1982, paid in May, 1982	140,000
Proposed final dividend for 1982, paid in 1983	350,000
ACT paid: 31 March, 1982	135,000
30 June, 1982	54,000
Mainstream corporation tax charge for 1982	520,000

REQUIRED:

The profit and loss account of Wookey Ltd. for 1982 and relevant balance sheet extracts at 31 December, 1982, not necessarily in a form suitable for publication but complying with the requirements of SSAP8.

Solution:

Profit and Loss Account for 1982

	£000	£000
Operating profit		1,000
Income from investments (£14,000 + £6,000 tax credit) 3/7ths		20
Profit before tax		1,020
Corporation tax:		
Charge for the year at 52%	520	
Tax credit on U.K. dividends received	6	
	—	526
Profit after tax		494
Less: Dividends—paid	140	
—proposed	350	
	—	490
Retained profit for the year		4

Relevant Balance Sheet extracts at 31 December, 1982

	£000
Current Assets	
Deferred asset: ACT recoverable	150 W1
Current Liabilities	
Proposed dividend	350
Tax due 30 September, 1983	331 W2
ACT due in respect of proposed dividend	150 W1

W1. £350,000 (proposed dividend) × 3/7ths

	£000	£000
W2. MCT charge for 1982		520
Less: ACT paid 31 March, 1982	135	
ACT paid 30 June, 1982	54*	
	—	189
		331

*Made up of ACT payable in respect of interim dividend, £60,000 (3/7ths × £140,000), minus tax credit in respect of dividend received, £6,000 (3/7ths × £14,000).

3.8.2 Deferred Taxation

In example 3.12, MCT was calculated at 52% of reported profit. In practice, however, the mainstream corporation tax charge often bears no relationship to reported profit. This is because there are significant differences between the procedures followed when calculating *reported profit* and *taxable profit*. These differences fall into two basic categories:

1. Permanent differences. Examples of transactions which give

rise to permanent differences between taxable profit and reported profit are tax free income, such as government grants, and business expenditure disallowed for tax purposes, such as charitable and political donations and most entertainment expenditure.

2. Timing differences. These arise when items of income and expenditure are taken into account in different accounting periods for the purpose of computing reported profit and taxable profit. These items therefore cause differences between the two profit figures which cancel out over time. Examples of timing differences are:
   (i) Interest receivable and payable which is included in the accounts on an accruals basis but taxed on a cash basis.
   (ii) General provisions for bad debts, which are not allowed for tax until they become specific.
   (iii) Expenditure on fixed assets, which results in depreciation being charged in the accounts whereas capital allowances are granted for tax purposes e.g. a first year allowance of 100% is given on plant and machinery.

Deductions from taxable profits in excess of the amount charged in the profit and loss account give rise to *originating* timing differences, whereas the opposite circumstances give rise to *reversing* timing differences.

The effect of timing differences on reported profit after tax is illustrated in example 3.13.

Example 3.13

Bulmore Ltd. was formed on 1st January, 19X1 and purchased plant costing £800,000. The plant was expected to have a four year life and no residual value at the end of that period. Annual profits before tax are £900,000 for the period 19X1–19X4 and the company's policy is to depreciate plant on the straight line basis.

Timing differences arising from the purchase of plant are as follows:

	19X1 £000	19X2 £000	19X3 £000	19X4 £000
First year allowance	800	—	—	—
Less: Depreciation	200	200	200	200
Originating (reversing) timing difference	600	(200)	(200)	(200)

Assuming there are no permanent differences and no other timing differences between reported and taxable profit, MCT is calculated as follows:

	19X1 £000	19X2 £000	19X3 £000	19X4 £000
Reported profit before tax	900	900	900	900
Less: Originating timing difference	600			
Add: Reversing timing difference		200	200	200
Taxable profit	300	1,100	1,100	1,100
MCT at 52%	156	572	572	572

On the basis of the above information, reported profit after tax is computed as follows:

	19X1 £000	19X2 £000	19X3 £000	19X4 £000
Profit before tax	900	900	900	900
Less: Corporation tax	156	572	572	572
Profit after tax	744	328	328	328

Profits after tax are often used as a basis for assessing corporate performance and, for this reason, it is thought that timing differences can result in wrong conclusions being reached by users of accounting reports. An examination of Bulmore's after tax profits suggests that the company was twice as profitable in 19X1 as in the following three years. This was, of course, not the case, and the only reason why Bulmore *appears* more profitable in 19X1 is because of the generous system of capital allowances used by the government in an attempt to encourage new investment.

The deferred tax account (DTA) is used as a device for neutralising the effect of timing differences on reported profits. The procedure is to make transfers of tax 'saved' from profit to the credit of the DTA when there are originating timing differences. When the differences reverse, an appropriate transfer is made from the DTA to the credit of the profit and loss account. *SSAP15 requires companies to show transfers to and from the DTA as a separate component of the corporation tax charge, either on the face of the profit and loss account or by way of a note.*

The following transfers would be required in the case of Bulmore Ltd.

	19X1 £000	19X2 £000	19X3 £000	19X4 £000
Originating (reversing) timing difference	600	(200)	(200)	(200)
Transfer to (from) DTA at 52%	312	(104)	(104)	(104)

The revised figures for reported profit after tax, and the balance sheet figures for deferred tax, are as follows:

Profit and Loss Account	19X1		19X2		19X3		19X4	
	£000	£000	£000	£000	£000	£000	£000	£000
Profit before tax............		900		900		900		900
Less: Corporation tax:								
Charge for the year	156		572		572		572	
Transfer to (from) DTA	312		(104)		(104)		(104)	
	—	468	—	468	—	468	—	468
Profit after tax..............		432		432		432		432

Balance Sheet Extract				
Credit balance on the DTA	312	208	104	—

The effect of using a DTA is that the total corporation tax charge each year is 52% of the pre-tax profit, while profit after tax is steady at £432,000. The DTA shows a credit balance of £312,000 in 19X1, and this amount is sometimes described as an interest free loan from the government. The loan arises because tax paid for 19X1 was £156,000, instead of £468,000, as the result of claiming the first year allowance, and it is repaid by three equal annual instalments of £104,000. It should be noted, however, that transfers between the profit and loss account and the DTA are merely book entries and do not affect the amount of tax paid, which is £156,000 for 19X1 and £572,000 for the following three years, irrespective of whether the adjustments are made. Nor does the creation and utilisation of a DTA affect the total profit reported over the four year period, although it does affect the amount reported in individual years:

	19X1	19X2	19X3	19X4	Total
	£000	£000	£000	£000	£000
Reported profit after tax:					
Without a DTA	744	328	328	328	1,728
With a DTA......................................	432	432	432	432	1,728

The main valuation requirements contained in SSAP15, entitled 'Accounting for Deferred Taxation', are:

1. *Deferred taxation should be accounted for on all short term timing differences.* These are differences which originate in one accounting period and reverse in the next, for example interest is reported in the accounts on an accruals basis but taxed on a cash basis.

2. *Deferred taxation should be accounted for on all other timing differences, except where it can be shown that the timing difference is unlikely to reverse in the foreseeable future.* For example, most companies purchase fixed assets each year, and the level of capital expenditure normally increases because of expansion and/or the effect of inflation. In these circumstances, originating timing differences in respect of new purchases will continuously exceed reversing timing differences in respect of fixed assets acquired in earlier years, and no additional liability to corporation tax will arise.

3. *The potential amount of the deferred tax liability on all timing differences should be disclosed by way of note.*

Note for students: As indicated in the *Accountancy* syllabus, students will not be required to make tax computations involving 'permanent differences', but they should be familiar with the adjustments to reported profit required to take account of 'timing differences'.

Example 3.14 (Taken from the April, 1983 *Accountancy* paper).

Lancaster Ltd. was incorporated and commenced business in January 1982. The following trial balance was extracted from the books at 31 December 1982.

	£	£
Share capital (ordinary shares of £1 each)		1,000,000
Trade creditors		264,500
Operating profit		315,000
Royalties		90,000
Dividends received		7,000
Fixed assets at cost (purchased January 1982) ...	200,000	
Provision for depreciation at 31 December 1982 ..		40,000
Stock, debtors and cash	1,469,500	
Interim dividend paid	35,000	
Advance corporation tax	12,000	
	£1,716,500	£1,716,500

The following additional information is provided:

1. Royalties consist of £65,000 received in cash and £25,000 outstanding at the year end.

2. The royalties outstanding give rise to a 'short-term' timing difference as defined by SSAP 15 entitled 'Accounting for Deferred Taxation'.

3. The directors intend to claim a first year allowance of 100% on the fixed assets purchased in January 1982. No provision for deferred taxation will be made in respect of the resulting timing difference as the directors are in possession of reliable evidence which suports their opinion that it will not reverse in the fore-seeable future.

4. Corporation tax is payable at 52% on *taxable* profits of £220,000.

5. The directors propose to pay a final dividend of 14p per share for 1982.

Required:

The profit and loss account of Lancaster Ltd. for 1982 and balance sheet at 31 December 1982, not necessarily in a form for publication, but complying with the provisions in SSAP 15.

NOTE:

Advance corporation tax should be taken as 3/7ths for the purpose of your calculations.

|20|

Solution:

Profit and Loss Account for 1982

	£	£
Operating profit		315,000
Royalties		90,000
Dividends received		10,000 W1
Net profit before tax		415,000
Corporation tax:		
Charge for year	114,400 W2	
Transfer to deferred tax account	13,000 W3	
Tax credit on investment income	3,000	
	———	130,400
Net profit after tax		284,600
Dividends: paid	35,000	
proposed	140,000	
	———	175,000
		109,600

W1. £7,000 (dividend received) + £3,000 (tax credit)
W2. £220,000 (taxable profits) × 52%
W3. £25,000 (short-term timing difference) × 52%

Balance Sheet at 31st December, 1982

	£	£
Fixed assets at cost		200,000
Less: Depreciation		40,000
		160,000
Current Assets		
Stock, debtors and cash	1,469,500	
Deferred tax account (Note 1)	47,000	
	1,516,500	
Current Liabilities		
Trade creditors	264,500	
Dividends	140,000	
Advance corporation tax	60,000	
Corporation tax payable (Note 2)	102,400	
	566,900	
Net Current Assets		949,600
		1,109,600
Share capital		1,000,000
Profit and loss account		109,600
		1,109,600

Notes:

1. The balance on the deferred tax account is made up as follows:

	£
Tax recoverable in respect of proposed dividend, £140,000 × 3/7	60,000
Less: Liability arising from short-term timing differences	13,000
	47,000

    In addition, there is a potential liability, not provided for, of £83,200 (originating timing difference 160,000 × 52%) in respect of timing differences relating to first year allowances claimed on the purchase of fixed assets.

2. Corporation tax payable consists of:

	£
Charge for the year	114,400
Less: Advance corporation tax on interim dividend (net)	12,000
	102,400

Examiner's comments:

Main student errors:

1. Dividends received were not 'grossed up'.
2. The transfer to the deferred tax account was not made.
3. ACT was not provided for in respect of the proposed dividend for 1982.
4. ACT paid during 1982 was not offset against the MCT charge for 1982 for the purpose of computing corporation tax payable on 30 September, 1983.

3.9 DISTRIBUTABLE PROFIT

The rules for the calculation of distributable profits differ between private and public limited companies. Identification of the particular category a company falls into is a simple matter: public limited companies are identified by the designatory letters p.l.c., whereas Ltd. after a company's name indicates that it is a private company. There are many differences between these two types of company; perhaps the most notable are that public companies have a minimum share capital requirement of £50,000, and private companies are not allowed to make a public issue of shares or debentures.

The 1980 Act defines distributable profits of private companies as:

Accumulated realised profits *minus* accumulated realised losses.

where:

Accumulated realised profits are realised profits which have not already been distributed as dividends or capitalised (see Chapter 4, section 2).

Accumulated realised losses are realised losses which have not been previously written off in either a reduction or reorganisation of capital (see Chapter 4, sections 3 and 7).

Profits or losses may be either capital or revenue in their origin.

The effect of these rules is that a company is legally entitled to declare a dividend out of realised profits brought forward but, if there are accumulated realised losses brought forward, these losses must be made good before a dividend can be paid. A company, with large accumulated realised losses, may therefore find it convenient to have a reduction of capital if it wishes to avoid a long delay before it can pay a dividend out of the profits accruing as the result of an improvement in trading conditions.

The Act does not define realised and unrealised profits and losses, but it does provide some guidance regarding the treatment of particular items:

1. Provisions as defined by the 1948 Act (i.e. 'Any amount that is either written off or retained in order to provide for depreciation, renewals or diminution in value of assets, or is retained in order to provide for any known liability whose amount cannot be determined with substantial accuracy') are to be treated as realised losses, except that private companies need not provide for an unrealised loss arising on revaluation of *all* a company's assets.

2. Any additional depreciation, which is charged as the result of

an upward revaluation of fixed assets, may be added back to reported profits for the purpose of computing distributable profits. This provision was introduced to avoid discouraging companies from revaluing their assets where they considered such a course appropriate.

3. Development expenditure, shown as a fixed asset, is to be treated as a realised loss for the purpose of computing distributable profit, unless there are 'special circumstances' justifying capitalisation, in which case the expenditure may be carried forward. Special circumstances are not defined in the Act, but it is likely that the capitalisation of development expenditure, which complies with the conditions laid down in SSAP13, will be acceptable.

In those circumstances not specifically covered by the Act, the determination of whether a profit or loss has been realised must be made in the light of generally accepted accounting principles. This would suggest that profit should be computed in accordance with the fundamental accounting concepts specified in SSAP2. In particular, revenues should be included in the profit and loss account only when they are realised, and provision should be made for all foreseeable losses. For example, if credit is taken for some or all of the profit expected to accrue on a long term contract, *only just begun*, this would contravene standard accounting practice and would have to be treated as unrealised for the purpose of computing distributable profits in accordance with the Companies Acts. A public company is bound by the same rules as a private company but, in addition, it must provide for net unrealised losses (unrealised profits *less* unrealised losses), if any, before declaring a dividend. For instance, a public company would have to make a provision for an unrealised loss arising on the revaluation of all its assets. The result is that public companies are subject to more stringent rules than private companies for the purpose of computing divisible profits.

Example 3.15

The following information is provided for Wendover Ltd. for 19X1:

	£
Depreciation charge (including £5,000 relating to the upward revaluation of fixed assets)	17,000
Operating profit for the year	100,000
Profit on the sale of fixed assets (extraordinary item)	20,000
Unrealised profit on the revaluation of fixed assets, credited to revaluation reserve	35,000

Distributable profits are computed as follows (taxation ignored):

	£
Operating profit	100,000
Add: Realised capital profit	20,000
Additional depreciation relating to revaluation of fixed assets	5,000
Distributable profit	125,000

3.10 QUESTIONS AND SOLUTIONS

Question 3.1 (Warmington Ltd.) tests students' ability to prepare and interpret the significance of accounting reports based on different valuation procedures. Question 3.2 (Milford Ltd.) tests students' knowledge of the valuation rules contained in the Companies Act 1981.

Question 3.1 (Taken from September, 1980 *Accountancy* paper).

Warmington Limited was incorporated in December, 1976, when it issued 600,000 ordinary shares of £1 each for cash. The company commenced business on 1 January, 1977, and, since that time, has traded in a single product, 'tint', which is both purchased and sold for cash, (i.e. there are no debtors or creditors).

The company purchased motor vehicles, fork lift trucks and other equipment at a total cost of £400,000 in December 1976. These fixed assets were expected to last nine years and have a combined residual value of £40,000.

The following information is provided in respect of the years 1977, 1978 and 1979.

		1977	1978	1979
1.	Number of items bought	13,000	14,000	14,000
	Number of items sold	10,000	12,000	14,000
2.	Average purchase price per item	£90	£100	£110
	Average sale price per item	£130	£140	£150

3. Expenditure on administration, finance, selling and distribution (other than depreciation) £305,000 £346,000 £402,000

4. Bank balance (overdraft) at 31 December £25,000 (£41,000) £117,000

Required:

(a) Summary trading and profit and loss accounts of Warmington Limited for each of the three years 1977 to 1979, together with the balance sheets at 31 December in each year:

    (i) using first in first out (FIFO) as the basis for valuing stocks;

    (ii) depreciating fixed assets on the straight line (equal instalment) basis.

(b) Summary trading and profit and loss accounts of Warmington Limited for each for the three years 1977 to 1979, together with the balance sheets at 31 December in each year:

    (i) using last in first out (LIFO) as the basis for valuing stocks;

    (ii) depreciating fixed assets on the reducing (diminishing) balance basis (depreciation rate 22·5 per cent).

(c) Calculations of the rate of return on capital employed for each year under both (a) and (b) above. For these purposes capital employed should be defined as the shareholders' equity in the balance sheet at 31 December of the relevant years.

(d) A full discussion of the results disclosed by your calculations under (a), (b) and (c), above.

NOTES:
1. *Ignore taxation.*
2. *Calculations to nearest £000.*
3. *No dividends were paid during the years 1977 to 1979.* [30]

Solution:

Workings:
1. Stock

Number of items in stock	Units	
1977	3,000	
1978	5,000	
1979	5,000	

FIFO: Stock valued at most recent purchase price.

		£000
1977	3,000 units at £90 each	270
1978	5,000 units at £100 each	500
1979	5,000 units at £110 each	550

LIFO: Stock valued at earliest purchase price.
		£000
1977	3,000 units at £90 each	270
1978	2,000 extra units at £100 each	200
		470
1979	No change in stock level, valued at 1977 and 1978 prices	470

2. Fixed Assets

		Straight line £000	Reducing balance £000
	Cost	400	400
1977	Depreciation	40	90
	Book value	360	310
1978	Depreciation	40	70
	Book value	320	240
1979	Depreciation	40	54
	Book value	280	186

(a)   Trading and Profit and Loss Accounts, £000

	1977		1978		1979
Sales		1,300		1,680		2,100
Purchases	1,170		1,400	1,540	
Opening stock	—		270	500	
Closing stock	(270)		(500)	(550)	
		900		1,170		1,490
Gross profit		400		510		610
Depreciation	40		40	40	
Administration etc.	305		346	402	
		345		386		442
Net profit		55		124		168

Balance sheets, £000

	1977	1978	1979
Share Capital	600	600	600
Retained profit	55	179	347
	655	779	947
Fixed assets at book value	360	320	280
Stock	270	500	550
Bank	25	(41)	117
	655	779	947

(b)   *Trading and Profit and Loss Accounts, £000*

	1977		1978		1979
Sales		1,300		1,680		2,100
Purchases	1,170		1,400		1,540	
Opening stock	—		270		470	
Closing stock	(270)		(470)		(470)	
		900		1,200		1,540
Gross profit		400		480		560
Depreciation	90		70		54	
Administration etc.	305		346		402	
		395		416		456
Net profit		5		64		104

Balance Sheets £000

	1977	1978	1979
Share Capital	600	600	600
Retained profit	5	69	173
	605	669	773
Fixed assets at book value	310	240	186
Stock	270	470	470
Bank	25	(41)	117
	605	669	773

(c) Rate of return on capital employed:

	1977	1978	1979
	%	%	%
(a)	8.4	15.9	17.7
(b)	0.8	9.6	13.5

(d) Points to be discussed include:
1. Both sets of calculations are based on the same business events.
2. The apparent performance of a business, as revealed by the rate of return on capital employed, may vary depending on the accounting policies followed, despite their consistent application over time.
3. Assuming the same period for writing off an asset, the reducing balance basis produces high charges in the early years, relative to the straight line basis, compensated for by lower charges later on.
4. The effect of using LIFO for stock valuation purposes is, when prices are rising and stock levels are increasing, to reduce profits and asset values compared with those which arise when FIFO is used.
5. The use of the reducing balance basis and LIFO under (b) has resulted in lower asset values to be carried forward and offset against future revenues.

Examiner's comments:
Main student errors: The opening stock for 1978 and 1979 was often omitted, while many students failed to accumulate retained profits when calculating the balance sheet figure for reserves. Very many candidates wasted time by writing out separate balance sheets and profit and loss accounts for each year, instead of using the columnar format.

Question 3.2 (Taken from the April, 1983 *Accountancy* paper).

The final accounts of Milford Ltd. are in the course of preparation, and it is intended to publish them in accordance with the formats prescribed by the Companies Act 1981. The draft profit and loss account and balance sheet, both of which comply with format 1, are set out below.

PROFIT AND LOSS ACCOUNT
FOR THE YEAR ENDED 31 DECEMBER 1982

	£	£
Turnover		862,150
Less: Cost of sales		484,500
Gross Profit		377,650
Less: Distribution costs	25,000	
Administration expenses	185,700	210,700
Operating profit		166,950
Less: Interest payable		12,000
Profit on ordinary activities before taxation		154,950
Tax on profit on ordinary activities		77,000
Profit on ordinary activities after taxation		77,950
Retained profit as at 1 January 1982		96,800
Retained profit as at 31 December 1982		£174,750

BALANCE SHEET
AS AT 31 DECEMBER 1982

	£	£
Fixed Assets		
Intangible assets: Development costs	24,100	
Goodwill	33,000	57,100
Tangible assets: Land and buildings	85,000	
Plant and machinery	126,600	211,600
		268,700
Current Assets		
Stocks	139,400	
Debtors	91,200	
Cash at bank and in hand	14,000	
	244,600	
Creditors: amounts falling due within one year		
Trade creditors	57,100	
Current corporation tax	77,000	
	134,100	
Net Current Assets		110,500
Total Assets Less Current Liabilities		379,200
Creditors: amount falling due after more than one year		
12% Debenture		100,000
		£279,200
Capital and Reserves		
Called up share capital		100,000
Share premium account		4,450
Profit and loss account		174,750
		£279,200

The following *additional information* is provided:

1. Development costs £24,100 are made up of:

	£
Research costs	15,000
Development expenditure	9,100
	£24,100

The development expenditure relates to a separately identifiable project which will undoubtedly produce a significant improvement in the quality of one of the company's product lines.

2. The figure for goodwill is stated at cost, and arose as the result of purchasing the business of a former competitor on 1 January 1982. It is thought that the goodwill possesses an economic life of five years.

3. Stock is valued at 'total' cost in the balance sheet set out above. Stock was valued at 'prime' cost, £75,000, for the purpose of the 1981 accounts, and this amount was used when computing the cost of sales figure appearing in the profit and loss account. The corresponding total cost valuation of stock at 31 December 1981 is £98,300 made up as follows:

	£
Prime cost	75,000
Production overheads	23,300
	£98,300

4. It has recently come to light that an invoice for £4,900, received from a supplier, has been erroneously omitted from the books. The goods referred to in the invoice were included in the physical stock-take.

5. The company's land and buildings are stated in the balance sheet at cost less depreciation. They were professionally revalued at £120,000 on 1 January 1982. It has now been decided to use this figure for the purpose of the accounts. Administration expenses include a depreciation charge of £2,000 which should be revised to £3,500 to take account of the revaluation.

Required:

(a) The profit and loss account of Milford Ltd. for 1982 and the balance sheet at 31 December 1982 redrafted, as necessary, to take account of the *additional information*. The revised accounts should comply, so far as the information permits, with the requirements of the Companies Act 1981 and Statements of Standard Accounting Practice.

[26]

(b) A calculation of the profit available for distribution according to the requirements of the Companies Act 1980.

[4]

NOTES:
Show all adjustments clearly.
Assume that the adjustments you make do not alter tax payable.

[Total marks for question—30]

Solution:

(a)   Profit and Loss Account for the year ended 31st December, 1982

	£	£
Turnover		862,150
Less: Cost of sales		534,300 W1
Gross profit		327,850
Less: Distribution costs	25,000	
Administration expenses	187,200 W2	
		212,200
Operating profit		115,650
Less: Interest payable		12,000
Profit on ordinary activities before taxation		103,650
Tax on profit on ordinary activities		77,000
Profit on ordinary activities after taxation		26,650
Retained profit brought forward		120,100 W3
Retained profit carried forward		146,750

Balance Sheet as at 31st December, 1982

Fixed Assets	£	£
Intangible assets: Development costs	9,100 W4	
Goodwill	26,400 W5	
		35,500
Tangible assets: Land and buildings	116,500 W6	
Plant and machinery	126,600	
		243,100
		278,600
Current Assets		
Stock	139,400	
Debtors	91,200	
Cash in hand	14,000	
	244,600	
Creditors: amounts falling due within one year		
Trade creditors	62,000 W7	
Current corporation tax	77,000	
	139,000	
Net current Assets		105,600
Total Assets less Current Liabilities		384,200
Creditors: amount falling due after more than one year		
12% Debenture		100,000
		284,200

128   VALUATION OF COMPANY ASSETS AND LIABILITIES

Capital and Reserves £

Called up share capital 100,000
Share premium account 4,450
Revaluation reserve 33,000 W8
Profit and loss account 146,750

284,200

Workings (not for publication):

£

W1. 484,500 + 15,000 (research costs) + 23,300 (increase in opening
valuation of stocks + 4,900 (invoice omitted) + 6,600 (goodwill
amortised) 534,300
W2. 185,700 + 1,500 (extra depreciation) 187,200
W3. 96,800 + 23,300 (increase in opening valuation of stocks) 120,100
W4. 24,100 − 15,000 (research costs) 9,100
W5. 33,000 − 6,600 (goodwill amortised) 26,400
W6. 120,000 − 3,500 (depreciation charged) 116,500
W7. 57,100 + 4,900 (invoice omitted) 62,000
W8. 120,000 − 87,000 (book value of land and buildings at 1st
January, 1982) 33,000
(b) Distributable profit: £
Accumulated profit balance 146,750
Add: Additional depreciation resulting from revaluation of
buildings 1,500

Profit available for distribution 148,250

Examiner's comments:
Main student errors:
1. Research costs not written off against profit.
2. The increase in the opening value of stock deducted from the figure given for cost of sales.
3. The increase in the opening value of stock not credited to retained profit brought forward.
4. Land and buildings shown in the balance sheet at the revalued figure of £120,000, but depreciation not deducted.
5. The revaluation reserve wrongly calculated.
6. Part (b) not attempted.

CHAPTER 4

Capital Reduction, Reorganisation and Reconstruction

4.1 INTRODUCTION

A company should have a balanced capital structure when it is established, that is, its assets should be funded by the appropriate types of finance. Long-term sources, such as equity capital and debentures, should cover the investment in fixed assets with sufficient excess to make a significant contribution towards the funding of current assets. If the often quoted ideal working capital ratio of 2:1 is desired, then half the value of current assets should be financed by long-term capital, and the remainder financed by short-term sources, such as creditors. Within long-term sources of funds a satisfactory relationship should be created between the various types available, the optimum structure depending on such factors as the nature of the trade undertaken and the likely stability of profits (See Chapter 8, section 6).

Once a company starts to trade, the financial structure established at the outset is affected by the results of trading and the passage of time. The initial equity investment is increased by the amount of profit earned and retained in the business, and is reduced by losses. As time passes, the repayment date for long-term loans gets closer and, near to the very end of their term, such sources must be classified as current liabilities. The rate at which debtors pay and creditors are paid affects the balance between current assets and liabilities, as do credit purchases of additional stock required to expand a successful company. In the longer term, success may encourage the acquisition of extra production capacity which must be funded by an appropriate type of finance if the capital structure of the business is to remain balanced.

The financial position of a business is subject to continuous change, unless the company is dormant and does not trade. Flows of resources take place with trading, and these have an impact on the enterprise which can be beneficial or detrimental. The result is that the business may be either a success or failure. A very successful business, in this context, is one which manages to expand; while survival, with an adequate level of return but no expansion, is regarded as a satisfactory performance. If a company goes into liquidation, or has to be reconstructed, it is a failure. There are certain courses of action which may be followed as a result of the success or failure of a business; it is the purpose of this Chapter to examine these alternatives and the accounting entries which are needed to reflect them. References to legislation are to the Companies Acts 1948, 1967, 1980 and 1981.

4.2 BONUS ISSUES

Bonus issues of shares are also referred to as 'Scrip Issues' or 'Capitalisation Issues'. To make such an issue, a company allots fully paid shares to its existing members and capitalises the corresponding value from its reserves, including any credit balance on its profit and loss account; the company does not receive any consideration for the issue. Each shareholder receives bonus shares in proportion to his existing stake in the company, for instance, the holder of 10% of the equity shares would receive 10% of any bonus issue. A company must have adequate reserves to make a bonus issue, and these will be possessed by a successful company which has retained a significant portion of its profits. A bonus issue may alternatively be made from any balance to the credit of a Share Premium Account or Capital Redemption Reserve. (The Capital Redemption Reserve is examined in section 4.4 of this Chapter).

A company can make a bonus issue only if authorised by its Articles of Association. A typical form for the articles to take is given in Table A of the 1948 Act as amended by the 1980 Act. These articles, which are usually adopted in the internal regulations tailor-made for particular companies, require the general meeting to approve the director's recommendation for a bonus issue before it may be made. A further consideration is that there must, of course, be sufficient authorised, but unissued, capital to enable the issue to take place.

Example 4.1—A Bonus Issue

The Good Company Ltd. has traded successfully for a number of years and has ploughed profits back into the company. Its balance sheet at 31 December, 19X1 is:

	£000		£000
Authorised Share Capital:			
4 million ordinary shares of £1 each ..	4,000		
Issued Share Capital:			
Ordinary Shares of £1 each..............	200	Fixed Assets	960
Share Premium	200	Working Capital	350
Profit and Loss Account....................	910		
	1,310		1,310

It is decided to make a bonus issue of shares, 4 bonus shares being given for each share currently held. The issue is to utilise the balance on the share premium account, with the remainder taken from the profit and loss account.

The balance sheet of the Good Company Ltd. as it will appear after the bonus issue is as follows:

Good Company Ltd. Balance Sheet 31 December, 19X1

	£000		£000
Authorised Share Capital:			
4 million ordinary shares of £1 each ..	4,000		
Issued Share Capital:			
Ordinary Shares of £1 each..............	1,000	Fixed Assets	960
Profit and Loss Account....................	310	Working Capital	350
	1,310		1,310

It can be seen that the bonus issue has not brought any new resources to the company; the only effect is an alteration in the composition of the company's equity, the total of which remains unchanged at £1,310,000. There is also no effect on the relative interest of each member in the company: prior to the issue a holder of 40,000 shares owned 20% of the company with a book value of 20% × £1,310,000 = £262,000; after the issue the holding has risen to 200,000 shares, which is still 20% of the issued shares and has the same book value.

If the directors do not wish to increase the amount of profit distributed, they must take steps to reduce proportionally the dividend per share. For example, to maintain a constant total cash distribution, after a 3 for 1 bonus issue, a company would have to reduce the dividend per share to one quarter of its former amount. However, as each shareholder after the issue has four times as many shares as previously, each receives an unchanged dividend in cash terms. The increase in the number of shares in issue does not affect the value of the company, as is shown by the case of a public limited company with quoted shares, where the market price per share should fall proportionally to compensate for the increased number of shares.

Example 4.2—A Bonus Issue

Traction plc is a listed company and has an issued share capital of 10 million ordinary shares with a nominal value of £1 each. The market value of each share is £6. You are required to illustrate the expected effect of a 2 for 1 bonus issue and a cut in the dividend per share from 12 pence to 4 pence on:

    (a) The market value of one share.
    (b) The market value of the entire company and the dividend it pays
    (c) The market value of a holding of 5,000 shares and the dividend received by the shareholder.

Solution

    (a) Where 1 share is held before the bonus issue, 3 are held after it. The value of the single share was £6, and the total value of the three shares into which it is converted is £6. Therefore, the value of a single share after the bonus issue is £2.

    (b)

	Value	Dividend Paid
Before bonus issue	10m. × £6 = £60m.	10m. × £.12 = £1.2m.
After bonus issue	30m. × £2 = £60m.	30m. × £.04 = £1.2m.

The gratuitous issue of an extra 20 million shares reduces the share price proportionally, and the total value of the company and cash dividend remain unchanged.

    (c)

	Value	Dividend Received
Before bonus issue	5,000 × £6 = £30,000	5,000 × £.12 = £600
After bonus issue	15,000 × £2 = £30,000	15,000 × £.04 = £600

Again, the total value of the shares and the dividend received remain unchanged.

It is therefore clear that the effect of a bonus issue is simply to increase the number of shares a company has in issue. This raises the question: 'Why would a company wish to make such an issue?' Possible reasons are:

    1. Theoretically, the balance on the profit and loss account is distributable as cash dividends; in practice this course may not be open to the company as the funds have been permanently invested in the substance of the business. For instance, in Example 4.1, the Good Company Ltd could not distribute the balance on its profit and loss account without liquidating a

substantial portion of its fixed assets. A bonus issue recognises the company's inability to distribute retained profits and brings the balance sheet into line with this reality.

2. The creation of an enlarged permanent equity capital base makes the company more attractive to potential investors, as the level of gearing cannot be increased by the withdrawal of profit which has been capitalised.

3. A bonus issue is sometimes taken as an indication of the fact that the directors intend to increase the overall level of dividend. If the investors believe this will happen, the shares become more attractive, and the price will fall less than would be expected otherwise. In example 4.2, the share price might finish up above £2.

4. The larger number of shares in circulation should help create a more active market as holdings are made more easily divisible.

5. A listed company which has a high and unwieldy share price may make a bonus issue to create a lower price per share. This is useful where, for example, a company acquires other companies by share exchanges and wishes to make the value of each of its own shares closer to that of likely acquisitions.

6. A successful company with substantial accumulated profits may receive favourable publicity from their capitalisation. The bonus issue draws attention to the success which has created the profits to enable the issue to take place.

7. The reduction in the dividend per share may help avoid any unfavourable publicity attached to the declaration of apparently high rates of dividend.

4.3 CAPITAL REDUCTION

Section 66 of the 1948 Act allows a company to reduce its share capital in any way it considers appropriate. The ability given in the Act is therefore a general one, but specific instances are also stated:

(a) Share capital which is lost or unrepresented by available assets may be cancelled (example 4.3 below).

(b) Share capital in excess of the needs of the company may be repaid (example 4.4 below).

(c) A company may extinguish or reduce the liability on any of its shares in respect of share capital not paid up.

In each of these cases, the right to reduce can be exercised only if certain conditions are met:

1. The company must be authorised to reduce its share capital by its Articles of Association. Article 46 of Table A contains an appropriate wording which many companies adopt.
2. The reduction must be agreed by a special resolution of the members, that is, a resolution passed by a majority of at least 75%.
3. The reduction must be confirmed by the court. This requirement is particularly important in relation to (b) and (c) above. The repayment of capital (b) actually reduces the assets of the company, while the reduction or cancellation of liability on unpaid share capital (c) reduces the funds on which a company can call if required. A creditor of a company, which decides to reduce its capital, such as a bank with which the company has an overdraft, may consider that its likelihood of repayment is jeopardised by the reduction. Such a creditor may object to the court, which can direct either that payment of the debt is secured or that an agreed amount is set aside to meet it.

The cancellation of share capital unrepresented by available assets, and the repayment of share capital to members, are each likely to have a substantial effect on the content of the balance sheet. They are considered further below.

When a company has either been trading unprofitably for a number of years or suffers abnormally large losses in a single year, it may show a large debit balance on its profit and loss account. Despite these losses, which have eroded capital, a company may still be viable and able to earn profits in the future. In these circumstances it is reasonable to recognise that some of the capital has been lost and to reduce its value accordingly. A further reason for engaging in capital reduction is that the Companies Acts prohibit the distribution of current profits before past losses have been made good (see Chapter 3, section 9), but they allow past losses to be removed from the calculation of distributable profits if they are written off in a capital reduction. Thus, a capital reduction scheme enables dividends to be paid from current profits despite the fact that losses have been made in the past. Also, a reduction scheme which removes a debit balance on the profit and loss account makes the company more attractive to prospective investors and sources of credit.

Example 4.3—Capital Reduction

Getting Better Ltd. is an old established company which, after trading profitably for a number of years, incurred substantial losses. Its balance sheet at 31 December, 19X1 is:

	£000		£000
Ordinary Shares of £1 each	1,000	Fixed Assets	520
Profit and Loss Account	(250)	Working Capital	230
	750		750

The company has rationalised its methods of production and distribution and has returned to profitability. It wishes to raise additional equity capital, and, as a preliminary step, decides to reduce its share capital to eliminate the debit balance on the profit and loss account.

The company's balance sheet, after the capital reduction has taken place, is as follows:

*Getting Better Ltd. Balance Sheet at 31 December, 19X1
after Capital Reduction*

	£000		£000
Ordinary Shares of £1 each	750	Fixed Assets	520
		Working Capital	230
	750		750

In this example the existing shareholders are issued with three shares for every four shares previously held. Alternatively, the company could keep one million shares in issue and reduce the nominal value of each share to 75 pence.

A company may find that it has assets in excess of its requirements, for instance, it may dispose of a substantial part of its assets but not wish to re-invest the cash received. The scale of the undertaking's activities is reduced, with the result that its share capital is now too large for its new, smaller, level of operations. It may be decided that it is appropriate to reduce the size of the company's share capital by repaying to the shareholders the amount in excess of requirements.

Example 4.4—Capital Reduction

Smaller Ltd. has sold to a competitor for cash a substantial number of its retail outlets. The bulk of the company's shares are owned by the directors, the balance being held by members of their families. The company's balance sheet after the sale is:

Smaller Ltd. Balance Sheet at 31 December, 19X1

	£000		£000
Ordinary Shares of £1 each	1,000	Fixed Assets	200
Profit and Loss Account..	100	Working Capital Requirements	150
		Surplus Cash	750
	1,100		1,100

The directors are nearing retirement age and, as they have no successors, decide to run the company at its reduced size and return the surplus assets to the shareholders. The reduction of capital is to be achieved by reducing the nominal value of each share to 25 pence and repaying 75 pence per share to the shareholders.

The company's balance sheet, after the capital reduction has been carried out, is as follows:

Smaller Ltd. Balance Sheet at 31 December, 19X1
after Capital Reduction

	£000		£000
Ordinary Shares of 25 pence each.....	250	Fixed Assets...........	200
Profit and Loss Account.................	100	Working Capital.....	150
	350		350

4.4 THE 1981 ACT

The 1981 Act contains provisions which allow companies, subject to certain conditions, to issue redeemable shares of all types and to purchase their own shares. These aspects of capital structure are new, and it will take some time for companies to become familiar with them and use them as a matter of routine. For the purpose of the Stage 2 *Accountancy* exam., candidates will only be expected to be familiar with the provisions and able to work simple examples.

4.4.1 Redeemable Shares

The 1981 Act allows companies to issue redeemable shares of any class. The issue of such shares must be permitted by the company's Articles of Association, and the shares may be redeemable on a stated date or at the option of the company. To prevent companies from redeeming the whole of their capital, and therefore having no members, redeemable shares can only be issued if there are already in issue shares which are not redeemable.

A number of conditions must be met when shares are redeemed:
1. The shares must be fully paid.

2. Companies must not convert shares into creditors; the terms of redemption must provide for payment on redemption.
3. Redeemable shares may only be redeemed out of distributable profits of the company or out of the proceeds of a fresh issue of shares made for the purpose of the redemption.
4. Any premium payable on redemption must be provided out of distributable profits unless the shares redeemed were themselves issued at a premium. In the latter case the premium payable on redemption may come from a new issue up to an amount equal to the lower of:
   (i) The premium received on the issue of the redeemable shares.
   (ii) The current balance on the share premium account, after crediting any premium received on the new issue.
5. Private companies may make redemptions out of capital (See Section 4.3 of this chapter).
6. Redeemed shares must be treated as cancelled.

Example 4.5—Redemption of Shares

Three existing public companies, Cup plc, Saucer plc and Spoon plc, each issued 200,000 redeemable shares of £1 each at a premium of 50 pence per share on 1 January, 19X0. After the issues, each company had a balance on its share premium account of £120,000. The shares are all redeemable on 1 January, 19X9 at £2 each.

Cup plc utilised £100,000 of the balance on its share premium account to issue fully paid bonus shares on 1 January, 19X5.

Saucer plc issued 50,000 ordinary shares of £1 each at a premium of 20 pence per share on 1 January, 19X6.

In December, 19X8, each company issued 200,000 ordinary shares of £1 each at a premium of 25 pence per share for the purpose of the imminent redemption. No transaction took place which had an effect on the company's share premium accounts other than those given above.

REQUIRED
Calculate for each company the minimum amount which must be provided from distributable profits on the redemption of the shares on 1 January, 19X9, and prepare the share premium accounts for each company to cover the period 1 January, 19X0 to 1 January, 19X9.

Solution

	Cup plc £000	£000	Saucer plc £000	£000	Spoon plc £000	£000
Nominal value of redeemed shares		200		200		200
Premium met from share premium account. Lower of:						
1. Premium on issue of shares being redeemed	100		100	100	100	100
2. Balance on share premium account after new issue (see below)...............	70	70	180		170	
Balance to be provided from distributable profit....................................		130		100		100
Total payable on redemption		400		400		400

Share Premium Accounts			
Balance 1 January, 19X0 brought down	20	20	20
Issue of redeemable shares 1 January, 19X0	100	100	100
Bonus Issue 1 January, 19X5..................	(100)	—	—
Issue of shares 1 January, 19X6	—	10	—
Issue of shares December, 19X8	50	50	50
Balance 31 December, 19X8....................	70	180	170
Redemption of shares 1 January, 19X9	(70)	(100)	(100)
Balance 1 January, 19X9 carried forward..	—	80	70

4.4.2 Purchase by a Company of Its Own Shares

The 1981 Act allows any company that has a share capital to purchase its own shares, subject to certain conditions, whether or not they are redeemable. This ability is of benefit to both public and private companies. Public companies are able, for example, to return to members any funds in excess of requirements by the purchase and cancellation of some of their shares, which avoids the need for a capital reduction, and companies can revise their capital structure more easily to bring it into line with current requirements. The main advantage to the owners of shares in private companies is the ability to realise their investment by selling their shares to the company, thereby overcoming any difficulty which would previously have been experienced in transferring their shares. For instance, close control of family companies may be retained by using the company's resources to acquire the shares of a member who dies or retires. However, the company is not bound to purchase its own shares, and can do so only if it has the resources available.

The conditions which a company must satisfy to purchase its own shares are largely similar to those which apply to redeemable shares, indeed, items 1 to 6 are virtually identical to those given in section 4.1 of this chapter. The conditions are:

1. The shares to be purchased must be fully paid.
2. The terms of acquisition must include cash payment on purchase.
3. The purchase may be made out of distributable profits of the company or out of the proceeds of a fresh issue of shares made for the purpose of the acquisition.
4. Any premium payable on purchase must be provided out of distributable profits unless the shares being bought were themselves issued at a premium. In the latter case, the premium payable on purchase may come from a new issue of shares up to an amount equal to the lower of:
   (i) The premium received on the issue of the shares being purchased.
   (ii) The current balance on the share premium account, after crediting any premium received on the new issue.
5. Private companies may make a payment out of capital (see section 4.3 of this chapter).
6. The shares purchased cannot be held by the company as an investment, they must be cancelled.
7. The company must be authorised to purchase its own shares by its Articles of Association.
8. Shares may not be purchased if, as a result of the purchase, the company would only have redeemable shares in issue.
9. After the purchase the company must have at least two members.
10. Public companies must have an allotted share capital in excess of the 'authorised minimum', which at present is £50,000. The purchase of its own shares must not reduce the allotted shares of a public company to below the authorised minimum.

The calculations in example 4.5 on the redemption of shares are the same for the purchase by a company of its own shares if, instead of the shares being redeemable, it is assumed that the companies purchased their own shares for £2 each.

The 1981 Act lays down detailed procedures to be followed that distinguish between off-market purchases and market purchases. In general, an off-market purchase occurs when the shares are not purchased on a recognised stock exchange, while a market purchase is one which is made on a recognised stock exchange. In the case of an off-market purchase, a specific contract of purchase must be approved by a special resolution of the membership; a market purchase requires only a general resolution which gives authority to purchase shares. The contract for an off-market purchase must state the names of the members who hold the shares to be bought; the authority for a market purchase need not relate to any particular shares, but must state the maximum number of shares to be acquired and the maximum and minimum prices to be paid. In both cases, for public companies, the authority lasts for a maximum of eighteen months, at the end of which, unless renewed, it lapses.

4.4.3 Redemption or Purchase out of Capital by Private Companies

Private limited companies are permitted by the 1981 Act to make a payment out of capital in respect of the redemption or purchase of their own shares. For example, a balance on a revaluation reserve account, which arose on the revaluation of a property, may be used. To make a payment out of capital a number of conditions must be satisfied, which include:

1. The payment must be authorised by the company's Articles of Association.
2. The payment must not exceed the 'permissible capital payment' which is the amount by which the price of the redemption or purchase exceeds the sum of the company's distributable profits and the proceeds of any new issue. The effect of this provision is to ensure that the company utilises its available profits and proceeds from any new issue before any payment out of capital is made.

Example 4.6—The Permissible Capital Payment

Jug Ltd., a private company, has in issue 40,000 redeemable shares of £1 each which are to be redeemed on 1 January, 19X4 at a premium of 25 pence per share. On 31 December, 19X3 the company has distributable profits of £15,000 and issues 10,000 shares of £1 each at a premium of 40 pence per share to finance the redemption.

REQUIRED

Calculate the permissible capital payment.

Solution

	£000	£000
Amount payable on redemption (40,000 × £1.25)......................		50
Less: Distributable profits...	15	
Proceeds of new issue (10,000 × £1.40).........................	14	
	—	29
		—
Permissible capital payment..		21
		—

3. The directors must make a declaration that specifies the permissible capital payment and gives their opinion that the company will be able to pay all its debts as they fall due and will continue as a going concern for at least one year after the proposed payment.
4. The company's auditors must report on the reasonableness of the directors' opinion expressed in 3 above.
5. The payment must be approved by a special resolution. After this has been passed, any member who did not support it, or any creditor, has five weeks in which to apply to the courts for the resolution to be cancelled.

4.4.4 The Capital Redemption Reserve The 1981 Act requires that, in certain circumstances, a transfer be made to a 'Capital Redemption Reserve' when a company redeems or purchases its own shares:
1. Where the redemption or purchase is made entirely out of profits, a sum equal to the nominal value of the shares redeemed or purchased must be transferred from profit to the capital redemption reserve.
2. Where the redemption or purchase is made wholly or partly out of a new issue, the sum to be transferred to the capital redemption reserve is the amount, if any, by which the nominal value of the shares redeemed or purchased exceeds the proceeds of the new issue.

Example 4.7—Capital Redemption Reserve *(Cases 1 and 2 above)*

The following is the balance sheet of Carpet Ltd., a private company, at 31 December, 19X2:

	£000
Share Capital	500
Distributable Profits	600
	1,100
Cash	400
Other Net Assets	700
	1,100

The company decides to purchase its own shares with a nominal value of £100,000 for £120,000 on 1 January, 19X3.

REQUIRED

Show the balance sheet of Carpet Ltd. as it would appear after the purchase of its own shares on the alternative assumptions that:
  (a) The company makes no new issue of shares. (Case 1)
  (b) The company issues at par for cash shares with a nominal value of £50,000 to finance the purchase. (Case 2)

Solution

	(a) £000	(b) £000
Share Capital	400	450
Capital Redemption Reserve	100(W1)	50(W3)
Distributable Profits	480(W2)	530(W4)
	980	1,030
Cash	280	330
Other Net Assets	700	700
	980	1,030

Workings

W1—The transfer to the Capital Redemption Reserve from distributable profit is the nominal value of the shares purchased, £100,000 (Case 1).

W2—The balance of distributable profit is £600,000 (original balance)—100,000 (transfer to Capital Redemption Reserve)—20,000 (premium on purchase) = £480,000.

W3—The transfer to the Capital Redemption Reserve from distributable profit is £100,000 (nominal value of the shares purchased)—50,000 (proceeds of new issue) = £50,000 (Case 2).

W4—The balance of distributable profit is £600,000 (original balance)—50,000 (transfer to Capital Redemption Reserve)—20,000 (premium on purchase) = £530,000.

3. Where the redemption or purchase is funded wholly or partly by a payment out of capital (private companies only), the amount to be transferred from capital to the Capital Redemp-

tion Reserve is the excess, if any, of the nominal value of the shares redeemed or purchased over the payment out of capital.

4. Where the purchase or redemption uses both the proceeds of a new issue and a payment out of capital (private companies only), the transfer is the amount of the excess, if any, of the nominal value of the shares purchased or redeemed over the sum of the proceeds from the new issue and the payment out of capital.

Example 4.8—Capital Redemption Reserve *(Cases 3 and 4 above)*
The balance sheet of Mat Ltd., a private company, at 31 December, 19X1 was:

	£000
Share Capital.........................	500
Distributable Profits...............	100
	600
Cash..................................	300
Other Net Assets	300
	600

The company decides to purchase its own shares with a nominal value of £80,000.

REQUIRED
Prepare the balance sheet of Mat Ltd. on the alternative assumptions that:
(a) The company purchases the shares for £160,000. (Case 3)
(b) The company purchases the shares for £160,000, but issues at par for cash shares with a nominal value of £40,000 to finance the purchase. (Case 4)

Solution

	(a)	(b)
	£000	£000
Share Capital..	420	460
Capital Redemption Reserve	20(W1)	20(W2)
	440	480
Cash..	140	180
Other Net Assets	300	300
	440	480

Workings

W1—The permissible capital payment is £160,000 (purchase price) – 100,000 (distributable profit) = £60,000.

The transfer to Capital Redemption Reserve is £80,000 (nominal value purchased) – 60,000 (permissible capital payment) = £20,000.

W2—The permissible capital payment is £160,000 (purchase price) – 100,000 (distributable profit) – 40,000 (proceeds from new issue) = £20,000.

The transfer to Capital Redemption Reserve is £80,000 (nominal value purchased) – (40,000 + 20,000) = £20,000.

There is an important difference between the effects of requirements 1 and 2 and 3 and 4 above which can be seen from examples 4.7 and 4.8. In example 4.7, in both cases, the transfer to Capital Redemption Reserve leaves the value of non-distributable equity at £500,000, while in example 4.8 it is reduced by £60,000 in case (a) and by £20,000 in case (b). The provisions therefore ensure that the value of non-distributable equity of public companies is maintained as they are not permitted to redeem or purchase their own shares out of capital.

The Capital Redemption Reserve can only be used for the issue of fully paid bonus shares or reduced only by the same procedure as if it were paid up share capital (see section 3 of this Chapter).

4.5 FAILURE, LOSSES AND CAPITAL EROSION

It is a fact that some companies will fail and will then have to be liquidated. Management and owners are often unwilling to face the likelihood of failure and attempt to struggle on until they are forced to accept the reality of the situation by, for example, the appointment of a receiver. Companies in financial difficulties need to obtain further finance, and the bank manager is often the first person approached for these resources. The optimistic attitude typically displayed by business management, often with little regard to the actual circumstances, is that the firm's position will improve and failure will be avoided provided it can survive for a further short period of time. It is therefore in the interests of banks, and all other potential providers of finance, to be able to judge which companies are merely going through a period of temporary difficulty and which companies are going to fail. It is important to ensure, as far as possible, that too pessimistic an assessment is not made, since the withdrawal of an existing financial provision by the bank may cause the failure of a company which would otherwise have recovered. Success or failure cannot be forecast with certainty, but there are a number of indicators which have been observed in failed companies and which can be looked for in companies suffering from financial difficulties in order to see whether they too are likely to fail.

4.5.1 The Causes of Failure The prime factor which causes companies to fail is inadequate management, which may misjudge costs, prices or markets, or base decisions on insufficient or out of date information. These shortcomings eventually cause the company to become insolvent and force it into liquidation. The causes of failure are therefore the factors which erode the liquidity of the company and leave it unable to attract further external finance or generate sufficient internal finance to continue in operation. When a bank manager is approached by a company with a request for an overdraft, an increased overdraft, or some other form of financial assistance, and the company's accounts reveal a poor liquidity position, the causes of the low liquidity ratio must be sought. If the causes are of a permanent nature, the provision of additional finance will merely postpone liquidation as the company will suffer another liquidity crisis as soon as the new funds have been used up. The causes of liquidity problems may be complex, but can be sought in such areas as:

1. Finance Costs. Interest charges on debt represent a fixed cost, they do not vary with the rate of output. A company with a high proportion of debt finance has to meet substantial interest payments, and it is possible for these to prove too great a burden, especially if there is a downturn in trading profit. Small companies often rely heavily on overdrafts for finance, and an increase in the rate of interest charged, particularly if it coincides with a fall in trading profits, can cause great difficulties.

2. Operating Costs. The high fixed costs associated with capital intensive production methods can prove an excessive drain on resources, particularly if there is a fall in the level of activity. Fixed costs do not respond to changes in the level of output, and may be completely outside the control of management; for example, local authorities set the rates payable by the occupiers of premises and these must be paid by businesses irrespective of their profitability. Also, the variable cost per unit of output may rise, for example, as the result of a pay increase granted to employees. If a firm cannot increase its selling price to recover increased operating costs, its profit margins are eroded, or even converted into losses, thereby reducing the level of cash flow into the business.

3. Overtrading. A company may be profitable, but management takes the unwise step of financing long-term developments with short-term funds, that is, they use money needed to meet operating costs to acquire fixed assets or to fund long-term activities such as research (see Chapter 9, section 9.2 for a fuller explanation of overtrading).

4. Market Failure. It is possible for a company to be efficient and, initially, to have a correctly balanced capital structure. However, it will still fail if it cannot sell its product at a price high enough to cover costs. The inability to charge an adequate price may be due to competitors having lower prices, or simply the fact that there is no longer a demand for the company's particular product.

Where symptoms such as those described above are shown by a company, a decision must be made whether they can be rectified in sufficient time and at a small enough cost to enable the company to continue in existence. If it is fairly certain that the company is going to fail, commercial losses are minimised by injecting no further finance. The likelihood of a firm, which appears to be failing, avoiding eventual liquidation depends to a large extent on the ability of management. To have reached the position where failure is a distinct possibility can be evidence of poor management, and a condition of financial help could be the injection of new managerial expertise. The bank's evaluation of the prospects of survival is likely to be based on forecasts made by management, and these must therefore be checked carefully for realism and compared with past results to see if they are consistent. Future sales of a product are unlikely to be substantially higher than in the past unless there is a convincing explanation for an anticipated upturn. Expectations should be expressed in the form of accounting reports, the contents of which can then be scrutinised. It is important not to accept management's statements without question; enough investigation should be carried out to reach an informed opinion on their reliability.

4.5.2 Losses and Capital Erosion Losses are caused by the failure to recover all costs through sales, and the solution lies in the company's ability to raise prices, cut costs, or produce a new product that can be sold profitably. It is unusual for companies to sell only one product, and diversification makes it more likely that poor results in one area will be offset by good results in others. The accounting system of a company should enable the identification of those lines which are being sold at a loss so that remedial action can be taken, but simply ceasing to trade in items which show a loss may not be the correct solution if they make a contribution to overhead costs. (See Chapter 10, section 5.4). A successful company must be able to adapt to changes in the market, and should always be developing new and improved lines to replace those which are likely to experience a fall in demand in the future. Both the time taken to develop and market a new product and the associated costs involved can be substantial, and so the process must be started well in advance and appropriate finance arranged. A firm whose current products are not in demand and which has no new developments to put into production is likely to fail.

A company which makes losses suffers an erosion of capital, which produces a corresponding reduction in net assets. The impact of losses on the viability of a company depends on their size relative to the company's resources, and on their duration. A relatively small annual loss is unlikely, in itself, to have a significant effect; the company still has a positive cash flow from trading if its depreciation charge is greater than the loss (see Chapter 9, section 7.1). The accumulation of a series of losses, even if individually small, has a more serious impact in the longer term; in these circumstances the cash flow represented by depreciation is used to finance running costs and the firm will probably be unable to attract finance when it is time for plant replacement. A company which continually makes losses is heading for likely failure; the size of the losses merely determines how long the process takes. The effect of large significant losses is more immediate and precipitates the crisis more quickly.

Example 4.9—The Effects of Losses

The balance sheet of Going Ltd. at 31 December, 19X0 is:

	£000
Share Capital	500
Profit and Loss Account	250
	750
Fixed Assets at written down value	400
Working Capital	350
	750

The fixed assets are expected to last a further five years, and to keep pace with inflation it is forecast that £20,000 per year must be invested in additional working capital.

REQUIRED

Prepare the balance sheet of Going Ltd. at 31 December, 19X5 on the alternative assumptions that it makes an annual loss of:

(a) £20,000

(b) £60,000

Solution

	(a)	(b)
	£000	£000
Share Capital	500	500
Profit and Loss Account	150	(50)
	650	450
Fixed Assets at written down value	—	—
Working Capital	450	450
Surplus Cash	200(W1)	—(W2)
	650	450

Workings (£000)

$$\text{5 years' losses} + \text{5 years' depreciation} - \text{5 years' additional working capital} = \text{Surplus Cash 31 December, 19X5}$$

W1	−100	+	400	−	100	=	200
W2	−300	+	400	−	100	=	0

No dividends have been paid throughout the five years, and in neither case does Going Ltd. have enough cash at the end of 19X5 to replace the exhausted fixed assets. The continual losses make it most unlikely that new external finance can be obtained. In case (b) the losses have eroded the book value of the share capital, while losses in excess of £60,000 would deplete working capital and therefore reduce the volume of trade the company is able to undertake.

The 1980 Act requires any director of a public company to call an extraordinary general meeting if he becomes aware of the fact that, as a result of business losses, the company's net assets are worth half or less of its called-up share capital. The meeting must be convened within 28 days of the loss becoming known and must be held within 56 days. This meeting is instructed to consider whether any, and if so what, measures should be taken to deal with the situation. For this purpose, the 'net assets' of a company are defined as 'the aggregate of its assets less the aggregate of its liabilities' and so their value is revealed by the balance sheet. The speed with which the erosion becomes apparent will therefore depend on the frequency of preparation of balance sheets.

The objective of this provision is to make the shareholders aware of the fact that the company has suffered major losses; once this has been done, they are able to meet to consider possible courses of action to prevent the accumulation of further losses. However, the legal requirement to call a meeting may give rise to problems. The fact that a meeting has been called may cause a withdrawal of finance by, for example, banks and trade creditors, thereby bringing about a failure which might have been averted. Assets are valued for accounting purposes on the assumption that the business is a going concern; in the circumstances which lead to the calling of a meeting under the 1980 Act, the liquidation basis may be more appropriate. The use of liquidation values would, although prudent, possibly reinforce the assumption that the company is bound to fail and hasten its end.

4.6   THE PROVIDERS OF FINANCE

The finance used to fund net assets is usually obtained from a variety of sources. A limited company must have in issue shares which are not redeemable, and it is likely also to use other types of finance such as debentures and trade credit. The terms on which funds are obtained are established at the time the company receives them, and each provider will normally insist on two conditions associated with investing and lending, namely, the right to convert the investment or loan back into cash and the right to a return in the form of dividends or interest. Reconversion to cash may involve selling the investment or debt, or being reimbursed by the company itself. Some debts, such as debentures, carry a right to a set rate of interest, others, such as trade creditors, receive no interest; the cost of overdrafts varies with changes in the general level of interest rates, and the return to shareholders depends on the company's profitability. The ability of a company to fulfill all of its obligations to the providers of finance relies on it being a going concern; a company which fails is unable to meet its obligations, and the rights of lenders and investors then become those which determine the disposition of available funds on liquidation. This section reviews the rights and expectations of those who finance companies, on the assumption that they are going concerns, and then examines the position on liquidation.

4.6.1   The Going Concern   A going concern may be defined as a company which is able to pay its debts as they fall due. Such debts include not only trade creditors, but also such items as loan interest and repayments, wages and salaries, and hire purchase instalments.

There are a great number of different sources of finance which a company may use, the main ones being:

1. Share Capital. A company may issue shares which possess a variety of rights as regards capital entitlements. Shares can be issued which are redeemable at a fixed, or indefinite, time in the future, and companies can also repay investors by purchasing their own shares. There can also be shares of different classes which have preferential rights on liquidation. Dividends can only be paid out of distributable profits (see Chapter 3, section 9), but some shares can be given preferential rights to dividends.

2. Debentures. A debenture is a written acknowledgement of a loan made to a company. It contains terms to cover the payment of interest and the repayment of capital. A debenture may also give the holder the option to convert the debt into shares at a predetermined rate. It is usual for a debenture to carry a charge on the company's assets, which may either be attached to particular assets or be a floating charge over the assets in general. The interest on debentures is payable whether or not the company makes profits.

3. Long-Term Loans. These can be secured or unsecured and may carry the right to interest at a fixed rate or at a rate which varies with the general rate of interest in the economy. The precise terms are set when the loan is made.

4. Bank Overdrafts. These are a major source of finance, especially for small and medium sized companies, and, although technically repayable at short notice, they usually have a degree of permanence. Banks usually require security, which may be given by a charge over the assets of the business, or a guarantee from, for example, a director who is also a major shareholder and who pledges his personal assets. The balance due fluctuates as deposits and withdrawals are made, and care must be taken to observe the trend: if it is upwards, then the company will encounter problems when its overdraft limit is reached. The rate of interest varies with changes in the general rate of interest in the economy, and the charge for a period is calculated on the daily balance outstanding.

5. Trade Creditors. Many trade creditors provide finance by allowing a period of time to elapse before requiring payment for the goods supplied. The period of credit is set by the normal terms of trade for a particular industry or profession. Interest is not usually charged, although some companies reserve the right to charge it on overdue debts, and a discount may be offered for prompt payment.

6. *Sundry Creditors*. Companies often have a number of short and medium-term debts which provide finance. For example, Value Added Tax and Income Tax collected by the company on behalf of the tax authorities are paid over periodically, and corporation tax is outstanding for at least nine months from the balance sheet date. The funds are available to the company from the time the tax is collected or the debt incurred to the time of payment, and, as one sum is paid, so another is accumulated. They therefore comprise a permanent source of finance.

4.6.2 Liquidation This is usually caused by a company being unable to pay its debts as they fall due. In determining the company's ability to pay its debts, the 1948 Act requires all contingent and prospective liabilities to be taken into account. Therefore, a company may currently be solvent, but may be forced into liquidation if it is apparent that it will be unable to meet some future obligation. When a company goes into liquidation, the administration of its affairs passes from the board of directors to an official known as a 'liquidator'. It is the duty of the liquidator to realise the assets of the company for as much as possible and use the proceeds to pay its creditors and members in a specified order. The order of repayment is as follows:

1. Debts secured with a fixed charge have first priority, and they are repayable out of the proceeds received from the sale of that asset. It is unlikely that the realised value of the asset will be exactly equal to the amount of the debt, and any surplus is used by the liquidator to meet the company's other liabilities. Great care must be exercised when there is a deficit, that is, the value of the secured asset is less than the debt. In these circumstances, the secured debt effectively divides into two separate parts; the first is covered by the secured asset to the extent of its value, and the second part ranks alongside, and therefore is added to, the unsecured creditors.
2. The costs of liquidation.
3. Preferential debts, which include certain taxes and sums due to employees.
4. Debts which carry a floating charge, that is, they are secured on the company's assets in general.
5. Unsecured creditors.
6. Shareholders. The priority for repayment where there exist different classes of shares is determined by the terms on which

the shares were issued. Preference shares are normally repaid in full before the ordinary shares, while the 1981 Act gives priority, within their particular class, to redeemable shares and any which the company has agreed to purchase, but has not acquired by the time of liquidation.

Each category listed above must be paid in full before the next group receives any payment whatsoever. Thus, all preferential debts must be paid before creditors with floating charges receive anything, and they in turn must be fully settled before any payment is made to unsecured creditors. A company which is insolvent when it is wound up is unlikely to be able to pay the full amount due to all of its creditors and classes of shareholders; some receive less than the amount due, and others receive nothing. Within the class where the liquidator runs out of money, the debts abate equally, that is, each creditor or class of shareholder receives the same proportional payment.

Example 4.10—Abatement

The liquidator of Gone Ltd. has sold all of the company's assets for £250,000 in cash. The sums to be met from this are:

	£000
Cost of liquidation	30
Preferential debts	20
Debts with floating charges	100
Unsecured creditors	200
Ordinary shareholders	250

REQUIRED

(a) Calculate how much is received by each class of creditor and shareholder, showing clearly the order of priority.

(b) Calculate the sum received by an unsecured creditor owed £2,500.

Solution

(a) The funds available are distributed as follows:

Order of Priority		£000
	Received from sale of assets	250
1.	*Less:* Cost of liquidation	30
		220
2.	*Less:* Preferential debts	20
		200
3.	*Less:* Debts with floating charges	100
4.	Available for unsecured creditors	100

Unsecured creditors are owed £200,000 and each receives 50 pence in the pound.

5.   Ordinary shareholders receive nothing.

(b) An unsecured creditor owed £2,500 receives 50 pence × 2,500 = £1,250.

There are two circumstances in which a bank may be interested in a company that is threatened with liquidation:

1. Where the bank is owed money by a company, the maximum amount it can expect to recover if the company fails is the sum due on liquidation. The extent of the bank's potential loss is then the difference between the sum lent and the receipts expected on liquidation.
2. The bank may hold shares in a company as security for a loan, in which case the sum receivable on the shares in a liquidation gives the value of the shares as a security.

Example 4.11 (Taken from the April, 1981 *Accountancy* paper).

One of your bank's customers, Jeremiah, has deposited 6,000 shares in Eastgate Ltd. as security for a personal bank overdraft on which £2,460 is at present outstanding. You have heard that, at a meeting between the directors and creditors of Eastgate Ltd. held on 20 April 1981, it was decided to liquidate that company. Certain facts and estimates were examined by the meeting. These included:

(i) *Balance Sheet of Eastgate Ltd. at 19 April, 1981*

	£	£		£	£
Share capital (£1 shares)		100,000	Goodwill at cost ...		22,000
Reserves at 31 December 1980	70,000		Freehold property at cost		45,000
Loss for 1981 to date	68,000		Plant and machinery at cost less depreciation		48,000
		2,000			115,000
		102,000	Quoted investments (market value £16,000)		12,000
12% debenture		50,000			
Current liabilities:			Current assets:		
Creditors	209,000		Stock	108,000	
Bank overdraft	68,000		Debtors	194,000	
		277,000			302,000
		£429,000			£429,000

(ii) The following asset values were considered to be relevant in a liquidation:

	£
Plant and machinery ..	10,000
Stock	47,000
Debtors	160,000

There was significant disagreement regarding the likely value of the freehold property. The majority accepted a valuation of £60,000 recently obtained from a firm of surveyors. A minority argued that, in view of development potential in the area where this property was located, a sale figure of £150,000 was likely to be much nearer the mark.

(iii) Eastgate Ltd.'s bank holds a fixed charge on the freehold property as security for the overdraft.

(iv) Of the £209,000 creditors, £57,000 were estimated as being preferential.

(v) The debenture is secured by a floating charge over the assets of Eastgate Ltd., other than the freehold property. There are no arrears of debenture interest.

(vi) Liquidation expenses are estimated at £6,000.

Required:

(a) Calculations of the amounts which would be received by each of the providers of finance, assuming that the majority view regarding the value of the freeholds is correct and that the other information proves accurate. You should show clearly the order of priority for repayment.

(b) An indication of the effect on the findings under (a) if the minority view regarding the value of the freeholds proves to be correct.

Note:

Ignore taxation.

[20]

Solution

(a)

Assets are expected to realise:	£000	£000
Freehold property		60
Less: Bank overdraft secured thereon		68
		—
To unsecured creditors		8
Quoted Investments		16
Plant and Machinery		10
Stock		47
Debtors		160
		—
		233

Priority	Repayment	£000	£000
1	Liquidation expenses...		6
			227
2	Preferential creditors...		57
			170
3	Debenture with floating charge....................................		50
			120
4	Unsecured creditors:		
	Bank overdraft residue	8	
	Other creditors (209–57)...	152	
		—	160
	Unsecured creditors receive 75 pence in the pound		—
	In total the bank receives £60,000 + (.75 × 8,000) = ...		66
	Unsecured creditors receive £152,000 × .75 = ...		114
5	Shareholders receive nothing		

(b) If the property sells for £150,000, the bank will recover the full overdraft of £68,000 out of its security and the non-preferential creditors will be repaid in full, £152,000. The amount available for the shareholders will be:

	£000
Increase in expected selling price of property.....................................	90
Less: additional amount due to bank and creditors............................	40
	50

Shareholders receive $\dfrac{£50,000}{100,000}$ = 50 pence per share.

Examiner's Comments

Points of weakness: 1. The treatment in (a) of the bank's deficit from its fixed charge. Many students gave it a first claim on the remaining assets.
2. The order of priority for repayment.
3. The abatement of amounts owing to the unsecured creditors.
4. Reserves were frequently included as an asset.

A 'receiver' may be appointed to enforce the terms of a secured debt if a company defaults in the payment of interest or capital when due, or behaves in a manner which threatens secured assets. The receiver takes control of the assets covered by the charge and realises them to provide funds to satisfy the terms of the loan. If the company remains solvent after the receiver has carried out his duties, management reverts to the directors. However, the appointment of a receiver is usually an indication that the company is failing and so liquidation, under the control of the liquidator, normally follows receivership.

4.7 CAPITAL RECONSTRUCTION

Liquidation is not the inevitable outcome of a company's insolvency. It may be worthwhile to attempt a rescue where the insolvency is due to specific, curable factors. For example, a company may have overtraded, and, if it is basically profitable, an injection of additional capital may save it; alternatively, a company may need time and finance to cease the production of unprofitable lines and bring to the market new, profitable products. In these circumstances, meetings of creditors and members are called to consider the acceptance of variations in their rights; to be acceptable it is anticipated that the proposed reconstruction must be more attractive to all parties than the alternative of liquidation.

4.7.1 The Variation of Rights The objective of a reconstruction scheme is to enable the company to continue as a going concern by the removal of the burden of immediate debts, the attraction of additional funds and the creation of a viable financial structure. The reconstruction can be carried out by altering the rights of creditors and members in the existing company, or the activities of the old company may be taken over by a newly established corporate entity which accepts revised obligations to the old company's creditors and members, with the old company being wound up or dissolved. It is possible to vary rights in a number of ways on reconstruction:

1. The nature of the debt may be changed, for example, debentures may be converted to share capital or creditors to secured loans.
2. The value of the liability may be changed; for example, the nominal value of ordinary shares, which are likely to be of little or no value on liquidation, can be greatly reduced, or creditors may agree to forego part of their debt.
3. The return on the debt may be varied. Trade creditors could be offered interest to delay their claims, or debenture holders given higher interest to extend the term of the debenture.
4. A combination of 1 to 3 above can be applied. 8% debentures with a face value of £100,000 repayable in one year's time may be cancelled in exchange for 75,000 ordinary shares of £1 each and £50,000 debentures carrying 12% interest and repayable in ten years' time.

The rights of creditors and members cannot be varied in an arbitrary manner; the 1948 Act provides for meetings of all classes to be called, and, if each of these approves of the proposed arrangement by a majority of at least 75%, then, with the sanction of the court, it becomes binding on all the interested parties.

4.7.2 Implementation of a Scheme of Reconstruction   When a company is reconstructed it is common to revalue the assets at realistic amounts and eliminate the debit balance on the profit and loss account, if any. When the reconstruction does not involve the creation of a new company, a Reconstruction Account is opened to complete the book-keeping double entries for the adjustments on reconstruction. This account is debited with reductions in the value of assets, the adverse profit and loss account balance, and the creation of liabilities; it is credited with reductions in liabilities and increases in the value of assets. The corresponding entries are in the appropriate asset or liability account.

Example 4.12—The Reconstruction Account

The following is the balance sheet of File Ltd. on 31 December, 19X1:

	£000	£000
Ordinary Shares of £1 each		250
Profit and Loss Account		(100)
		150
8% Secured Debentures repayable 31 December, 19X2		130
		280
Fixed Assets at written down value		180
Goodwill		50
Stock	90	
Debtors	85	
	175	
Trade Creditors	85	
Bank Overdraft	40	
	125	
Working Capital		50
		280

The company's activities have been partially reorganised and a number of loss-making branches closed. It is forecast that profits will be made in the future, but reconstruction is necessary to enable the company to raise further equity capital needed to complete the reorganisation. The following scheme has been accepted by all interested parties:

1. The assets are to be written down to realistic current values:

	£000
Fixed Assets...............	80
Goodwill...................	—
Stock........................	70
Debtors.....................	80

2. The debit balance on the profit and loss account is to be eliminated.
3. The existing 8% debentures are to be cancelled. In return the debenture holders are to receive 12% debentures with a nominal value of £90,000 and 35,000 ordinary shares of £1 each fully paid.
4. The trade creditors are to be reduced by £25,000, and they agree, in return for an interest payment, to wait one year for their money.
5. Each existing ordinary share of £1 is to be written down to 2 pence. The 2 pence shares are to be consolidated into shares with a nominal value of £1 each. The ordinary shareholders agree to subscribe in cash for 60,000 shares of £1 each at par.

REQUIRED

(a) Prepare the Reconstruction Account of File Ltd. to put the scheme into effect.
(b) Prepare the Balance Sheet of File Ltd. after the scheme has been effected.

Solution

Reconstruction Account

	£000		£000
Fixed Assets...	100	8% Debentures..........	130
Goodwill..	50	Creditors..................	25
Stock...	20	Ordinary Shares.........	245
Debtors..	5		
Profit and Loss Account...........................	100		
12% Debentures.......................................	90		
Ordinary Shares (for debenture holders).......	35		
	___		___
	400		400

Balance Sheet after Reconstruction

	£000		£000	£000
Ordinary Share Capital...................	100(W1)	Fixed Assets...		80
12% Debentures...........................	90	Stock............	70	
Creditors (deferred for one year).......	60	Debtors.........	80	
		Cash (W2).....	20	
			—	170
	___			___
	250			250

Workings

W1 Ordinary Share Capital	£000
Issued to Debenture holders..............	35
Ordinary shareholders (reduced).........	5
Issued for cash............................	60
	100

W2 Cash	
Overdraft.....................................	(40)
Cash from issue of shares................	60
	20

Note. In this example the amounts written off assets together with the removal of the accumulated loss were exactly balanced by adjustments to the claims from various providers of finance. The credit balance, which sometimes remains on the reconstruction account after the adjustments have been made, is a capital reserve and is shown in the balance sheet as part of equity.

In questions on reconstruction, care must be taken to show how the revised figures in the balance sheet after reconstruction have been computed. The following example shows this need clearly, as the value of ordinary shares in the new company's balance sheet involves a fairly complex calculation. Failure to show detailed workings may make it impossible for the examiner to detect the nature of particular errors and give due credit for calculations correctly made.

Example 4.13 (Taken from the April, 1980 *Accountancy* paper).

Arches Limited has incurred trading losses during each of its last three accounting periods and is now in severe financial difficulty. The company's balance sheet at 31 March, 1980 is as follows:

Balance Sheet

	£		£
Ordinary Shares (£1 each)	200,000	Fixed assets at cost	
Profit and loss account ..	(30,000)	*less* depreciation ..	239,000
	170,000	Goodwill	37,000
12% debenture stock ..	100,000	Stock	90,000
Bank overdraft (secured)	67,000	Trade debtors ..	64,000
Trade creditors ..	93,000		
	430,000		430,000

A reorganisation of the company's activities during March 1980 resulted in a transfer of resources from loss-making to profitable product lines.

A meeting of all parties involved is held on 2 April, 1980 to consider a scheme of reconstruction under the Companies Acts. The proposal made by the directors is that a new company called Arches (1980) Limited be formed to take over the assets, liabilities and business activities of Arches Limited. It is estimated that the annual trading profits of Arches (1980) Limited, for the foreseeable future, will be £43,500 before charging debenture interest (see below). After debenture interest has been deducted 50 per cent of the balance remaining is to be paid out as dividends.

Arches (1980) Limited would take over the fixed assets at their depreciated replacement cost, estimated at £156,000; stock, trade debtors, trade creditors and the bank overdraft would be transferred at the figures appearing in the above balance sheet.

Arches (1980) Limited would issue 20p ordinary shares and 15 per cent debenture stock as follows:

(1)   The existing debenture holders of Arches Limited would receive £10 of 15 per cent debenture stock for every £20 of 12 per cent debenture stock presently held. They would also receive the number of 20p ordinary shares which causes the dividend plus debenture interest receivable from Arches (1980) Limited to be equal to the amount of debenture interest previously received from Arches Limited.

(2)   The issued share capital of Arches (1980) Limited would consist of 500,000 ordinary shares of 20p each. After the issue of ordinary shares referred to above, the balance of the 500,000 shares would be issued on a pro rata basis in exchange for the ordinary shares held in Arches Limited.

If the reconstruction proposal is accepted the existing ordinary shareholders of Arches Limited have agreed to subscribe in cash for an additional 400,000 ordinary shares of 20p each at par. The proceeds would be used primarily to repay the bank overdraft.

Required:

The opening balance sheet of Arches (1980) Limited assuming the proposed reconstruction is adopted and put into effect. The balance sheet should show clearly the number of ordinary shares issued to the debenture stock holders of Arches Limited and the number of shares issued to the ordinary shareholders of Arches Limited, distinguishing those paid for in cash.

NOTES:

(i) *Ignore taxation and any arrears or accruals of dividends or interest.*

(ii) *Assume that no changes have occurred since the balance sheet date.*

[20]

Solution

Balance Sheet of Arches (1980) Ltd.

	£	£
Ordinary Shares:		
Issued to debenture holders (W2)		45,000
Issued to shareholders for cash (W3)		80,000
Issued to shareholders on reconstruction (W3)		55,000
900,000 shares at 20 pence each		180,000
15% Debenture Stock (W1)		50,000
		230,000
Fixed Assets at valuation		156,000
Stock	90,000	
Trade Debtors	64,000	
Bank (80,000 − 67,000)	13,000	
	167,000	
Less: Trade Creditors	93,000	
		74,000
		230,000

Workings
W1—15% Debentures issued: $10/20 \times 100,000 = £50,000$
W2—Interest payable on new debentures: $15\% \times £50,000 = £7,500$

	£
Debenture holders of Arches Ltd. received interest of	12,000
Less: Interest on new debentures in Arches (1980) Ltd.	7,500
Balance to be received as dividends	4,500

Calculation of Dividends:

	£
Forecast profit before finance charges..	43,500
Less: Finance Charge (W2)	7,500
	36,000
Dividend (50% × £36,000)..	18,000
Profit retained	18,000

Shares issued to debenture holders of Arches Ltd. are therefore:

$$\frac{4,500}{18,000} \times 900,000 = 225,000 \text{ shares}$$

225,000 at 20 pence = £45,000
W3—Shares issued to shareholders of Arches Ltd.:
For cash: 400,000 at 20 pence = £80,000
On reconstruction: 500,000 − 225,000 (W2) = 275,000 at 20 pence
= £55,000

Examiner's comments
Areas of weakness: 1. Errors in the calculation of shares to be issued to debenture holders.
2. Failure to use the cash received from the issue of shares to pay off the overdraft.

4.7.3 The Evaluation of Reconstruction Schemes   The providers of finance, when asked to participate in a scheme of reconstruction, should weigh the benefits they might obtain from its implementation with the alternative, which is usually liquidation. A first step in the review of any scheme is to consider the rights of each class on liquidation and reconstruction. The likely outcomes must be based on forecasts, and so cannot be guaranteed as accurate, but because liquidation is more immediate its results are open to less doubt. Presentation and assimilation of the outcome of liquidation and reconstruction, as alternatives, is achieved by the use of a tabular format. Such an analysis for Arches Ltd. (example 4.13), *on the assumption that in a liquidation its fixed assets would be worth their depreciated replacement cost*, is:

Provider of Finance	Position on Liquidation	Position on Reconstruction
Shareholders	Receive £50,000 (W1) less liquidation expenses	Receive £55,000 shares and buy £80,000. This entitles them to expected dividends of £13,500. They own 75% of the company.
Debenture Holders	Receive £100,000 cash	Receive £50,000 of debentures and £45,000 of shares. No reduction in income occurs. They own 25% of the company.
Creditors	£93,000 received	£93,000 received. Future custom.
Bank	£67,000 received	£67,000 received. Future custom.

W1. Assets £310,000 (156,000 + 90,000 + 64,000) − Liabilities £260,000 (100,000 + 93,000 + 67,000).

Provided that the profit forecast is accurate, it appears that all parties are left no worse off, or indeed benefit, from the reconstruction of Arches Ltd.

The timing of any prospective payments is also important when assessing the merits of a reconstruction scheme. For example, if the creditors of Arches Ltd. in example 4.13 were asked to wait a year before payment, they would expect some compensation for this delay. On liquidation they would be paid in the near future, and the cash received could be invested; to wait a year they would require reimbursement for the interest foregone, plus perhaps an additional amount for the risk of leaving their money in a company which has been on the brink of failure. When the payment of sums of money is offered on different dates, an adjustment for interest is needed to enable comparison. For example, if funds can be invested at 10% per annum and a creditor is offered the choice between £1,000 on immediate liquidation or £1,050 in one year's time, liquidation is preferable since £1,000 could be invested for a year at 10% to give £1,100 at the end of the year.

Some of the costs and benefits associated with reconstruction schemes are intangible, and hence difficult to quantify; they should be considered nevertheless. For example, a bank may wish to avoid unfavourable publicity which might result from putting a customer into liquidation. The social consequences of liquidation, like unemployment, should also be considered, together with the benefit of future custom which will come from the firm's continued existence.

An important matter to investigate is whether the factors which produced the need for a reconstruction are eliminated by the proposed scheme. If they are not, reconstruction is not worthwhile. For example, if the underlying fact is that there is no demand for a company's product, then a reconstruction will not create a demand; the losses will continue unless there are new, profitable, products ready to be marketed. In addition, a check should be made that the reconstructed company will at least start off in a viable condition; a forecast balance sheet will reveal if it will have an acceptable level of liquidity and working capital, and whether the proposed gearing is satisfactory.

Example 4.14 (Taken from the September, 1979 *Accountancy* paper).

The balance sheet of Thornton Ltd, as at 31 August 1979, is as follows:

Balance Sheet

	£		£
Share capital (£1 shares)	40,000	Goodwill	12,000
Reserves	(550)	Freehold property	8,000
10% debenture, 1990 ..	10,000	Equipment at cost	
Bank overdraft ..	25,000	*less* depreciation ..	24,000
Rates & taxes	9,000	Stock	46,100
Other creditors	31,350	Debtors	24,700
	£114,800		£114,800

The bank overdraft carries a fixed charge over the freehold property and the debenture is secured by a floating charge over the remaining assets of Thornton Ltd.

The company was formed some years ago. After a period of profitable activity, business has steadily declined and a loss was reported for each of the last three years. The present position of the company has been further aggravated by the fact that the market for certain product lines has completely collapsed. As a result the company is now in severe financial difficulty and a meeting of the creditors is called for 2 September 1979 to consider its affairs.

The following proposals are put forward for consideration:

(i) *Immediate liquidation of the company*

In these circumstances it is estimated that the assets would realise the following amounts:

	£
Freehold property	15,000
Equipment	9,000
Stock	19,200
Debtors	24,700

It is discovered that 'other creditors' includes £9,350 that would rank as preferential in a liquidation, as well as the amounts due for rates and taxes. The liquidation expenses are estimated at £8,550.

(ii) *Reorganisation and capital reconstruction*

The management of Thornton Ltd have informed the creditors that a complete reorganisation is presently taking place and that the removal of unprofitable lines will reverse the present trend within a couple of months. Accordingly, the directors have prepared a scheme of capital reconstruction for consideration. The plan is to revalue tangible assets at their liquidation values, and to write off goodwill and the debit balance on reserves. The shareholders would be asked to accept shares with a nominal value of 1p each in a 'one for one' exchange for shares presently held. After the exchange has taken place the shares will be consolidated into £1 shares. The bank and the non-preferential other creditors would be asked to reduce their claims to 95% and 70% of their present balances respectively. The non-preferential other creditors would obtain repayment of this revised amount in three months' time, and the bank would receive its repayment in twelve months' time. The shareholders have indicated their willingness to take up a further 20,000 £1 shares at par, to finance working capital requirements, if this proposal is adopted.

Required:

(a) A calculation of the amounts which would be received by each of the providers of finance under proposal (i), assuming the information proves accurate. You should show clearly the order of priority for repayment.

(b) The revised balance sheet of Thornton Ltd at 2 September 1979 under proposal (ii).

(c) A consideration of the relative merits of the two proposals from the respective viewpoints of the bank, of the non-preferential other creditors, and of the shareholders.

NOTE: The current interest rate on all forms of borrowing is 10%. The £25,000 overdraft includes interest to date.

You may assume that no changes have occurred since the balance sheet date and the selected proposal will be implemented immediately.

[30]

Solution

(a) Immediate Liquidation

	£
Assets expected to realise	
(i) Freehold property	15,000
Less: Bank overdraft secured thereon	25,000
To unsecured creditors	10,000
(ii) Plant and machinery	9,000
Stock	19,200
Debtors	24,700
	52,900
Less:	
1. Liquidation expenses	8,550
	44,350
2. Preferential creditors	18,350
	26,000
3. Debentures secured by floating charge	10,000
Available for unsecured creditors	16,000
Unsecured creditors: Bank	10,000
Other creditors	22,000
	32,000

Therefore unsecured creditors get 50 pence in the pound. In total the bank gets £15,000 + £5,000 = £20,000.

Non-preferential creditors get 50% of £22,000 = £11,000.

The shareholders receive nothing.

(b) Revised Balance Sheet

	£	£
Share Capital (20,000 + 400).....................................		20,400
10% Debentures...		10,000
		30,400
Freehold property...		15,000
Equipment		9,000
		24,000
Stock	19,200	
Debtors	24,700	
Cash	20,000	
	63,900	
Less: Bank Overdraft..	23,750	
Rates and Taxes...	9,000	
Other creditors...	24,750	
	57,500	
Working Capital..		6,400
		30,400

Reconstruction Account

		£	£
Amounts written off:	Goodwill		12,000
	Equipment		15,000
	Stock		26,900
	Reserves		550
			54,450
Provided by:	Share capital	39,600	
	Freeholds..	7,000	
	Bank...	1,250	
	Other creditors..	6,600	
			54,450

(c)

	Liquidation	*Reconstruction*
(i) bank	£20,000 + 10% = £22,000	£23,750
(ii) non-preferential other creditors	50% of £22,000 = £11,000 + 2.5% = £11,275	£22,000 × 70% = £15,400
(iii) shareholders	Nil	?

For both the bank and the non-preferential other creditors the reconstruction would seem to be the better choice even after adding interest at the rate of 10% per annum to the amounts received on liquidation in order to achieve comparability. But reconstruction involves risk for which the bank is perhaps not adequately compensated.

Under liquidation the shareholders get nothing. Under reconstruction they will reap the benefit if the company does recover, but they have to risk a further £20,000.

Examiner's Comments
Area of weakness: 1. The treatment as secured of the unsecured portion of the bank overdraft on liquidation.
2. The order of repayment on liquidation, for example, the floating
charge was often given priority over the preferential creditors.
3. The abatement of amounts owing to unsecured creditors.
4. The effect of timing on the payments in part (c).

CHAPTER 5

Group Accounts

5.1 INTRODUCTION

There has been a substantial increase in the average size of the business unit during the present century which started with many industries still characterised by the 'one man business'. Today the sole trader remains an important feature of business life but, in many industries, the large scale corporation is now dominant. This development has occurred as the result of both internal and external growth. Internal expansion involves the development of the existing company's business, whereas external growth involves combining together the activities of two or more separate entities in order to achieve particular business objectives. For instance, a company may wish to safeguard its source of essential raw materials, which are in scarce supply, or guarantee wholesale and retail outlets for the products which it manufactures. The economic term used to describe the process whereby companies expand backwards or forwards along the chain of production and distribution is *vertical integration*. In contrast, *horizontal integration* occurs when companies, at the same stage in the chain, join together; this strategy may be adopted in order to reduce competition, and perhaps also to reap some of the benefits commonly associated with large scale production. *Diversification* occurs when companies expand into unrelated fields for such reasons as risk-spreading or to utilise available funds when there is no room for further expansion in their present line of business. Obviously a company may, at different times, or even at the same time, expand in all three directions.

5.2 COMBINATIONS BASED ON ASSETS OR SHARES

Business combinations may take the form of either an acquisition or a merger. There are a number of factors which determine the procedure followed, but perhaps the most important is the relative size of the two enterprises. In the case of an acquisition, a larger company normally takes over a smaller company, whereas a merger usually involves two or more companies of roughly the same size. In either of these cases, the combination may be based on assets or shares.

5.2.1   Combinations Based on Assets

Where one company, company A, acquires the assets of another company, company B, ownership of B's assets is transferred to A; B then goes into liquidation and A carries on the combined activities formerly undertaken by two companies. In the case of a merger, a new company, C, may be formed to acquire the assets of both A and B whose shareholders may well receive shares in the new company in exchange for their present holdings. Companies A and B may then be wound up and a single legal entity, company C, emerges to carry on the activities previously undertaken by the two companies. In both the takeover and merger, it will be necessary to value the assets transferred for inclusion in the acquiring company's books. Once this has been done, however, the assets are accounted for in the normal way and the reporting problems which arise when the combination is based on shares (see sections 4 to 7 of this Chapter) are avoided.

5.2.2   Combinations Based on Shares

Where one company, company A, purchases the shares of another company, company B, an agreement is reached between company A and the *shareholders* of company B; the transaction does not affect company B directly, and it remains in existence as a separate legal entity. Similarly a merger, based on shares, will result in the formation of a new company to acquire the shares of two or more existing companies, which again remain in existence as separate legal entities.

Up to the end of the nineteenth century, in Great Britain, acquisitions and mergers were invariably based on assets, and they resulted in the liquidation of either the company which had been taken over or the various companies which had been amalgamated. Around the turn of the century, managers began to recognise certain advantages accruing to the potentially looser form of business combination which results when shares are acquired rather than assets. These include:

  1. Economy. It is not necessary to purchase all the company's

shares, merely enough to ensure effective control over its activities.
2. Continuity. Where the acquired company maintains a separate identity, the goodwill specific to the purchased or merged company is more likely to survive unimpaired.
3. Decentralisation of both managerial and decision-making processes is facilitated where companies retain their own identity.

5.3 THE GROUP

Combinations based on shares (section 2.2 of this chapter) give rise to a *group* of companies within which the company which purchases the shares is called the 'holding company' and the company whose shares are acquired is called the 'subsidiary company'.

Figure 5.1

HC Ltd. purchased the entire share capital of SC Ltd. The relationship between the two companies can be shown diagrammatically as follows:

The arrow indicates that HC is the holding company and SC is the subsidiary, while the percentage superimposed on the arrow indicates the extent of the shareholding. Together HC and SC comprise a *group* of companies.

The external reporting requirements imposed by the Companies Acts, up until 1948, applied only to separate legal entities. In figure 5.1, for instance, HC and SC would each have had to publish separate accounts, but these accounts would have been confined to the transactions directly affecting them as separate legal entities. The accounts published by HC would therefore have included cash actually received from SC in the form of dividends, but any profits earned and retained by the subsidiary would not have been reported by the holding company. This provided management with enormous scope for publishing misleading financial information if it was inclined to do so. For instance, when the holding company's profits were low, management was often able to conceal this fact by making large undisclosed transfers of dividends from profitable subsidiaries. In different circumstances, management might allow subsidiaries to retain all their profits, and even make generous provisions for actual or potential losses of subsidiaries in order to depress a highly favourable profit figure which might otherwise become the basis for unwelcome wage demands or dividend claims. Admittedly, these are extreme examples, but they indicate the scope for potential abuse where accounting reports are confined to the legal entity.

Where abuses occurred, the holding company's accounts were of little use either for assessment purposes or as a basis for resource allocation decisions. The legislature's response, contained in the 1948 Act, was to require holding companies to supplement their legal entity based accounts with financial statements based on the affairs of the entire economic entity. Referring back to figure 5.1, both HC and SC are separate legal entities which continue to publish legal entity based accounts but, in addition, HC is required to publish group accounts dealing with the affairs of the economic entity formed by SC and itself.

5.3.1 Group Accounting Regulations The main reporting obligations imposed on the directors of holding companies are contained in the Companies Acts 1948, 1967 and 1981, and in Statement of Standard Accounting Practice (SSAP) 14, entitled 'Group Accounts', issued in 1978. Group accounts questions included in the *Accountancy* paper concentrate on the main principles, and candidates are not required to *present* consolidated balance sheets in accordance with the publication requirements contained in the Companies Acts (see syllabus). The provisions with which candidates are expected to be familiar are examined below.

The holding company/subsidiary company relationship exists in three basic situations, i.e. a company is a holding company and another company its subsidiary:

(i) where the first company is a member of the second company and controls the composition of its board of directors;

(ii) where the first company holds more than half, in nominal value, of the equity share capital of the second company.

Often both these tests produce the same result. For example, where a company's share capital consists entirely of ordinary shares possessing identical voting rights (e.g. one vote per share), it will be necessary to acquire more than half the equity shares (test ii) in order to control the composition of the board of directors (test i).

Example 5.1

HC Ltd. purchased 102,000 ordinary shares in SC Ltd. on 1 January, 19X1. The issued share capital of SC consists of 200,000 ordinary shares of £1 each, which carry equal voting rights.

HC is therefore the holding company of SC, as from 1 January, 19X1, on both bases:

1. It holds more than half the voting power, and is therefore able to control the composition of the board of directors.
2. It owns more than half the equity share capital, and the relationship between the two companies can be presented as follows:

HC

51%

SC

However, it is possible to hold much less than half the equity share capital, but still control the composition of the board of directors. This can occur for a variety of reasons, which include the existence of non-voting shares or restricted voting shares, or because of the possession of contractual rights to appoint the majority of the directors. In any of these circumstances, a holding company/subsidiary company relationship may exist applying test (i) but not test (ii).

Example 5.2

HC Ltd. purchased 50,000 A ordinary shares in SC Ltd. on 1 January, 19X1. The issued share capital of SC consists of 75,000 A ordinary shares and 125,000 B ordinary shares. Category A shares are voting shares and category B non-voting.

Test (i) HC is a holding company because it owns a majority of the voting shares and is therefore able to control the composition of the board of directors.

Test (ii) HC is not a holding company because it owns only 25% of the equity shares.

Because only one of the tests has to be satisfied, HC is the holding company of SC.

In the remainder of this chapter, it should be assumed that all equity shares carry equal voting rights, so that a holding company/subsidiary company relationship exists only where a majority of the equity shares are held.

(iii) where one company, company 1, is the holding company of another company, company 2, which is in turn the holding company of a third company, company 3, then company 3 is the sub-subsidiary of company 1.

Example 5.3

HC Ltd. has an 80% holding in SC1 Ltd. In addition, SC1 has a 55% holding in SC2 Ltd. The relationship between the three companies is as follows:

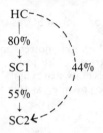

Notes:
1. HC is the holding company of SC1 by virtue of its 80% holding.
2. HC is also the holding company of SC2, since SC2 is the subsidiary of SC1. It should be noted that this situation arises despite the fact that HC has an indirect interest of only 44% (80% of 55%) in the assets and profits of SC2.

Sub-subsidiaries are examined in section 7 of this Chapter.

Group accounts can take a variety of different forms, but SSAP 14 stipulates that they should normally consist of a consolidated balance sheet dealing with the combined state of affairs of the holding company and its subsidiaries, as if they were a single entity, and a consolidated profit and loss account dealing with the combined profits and losses of the group. Steps should be taken to ensure that, as far as possible, uniform accounting policies (see Chapter 3, section 2) are employed when preparing the accounts of companies which are to be consolidated. When this is impracticable, however, details should be given of the different accounting policies used, their financial effect, and the reasons for the divergent treatment.

A further technical problem arises where a subsidiary is acquired whose accounting year-end differs from that of the holding company. Where this occurs, the directors are encouraged to take steps to obtain a coincidence of accounting dates or to use special financial statements, which have been drawn up to the same date as those of the holding company, for consolidation purposes. Where neither course is feasible the consolidated accounts must incorporate the last audited accounts of the subsidiary company, and care should be taken to adjust for significant post-balance sheet events so that the shareholders of the holding company are not misled. Events which require adjustment include:

ADJUSTMENTS

(i) intra-group transfers of cash or assets;
(ii) losses sustained by subsidiaries;
(iii) capital expenditures (or capital receipts) of subsidiaries.

The group accounting regulations recognise the existence of circumstances which justify the omission of one or more subsidiaries from the consolidated accounts published by the holding company. These are as follows: *EXEMPTIONS*

(i) where the subsidiary's activities are so dissimilar from those of other companies within the group that consolidated financial statements would be misleading, e.g. where a large industrial company acquires a small financial institution, the structure of the two balance sheets will be so different that consolidation would produce a meaningless and perhaps even misleading document;

(ii) where the holding company owns more than half the equity capital but, for some reason, e.g. the shares do not carry more than half the votes, it is unable to appoint the majority of the board of directors;

(iii) where the subsidiary operates under restrictions, e.g. exchange control restrictions, which significantly impair control by the holding company over the subsidiary's assets and operations for the foreseeable future;

(iv) where control is intended to be temporary;

(v) where it is impracticable or would be of no real value to members in view of the insignificant amounts involved or because it would involve undue expense or delay.

Where any of the above circumstances apply, holding companies are required to publish alternative financial information to help users make an assessment of the subsidiary company's performance. The information is specified in paragraphs 23–27 of SSAP *14* 14, but candidates will not be expected to memorise these provisions for examination purposes.

5.4 THE CONSOLIDATED BALANCE SHEET The basic concept underlying the preparation of consolidated accounts is extremely simple. The objective is to provide the shareholders of the holding company with full information concerning the activities of the entire economic unit in which they have invested, and this is achieved by combining the assets and liabilities of the holding company and its subsidiary into a single balance sheet so as to disclose the overall financial position of the group. In addition, the profits and losses of subsidiaries are combined with those of the holding company by means of a consolidated profit and loss acount which consequently reveals the aggregate increase or decrease in the book value of the shareholders' investment. The consolidated accounts are published in addition to legal entity based accounts, except that the holding company's own profit and loss account *may* be omitted provided the consolidated profit and loss account is amended to incorporate information which would otherwise be lost.

Example 5.4

The summarised balance sheets of HC Ltd. and SC Ltd. at 31 December, 19X1 are as follows:

Balance Sheet at 31 December, 19X1

	HC Ltd.	SC Ltd.
	£	£
Share capital (£1 ordinary shares)	60,000	25,000
Retained profits	36,000	10,000
	96,000	35,000
Liabilities	15,000	8,000
	111,000	43,000
Fixed assets at book value	36,000	27,000
Current assets: Stocks	20,000	7,000
Debtors	18,000	8,000
Bank	+37,000	1,000
	111,000	43,000

HC Ltd. purchased the entire share capital of SC Ltd. for £35,000 on 31 December, 19X1. The revised balance sheet of HC Ltd. at 31 December, 19X1 is as follows:

Revised Balance Sheet of HC Ltd. at 31 December, 19X1

	£
Share capital (£1 ordinary shares).........	60,000
Reserves.......................................	36,000
	96,000
Liabilities.....................................	15,000
	111,000
Fixed assets at book value	36,000
(BANK) – Investment in SC Ltd.	35,000 X
Current assets: Stocks	20,000
Debtors	18,000
Bank.......................	2,000 X
	111,000

In the separate balance sheets of HC Ltd. and SC Ltd. the only change involves a redistribution of HC Ltd.'s assets; £35,000 is transferred from 'Bank' to 'Investment in SC Ltd.' The balance sheet of SC Ltd. remains unchanged; the transaction is with the shareholders of SC Ltd. and no resources transfer into or out of the subsidiary company as a result of the share purchase.

Turning to the preparation of the consolidated balance sheet. Attention has already been drawn to the fact that the basic reason for producing consolidated accounts, is that the group of companies is in fact, though not in law, a single undertaking. It therefore follows that the essence of consolidation procedures is the cancellation of inter-company transactions. Items which appear as an asset in the balance sheet of one member of the group and as a liability in the balance sheet of another member of the group must be offset against one another for consolidation purposes. HC Ltd.'s revised balance sheet contains an asset entitled 'Investment in SC Ltd., £35,000', whereas SC Ltd.'s balance sheet shows a similar amount 'owing' to its shareholders, namely HC Ltd. These two balances therefore cancel out, and the remaining assets and liabilities are aggregated to produce the following consolidated balance sheet.

CONSOLIDATION.

Consolidated Balance Sheet of HC Ltd. and Subsidiary

Inter debts not to be included

	Workings: HC	SC	
	£	£	£
Share capital	60,000	*	60,000
Reserves	36,000	*	36,000
	96,000		96,000
Liabilities	15,000 +	8,000	23,000
			119,000
Fixed assets at book value	36,000 +	27,000	63,000
Current assets: Stocks	20,000 +	7,000	27,000
Debtors	18,000 +	8,000	26,000
Bank	2,000 +	1,000	3,000
			119,000

*Set off against the balance described as Investment in SC Ltd. in HC Ltd.'s balance sheet.

Example 5.4 illustrates the essence of consolidation procedures but it is an over-simplification. It is very unlikely that the price paid on acquisition will be exactly equal to the figure for shareholders' equity in the subsidiary company's balance sheet. Furthermore, a period of time will usually elapse betwen the date when the shares were acquired and the consolidation date. Finally the investing company may well take the opportunity, which this form of business combination permits, to achieve control while purchasing less than the entire share capital. Consequently the preparation of consolidated accounts, based on the separate accounts of the holding company and one or more subsidiaries, is generally preceded by three 'primary' calculations, namely, the calculation of:
  Goodwill
  Post-acquisition profits
  Minority interest
The calculation of the balances covered by each of these descriptions is examined in sections 4.1–4.3 of this Chapter

5.4.1 Goodwill   Goodwill arising on consolidation is defined as the difference between the price paid by the holding company and the 'fair' value of the net tangible and identifiable intangible assets belonging to the subsidiary company at the date of acquisition.

Often the price paid significantly exceeds the 'book' value of the net assets of the subsidiary company. Part of this surplus will be attributable to the favourable trading connections, or goodwill, built up by the subsidiary company over the years; the residual difference will be a consequence of the fact that there exists a disparity between the book value and the current or *fair value* of the assets at the time when an interest was acquired. It is for this reason that management is required by SSAP14 to restate the subsidiary company's assets at their fair value for the purpose of computing goodwill. The adjustments required need not necessarily be written into the books of the acquired company and used for the purpose of its legal entity based accounts, but they must be made for consolidation purposes.

Example 5.5

The summarised balance sheets of A Ltd. and B Ltd. at 31 December, 19X1 are as follows:

	A Ltd. £	B Ltd. £
Share capital (£1 ordinary shares)	100,000	50,000
Retained profits	70,000	12,000
	170,000	62,000
Liabilities	25,000	16,000
	195,000	78,000
Fixed assets at book value	60,000	46,000 54
Investment in B Ltd.	75,000	
Current assets: Stocks	32,000	13,000
Debtors	27,000	17,000
Bank	1,000	2,000
	195,000	78,000

A Ltd. purchased the entire share capital of B Ltd. on 31 December, 19X1. The fixed assets of B Ltd. are considered to possess a fair value of £54,000, but there are no material differences between the book values and fair values of the remaining assets.

The fixed assets must be included at their fair value for the purpose of calculating goodwill.

SSAP 14 = "ASSETS MUST BE AT FAIR VALUE"

Calculation of goodwill arising on consolidation (net asset
approach)

	£	£
Price paid		75,000
Less: Value of business acquired:		
Fixed assets..	54,000	
Stock..	13,000	
Debtors...	17,000	
Bank...	2,000	
Liabilities..	(16,000)	
		70,000
Goodwill..		5,000

When solving examination questions, it is generally necessary to
calculate the 'value of business acquired' using the equity components rather than the net asset approach. The result is the same,
but the former procedure is followed because, in most group
accounting questions, a period of time will have elapsed between
the dates of takeover and consolidation. Consequently the figures
for assets and liabilities at the date of takeover are unlikely to be
available, but sufficient information will be provided to build up
the shareholders' equity interest at that date. In example 5.5, the
re-statement of fixed assets at their fair value produces a revaluation surplus, which increases the book value of the shareholders'
equity by £8,000. The calculation of goodwill, on consolidation,
using the shareholders' equity approach is as follows:

Calculation of goodwill arising on consolidation (shareholders'
equity approach)

	£	£
Price paid:		75,000
Less: Value of business acquired:		
Share capital	50,000	
Revaluation surplus	8,000	
Retained profits	12,000	
		70,000
Goodwill..		5,000

Consolidated Balance Sheet of A Ltd. and Subsidiary at 31 December, 19X1

	£
Share capital (£1 ordinary shares)	100,000
Retained profits	70,000
	170,000
Liabilities	41,000
	211,000
Goodwill arising on consolidation.......	5,000
Fixed assets at book value.................	114,000*
Current assets: Stocks......................	45,000
Debtors....................	44,000
Bank	3,000
	211,000

60 + 54

*Includes the fair value of B Ltd.'s fixed assets.

It should be noted that the figure for retained profits, in the consolidated balance sheet, consists only of the retained profits of A Ltd. and includes no part of the retained profits of the subsidiary at the takeover date. Profits earned prior to the date of acquisition (pre-acquisition profits) are not available for distribution to the shareholders of the holding company, and are instead treated as part of the capital value of the business at the takeover date. This is clearly demonstrated in the above calculation of goodwill, using the shareholders' equity approach; the retained profits and revaluation surplus, which is also pre-acquisition, are added to share capital to produce a figure of £70,000 for shareholders' equity. This is offset against the price paid, £75,000, and results in a balance of £5,000 which is described as goodwill arising on consolidation in the consolidated balance sheet. Profits earned since the date of acquisition accrue to the holding company's shareholders, and their accounting treatment is examined in section 4.2 of this Chapter.

Sometimes the price paid by the holding company is less than the book value of the company acquired. In such circumstances, it is quite likely that a downward revision of asset values will be needed. Where a credit balance remains, even after any necessary adjustments to book value have been made, it is reported as 'capital reserve' in the consolidated balance sheet. This reserve is not available for distribution.

5.4.2 Post-Acquisition Profits A period of time will usually have elapsed between the acquisition of a controlling interest in another company and the date of the consolidated accounts. The subsidiary company may have generated profits during the interim period, and these profits, when transferred, are available for distribution to the shareholders of the holding company. Their accounting treatment is dealt with in the following example:

Example 5.6

The same information as for example 5.5, except that a share acquisition date of 31 December, 19X0 is assumed, at which time the retained profits of B Ltd. amounted to £9,500.

Calculations:

		£	£
(i)	Goodwill:		
	Price paid		75,000
	Less: Value of business acquired:		
	Share capital	50,000	
	Revaluation surplus	8,000	
	Retained profits	9,500	
			67,500
			7,500
(ii)	Post-acquisition profits of B Ltd.:		
	Retained profits at 31 December, 19X1		12,000
	Less: Retained profits at 31 December, 19X0		9,500
			2,500

The post-acquisition profits of £2,500 are earned during a period when B Ltd. is a member of the group. These profits therefore accrue to the shareholders of the holding company and must be added to A Ltd.'s retained profits of £70,000 to produce a combined total of £72,500 for inclusion in the following consolidated balance sheet;

Consolidated Balance Sheet of A Ltd. and Subsidiary at 31 December, 19X1

	£
Share capital (£1 shares)	100,000
Retained profits	72,500
	172,500
Liabilities	41,000
	213,500
Goodwill arising on consolidation	7,500
Fixed assets at book value	114,000
Current assets: Stocks	45,000
Debtors	44,000
Bank	3,000
	213,500

There are two further matters which require emphasis in connection with the calculation of distributable profits for inclusion in the consolidated balance sheet:

1. Losses suffered by a subsidiary company, since the acquisition date, are attributable to the shareholders of the holding company, in the same way as profit earned. Post-acquisition losses must therefore be deducted from the holding company's balance of retained profits, and the result will be that the consolidated balance sheet will show a lower figure for retained profit than does the legal entity based financial statement published for the holding company.

2. To the extent that post-acquisition profits earned by a subsidiary are transferred to the holding company by way of dividends, the amount to be aggregated when consolidation takes place is correspondingly reduced, e.g. assume B Ltd. had paid an interim dividend of £1,000 during July 19X1. A Ltd.'s retained profits would then be £71,000 and the retained profit of B Ltd. would be £11,000: the post-acquisition retained profits of the latter company would amount to £1,500 (£11,000–£9,500) but the consolidated profit balance remains unchanged at £72,500 (£71,000 + £1,500).

5.4.3 Minority Interest   In many cases the holding company may either choose, in the interests of economy, or be forced to accept, in view of the obstinacy of certain shareholders, a controlling interest of less than 100%. In these circumstances, the investment confers an interest in the subsidiary company's net assets, based on the proportion which the number of equity shares acquired bears to the total number of equity shares then in issue. This must be taken into account when preparing consolidated balance sheets. The procedure followed is to include the full amount of the subsidiary's assets and liabilities, in the consolidated balance sheet, with that part which is financed by investors outside the group represented by a credit balance described as 'Minority interest'. This is shown as a separate item, normally immediately following shareholders' equity. The minority interest consists of an appropriate proportion of the share capital plus reserves and any other credit balances which accrue to the equity shareholders at the accounting date.

Example 5.7

The summarised balance sheets of C Ltd. and D Ltd. at 31 December, 19X1 are as follows:

	£	C Ltd. £	£	D Ltd. £
Share capital (£1 ordinary shares)............		200,000		80,000
Retained profits at 1 January, 19X1.........	77,000		7,000	
Add: Profit for 19X1	18,000		6,000	
		95,000		13,000
		295,000		93,000
Current liabilities: Trade creditors...........		106,000		25,000
Bank overdraft				
(North Bank).............				17,000
		401,000		135,000
Fixed assets at book value.....................		94,000		58,000
Investment in D Ltd.		90,000		
Current assets: Stocks..........................		103,000		52,000
Debtors........................		79,000		25,000
Bank Balance (South Bank)		35,000		
		401,000		135,000

Notes:
1. The investment in D Ltd. consists of 60,000 ordinary shares purchased on 1 January, 19X1.
2. It may be assumed that there are no significant differences between the book value and fair value of D Ltd.'s assets.

The relationship between C Ltd. and D Ltd. may be presented in the following diagram, which is a useful starting point for answering questions involving the preparation of consolidated accounts.

C Ltd.
|
75% shareholding
↓
D Ltd. (pre-acquisition profit £7,000)

Calculations:

		£	£
(i) Goodwill: Price paid:......			90,000
Less: Value of business acquired:			
Share capital............		80,000	
Retained profit............		7,000	
		87,000	
Proportion of shares acquired 75%			65,250
			24,750
(ii) Retained profits: C Ltd........			95,000
D Ltd, 6,000 × 75%.........			4,500
			99,500
(iii) Minority interest.			
Total equity of D Ltd: Share capital			80,000
Retained profits.........			13,000
			93,000
Proportion attributable to minority shareholders, 25% × 93,000			23,250

The figures for goodwill, post-acquisition profit and minority interest may alternatively be calculated using a tabular format (see below). Firstly, the total equity of D Ltd. is distributed between the holding company, distinguishing between the position 'at' and 'since' acquisition, and the minority interest. The value of the subsidiary 'at acquisition' is then compared with the price paid to calculate goodwill, while profits arising since acquisition are added to the holding company's retained profits to produce the group figure for inclusion in the consolidated balance sheet.

D Ltd.	Total Equity £	C Ltd. 75% At Acquisition £	Since Acquisition £	Minority Interest 25% £
Share capital	80,000	60,000		20,000
Retained profits: At acquisition	7,000	5,250		1,750
Since acquisition ...	6,000		4,500	1,500
	93,000	65,250	4,500	23.250
Price paid		90,000		
Goodwill		24,750		
Retained profits C Ltd.			95,000	
Group retained profits			99,500	

An advantage of the above presentation is that it is easy to check whether total equity has been fully allocated for the purpose of calculating goodwill, retained profits and minority interest. Also, provided the additions and cross-casts are checked, the possibility of arithmetical error is reduced.

Consolidated Balance Sheet of C Ltd. and Subsidiary

	£
Share capital	200,000
Retained profits	99,500
	299,500
Minority interest	23,250
Current Liabilities: Trade creditors	131,000
Bank overdraft*	17,000
	470,750
Goodwill arising on consolidation	24,750
Fixed assets at book value	152,000
Current assets: Stocks	155,000
Debtors	104,000
Bank balance*	35,000
	470,750

*The bank overdraft and bank balance are at different banks. Best accounting practice therefore, requires these items to be shown separately and not offset against one another; if they were, both current assets and current liabilities would be understated.

A further illustration of consolidation procedures, incorporating the matters considered so far and involving two subsidiaries, is given in example 5.8. As usual, students are reminded to work the question *before* referring to the solution.

Example 5.8

The summarised balance sheets of Clubs Ltd. and its subsidiary companies Diamonds Ltd. & Hearts Ltd. at 31 December, 19X1 were as follows:

	Clubs Ltd. £	Diamonds Ltd. £	Hearts Ltd. £
Share capital (£1 shares)	200,000	80,000	40,000
Profit and loss account at			
31 December, 19X0	36,000	33,200	7,200
Profit for 19X1	7,000	11,400	3,600
Creditors	65,000	37,400	18,400
	308,000	162,000	69,200
Fixed assets at book value	59,000	99,500	39,700
80,000 shares in Diamonds Ltd.	126,000		
30,000 shares in Hearts Ltd.	44,000		
Current assets	79,000	62,500	29,500
	308,000	162,000	69,200

Clubs Ltd. acquired the shares in both subsidiaries on 31 December, 19X0. Neither subsidiary paid a dividend in respect of 19X0 and none are proposed for 19X1.

REQUIRED:
The consolidated balance sheet for the group at 31 December, 19X1, presented in vertical format to disclose the balance for working capital.
Notes:
Ignore taxation.
Assume no differences between the book value and fair value of the assets and liabilities of Diamonds Ltd. and Hearts Ltd.

Solution

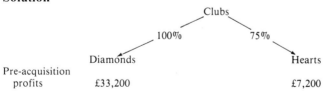

	Clubs	
	100% 75%	
	Diamonds Hearts	
Pre-acquisition profits	£33,200 £7,200	

Calculations:

Diamonds	Total Equity £	At Acquisition £	Since Acquisition £	Minority Interest £
Share capital	80,000	80,000		
Profit and loss account: At acquisition	33,200	33,200		
Since acquisition	11,400		11,400	
	124,600	113,200	11,400	

Hearts				
Share capital	40,000	30,000		10,000
Profit and loss account: At acquisition	7,200	5,400		1,800
Since acquisition	3,600		2,700	900
	50,800	35,400	2,700	12,700

Totals (Diamonds and Hearts)	175,400	148,600	14,100	12,700
Total price paid (£126,000 + £44,000)		170,000		
Goodwill		21,400		
Profit and loss account, Clubs Ltd.			43,000	
Group profit and loss account			57,100	

Consolidated Balance Sheet of Clubs Ltd. and
Subsidiaries at 31 December, 19X1

	£	£
Share capital (£1 shares)		200,000
Profit and loss account		57,100
		257,100
Minority interest		12,700
		269,800
Goodwill		21,400
Fixed assets at book value		198,200
Current assets	171,000	
Less: Current liabilities	120,800	
Working capital		50,200
		269,800

The three 'primary' adjustments, discussed above, need to be made in most questions requiring the preparation of a consolidated balance sheet. There are a number of other accounting complications with which the student must be familiar. The main 'second-ary' adjustments are:

> Inter-company balances.
> Inter-company unrealised profits.
> Dividends paid out of pre-acquisition profits.

The adjustments required to take account of these matters are now considered in sections 4.4–4.6 of this Chapter.

5.4.4 Inter-Company Balances It is quite likely that transfers of cash and goods will be made between the members of a group of companies. Indeed, an important reason for takeovers and mergers is that they provide scope for achieving a more effective utilisation of available resources. Where, for instance, a public company with significant and readily available sources of finance acquires a con-trolling interest in a small family concern, which has good potential for expansion but finds it difficult to raise funds, a transfer of cash, via inter-company loan accounts, may follow almost immediately. The loan will, of course, be reported respectively as an asset and liability in the separate accounts published for the holding company and subsidiary. Group accounts, however, regard these separate legal entities as a single undertaking and, in these circumstances, inter-company balances must be cancelled out. Sometimes a residual difference will remain after the balance sheet items have been offset against one another. This will be attributable to cash or goods-in-transit, and the transaction should be recorded in the transferee's books in order to achieve equality between debits and credits.

An accounting complication sometimes arises as the result of one company drawing a bill of exchange on another company within the group. Where the bill is still held by the drawer at the consolidation date, the inter-company indebtedness will cancel out in the normal way. Where, however, the drawer has discounted the bill, the amount involved must be shown as a contingent liability in the notes attached to the drawer's legal entity based accounts. In the consolidated balance sheet, however, no contingent liability need be reported since the actual liability will be disclosed under the description 'Bill payable'.

5.4.5 Inter-Company Unrealised Profits The accounting con-vention, that a 'transfer at arms length' must occur before an increase in corporate wealth is recognised, must be applied on a group basis when preparing consolidated accounts. It is likely that intra-group transfers of stock will be made, particularly where the share purchase has resulted in an element of vertical integration designed to safeguard either sources of raw materials or consumer outlets. These transfers will normally be made at a figure which approximates market price, both to enable the performance of individual companies to be fairly assessed and to avoid unnecessary complications where minority shareholdings exist. Provided that the recipient company has resold the items transferred, either in their original form or incorporated in a different product, it is perfectly legitimate to recognise both elements of profit in the consolidated accounts, i.e. the profit arising on the intra-group transfer and the profit arising on the sale of the product to an external party. Where, however, the items transferred remain unsold by the transferee company, at the end of the accounting period, a consolidation adjustment must be made to reduce the value of the stock to a figure which represents its original cost to the group. This adjustment may take either of two forms:

(i) Remove the entire inter-company unrealised profit.

(ii) Remove only that part of the inter-company unrealised profit which is attributable to the shareholders of the holding company, on the grounds that 'a transfer at arms length' has occurred, from the point of view of the minority shareholders.

Either approach represents acceptable accounting practice, but the former enjoys the practical advantage of being a rather more straightforward adjustment.

Example 5.9

Small Ltd. is a wholly owned subsidiary of Large Ltd. During 19X1 Small Ltd. transferred to Large Ltd., for £18,000, stock which had cost Small Ltd. £12,000. Large Ltd. had resold threequarters of this stock for £15,500 by 31 December, 19X1.

The above transactions produce the following financial effects for accounts prepared for Small Ltd., Large Ltd. and the group.

1. Small Ltd. takes credit for £6,000 profit (£18,000–£12,000) in its legal entity based accounts.

2. Large Ltd. takes credit for £2,000 profit (£15,500–¾ × £18,000) in its legal entity based accounts.

3. Stock purchased from Small Ltd. for £4,500 remains unsold at the balance sheet date. The stock is included in Large Ltd.'s legal entity based accounts at £4,500, but must be reduced to cost, (¼ × £12,000) £3,000, for consolidation purposes.

The unrealised profit may be eliminated from the consolidated accounts by means of the following journal entry (narrative omitted):

	£	£
Dr. Consolidated profit and loss account......................	1,500	
Cr. Stock in trade...		1,500

Note:

If only 60% of the equity share capital of Small Ltd. is owned, management *may* choose to consider £900 (60% × £1,500) as unrealised profit and the remainder as realised from the viewpoint of the minority shareholders in Small Ltd. Where this alternative is followed both stocks and minority interest will be £600 higher than if the entire unrealised profit was eliminated.

5.4.6 Dividends Paid Out of Pre-Acquisition Profits Where a controlling interest is purchased soon after the directors of the acquired company have proposed the payment of a dividend, the shares may well be acquired with dividend rights attaching (i.e. cum. div.) The source of the dividend, when paid, is pre-acquisition profits: it must not, therefore, be treated as revenue by the holding company, but must instead be accounted for as a partial return of the capital cost. In the books of the holding company the following journal entry may be used to record the dividend received:

	£	£
Dr. Cash...	xxx	
Cr. Investment in subsidiary company		xxx

Being dividend from subsidiary company paid out of pre-acquisition profits and treated as a reduction in the capital cost of the investment.

In examination questions, it sometimes happens that a holding company wrongly credits to its profit and loss account a dividend received out of a subsidiary's pre-acquisition profits. This error is corrected by making an appropriate transfer from profit to the credit of the investment in subsidiary company account.

Example 5.10 illustrates the calculations needed to give effect to the three secondary adjustments, discussed above, as well as the three primary adjustments.

Example 5.10

The summarised balance sheets of E Ltd. and F Ltd. at 31 December, 19X2 are as follows:

	E Ltd. £	F Ltd. £
Share capital (£1 ordinary shares)	200,000	40,000
Reserves	75,000	20,000
	275,000	60,000
Loan from E Ltd.		5,000
Other liabilities	36,000	7,000
	311,000	72,000
Fixed assets at book value	172,000	27,000
30,000 shares in F Ltd. at cost	36,000	
Loan to F Ltd.	7,000	
Current assets: Stocks	27,000	17,000
Debtors	39,000	18,000
Bank	30,000	10,000
	311,000	72,000

The shares in F Ltd. were purchased on 31 December, 19X1 when the balance sheet of the company included reserves amounting to £12,000 and a proposed dividend of £4,000 subsequently paid on 31 January, 19X2. E Ltd.'s share of the proposed dividend is included in Reserves £75,000 in the above balance sheet. At 31 December, 19X2 the stocks of F Ltd. include goods transferred from E Ltd., at cost plus 50%, amounting to £3,000. On 29 December, 19X2 F Ltd. despatched a cheque for £2,000 to E Ltd. which was received by the latter company on 3 January, 19X3.

REQUIRED:
The consolidated balance sheet of E Ltd. and subsidiary at 31 December, 19X2.
Notes:
The assets and liabilities of F Ltd. were revalued on 31 December, 19X1 and the revised figures were written in to the books of that company. Ignore taxation.

Solution

E Ltd.
|
75%
↓
F Ltd. (pre-acquisition profits £12,000)

Students may find it useful to use journal entries (J.E.) to identify the correct treatment of the 'secondary' adjustments for consolidation purposes:

J.E.1   Inter-company balances
Dr.   Cash-in-transit £2,000
Cr.   Loan to F Ltd. £2,000

Being cash-in-transit from F Ltd. to E Ltd. at the year end.

J.E.2 Inter-company unrealised profits
Dr.   Reserves (E Ltd.).. £1,000
Cr.   Stocks £1,000

Being unrealised profit on intra-group transfers of stock at cost plus 50%.

J.E.3 Dividends paid out of pre-acquisition profits
Dr.   Reserves (E Ltd.).. £3,000
Cr.   Investment in F Ltd. at cost...   £3,000

Being dividend received out of pre-acquisition profits, 75% × £4,000.

Calculations:	Total Equity £	At Acquisition £	Since Acquisition £	Minority Interest £
Share capital	40,000	30,000		10,000
Reserves: At acquisition	12,000	9,000		3,000
Since acquisition..........	8,000		6,000	2,000
	60,000	39,000	6,000	15,000
Price paid...............................		33,000 W1		
Capital reserve..........................		6,000		
Reserves, E Ltd.........................			71,000 W2	
Group reserves..........................			77,000	

Workings		£	£
W.1	Price paid as per question		36,000
	Less: Dividend received out of pre-acquisition profits (J.E.3)......		3,000
			33,000
W.2	Reserves of E Ltd. as per question..		75,000
	Less: Pre-acquisition dividend wrongly credited to reserves (J.E.3)	3,000	
	Unrealised profit on stocks (J.E.2)................................	1,000	
			4,000
			71,000

Consolidated Balance Sheet of E Ltd. and Subsidiary at 31 December, 19X2

		£
Share capital (£1 shares)		200,000
Capital reserve on consolidation		6,000
Reserves		77,000
		283,000
Minority interest		15,000
Liabilities		43,000
		341,000
Fixed assets at book value		199,000
Current assets:	Stocks £44,000 – £1,000 (J.E.2)	43,000
	Debtors	57,000
	Bank	40,000
	Cash-in-transit (J.E.1)	2,000
		341,000

5.5   SHARE EXCHANGES

In each of the examples worked so far, the holding company has purchased the shares for cash. In practice, consideration may take a number of different forms, depending on the wishes of the directors of the holding company and the shareholders of the subsidiary. The subsidiary company's shareholders may agree to accept shares in the holding company in exchange for their present holdings; they may alternatively accept an issue of loan stock from the holding company; finally they may agree to accept some combination of shares, loan stock and cash. It is of course also possible for different groups of shareholders to make separate arrangements with the holding company: those who refuse to accept any of the terms offered will together retain a 'minority interest' in the subsidiary company.

Where the consideration takes the form of securities, it will be necessary to allocate a value to them for accounting purposes.

Example 5.11

Great Ltd. agrees to purchase the entire share capital of Little Ltd. for £500,000. The share capital of Little Ltd. consists of 100,000 ordinary shares of £1 each. Under the terms of the agreement the shareholders of Little Ltd. receive £75,000 cash, and 5 shares in Great Ltd. (nominal value 50p each) for every two shares presently held.

The value of each of the shares issued by Great Ltd. is calculated as follows:

	£
Purchase price	500,000
Less: Consideration in cash........................	75,000
Total value of shares issued........................	425,000
Number of shares issued, $100,000 \times 5/2$.........	250,000
Value of each share (nominal value 50p)	
$£425,000 \div 250,000 =$	£1.70

The acquisition may then be recorded in Great Ltd.'s books using the following journal entry (narrative omitted):

		£	£
Dr.	Investment in Little Ltd......................................	500,000	
Cr.	Cash..		75,000
Cr.	Share capital $(250,000 \times 50p)$		125,000
Cr.	Share premium account $(250,000 \times £1.20)$................		300,000
		500,000	500,000

It may happen that no formal agreement is reached regarding the price to be paid. For instance, the parties may simply agree to exchange shares in certain proportions without specifying a total purchase price. In these circumstances, the total purchase price must be computed on the basis of the quoted market price of one or other of the company's shares. Where neither company is quoted, a share valuation will have to be made using the procedures explained in Chapter 7.

Example 5.12

The following are the summarised balance sheets of Big Ltd. and Small Ltd. at 31 December, 19X1.

	Big Ltd.	*Small Ltd.*
	£	£
Issued ordinary share capital (£1 shares)	700,000	250,000
Revenue reserves...	450,000	150,000
Liabilities	260,000	160,000
	1,410,000	560,000
Assets...	1,410,000	560,000

On 31 December, 19X1 Big Ltd. offered the shareholders of Small Ltd. three shares in Big Ltd. for every two shares presently held. Holders of 200,000 shares in Small Ltd. accepted this offer and the exchange took place on the same day. It was agreed that the shares in Small Ltd. were worth £1.80 each.

REQUIRED:
The consolidated balance sheet of Big Ltd. and subsidiary, after the above transaction is complete.

Solution

Big Ltd.
|
80%
↓
Small Ltd.

Calculations: £

Purchase price, 200,000 × £1.80   360,000

Number of shares issued, 200,000 × 3/2   300,000

Nominal value of shares issued, 300,000 × £1   300,000

Share premium, £360,000 − £300,000   60,000

	Total Equity £	At Acquisition £	Minority Interest £
Share capital..............	250,000	200,000	50,000
Revenue reserves.........	150,000	120,000	30,000
	400,000	320,000	80,000
Price paid		360,000	
Goodwill..................		40,000	

Consolidated Balance Sheet of Big Ltd. and
Subsidiary at 31 December, 19X1

	£	
Issued ordinary share capital (£1 shares).........	1,000,000	W1
Share premium account	60,000	
Revenue reserves	450,000	
	1,510,000	
Minority interest	80,000	
Liabilities...	420,000	
	2,010,000	
Goodwill	40,000	
Other assets..	1,970,000	
	2,010,000	

W1. £700,000 + £300,000 (share exchange)

5.6 THE CONSOLIDATED PROFIT AND LOSS ACCOUNT

The *Accountancy* syllabus makes it clear that examination questions will not be set which require candidates to prepare a consolidated profit and loss account. It is, however, quite likely that students will be required to make adjustments to the profit figures, given in the question, to arrive at the balance for inclusion in the consolidated balance sheet which they are asked to prepare. These adjustments fall into two categories:

1. Adjustments to take account of normal trading items, for instance, provisions for bad debts, and accruals for general expenses.
2. Consolidation adjustments, such as unrealised profit on intra-group stock transfers, and additional depreciation which needs to be charged as the result of restating the subsidiary's fixed assets at their fair value.

Some of these adjustments have already been illustrated, and further instances arise in the examples and questions which follow.

5.7 SUB-SUBSIDIARY COMPANIES

When preparing the consolidated balance sheet of a group containing a sub-subsidiary, it is recommended that the exercise should proceed in two stages.

1. Consolidate the balance sheets of the subsidiary and the sub-subsidiary.
2. Consolidate the balance sheet of the ultimate holding company with the consolidated balance sheet of the sub-group prepared under stage 1.

This procedure is demonstrated in the following example:

Example 5.13

The summarised balance sheets of G Ltd., H Ltd. and I Ltd. at 31 December, 19X2 were as follows:

	G Ltd. £	H Ltd. £	I Ltd. £
Share capital (£1 ordinary shares)	25,000	30,000	50,000
Revenue reserves	19,850	17,800	14,000
	44,850	47,800	64,000
12% Debentures	26,000	42,500	45,000
Loan from G Ltd.	—	7,000	—
Proposed dividend	—	5,000	—
Current liabilities	6,650	18,200	82,000
	77,500	120,500	191,000
Fixed assets	19,000	32,500	92,000
22,500 shares in H Ltd. at cost	40,000	—	—
50,000 shares in I Ltd. at cost	—	75,000	—
Loan to H Ltd.	7,000	—	—
Current assets	11,500	13,000	99,000
	77,500	120,500	191,000

G Ltd. acquired its shares in H Ltd. when the revenue reserves of H Ltd. were £14,000. H Ltd. acquired its shares in I Ltd. when the revenue reserves of I Ltd. were £22,000. At the time of these acquisitions no dividends were proposed, none have since been paid and no changes have occurred in the issued share capital of either subsidiary since acquisition. The dividend receivable by G Ltd. from H Ltd. has not been accrued by the former company.

REQUIRED:

The consolidated balance sheet of the group at 31 December, 19X2.

Notes:

Assume no differences between the book value and fair value of the assets and liabilities of H Ltd. and I Ltd.

Ignore taxation.

Solution

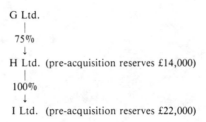

G Ltd.
|
75%
↓
H Ltd. (pre-acquisition reserves £14,000)
|
100%
↓
I Ltd. (pre-acquisition reserves £22,000)

Calculations:

Stage 1: Consolidation of H Ltd. and I Ltd.

I Ltd.

	Total Equity £	At Acquisition £	Since Acquisition £
Share capital	50,000	50,000	
Revenue reserve: At acquisition	22,000	22,000	
Since acquisition	(8,000) W1		(8,000)
	64,000	72,000	(8,000)
Price paid		75,000	
Goodwill		3,000	
Revenue reserves, H Ltd.			17,800
Revenue reserves of sub-group			9,800

W.1 £72,000 (equity at date of acquisition) – £64,000 (equity at 31 December, 19X2).

*Consolidated Balance Sheet of Sub-Group at
31 December, 19X2*

	£
Share capital (£1 ordinary shares)	30,000
Revenue reserves	9,800
	39,800
12% Debentures	87,500
Loan from G Ltd.	7,000
Proposed dividend	5,000
Current liabilities	100,200
	239,500
Goodwill	3,000
Fixed assets	124,500
Current assets	112,000
	239,500

Note:

The preparation of the consolidated balance sheet of the sub-group is not essential, but it is useful for a number of reasons. It is a check on arithmetic accuracy at the end of stage 1 calculations; it adds together the figures for two companies, leaving only one further company to be added at stage 2; and it discloses the figure for the equity interest in H Ltd. (£39,800) which is allocated between the holding company and minority interest under stage 2.

Stage 2: Consolidation of G Ltd. with sub-group.

Sub-group	Total Equity	At Acquisition	Since Acquisition	Minority Interest
Share capital....................	30,000	22,500		7,500
Revenue reserves:				
At acquisition...............	14,000	10,500		3,500
Since acquisition...........	(4,200) W1		(3,150)	(1,050)
	39,800	33,000	(3,150)	9,950
Price paid.......................		40,000		
Goodwill........................		7,000		
Revenue reserves, G Ltd.....			23,600 W2	
Group revenue reserves			20,450	

W.1   £44,000 (equity at date of acquisition) – £39,800 (equity at 31 December, 19X2, see sub-group consolidated balance sheet).

		£
W.2	Revenue reserves of G Ltd. per question	19,850
	Add: Dividend receivable from H Ltd. £5,000* × 75%	3,750
		23,600

Note: The remainder of the proposed dividend, £1,250 is payable to H Ltd.'s minority shareholders.

Consolidated Balance Sheet of the Group at
31 December, 19X2

	£
Share capital (£1 ordinary shares)	25,000
Revenue reserves	20,450
	45,450
Minority interest...	9,950
12% Debentures...	113,500
Dividend payable to minority shareholders.........	1,250
Current liabilities.......................................	106,850
	277,000
Goodwill (£3,000 + £7,000)............................	10,000
Fixed assets...	143,500
Current assets	123,500
	277,000

5.8   INTERPRETING CONSOLIDATED BALANCE SHEETS

The opening paragraph to section 4 of this chapter draws attention to the fact that the basic objective of consolidated accounts is to provide the shareholders of the holding company with full information concerning the activities of the entire economic unit in which they have invested. We have examined the various procedures followed when preparing a consolidated balance sheet, and it is now possible to consider more fully what is meant by this statement. The holding company's legal entity based accounts deal with the results of a single organisation, whereas group accounts set out the combined results of at least two, and perhaps a much larger number of legally separate businesses. Therefore, it is not surprising that there are often significant differences between the two sets of accounts. Some important differences may well be clearly visible from a simple comparison of the totals appearing in the balance sheets. For instance, the holding company's balance sheet may contain a large overdraft, whereas the consolidated balance sheet shows a healthy cash surplus, indicating that the subsidiaries are in possession of substantial amounts of cash. A more searching comparison can be made of the information contained in economic entity and legal entity based accounts, by using techniques such as ratio analysis (Chapter 8) and fund flow analysis (Chapter 9).

For illustrative purposes, a comparison is made below of the information contained in G Ltd.'s own balance sheet (example 5.13) and the balance sheet of the group. The main points of interest are as follows:

1. Revenue reserves: G Ltd.   £19,850
   Group   £20,450

   This shows that the net post-acquisition retained profits of the two subsidiaries are minimal, and suggests that they may not be particularly profitable companies. In fact, the post-acquisition profits of H Ltd. are roughly the same as the post-acquisition losses of I Ltd.

2. Fixed assets: G Ltd.   £19,000
   Group   £143,500

   This shows that a large percentage of the group's fixed assets are owned by the subsidiary companies, and this information would be of particular interest to prospective creditors of the holding company who might be keen to ensure that their advance is adequately secured.

3. Solvency:
   Working capital ratio (see Chapter 8, section 3): G Ltd. 1.73:1
   Group 1.14:1

   The working capital position of G Ltd. appears satisfactory, but that of the group totally inadequate. This would suggest that there are underlying financial difficulties which are not evident in G Ltd.'s own balance sheet. An examination of the subsidiary companies' balance sheets show that the problem is at H Ltd. where current liabilities significantly exceed current assets.

4. Gearing:

Debt/equity ratio (see Chapter 8, section 6): G Ltd. 58%

Group 250%

Inter-company shareholdings cancel out on consolidation, whereas the debentures, all held outside the group, must be aggregated. Consequently, the consolidated statement reveals a much higher level of gearing than is evident from an examination of the individual balance sheets of G Ltd. and the other companies within the group. The group pays annual interest to debenture holders totalling £13,620 (£113,500 × 12%). Annual profit figures are not given but the interest charge is nearly 70% of the total retained profits and this would suggest that the group will find it difficult to meet its interest charges unless trading results improve.

Conclusion: The group accounts point to the existence of significant financial difficulties which are not evident from G Ltd.'s own balance sheet.

5.9 ASSOCIATED COMPANIES

During the 1960s, it was a growing practice for companies to conduct part of their activities through other companies in which a less than 50% equity interest was acquired, and which, consequently, escaped the group accounting provisions of the 1948 Act. Effective control was exercised, however, either through the existence of some form of partnership agreement or because of a wide dispersion of shares. Consequently, the directors of the investing company were able to influence both the commercial and financial policies of the 'associated' company. The growing demand for fuller disclosure was therefore fully justified:

(i) to remove obvious opportunities for the managers of investing companies to manipulate their reported results. For instance, by building up undisclosed profits, in the accounts of the associated company, which could, when required, be transferred to the investing company in the form of a dividend.

(ii) to provide more meaningful performance data concerning the activities of the entire economic unit over which some influence was exercised. In this context, the growing popularity of the price/earnings ratio emphasised the increasing significance attached to reported earnings as a performance indicator. It was therefore important to take steps to ensure that the investing companies' published earnings fairly represented their actual performance.

The matter was referred to the Accounting Standards Committee which concluded that, where management assumes a measure of direct responsibility for the performance of its investment, by actively participating in the commercial and policy making decisions of an associated company, it must present a full account to its members. Accordingly, it was decided that group accounts, prepared in accordance with the Companies Act, should be extended to incorporate additional information concerning the activities of these associated companies. This decision obliged the committee to draft requirements covering two matters:

(i) A precise definition of the associated companies in relation to which further disclosures are required.
(ii) The additional information to be published.

The requirements are contained in SSAP1, entitled 'Accounting for the results of associated companies', and are examined below:

5.9.1 Definition of an Associated Company SSAP 1 identifies two situations in which an investing company/associated company relationship is considered to subsist. These can be described in general terms as follows:

(a) where a number of companies which act together own and control another company, as in the case of a consortium, or;
(b) where an investing company has an interest in another company which is both substantial and long term. Also, because the shareholdings are widely distributed, the investing company is in a position to exercise a significant influence over that company. Where the investing company holds more than 20% of the equity voting rights, it should be presumed that the company has the ability to exercise significant influence unless it can clearly be demonstrated otherwise. For example, there may exist one or more other large shareholdings which prevent the investing company exerting such influence.

Significant influence over a company essentially involves participation in the financial and operating policies of that company, but it need not necessarily amount to control of those policies. Representation on the board of directors is one indication of such participation but it is not conclusive proof.

5.9.2 Equity Accounting for the Results of Associated Companies It would be unrealistic to extend traditional consolidation procedures to associated companies, without modification, since such a course would result in the inclusion of assets in which the shareholders of the holding company have only a minor proprietary interest, and it could result in a situation where the assets financed by 'outsiders' exceeded the aggregate assets belonging to the group. Furthermore the term minority interest would have to be replaced by a description such as majority interest. In order to avoid these, and other anomalies, modified consolidation procedures are used to account for the results of associated companies. These modified procedures are commonly described as 'equity accounting'.

The following two calculations must be made:
1. The price paid is allocated between:
    (i) The investing company's share of the net assets, other than goodwill, of the associated company at the acquisition date. For this purpose net assets should be restated at their fair value.
    (ii) The investing company's share of any goodwill appearing in the balance sheet of the associated company at the acquisition date.
    (iii) The premium paid (or discount arising) on the acquisition of the interest in the associated company. This calculation is analogous to the calculation of goodwill or capital reserve arising on the consolidation of a subsidiary company.

Example 5.14

On 31 December, 19X1, Investment plc purchased 25% of the equity share capital of Associated plc for £1,000,000. The balance sheet of Associated plc at the acquisition date included net assets, other than goodwill, restated at a fair value of £2,800,000. Goodwill amounted to £800,000. Investment plc is able to exert a significant influence over the affairs of Associated plc. The price paid is allocated as follows:

	£	£
Price paid for shares..		1,000,000
Allocated as follows:		
Share of net assets, 25% × £2,800,000......................	700,000	
Share of goodwill, 25% of £800,000	200,000	
		900,000
Premium paid on acquisition..................................		100,000

The above allocation may either be disclosed on the face of the balance sheet or by way of note.

2. The investing company's share of the undistributed post-tax profits less losses of associated companies must be computed. This amount is then brought into the investing company's balance sheet as an addition to retained profits (credit) and to the value of the investment in the associated company (debit). Refer back to example 5.14, and assume that, in 19X2, Associated plc earns a profit of £300,000, of which £140,000 is paid out as a dividend during the year (ignore taxation). Investment plc receives £35,000 (£140,000 × 25%) during the year, which is credited to dividend received and debited to cash. At the year end Investment plc's share of the post-acquisition retained profit is £40,000 (£160,000 × 25%), and this amount is credited to reserves and debited to the book value of the investment in the associated company which becomes £1,040,000 (£1,000,000 + £40,000).

Example 5.15

The results of J plc and its subsidiaries have already been consolidated. The results of K plc, an associated company, must now be incorporated by applying the instructions contained in SSAP 1. The following information is provided.

Summarised Balance Sheets at 31 December, 19X5

	J plc (group)		K plc	
	£m	£m	£m	£m
Fixed assets at cost less depreciation		54		178
Investment in K plc at cost...................................		80		
Current assets..	95		364	
Less: Current liabilities......................................	55		192	
Net current assets...		40		172
		174		350

Financed by:	£m	£m
Share capital (£1 ordinary shares)...........................	137	170
Reserves...	21	180
	158	350
Minority interest...	16	—
	174	350

J plc acquired 25% of the share capital of K plc on 31 December, 19X3, at which date the reserves of K plc stood at £40,000,000. At 31 December, 19X3, the balance sheet of K plc contained no figure for goodwill and the net assets were estimated to possess a fair value of £260,000,000.

REQUIRED:
The consolidated balance sheet of the group as at 31 December, 19X5, incorporating the results of its associated company K plc.
Note:
Ignore advance corporation tax.

Solution
Calculations:

1. Allocation of purchase price:	£m
Price paid for shares..	80
Less: Share of net assets, £260m × 25%................................	65
Premium paid on acquisition...	15

2. J plc's share of the post acquisition retained profits of K plc:	
Reserves at 31 December, 19X5..	180
Less: Reserves at date of acquisition....................................	40
Post-acquisition retained profits...	140
Attributable to J plc, £140m × 25%.......................................	35

Consolidated Balance Sheet as at 31 December, 19X5

	£m	£m
Fixed assets at cost less depreciation		54
Investment in associated company (see note)............................		115
Current assets..	95	
Less: Current liabilities	55	
Net current assets...	—	40
		209

	£m
Financed by:	
Share capital (£1 ordinary shares)	137
Reserves	56
	193
Minority interest	16
	209

Note:
Investment in K plc:
Groups share of net assets:

	£m
Fair value at takeover date	65
Share of post-acquisition undistributed profit	35
	100
Premium on acquisition	15
	115

5.10 LIMITATIONS OF GROUP ACCOUNTS

The problem of deciding which companies are to be treated as members of the group, for the purpose of preparing consolidated accounts (the form which group accounts commonly takes), has proved difficult. At present, subsidiary and associated companies are defined primarily in terms of the percentage of equity share capital owned, but this solution has provided scope for abuse. A reduction in the equity interest to 50% or less will usually result in the exclusion of a company's assets and liabilities from the consolidated balance sheet. Then again, the reduction of a trade investment to a figure which is marginally below a 20% interest will often allow management to conceal, from its shareholders, the full significance of that company's profit or loss making activities for the overall position and progress of the group.

Certain other difficulties, associated with consolidated accounts, arise directly from the obligation to aggregate the assets and liabilities as well as the profits and losses of subsidiaries. Whereas a particular company will normally take steps to ensure that common accounting policies are adopted throughout the firm, such uniformity is less likely to exist throughout a group of companies. Where the group includes overseas subsidiaries, which have to comply with local legal requirements for disclosure or taxation purposes, the diversity of accounting policies is likely to increase. These aggregation problems are compounded where group members fulfil a wide range of commercial functions, and some doubt must be cast on the utility of positional statements which consist of a collection of diverse assets and the summation of capital structures which are appropriate for a wide range of different types of company. A further problem, of increasing importance in recent years, is the large quantities of assets belonging to overseas subsidiaries located in economically and/or politically sensitive areas. In these circumstances it may be necessary to omit certain subsidiaries from consolidation, and instead give the information specified in SSAP 14 (paras 23–27), which is often the same as the disclosures required for associated companies, i.e. subsidiaries are accounted for on the equity basis.

The present system of group accounts has developed gradually over the last seventy years (many companies voluntarily published group accounts prior to the introduction of a legal requirement in 1948), and there is widespread support for the view that the reporting accountant has dealt in an effective manner with most of the difficulties which have been encountered. The result is the publication of useful information concerning the progress and financial position of holding companies, their subsidiaries and their investments. The limitations of group accounts must not, however, be forgotten. Economic entity based accounting information is prepared primarily for the holding company's shareholders. Bankers and creditors of constituent companies, examining a set of consolidated accounts, must remember that, in the absence of cross-guarantees within the group, the fund against which they may proceed in law for repayment of their debt is restricted to the assets of the particular company with which a contractual relationship exists. At the same time, the holding company's bank may quite properly regard group accounts a useful means of finding out about the nature and value of assets underlying investments in subsidiaries.

5.11 QUESTIONS AND SOLUTIONS
The following four questions test the student's ability to prepare and interpret the significance of consolidated accounts. Questions 5.1 and 5.2 involve a holding company and a subsidiary company, question 5.3 also includes a sub-subsidiary company, while question 5.4 includes an associated company.

Questions 5.1 (taken from the September, 1978 *Accountancy* paper).

The following are summarised draft balance sheets of Nut Ltd. and Bolt Ltd. at 31 December, 1977:

	Nut Ltd. £	Bolt Ltd. £
Issued share capital (£1 ordinary shares)	200,000	60,000
Profit and loss account at 31 December, 1976 ..	47,000	87,000
Profit 1977	13,600	16,500
Loan from Nut Ltd.	—	20,000
Sundry creditors	61,400	33,500
	£322,000	£217,000
Freehold property at cost	20,300	80,000
Equipment, net of depreciation	63,700	40,000
36,000 shares in Bolt Ltd. at cost	106,000	—
Loan to Bolt Ltd.	20,000	—
Current assets	112,000	97,000
	£322,000	£217,000

Nut Ltd. acquired its shares in Bolt Ltd. on 31 December, 1976.

No dividends were paid by either company during 1977, but Nut Ltd. proposes to pay a dividend of £10,000 and Bolt Ltd. is proposing a dividend of £24,000. The effects of these proposals are to be recorded in the finalised balance sheets.

Nut Ltd. has recently approached its bank for an overdraft limit of £30,000.

Required:

  (a) The consolidated balance sheet of the group at 31 December, 1977, incorporating the effect of proposed dividends where appropriate.

  (b) *Brief* comments, concerning *security* for a bank overdraft, which may be suggested by the accounting information given.

Note: Ignore taxation

[20]

Solution

Nut
|
60%
↓
Bolt (pre-acquisition profit £87,000)

(a) *Calculations:*

	Total £	At Acquisition £	Since Acquisition £	Minority Interest £
Share capital................	60,000	36,000		24,000
Profit and Loss Account:				
At acquisition...........	87,000	52,200		34,800
Since acquisition........	16,500		9,900	6,600
	163,500	88,200	9,900	65,400 W1
Price paid		106,000		
Goodwill.....................		17,800		
Retained profits, Nut Ltd............................			50,600 W2	
Retained profits, group..			60,500	

W1. This includes the minority interest in the dividend proposed by Bolt Ltd. i.e.
£24,000 × 40% = £9,600. For balance sheet purposes the total minority interest
may be allocated as follows:

	£
Minority interest	55,800
Dividend payable to minorities..	9,600
	65,400

W2. This is calculated after deducting the dividend proposed by Nut Ltd. from the
profit figure given in the draft balance sheet.

Consolidated Balance Sheet of Nut Ltd. and
Subsidiary at 31 December, 1977

Fixed Assets	£	£
Goodwill arising on consolidation		17,800
Freehold property at cost		100,300
Equipment, net of depreciation		103,700
		221,800
Current Assets	209,000	
Less: Current liabilities		
Sundry creditors	94,900	
Proposed dividends:		
Shareholders of Nut Ltd	10,000	
Minorities	9,600	
	114,500	
Working capital		94,500
		316,300
Financed by:		
Issued share capital (£1 ordinary shares)		200,000
Retained profits		60,500
		260,500
Minority interest		55,800
		316,300

(b) The balance sheet of Bolt, which includes freehold properties with a book value of £80,000, appears to offer better security than that of Nut Ltd. In addition, Bolt's current assets are three times its current liabilities (excluding the loan from Nut). If the advance is made to Bolt, the bank should arrange for repayment to be guaranteed by the holding company.

Examiner's comments:
Main student error: The holding company's profit and loss account was credited with a full share of the dividend proposed by Bolt, namely 60% × £24,000 = £14,400. The post-acquisition profits of Bolt, attributable to Nut, amount only to £9,900 (see 'calculations') and so £4,500 of the dividend is payable out of pre-acquisition profits. It is not necessary to record the proposed transfer (see 'calculations') before preparing the consolidated accounts but, if this is done, both the profit balance 'at acquisition' and the price paid for the shares in Bolt must be reduced by the amount of the dividend payable out of pre-acquisition profits. Goodwill remains unchanged at £17,800.

Question 5.2 (taken from the April 1982 *Accountancy* paper)

The summarised balance sheets of Belmont plc. and Tredegar plc. (both public limited companies) as at 31 December 1981 were as follows:

	Belmont £000	Tredegar £000
Issued share capital (£1 ordinary shares)	1,000	400
Reserves at 1 January 1981	750	120
12% debentures	—	100
Trade creditors and accruals	461	190
Bank overdraft (North Bank)	103	—
Profit before depreciation for 1981	308	150
Provision for depreciation of plant and machinery, 1 January 1981	426	240
	3,048	1,200
Plant and machinery at cost	1,420	600
Investment in Tredegar:		
Debenture stock at cost (nominal value £60,000)	60	—
Stocks	1,041	340
Trade debtors and prepayments	527	203
Bank balance (South Bank)	—	57
	3,048	1,200

Belmont purchased the debentures in Tredegar when they were first issued some years ago.

On 1 January 1981 Belmont purchased, by way of a share exchange, 300,000 £1 ordinary shares in Tredegar. The shares of Belmont were valued, at 1 January 1981, at £3.00 each and the terms of the acquisition were that the vendor shareholders of Tredegar would receive two shares in Belmont for every three shares held in Tredegar. In arriving at the purchase price of the shares in Tredegar, the plant and machinery of that company were revalued at £500,000. No records were made of the transactions and valuations referred to in this paragraph before preparing the balance sheets set out above.

On 31 March 1981, Tredegar paid a dividend of £60,000 in respect of 1980. Belmont's share of this dividend, £45,000, has been credited to the profit and loss account balance reported in the balance sheet shown above.

Depreciation is to be charged at the rate of 10% for 1981. In the case of Belmont the charge is to be based on the original cost of plant and machinery whereas, in the case of Tredegar, the charge is to be based on the revalued figure of £500,000.

Required:

(a) The consolidated balance sheet of Belmont plc. and its subsidiary company as at 31 December 1981. The consolidated balance sheet should be presented in vertical format and prepared in accordance with normal accounting practice.

[26]

(b) A clear explanation for your treatment of the dividend paid by Tredegar plc. to Belmont plc.

[4]

Notes:

Ignore taxation.

No dividends were paid or proposed by either of the companies for 1981.

[Total marks for question—30]

Solution

Belmont
|
75%
↓
Tredegar (pre-acquisition profits £120,000)

(a) *Calculations:*
Journal entries:

	£000	£000
Belmont's books:		
J.E.1 Dr. Investment in Tredegar	600	
Cr. Share capital		200
Cr. Share premium account		400
	600	600

To record the issue of 200,000 shares in Belmont (£1 nominal value) at £3 each, in consideration for the acquisition of 300,000 shares in Tredegar.

J.E.2 Dr. Profit and loss account	45	
Cr. Investment in Tredegar		45

To transfer to 'Investment in Tredegar', the pre-acquisition dividend wrongly credited to the profit and loss account.

For consolidation purposes:

J.E.3 Dr. Plant and machinery of Tredegar at revalued figure 500
      Dr. Provision for depreciation at 1 January, 1981 240
      Cr. Plant and machinery of Tredegar at cost   600
      Cr. Revaluation surplus   140

                                                                    740   740

Being adjustment needed to restate the assets of Tredegar at their fair value.

Tredegar	Total	At Acquisition	Since Acquisition	Minority Interest
	£000	£000	£000	£000
Share capital	400	300		100
Revaluation surplus	140	105		35
Reserves: At acquisition	120	90		30
Since acquisition ...	100 W1		75	25
	760	495	75	190
Price paid		555 W2		
Goodwill		60		
Profit, Belmont			121 W3	
Group profit			196	

W1. Profit before depreciation, £150,000, less depreciation, £50,000.
W2. Total consideration, £600,000 (J.E.1), less dividend received out of pre-acquisition profits £45,000 (J.E.2).
W3. Profit before depreciation, £308,000, less depreciation, £142,000, and less dividend wrongly credited, £45,000 (J.E.2).

Consolidated Balance Sheet of Belmont plc and Subsidiary
at 31 December, 1981

	£000	£000
Plant and machinery at cost or revalued amount 1,420 + 500		1,920
Less: Depreciation 568 + 50		618
		1,302
Goodwill arising on consolidation		60
Current Assets:		
Stocks	1,381	
Trade debtors and prepayments	730	
Bank balance	57	
	2,168	
Less: Current Liabilities		
Trade creditors and accruals	651	
Bank overdraft	103	
	754	
Working capital		1,414
		2,776
Financed by:		
Issued share capital		1,200
Share premium account		400
Reserves at 1 January, 1981	750	
Profit for 1981	196	
		946
		2,546
12% Debentures		40
Minority interest		190
		2,776

(b) The shares in Tredegar were purchased on 1 January, 1981. The profits earned by that company prior to 1 January are designated pre-acquisition profits and are not available for distribution to the shareholders of the acquiring company. Any dividend paid out of pre-acquisition profits is a return of the acquirer's capital investment and should be deducted from the price paid for shares purchased.

Examiner's comments:
Main student errors:
1. Failure to transfer the dividend received from Belmont's profit and loss account to its investment account.
2. The calculation of the revaluation surplus by comparing the revaluation with the cost of plant rather than book value.
3. Tredegar's depreciation charge based on cost rather than the revalued figure.
4. Share premium arising on the share exchange wrongly calculated.

Question 5.3 (taken from the September, 1980 *Accountancy* paper).

The summarised balance sheets of Hide Limited and its subsidiaries Watkin Limited and Davey Limited at 31 December 1979
were as follows :

	Hide Ltd £	Watkin Ltd £	Davey Ltd £
Ordinary share capital (£1 shares) ..	800,000	240,000	160,000
Reserves at 31 December, 1978 ..	180,000	67,200	18,000
Net profit(loss) for 1979	80,000	60,000	(12,400)
Less: preference dividend for 1979 ..	—	(5,000)	—
	1,060,000	362,200	165,600
10% Preference shares	—	50,000	—
Loan from Watkin Ltd.	10,000	—	—
Trade creditors	365,100	103,100	76,200
Preference dividend payable	—	5,000	—
	£1,435,100	£520,300	£241,800

Fixed assets at book value	671,800	151,700	140,000
180,000 ordinary shares in Watkin Ltd. at cost (purchased 31 December, 1976)	272,000	—	—
160,000 ordinary shares in Davey Ltd. at cost (purchased 1 January, 1979)	—	205,100	—
Loan to Hide Ltd.	—	12,000	—
Current assets	491,300	151,500	101,800
	£1,435,100	£520,300	£241,800

The following additional information is provided :

1. The balance on Watkin Limited's reserve account was £52,000
   at 31 December 1976.

2. During 1979 a cheque made out for £2,000 was received by
   Watkin Limited from Hide Limited and wrongly credited to a
   customer's account.

3. No ordinary dividends have been paid by Watkin Limited and
   Davey Limited since 1975.

Required:

(a) The consolidated balance sheet for the Hide Limited group fo
   companies as at 31 December 1979.

(b) A discussion of the uses and limitations of group accounts from the viewpoint of:

    (i) the shareholders of the holding company; and

    (ii) the creditors of the holding company.

NOTE: Ignore taxation.

[30]

Solution

Hide
|
75%
↓
Watkin (pre-acquisition reserves £52,000)
|
100%
↓
Davey (pre-acquisition reserves £18,000)

(a) *Calculations:*
  (i) Consolidate sub-group

Davey	*Total* £	*At Acquisition* £	*Since Acquisition* £
Share capital	160,000	160,000	
Reserves: At acquisition	18,000	18,000	
Since acquisition	(12,400)		(12,400)
	165,600	178,000	(12,400)
Price paid		205,100	
Goodwill		27,100	
Reserves, Watkin			122,200 W1
Reserves sub-group			109,800

W1. £67,200 + £60,000 − £5,000

Extract from Consolidated Balance Sheet of Sub-Group

	£
Share capital (£1 shares)	240,000
Reserves	109,800
	349,800

  (ii) Consolidate Hide with sub-group.
  Journal entry to take account of cheque wrongly credited to customer's account in Watkin's books.

	£	£
Dr. Current assets	2,000	
Cr. Loan to Hide		2,000

Sub-Group	Total £	At Acquisition £	Since Acquisition £	Minority Interest £
Share capital............	240,000	180,000		60,000
Reserves:				
At acquisition	52,000	39,000		13,000
Since acquisition....	57,800 W1		43,350	14,450
	349,800	219,000	43,350	87,450
Price paid................		272,000		
Goodwill................		53,000		
Reserves, Hide			260,000	
Group reserves			303,350	

W1. £109,800 (see extract from consolidated balance sheet of sub-group) − £52,000 (reserves at date of acquisition).

Consolidated Balance Sheet of Hide and Subsidiary as at 31 December, 1979

	£	£
Goodwill (£27,100 + £53,000).....................................		80,100
Fixed assets at book value		963,500
Current assets	746,600	
Current liabilities: Trade creditors.............................	544,400	
Preference dividend payable............	5,000	
	549,400	
Working capital...		197,200
		1,240,800
Financed by: Share capital (£1 shares)		800,000
Reserves		303,350
		1,103,350
10% Preference shares...		50,000
Minority interest...		87,450
		1,240,800

(b) (i) Company accounts are intended to provide shareholders with useful information concerning the progress of their investment. The accounts of the holding company show only the book value of the investment in subsidiaries and the amount of dividends received and receivable in respect of the year just past. In particular there may be wide differences between the dividends declared by subsidiaries and the profits earned or even losses suffered by them. Consolidated accounts are designed to focus attention on the overall results achieved by the economic entity, and therefore include the total profits attributable to the holding company's shareholders, and all assets and liabilities in which the shareholders possess a 'proprietorial' interest.

(ii) In the absence of guarantees from other parties, the claims of creditors are confined to the legal entity to which they have extended credit or provided finance. For this reason, creditors will be principally interested in legal entity based accounting information. Group accounts are of some use to the creditors of the holding company, because they provide an indication of asset values underlying the figure for investments in subsidiaries, but the fact that they include resources against which a claim cannot be made must always be borne in mind.

Examiner's comments:
Main student errors:
 1. Incorrect treatment of the post-acquisition loss of Davey Ltd., both for the purpose of computing the minority interest and the profit balance attributable to the shareholders of the holding company.
 2. Failure to draw attention, under (b), to the fact that creditors claims are legally restricted to the assets actually belonging to the holding company.

Question 5.4

Langland plc is a manufacturing company which has been in business for a number of years. Early in 19X1, the directors decided to diversify their activities and subsequently purchased shareholdings in both Caswell Ltd. and Oxwich Ltd. Directors were appointed by Langland to the boards of each company so as to take an active part in their operational and financial decisions.

The following information was extracted from the companies' books as at 31 December, 19X2.

	Langland £000	Caswell £000	Oxwich £000
Credit balances:			
Issued share capital (£1 ordinary shares)..........	1,500	500	600
Reserves	738	210	80
10% Debentures.........................	100	—	—
Proposed dividend......................	—	—	40
Current liabilities.......................	256	750	594
	2,594	1,460	1,314
Debit balances:			
Goodwill at cost........................	—	—	250
Freehold property at cost	—	—	500
Equipment at cost less depreciation........	873	310	276
Current assets..........................	721	1,150	288
Investments............................	1,000	—	—
	2,594	1,460	1,314

The following information is provided in respect of the investments.

	Caswell	Oxwich
Price paid......................	£700,000	£300,000
Numbers of shares held	450,000	180,000
Date of acquisition	30 March, 19X1	1 January, 19X2
Balance on reserves at date of acquisition	£150,000	£70,000

The freehold property of Oxwich possessed a fair value of £720,000 on 1 January, 19X2. There were no other significant differences between the fair value and book value of the assets of Caswell and Oxwich at the acquisition dates.

Credit has not been taken in the books of Langland for its share of the dividend proposed by Oxwich.

REQUIRED:

A consolidated balance sheet of the group as at 31 December, 19X2.

Notes:

Ignore taxation and depreciation of goodwill and freehold property.

Solution

Langland

90%   30%

Caswell   Oxwich
(pre-acquisition reserves £150,000)   (pre-acquisition reserves £70,000)

		At	Since	Minority
Calculations:	*Total*	*Acquisition*	*Acquisition*	*Interest*
(i) Caswell	*£000*	*£000*	*£000*	*£000*
Share capital	500	450		50
Reserves: At acquisition	150	135		15
Since acquisition	60		54	6
	710	585	54	71
Price paid		700		
Goodwill		115		

(ii) *Oxwich*

Allocation of purchase price:	*£000*	*£000*
Price paid		300
Less: Goodwill, £250,000 × 30%	75	
Other net assets at fair value, (600,000 + 70,000 + 220,000* − 250,000) × 30%	192	
		267
Premium paid on acquisition		33
Share of post-acquisition retained profits (80,000 − £70,000) × 30%		3

*Difference between fair value and book value of freeholds.

*Consolidated Balance Sheet of the Group as at
31 December, 19X2*

Fixed Assets	£000	£000
Goodwill arising on consolidation		115
Equipment at cost less depreciation		1,183
Investment in associated company:		
Share of net assets, other than goodwill at takeover date	192	
Share of post-acquisition undistributed profits......................	3	
	195	
Goodwill and premium on acquisition:		
Share of goodwill	75	
Premium on acquisition	33	
		303
Current Assets		
(including dividend receivable from Oxwich, £40,000 × 30%) ...	1,883	
Less: Current Liabilities	1,006	
		877
		2,478
Financed by:		
Issued share capital (£1 ordinary shares)............................		1,500
Reserves		807 W1
		2,307
Minority interest...		71
10% Debentures..		100
		2,478
W1. Reserves: Langland		738
Dividend receivable from Oxwich £40,000 × 30% .		12
		750
Caswell ....,.........................		54
Oxwich...		3
		807

CHAPTER 6

✳ SSAP 16 SUSPENDED ·1·86

Current Cost Accounting

6.1 HISTORICAL COST AND CURRENT VALUE

The accounting reports prepared for both internal and external consumption have been based, traditionally, on the concept of historical cost. That is, assets are normally reported at the price paid when the initial acquisition took place, less, in the case of fixed assets, an appropriate deduction for depreciation; while liabilities are reported at their face value. In recent years, however, businessmen and accountants have increasingly asked themselves the question: 'Is historical cost the correct basis of valuation?'. The reason for this uncertainty is a growing suspicion that the widespread use of historical cost as the basis for financial reports is more a consequence of the way in which accountancy has evolved than the result of any rational assessment of the available alternatives.

Historically, the primary objective of accountancy was to provide management with a permanent financial record of business transactions to help them regulate and control the transfer of resources between the company and the rest of the economy. For example, management required a detailed record of goods received from suppliers in order to ensure that the resulting debts were properly discharged when they fell due for payment. It was therefore natural and, indeed, inevitable that transactions should be recorded at the price ruling when the initial transfer took place. Although this book-keeping exercise no longer dominates the accounting process, which is increasingly concerned with the preparation of accounting reports, record-keeping nevertheless remains an important function which continues to oblige companies to record transactions initially in terms of historical cost.

For the purpose of financial reporting, however, it is often suggested that 'current values' are more relevant than historical costs. Consider the following three examples:

Example 6.1

Hanley Ltd. purchased a piece of land for £20,000 some years ago, and it was reported at this figure in a recently prepared balance sheet. The following additional information is provided:

1. The directors have been offered an annual rental of £3,000 for this land by a local farmer.
2. The current value of the land is now £50,000, but no further increase is expected to occur in the foreseeable future.
3. The company invests money at 12%.

Which figure is likely to be more relevant for the purpose of helping management decide what to do with the land—historical cost or current value? Clearly current value. The land can be rented out for £3,000, which represents a return of 15% on historical cost (£20,000), but only 6% on current value (£50,000). It is therefore advisable to sell the land and invest the proceeds at 12% to produce £6,000 per annum.

Example 6.2

Fawley Ltd., purchased a freehold property some years ago and it was reported at £100,000 (historical cost less depreciation) in a recently prepared balance sheet. The company has since approached the bank for a loan of £250,000. In the bank's view, none of the company's other assets represents a satisfactory security, but there is reliable evidence which shows that the property's current value is in the region of £500,000.

Which figure is likely to be more relevant for the purpose of helping the bank decide whether the property is an acceptable security for the proposed loan? Again the answer is current value, and the result is that a loan will be granted which would have been refused if the security had been assessed only on the basis of its historical cost less depreciation.

Example 6.3

Crawley Ltd., reported profits for 19X1 of £500,000, and the balance sheet at 31 December, 19X1, prepared on the historical cost basis, showed net assets of £2,000,000. The current value of net assets is estimated to be £10,000,000.

	Historical cost	Current value
Rate of return on net assets	25%	5%

An assessment of management's performance, based on historical cost accounts, shows them to have achieved an apparently satisfactory return of 25%. However, management has at its disposal assets whose *true* value is £10,000,000 and, using this figure, a much lower rate of return is computed and a more critical assessment of managerial performance is likely to result. (*Note.* It is recognised that the use of current values will reduce profit, and therefore the real rate of return will be even lower, but that complication is ignored at this stage).

In the above examples current values, rather than historical cost, appear to be more relevant for the purpose of assessments made and decisions reached by management, creditors and shareholders. It is only during the last ten years, however, that inflation accounting has become a major topic of debate. The reason for this is examined in the next section.

6.2 THE IMPACT OF INFLATION ON ACCOUNTING REPORTS

Why has inflation accounting been a major topic of debate during the last decade? The answer is the consistently high level of inflation demonstrated in figure 6.1.

Figure 6.1 Retail Price Index (Jan. 1974 = 100)

Date: January	Index	% increase over twelve months
1973	89.3	7.7
1974	100.0	12.0
1975	119.9	19.9
1976	147.9	23.4
1977	172.4	16.6
1978	189.5	9.8
1979	207.2	9.3
1980	245.3	18.3
1981	277.3	13.0
1982	310.6	12.0
1983	325.9	4.9

Historical cost accounting is satisfactory when prices are relatively stable, as was the case in Britain prior to 1973. Admittedly prices have moved steadily upwards throughout the present century, but the average annual rate of increase until 1973 was just 2.75% as compared with 14% over the following ten years. Fairly compelling reasons were needed to convince businessmen that they should critically re-examine the well tried historical cost accounting procedures which, for many years, had enabled annual accounts to be prepared with the minimum of fuss. Prior to 1973 these reasons simply did not exist, but now they do, since an annual increase of 14% causes prices to double in just over five years; the result is that there are substantial differences between the historical cost and current cost of assets belonging to most British companies.

During the 1970s British companies, with encouragement from the Government and the accounting profession, experimented with a variety of different methods of inflation accounting. Usually, these companies continued with historical cost as the basis for their main accounts, and the inflation adjusted accounts were published as supplementary information for the use of shareholders, creditors and other interested parties. Current cost accounting (CCA) is the version at present favoured by the accounting profession, and

SSAP 16,* which contains detailed procedures for companies to follow, is examined in section 5 of this chapter. For the purpose of discussion, however, it is useful to outline, at this stage, the essential features of CCA. They are as follows:

1. Assets are shown in the balance sheet at their *current* cost, i.e. at what it would cost to replace them at the balance sheet date.
2. Profit is measured by matching the *current* cost of assets sold or used up during the course of the business process against sales revenue.

CCA and historical cost accounting (HCA) are compared and contrasted in the following simple example:

Example 6.4

Lakeside Ltd. was incorporated on 1 January, 19X1 with an issued share capital of £1,000 which was immediately invested in 5 units of stock costing £200 each. The current replacement cost rose to £230 per unit on 20 January and remained at that figure for the rest of the month. The entire stock was sold on 31 January for £1,400 in cash. All other costs and taxation are ignored.

Required:

(a) The HCA and CCA balance sheets as at 20 January, 19X1.
(b) The HCA and CCA profit and loss account for January, 19X1, and HCA and CCA balance sheet as at 31 January, 19X1.

Solution

(a) *Balance Sheets at 20 January*

	HCA £	CCA £
Share capital...	1,000	1,000
Current cost reserve	—	150
	1,000	1,150
Stock	1,000	1,150

The historical cost accounts show that the cash raised on incorporation was invested in stock which continues to be reported at its historical cost of £1,000. The current cost accounts recognise that the stock is now worth £1,150, and the increase in value is credited to current cost reserve. The £150 is called a 'holding gain', i.e. a gain which arises simply as a result of holding an asset when prices are rising, rather than a profit which is earned as the result of business operations.

---

*Statement of standard accounting practice No. 16; *Current Cost Accounting*. The Institute of Chartered Accountants in England and Wales, March 1980.

NB ❋ SUSPENDED ❋

(b)   *Profit and Loss Accounts for January*

	HCA £	CCA £
Sales	1,400	1,400
Less: Cost of goods sold	1,000	1,150
Net profit	400	250

Balance Sheets at 31 January

	HCA £	CCA £
Share capital	1,000	1,000
Current cost reserve	—	150
Net profit	400	250
	1,400	1,400
Cash	1,400	1,400

The above calculations of profit reflect the different objectives of historical cost accounting and current cost accounting which are as follows:

HCA: Money is raised from shareholders when a company is formed, and this money is then invested in business assets. The profit measurement process is designed to maintain intact the 'money' value of the shareholder's original investment by charging against revenue the historical cost of resources used up during the course of trading activity. One of the reasons for measuring profit is to identify surplus resources which may be paid out in the form of dividends. If the full £400 profit is paid out in dividends, cash will nevertheless be left in the company equal to the money value of the shareholders original investment. In this sense, the profit measurement process has done its job which is to protect the shareholders' initial investment. It may be pointed out that the company does not possess enough money to replace its stock, but that is not the aim of the measurement process.

CCA: Current cost accounting is concerned with maintaining intact a company's productive capacity rather than the money value of the shareholders' investment. Capital is therefore defined as the company's operating assets, while current cost profit is the surplus left over after full provision has been made for the replacement cost of assets sold or used up during the course of business activity. In example 6.4, sales revenue less the replacement cost of stock sold produces a current cost profit of £250. The company may therefore distribute its entire current cost profit, but still leave an amount of cash which is sufficient to finance stock replacement at £230 per unit, i.e. 5 × £230 = £1,150.

We can therefore see that HCA and CCA have quite different objectives: the former is concerned with protecting the money value of the shareholder's investment, while the latter is designed to preserve the company's capacity to generate revenue in the future. Published accounting information will differ a great deal depending on which method is employed. More specifically, the profit figure will be usually lower and the balance sheet value of assets usually higher under CCA. The former point is illustrated in figure 6.2 which gives a comparison of historical cost and current cost profit, by industry, for a selected range of public companies.

Figure 6.2   Comparison of Published Profit Figures, 1981

Industry	1 Number of Companies	2 HC profit (loss)	3 CC profit (loss)	4 $\frac{CC}{HC} \times 100$
		£m	£m	%
Building materials	16	308.4	144.1	47
Contracting and constructing	14	196.0	137.0	70
Engineering contractors	6	70.6	45.1	64
Metals and metal forming	9	14.8	(143.4)	—
Motors	16	31.4	(107.3)	—
Brewers and distillers	7	516.9	263.7	51
Food manufacturing	11	536.1	298.0	56
Food retailing	9	94.9	76.1	80
Chemicals	9	(11.0)	(295.0)	—
Shipping and transport	6	110.1	59.9	54
Total	103	1,868.2	478.2	26

SOURCE: Columns 1–3 were extracted from a more comprehensive table contained in R. N. Berry and S. J. Gray, 'The impact of current cost accounting: some industry comparisons,' *The Accountant's Magazine*, January, 1982, p.14.

The above table shows that the relationship between HC profit and CC profit (column 4) varies significantly from one industrial sector to another. There are two main reasons for this:

1. Variations in the rate at which costs are rising, e.g. the costs of chemical companies may be increasing rapidly due to the rise in the price of oil, while the costs of food manufacturers may be more stable due to a fall in the price of imported raw materials.

2. Variations in the rate of turnover of fixed assets and stock. The slower the rate of turnover, the more costs are likely to rise between the date an asset is acquired and the date it is sold or used up.

The extent of the difference between HC profit and CC profit may therefore vary from industry to industry, but the overall trend is consistent. All industries show a lower profit, or higher loss, on the latter basis, and the total current cost profit is only 26% of the historical cost level.

6.3   THE RELATIVE MERITS OF CCA AND HCA

Financial information is required for a number of purposes, and probably neither CCA nor HCA is superior in every respect. It is for this reason that many people favour the publication of both current cost and historical cost based financial information, at least by large companies. The respective claims made by the advocates of CCA and HCA are examined below.

Claims made by the advocates of CCA:

1. *CCA produces more realistic asset values*   This is particularly the case with fixed assets which, under HCA, are often reported at only a fraction of their real value.

2. *CCA matches like items with like*   Price indices and asset revaluations are used to restate original costs in terms of current costs for the purpose of measuring periodic profit. The historical cost approach, which mixes together £s of different generations, e.g. sales revenues expressed in present day £s and the depreciation charge expressed in £s representing values which ruled some years ago, has been likened to the consolidation of a foreign subsidiary without first converting the overseas currency into sterling. In either case the results are considered meaningless.

3. *CCA identifies 'true' profits*   It is argued that, during a period of inflation, HCA profit consists of two elements, namely 'true' profit and an inflationary element called the 'holding gain'. In example 6.4, CCA procedures analyse the historical cost profit of £400 into 'true profits of £250 and a 'holding gain' of £150, representing resources which must be retained within the business in order to protect the entity's capacity to generate future revenue. The current cost profit figure is therefore thought to be more relevant for the following purposes:

(a) *Taxation*   HCA results in over-taxation, since tax is levied on holding gains which must be retained in full in order to avoid an erosion of the company's operating capacity. Stop-gap measures introduced in the 1970s, such as the 100% first year allowance and stock appreciation relief, have helped to ameliorate the damage, but the complete adoption of CCA profits for taxation purposes is considered a better solution.

(b) *Dividend policy*   Despite declining real profitability, the HCA profits of many companies have remained at a reasonable level due to the effect of inflation i.e. reported profit has contained large holding gains. It has therefore been difficult for management to justify a lower dividend in spite of the harmful effect on financial stability of maintaining the previous level of payout. The publication of CCA profits should help to explain to shareholders the need for lower dividends in certain cases.

(c) *Collective bargaining*   Trade union reference to reported profit levels during the course of wage negotiations is an established practice. The disparity which commonly exists between management's plea that they cannot afford to increase wages and certain financial facts appearing in the accounts is a source of acute embarrassment which might be partly avoided by the adoption of CCA.

(d) *Performance assessment and resource allocation*   CCA causes the profits and asset values of different companies to be computed on a comparable basis, and this provides shareholders with a more rational foundation for investment decisions. Similarly CCA data, which incorporates current costs in the calculation of both periodic profit and capital employed, provides management with a more meaningful measure of the relative profitability of products, departments and geographical areas, both as a basis for assessing past performance and to support future resource allocation decisions.

4. *CCA facilitates asset replacement*   It is necessary to charge revenue with the current cost of stocks sold and fixed assets used up, during the course of the productive process, in order to indicate clearly the quantity of resources which must be retained to finance asset replacement. The failure of companies to amend their profit measurement procedures and then to base distribution decisions on the revised figures has resulted in them needing to raise additional finance merely to pay for asset replacements. The growing figures

for bank loans and overdrafts in the balance sheets of many companies can be entirely explained in these terms.

5. *CCA improves pricing policy*   Full knowledge of the current costs of business activity is an essential element in the development of a rational system for pricing goods and services.

The above arguments comprise a strong case for CCA. The following are the main reasons why CCA has not yet superceded HCA, and why many doubt whether it will ever prove more acceptable:

(a) *HCA data is readily available*   As explained above, all transactions must initially be recorded at historical cost. Obtaining current costs for the various assets belonging to a company is a time consuming and expensive process.

(b) *HCA data is broadly factual*   The calculation of current costs provides increased scope for subjective judgement, error and the fraudulent manipulation of accounting reports.

(c) *HCA data is more easily verified*   Any departure from historical cost adds to the difficulties facing the auditor, whose job it is to report on the truth and fairness of the information contained in the accounts.

(d) *HCA procedures are well understood* and their major defects widely recognised. CCA procedures are at an early stage of development, and their potential and limitations continue to be matters for conjecture.

6.4   SOME PARTIAL SOLUTIONS

Many people acknowledge the fact that inflation shows up the deficiencies of HCA, but they do not agree that there is a real need for major change. Instead they argue that it is possible to accommodate the effects of inflation by making some relatively simple changes within the historical cost framework. The main proposals, which have been used by certain companies for many years, are as follows:

1. Periodic revaluation of fixed assets. Inflation will result in differences between the original cost and current cost of all tangible assets, but the discrepancies will be greater in the case of those assets which have been owned for a long period of time. The result is that the need for restatement has always seemed greater for fixed assets than for current assets and, within the former group, it is land and buildings that have more often been the subject of periodic revaluation. I.C.I.

and Unilever are examples of British companies which voluntarily revalued their fixed assets in the 1960s and transferred the surplus arising to a revaluation reserve.

2. Base depreciation on replacement cost. Companies which revalued their fixed assets, often then based their depreciation charge on the revised figure. Other companies chose not to restate their fixed assets but made an *appropriation* of profits to replacement reserve to cover the additional cost of replacing fixed assets. Early British examples include John Summers & Sons Ltd., and Joseph Lucas (Industrial) Ltd.

3. Use the LIFO basis for issuing stock to production and matching finished goods with sales. The effect is demonstrated in Example 6.5.

Example 6.5

The following information is provided for Farnwell Ltd., which commenced business on 1 January, 19X0:

	No. of items	Purchase price £	Sales price £
1 January	1	200	—
8 January	1	220	—
9 January	1	—	228
27 January	1	232	—
28 January	1	—	241

Summarised Trading Accounts for January, 19X0

	FIFO £	FIFO £	LIFO £	LIFO £
Sales..		469		469
Less: Purchases..............................	652		652	
Closing stock	(232)		(200)	
Cost of goods sold...................	—	420	—	452
Gross Profit...................................		49		17

LIFO *assumes* that most recent purchases are sold first and therefore reports a much lower profit figure than FIFO during a period when prices are rising. The LIFO cost of goods sold figure will still be lower than the corresponding figure computed on a strict current cost basis, but the difference will be small. In example 6.5, the item purchased on 8 January is matched with the sale on 9 January, using LIFO; similarly the purchase on 27 January is matched with the sale price on 28 January. The purchase price may have risen between 8 and 9 January and/or between 27 and 28 January, of course, but the increase is unlikely to have been significant and LIFO therefore produces a cost of goods sold figure which closely approximates current cost.

LIFO has never been popular in Britain, probably because it is unacceptable for tax purposes. There are other disadvantages. In Example 6.5, closing stock is reported under LIFO at £200 in the balance sheet—well below its true value. In the case of a company which has been in business for many years, the LIFO basis will result in an utterly meaningless balance sheet figure for stocks. A further drawback of LIFO is that it works well only when the volume of purchases exceeds sales. For instance, assume that, without making a further purchase, Farnwell sold the item in stock at 31 January for £245 on 1 February, 19X0.

	FIFO £	LIFO £
Sales........................	245	245
Cost of sales..............	232	200
Gross profit	13	45

In these circumstances LIFO reports a far *higher* profit than FIFO, because stocks have been run down and the 'old' purchase price must be matched with current sales revenue.

4. Transfer to reserves. The fact that profits are overstated does not necessarily mean that a company will run short of money because excessive dividends have been paid. It has always been a common practice for companies to finance *expansion* out of retained profits; in more recent times prudent corporate managers have also made large transfers to reserves in recognition of the fact that profits are needed to finance asset replacement and are therefore unavailable for distribution.

6.5   STATEMENT OF STANDARD ACCOUNTING PRACTICE (SSAP) 16

In the 1970s, a number of methods of inflation accounting were proposed, both by the government and the accounting profession, in the attempt to improve the quality of published financial information during a period of rapidly rising prices. SSAP7, issued in 1974, encouraged companies to publish a supplementary statement which showed the effect of changes in the *general* price level on shareholders' funds. In 1975, however, a government committee (the Sandilands Committee), rejected SSAP7, and instead recommended that accounts should be drawn up in accordance with the principles of current cost accounting, i.e. that accounts should take account of changes in the prices of the assets actually belonging to the company rather than changes in the general price level.

In response to the findings of the Sandilands Committee, the accounting profession subsequently issued Exposure Draft 18

(1977) which, among other things, proposed the *replacement* of HCA by CCA. The system recommended was complicated, and it was rejected at a special meeting held by the members of the Institute of Chartered Accountants in England and Wales. Following this reversal, the accounting profession instead issued the 'Hyde Guidelines' which encouraged quoted companies to publish supplementary information which showed some of the effects of changing prices on their published historical cost profit figures. SSAP16, issued in 1980 for a trial period of three years, is therefore the most recent in a series of proposals designed to tackle the problem of accounting in times of inflation. It is not likely to be the definitive answer, and some further changes may be expected in due course.

The statement applies to quoted companies and other large companies whose turnover, gross assets and number of employees exceed certain specified thresholds. The statement requires these companies to publish CCA information as a supplement to the main accounts which will normally continue to be based on historical cost. The purpose of the statement is to provide data which is helpful in assessing the financial viability of the business, and in making decisions designed to maintain the company's operating capability. The main features of the current cost accounts are:

1. Disclosure of *current cost operating profit.* This makes full allowance for the impact of price changes on the company's operating assets, but takes no account of the way in which the company is financed. Broadly speaking, this means that full provision is made for the additional cost of replacing business assets i.e. the extra £150 in example 6.4.

2. Disclosure of the *current cost profit attributable to shareholders.* This is determined after making the gearing adjustment which assumes that 'borrowing' will continue to finance a similar proportion of operating assets as in the past. If, in example 6.4, some of the stock was financed by borrowing, it would be unnecessary for shareholders to meet the full additional cost of replacement, as a proportion of the extra cost would be financed by creditors.

3. Operating assets are reported in the balance sheet at their current replacement cost.

No significant revision of the way in which the balance sheet is presented is required to take account of the provisions of SSAP16, but asset values are likely to increase a great deal, and a current cost reserve must be opened to take account of these changes. The format of the profit and loss account is subject to more substantial changes, and a typical presentation is reproduced as Figure 6.3.

Figure 6.3 Current Cost Profit and Loss Account

	£	£
Profit before interest and taxation on the historical cost basis........		*
Less: Current cost operating adjustments:		
Cost of sales adjustment	*	
Monetary working capital adjustment	*	
	—	
Total working capital adjustment........................	*	
Depreciation adjustment	*	*
	—	—
Current cost operating profit		*
Less/Add: Gearing adjustment	*	
Interest payable less receivable	*	*
	—	—
Current cost profit before tax		*
Taxation..		*
		—
Current cost profit attributable to shareholders.........................		*
Dividends..		*
		—
Retained current cost profit for the year.................................		*
		—

The main adjustments required to convert HCA to CCA are considered below.

6.5.1 Fixed Assets and the Depreciation Adjustment The government has taken steps to simplify and reduce the cost of adopting CCA by arranging for the publication of index numbers which may be used by companies for the purpose of obtaining current values for plant and stocks. Separate indices are published for each industry and for each category of plant and stock, and it is up to companies to choose those which are appropriate for their type of business. Management may alternatively arrange for their assets to be valued, or take steps to construct an internal index tailor-made for their particular company. In general, these alternative approaches are less popular since they involve extra work and cost, but periodic revaluations must be obtained for land and buildings for which there exists no suitable government index.

Computations of the depreciation adjustment, for inclusion in the profit and loss account, and the balance sheet figures for the gross cost of assets and the related accumulated depreciation are illustrated in Example 6.6.

Example 6.6

Treen Limited purchased a freehold property for £750,000 (including land £150,000) on 1 January, 19X0, and depreciates the building assuming a twenty five year life and zero value at the end of that period. An annual depreciation charge of £24,000 (£600,000 × 1/25) was therefore made in the historical cost accounts for 19X0. For the purpose of the current cost accounts, the following open market valuations for land and buildings, in their existing use, were obtained from a firm of chartered surveyors.

	Buildings £	Land £	Total £
Average values during 19X0	625,000	175,000	800,000
Values at 31 December, 19X0	660,000	180,000	840,000

The relevant information for inclusion in the current cost accounts for 19X0 is computed as follows:

(i) Depreciation adjustment: The company has benefitted from using the asset throughout 19X0 and the current cost depreciation charge should therefore be based on its average current value during that period. The depreciation adjustment is computed as the difference between the current cost charge and the historical cost charge *already* made in the accounts.

	£
CC charge £625,000 × 1/25..............	25,000
Less: HC charge..........................	24,000
Depreciation adjustment.........	1,000

The following journal entry may be used to record the depreciation adjustment in the current cost accounts (narrative omitted):

	£	£
Dr. Depreciation adjustment (reported in CC profit and loss account)	1,000	
Cr. Accumulated depreciation (reported in CC balance sheet)...		1,000

(ii) Current cost of freehold property at 31 December, 19X0   840,000

The difference between historical cost and current cost, i.e. £90,000, is credited to the current cost reserve by means of the following journal entry (narrative omitted):

	£	£
Dr. Freehold property (reported in CC balance sheet)	90,000	
Cr. Current cost reserve (reported in CC balance sheet)		90,000

(iii) Accumulated CC depreciation charge to 31 December, 19X0. The remaining useful life of the buildings is now 24 years, and so accumulated depreciation, at 31 December, 19X0, must be computed as 1/25 of the current cost at that date.

i.e.   £660,000 × 1/25 = £26,400

This calculation gives rise to backlog depreciation which is now examined.

6.5.2 Backlog Depreciation
Backlog depreciation is the excess of accumulated depreciation, computed for inclusion in the current cost balance sheet, over the aggregate charges, made to date, in the current cost profit and loss account. Backlog depreciation arises because, during a period of rising prices, previous depreciation charges, debited to the current cost profit and loss account, will have been based on lower figures for current cost. Treen Ltd. (see example 6.6) has owned the freehold property for only one year and the calculation is straightforward.

	£	£
Accumulated CC charge to 31 December, 19X0............		26,400
Less: HC charge for 19X0......................................	24,000	
Depreciation adjustment for 19X0.....................	1,000	25,000
Backlog Depreciation		1,400

The problem is how to dispose of backlog depreciation. One suggestion put forward is that backlog depreciation should be deducted from profit, but this idea has been rejected on the grounds that it would understate profits since £25,000 (not £26,400) represents the value of resources used up *during* 19X0. The preferred solution is to deduct backlog depreciation from the current cost reserve. The following journal entry records this adjustment (narrative omitted):

		£	£
Dr.	Current cost reserve (reported in CC balance sheet).........	1,400	
Cr.	Accumulated depreciation (reported in CC balance sheet).		1,400

The relevant current cost balance sheet entries relating to the freehold property purchased by Treen are as follows:

Extracts from Current Cost Balance Sheet of Treen Ltd.

Fixed Assets	£
Freehold property at current cost...................................	840,000
Less: Accumulated depreciation	26,400 W1
	813,600
Financed by:	
Share capital...	xxx
Current cost reserve	88,600 W2

W1.	Historical cost depreciation charge.........................	24,000
	Add: Depreciation adjustment	1,000
	Backlog depreciation.....................................	1,400
		26,400

W2.	Surplus arising from revaluation of freehold property ..	90,000
	Less: Backlog depreciation...................................	1,400
		88,600

Example 6.7 illustrates the use of specific index numbers in order to obtain current cost figures for fixed assets purchased in a previous accounting period.

Example 6.7

Usk Ltd., purchased plant costing £600,000 on 1 January, 19X1. It was estimated that the plant would have an eight year life and a zero residual value at the end of that period. For 19X3, a depreciation charge of £75,000 (£600,000 × 1/8) was made in the HC profit and loss account, and plant was reported in the HC balance sheet at cost £600,000 less accumulated depreciation £225,000. The following relevant index numbers are provided for plant.

1 January, 19X0	120
Average for 19X3	150
31 December, 19X3	155

The information for inclusion in the current cost accounts for 19X3 is computed as follows:

(i) Depreciation adjustment   £

$$\text{CC charge} = \text{HC charge} \times \frac{\text{Average index for the year}}{\text{Index at date of acquisition}}$$

$$= £75,000 \times \frac{150}{120} = \quad\dots\dots\dots\dots\dots\dots\dots\dots\dots\dots\dots \quad 93,750$$

Less: HC charge   75,000

                    18,750

(ii) Current cost at 31 December, 19X3

Historical cost $\times \dfrac{\text{Index at the year end}}{\text{Index at the date of acquisition}}$

£600,000 $\times \dfrac{155}{120} = $ 775,000

(iii) Accumulated CC charge

£775,000 (current cost) $\times$ 3/8 (3 years old) = ...   290,625

(iv) Backlog depreciation	£	
Accumulated CC charge....................................		290,625
Less: HC charge to date.....................................	225,000	
Depreciation adjustment for 19X3	18,750	
		243,750
		46,875

(v) Net transfer to current cost reserve	
Excess of CC over HC of plant	175,000
Less: Backlog depreciation.................................	46,875
	128,125

Journal entries, prepared along the lines described in sections 5.1 and 5.2 of this chapter, may be used as the basis for recording the above information.

6.5.3 Stocks and the Cost of Sales Adjustment   Ideally, the cost of sales should be computed by determining, at the date of each sale, the current replacement cost of the item sold but, in practice, this would impose an intolerable burden upon companies. Instead, a satisfactory approximation to current replacement cost will usually be achieved by applying 'the averaging method', which uses an index of changes in stock prices to calculate the cost of sales adjustment (COSA). The procedure is as follows:

1. Deduct the opening HC value of stock from the closing HC value of stock.

2. Restate the closing book value of stock at the average price of stock for the year using the formula:

$$\text{Closing stock} \times \frac{\text{Average index for the year}}{\text{Index at the date of acquisition}}$$

3. Restate the opening book value of stock at the average price of stock for the year using the formula:

$$\text{Opening stock} \times \frac{\text{Average index for the year}}{\text{Index at the date of acquisition}}$$

4. Deduct 3 from 2 to find the increase in the volume of stock held.
5. Deduct 4 from 1 to find the increase in the price of stock held (COSA).

In the HCA, closing stock will normally exceed opening stock, but the difference is likely to be due to *both* rising prices and an increase in the value of stocks held. Calculations 2 and 3 restate opening and closing stocks at comparable prices, and calculation 4 therefore identifies any increase in the volume of stock held. The effect of calculation 5 is then to identify the increase in stock value due to inflation.

Example 6.8

The following information is provided for Tilgate Ltd.

	£
HC value of stock held at 31 December, 19X0.........	590,000
HC value of stock held at 31 December, 19X1.........	740,000
Stock indices:	
Average for December, 19X0.............................	100
At 31 December, 19X0	101
Average for 19X1...	108
Average for December, 19X1	116
At 31 December, 19X1	118

Opening and closing stock each represent one month's purchases.

COSA is calculated as follows (£000)

1. Increase in book value (740 – 590)........................		150
2. Restate closing stock $740 \times \dfrac{108}{116*}$..........................	689	
3. Restate opening stock $590 \times \dfrac{108}{100*}$	637	
4. Increase due to volume change...............................		52
5. Increase due to inflation.......................................		98

*NB. The average indices for December must be used because opening and closing stock each represent one month's purchases, i.e. they were made at prices ruling *during* December. A common student error is to use the year end indices.

The following journal entry records the COSA in the current cost accounts (narrative omitted):

	£	£
Dr. COSA (reported in the CC profit and loss account)	98,000	
Cr. Current cost reserve (reported in the CC balance sheet).		98,000

COSA is deducted from historical cost profit (see figure 6.3), and this has the effect of eliminating from reported profit gains realised as the result of holding stock during an inflationary period, i.e. realised holding gains. The double entry is completed by crediting £98,000 to the current cost reserve.

It is also necessary to restate closing stock at current cost for balance sheet purposes, by using the following factor:

$$\frac{\text{Index at the year end}}{\text{Index at the date of acquisition}}$$

The current cost of Tilgate's closing stock therefore becomes:

$$£740,000 \times \frac{118}{116} = £752,758$$

The following journal entry records the unrealised holding gain of £12,758 (£752,758 – £740,000), narrative omitted:

	£	£
Dr. Closing stock (reported in the CC balance sheet)	12,758	
Cr. Current cost reserve (reported in the CC balance sheet).		12,758

In most companies this adjustment will not be large because, in Great Britain, FIFO is the method commonly used to match purchases with sales, and this causes closing stock to be valued already at the most recent purchase prices.

Readers should now test their understanding of the calculations explained so far by working Rociety Ltd., taken from the April, 1981 examination paper.

Example 6.9

The summarised profit and loss account and balance sheet of Rociety Ltd., a trading company, prepared under the historical cost convention, were as follows:

PROFIT AND LOSS ACCOUNT FOR 1980

	£000	£000
Sales		1,400
Less: Opening stock	156	
Purchases	1,024	
Closing stock	(196)	
Cost of goods sold		984
Gross profit		416
Less: Depreciation	50	
Other running costs	300	350
Net profit		66

BALANCE SHEET AT 31 DECEMBER 1980

	£000	£000
Fixed assets purchased 1 January 1979		500
Less depreciation (10% straight line)		100
		400
Stock	196	
Debtors	160	
Bank	20	
	376	
Less creditors	136	240
		640
Share capital		300
Reserves at 1 January 1980	274	
Profit for 1980	66	340
		640

The following price indices are provided for the company's stock and fixed assets:

	Stock	Fixed Assets
1 January 1979	*	80
Average for November/December 1979	120	*
31 December 1979	*	90

Average for 1980	130	96
Average for November/December 1980	140	*
31 December 1980	142	104

Stock turns over, on average, once every two months.

*indices not provided.

Required:

A summarised profit and loss account for 1980 and balance sheet at 31 December 1980, prepared on the *current cost basis*. The profit and loss account should contain a cost of sales adjustment and a depreciation adjustment, whilst the balance sheet should contain a current cost reserve.

Notes:

1. **Ignore (i) the monetary working capital adjustment, (ii) the gearing adjustment, (iii) taxation, (iv) dividends.**
2. **Calculations to nearest £000.**

[20]

Solution

(a) *Workings* (nearest £000):
  Fixed assets and the depreciation adjustment:
  (i) Depreciation adjustment

CC charge: $50 \times \dfrac{96}{80}$		60
Less: HC charge		50
		10

  (ii) Current cost at 31 December, 1980

$500 \times \dfrac{104}{80}$		650

  (iii) Accumulated CC charge

$650 \times 10\% \times 2$ (assets 2 years old)...		130

  (iv) Backlog depreciation

Accumulated CC charge..		130
Less: HC charge to date...	100	
Depreciation adjustment for 1980	10	110
		20

(b) Stock and the cost of sales adjustment.

    (i) COSA

Increase in book value (196 – 156)	40
Restate closing stock $196 \times \dfrac{130}{140}$	182
Restate opening stock $156 \times \dfrac{130}{120}$	169
Increase due to volume change	13
Increase due to inflation	27
(ii) Current cost of closing stock $196 \times \dfrac{142}{140}$	199

(c) Current cost reserve.

Current Cost Reserve Account

Backlog depreciation	20	Revaluation of plant (650 – 500)	150
Closing balance	160	COSA	27
		Revaluation of stock (199 – 196)	3
	180		180

Summarised Profit and Loss Account for 1980

	£000	£000
Profit on the historical cost basis		66
Less: Current cost operating adjustments:		
COSA	27	
Depreciation adjustment	10	37
Current cost operating profit		29

Summarised Balance Sheet at 31 December, 1980

	£000	£000
Fixed assets at current cost		650
Less: Accumulated depreciation		130
		520
Stock	199	
Debtors	160	
Bank	20	
	379	
Less: Creditors	136	
		243
		763

	£000	£000
Share capital...........................		300
Reserves at 1 January, 1980.............	274*	
Add: Current cost profit for 1980.....	29	
	—	303
Current cost reserve		160
		—
		763

*Technically, retained profits should be reduced and the current cost reserve should be increased by the total of previous years' depreciation and cost of sales adjustments, but in the absence of necessary additional information this cannot be done.

Examiner's comments:
Most common errors:
  1. The stock indices at 31 December in each year were erroneously used to restate opening and closing stock for the purpose of computing COSA.
  2. The current cost charge for depreciation was based on the current cost of fixed assets at 31 December, 1980 instead of their average current cost during 1980.
  3. Backlog depreciation was omitted.

6.5.4 The Monetary Working Capital Adjustment

The monetary working capital adjustment (MWCA) has close similarities to COSA, both as regards its purpose and in the manner of its calculation. COSA measures the effect of price changes on the value of stock used up during an accounting period, and it also indicates the additional amount of resources required to finance higher-priced stocks. Most businesses, however, have other working capital besides stocks involved in their day to day operating activities. In particular, where goods are sold on credit, a large quantity of resources will be tied up in debtors. On the other hand, credit is normally obtained from suppliers of goods and services, and this reduces the amount of finance which a company must provide to support its working capital requirements.

The MWCA is designed to identify the amount of finance needed to cover additional monetary working capital requirements brought about by price increases. Monetary working capital is, for this purpose, usually defined as trade debtors less trade creditors, though an element of cash may need to be included where it is an essential element of business operations. Examination questions will indicate the amount of cash, if any, to be included when calculating the MWCA. COSA and MWCA together allow for the impact of price changes on the total amount of working capital used by a business. The two adjustments are usually combined for presentation purposes (see figure 6.3). Where trade creditors exceed trade debtors, as in the case of a retail outlet, the MWCA will be negative and the need for a COSA correspondingly reduced.

MWCA is computed using 'the averaging method' and an appropriate price index. A separate index may be used for trade debtors and trade creditors, but often a single index is applied to the net difference between the two totals where the periods of credit received and allowed are similar. The stock index is often considered appropriate since the bulk of the creditors and debtors will relate to purchases and sales of stock.

Example 6.10

Tor Ltd., purchases and sells goods on credit. One month's credit is both allowed to customers and received from suppliers. The following information is provided:

		£
Debtors:	31 December, 19X1	760,000
	31 December, 19X2	950,000
Creditors:	31 December, 19X1	470,000
	31 December, 19X2	360,000
Index:	Average for December, 19X1	100
	Average for 19X2	107
	Average for December, 19X2	115

Monetary working capital is first computed:

	31 December	
	19X1	*19X2*
	£000	*£000*
Debtors	760	950
Less: Creditors	470	360
Monetary working capital	290	590

Calculation of MWCA (nearest £000):

1. Increase in book value of MWC (590 – 290) 300

2. Restate closing MWC $590 \times \dfrac{107}{115*}$ 549

3. Restate opening MWC $290 \times \dfrac{107}{100*}$ 310

4. Increase due to volume change 239

5. Increase due to inflation 61

*N.B. The calculations are based on the average indices for December because one month's credit is obtained from suppliers and allowed to customers.

The following journal entry records the MWCA in the current cost accounts (narrative omitted):

		£	£
Dr.	MWCA (reported in the CC profit and loss account)...	61,000	
Cr.	Current cost reserve (reported in the CC balance sheet)		61,000

6.5.5 The Gearing Adjustment A company's operating assets are usually financed partly by equity and partly by borrowing. Often companies will expect to maintain a fairly constant relationship between debt and equity finance, although levels will vary depending on the characteristics of the particular industry (see Chapter 8, section 6). The current cost operating adjustments considered above (namely the depreciation adjustment, COSA and MWCA) make full provision for the additional cost of replacing assets used up during the course of business activity, and this assumes that the entire burden will fall on the equity shareholders. In practice this will not be the case; in a company where loan creditors have financed 25% of the operating assets in the past, they will be expected to finance a similar proportion in the future. The gearing adjustment acknowledges this fact by adding back to profit an appropriate proportion of the current cost operating adjustments—in this case 25%.

The presentation of the gearing adjustment in the current cost profit and loss account is demonstrated in figure 6.3 of this chapter. It should be noted that, for presentation purposes, interest payable (less receivable) is deducted from the gearing adjustment, and the net difference is then added to or subtracted from the 'current cost operating profit'. Where the gearing adjustment exceeds interest payable, the surplus accrues to the shareholders who benefit from the fact that a portion of total business activity is financed from borrowed funds; where interest payable exceeds the gearing adjustment, the difference represents the net cost of borrowed funds. The gearing adjustment is calculated using the following formula:

$$\frac{\text{average net borrowings}}{\text{average net operating assets}} \times \frac{\text{total current cost}}{\text{operating adjustments}}$$

where:
1. *net borrowings* are defined as
   (i) all liabilities, other than proposed dividends and any items included when computing the MWCA (usually only trade creditors), less
   (ii) current assets, other than items included in the COSA and MWCA. Normally this will leave only cash, where there is any.
2. *net operating assets* are defined as fixed assets plus stock and monetary working capital.

3. *the average* is calculated from figures contained in the *current cost* balance sheets which set out the company's financial position at the beginning and the end of the accounting period.

Example 6.11

The following current cost accounts of Ogmore Ltd., for 19X1 have been prepared, except that a gap has been left for the gearing adjustment which has not yet been calculated.

Current Cost Profit and Loss Account

	£000	£000
Profit before interest and taxation on the historical cost basis .		5,620
Less: Current cost operating adjustments:		
COSA	600	
MWCA...	250	
Total working capital adjustment............................	850	
Depreciation adjustment...	700	
		1,550
Current cost operating profit...		4,070
Less: Gearing adjustment..	—	
Interest payable less receivable.................................	110	
		110
Current cost profit before tax...		3,960
Taxation		2,020
Current cost profit attributable to shareholders...................		1,940
Dividends..		500
Retained current cost profit for the year...........................		1,440
Retained current cost profits at 1 January........................		3,600
Retained current cost profits at 31 December.....................		5,040

Current Cost Balance Sheet

1980 £000		£000	£000
14,300	Fixed assets at current cost		18,600
7,900	*Less:* Accumulated depreciation		8,700
6,400			9,900
	Current Assets		
4,500	Stocks	5,200	
2,600	Debtors	3,700	
300	Cash at bank	200	
7,400		9,100	
	Less: Current liabilities		
400	Proposed dividend	500	
1,650	Taxation payable 30 September	1,700	
2,050	Creditors	2,800	
4,100		5,000	
3,300	Net current assets		4,100
9,700			14,000
	Financed by:		
2,000	Share capital...		2,000
2,370	Current cost reserve		4,910
3,600	Retained profits		5,040
7,970			11,950
530	Deferred taxation		850
1,200	12% Debenture		1,200
9,700			14,000

Notes: Monetary working capital consists of debtors and creditors.
Ignore advance corporation tax.

REQUIRED
Calculate the gearing adjustment for 19X1 and indicate the effect of incorporating it in the above current cost accounts.
Note: Calculations to the nearest £000.

Solution £000:

		19X0	19X1
1. Average net borrowing:			
Liabilities: Taxation payable 30 September		1,650	1,700
Deferred taxation		530	850
12% Debenture		1,200	1,200
		3,380	3,750
Assets: Cash at bank		300	200
		3,080	3,550

Average = (£3,080 + £3,550) ÷ 2 = £3,315.

		19X0	19X1
2. Average net operating assets:			
Assets: Fixed assets		6,400	9,900
Stocks		4,500	5,200
Monetary working capital		550	900
		11,450	16,000

Average = (£11,450 + £16,000) ÷ 2 = £13,725.

3. Gearing adjustment = $\dfrac{3,315}{13,725} \times 1,550$ (total current cost operating adjustments)

= 374

The gearing adjustment is credited to the profit and loss account and debited to the current cost reserve. The effect will be to increase 'current cost profit attributable to shareholders' by £374,000 and reduce current cost reserve by a similar amount.

6.6   RESPONSE TO SSAP16

The standard came into operation for accounting periods beginning on or after 1 January, 1980 and, on the whole, it has proved more acceptable than have previous attempts to implement a system of inflation accounting. Some of the main opposition has come from within the accounting profession itself, and in July, 1982 the members of the Institute of Chartered Accountants in England and Wales met to consider a motion calling for its immediate withdrawal. The motion was narrowly defeated and it is expected that some amendments will be required, in due course, to make SSAP16 more acceptable, but it seems likely that a revised version of CCA will continue as a permanent feature of the financial reporting procedures of many large companies. For the majority of companies, however, extensive current cost accounting requirements are unlikely to be introduced in the foreseeable future. The accounting systems of these companies are generally less sophisticated, and the additional cost of producing CCA data would be disproportionate to the benefits obtained.

One of the virtues of CCA is that it underlines the fact that accountancy is not a precise science and that the level of reported profit is heavily dependent on views held concerning the value of a company's assets. Historical cost accounts are familiar to users of accounting reports, and their contents are fairly well understood, but they do suffer from some important limitations which are discussed in section 3 of this chapter. Similarly, current cost accounts suffer from certain limitations, but they also display important virtues in areas where historical cost accounts reveal severe shortcomings. It is therefore perhaps appropriate for most large companies to continue with historical cost as the basis for their main accounts and with CCA data published as useful supplementary information.

6.7 QUESTIONS AND SOLUTIONS

Question 6.1 examines the effect on reported profit of using FIFO and LIFO as methods of valuing stock during a period of inflation. Questions 6.2 and 6.3 are designed to test students' ability to prepare current cost accounts containing the various adjustments described in this chapter.

Question 6.1 (Taken from the September, 1981 *Accountancy* paper).

Canvas Ltd. was incorporated in December 1975 to trade in a single product called 'Como'. The company began trading on 1 January 1976. Purchases and sales for the five years to 31 December, 1980, when the company discontinued 'Como' in favour of a more profitable line, were as follows:

	Purchases		Sales	
	Units	Price per unit £	Units	Price per unit £
1976	100	400	80	500
1977	100	450	80	550
1978	100	500	80	600
1979	100	550	80	650
1980	—	—	80	700

Required:

(a) Using (i) the first in first out (FIFO) basis and (ii) the last in first out (LIFO) basis of stock valuation, calculate the gross profit of Canvas Ltd. for each of the five years to 31 December, 1980. You should present your answer in columnar format.

(b) Compare the results of your calculations and consider the relative merits of FIFO and LIFO as bases for valuing stock during a period of inflation.

[20]

Solution

(a) (i)   *Trading and Profit and Loss Accounts, FIFO Basis*

	1976	1977	1978	1979	1980
	£	£	£	£	£
Sales	40,000	44,000	48,000	52,000	56,000
Opening stock	—	8,000	18,000	30,000	44,000
Purchases	40,000	45,000	50,000	55,000	—
Closing stock	(8,000)	(18,000)	(30,000)	(44,000)	—
Cost of goods sold	32,000	35,000	38,000	41,000	44,000
Gross profit	8,000	9,000	10,000	11,000	12,000

(ii)   *Trading and Profit and Loss Account, LIFO basis*

	1976	1977	1978	1979	1980
	£	£	£	£	£
Sales	40,000	44,000	48,000	52,000	56,000
Opening stock	—	8,000	17,000	27,000	38,000
Purchases	40,000	45,000	50,000	55,000	—
Closing stock	(8,000)	(17,000)	(27,000)	(38,000)	—
Cost of goods sold	32,000	36,000	40,000	44,000	38,000
Gross profit	8,000	8,000	8,000	8,000	18,000

(b) Total profits over 5 year period.

	FIFO	LIFO
	£	£
1976	8,000	8,000
1977	9,000	8,000
1978	10,000	8,000
1979	11,000	8,000
1980	12,000	18,000
	50,000	50,000

The total profits, over the five year period 1976–80, are the same in each case and the method of stock valuation employed merely affects the allocation of the profits between each of the five years.

When stock levels are rising, profits are lower under the LIFO method of stock valuation. This happens because, under LIFO, the most recent, or 'current', costs are matched against sales proceeds for the purpose of calculating profit, whilst items in stock are valued at the earliest purchase prices. The lower profits reported under LIFO, during each of the first four years, are compensated in year 5 when stocks are run down to zero and the 'old' costs are matched against sales.

At Canvas Ltd., it appears that the annual selling price has been increased by an amount sufficient to recover from customers the increased cost of purchases. Each year 80 items are sold at a price £100 in excess of the current purchase price. If the company could operate without holding stocks, a profit of $80 \times £100$, or £8,000, would be earned and reported each year. Where stocks are held, during a period of inflation, the difference between the original purchase price and current sales price is considered to comprise two elements—'real' profits and an inflationary element or holding gain. If Current Cost Accounting procedures are applied, FIFO, which is more likely to correspond with the actual movement of goods, reports a 'real' or current cost profit of £8,000 each year plus an annual holding gain of £1,000 in 1977, £2,000 in 1978, £3,000 in 1979 and £4,000 in 1980 (the holding gain arises from the items in stock, since their replacement cost rises by £50 per unit between the dates of purchase and sale). Under the historical cost system, LIFO does in fact report a profit of £8,000 for each of the years 1976–1979. It is for this reason that LIFO has sometimes been considered a more appropriate basis for matching the cost of purchases with sales during a period of rising prices. However, there are disadvantages with using LIFO. These include the following:

(i) It results in an artificially low balance sheet figure for stock, with a consequent understatement of capital employed.

(ii) It achieves the desired effect only when purchases exceed sales. When sales exceed purchases LIFO reports a profit figure which is even further removed from reality than that reported under FIFO, e.g. Canvas Ltd., 1980.

Examiners' comments:
Most common errors:

1. Closing stock of one period not brought forward as opening stock of the next.
2. Failure to appreciate the fact that total profits over the five year period are the same under either method.
3. Comments on the relative merits of the two methods during a period of inflation were superficial.

Question 6.2 (Taken from the September, 1982 *Accountancy* paper).

The summarised accounts of Tisch plc for 1981, prepared on the historical cost basis, are as follows:

PROFIT AND LOSS ACCOUNT, YEAR ENDED 31 DECEMBER 1981.

	£000s
Operating profit	355
Less: Interest payable	60
Net profit before taxation	295
Less: Corporation tax	150
Net profit after taxation	145
Add: Retained profit at 1 January 1981	180
Retained profit at 31 December 1981	325

BALANCE SHEET AT 31 December 1981

1980			
£000		£000	£000
1,000	Fixed Assets at cost		1,000
250	*Less:* Depreciation		375
750			625
	Current Assets		
600	Stock (December purchases)	900	
30	Cash	50	
630		950	
	Less: Current Liability		
100	Corporation tax payable	150	
530	*Net Current Assets*		800
1,280			1,425
	Financed by:		
700	Share capital (£1 ordinary shares)		700
180	Reserves		325
880			1,025
400	15% Debenture repayable 1990		400
1,280			1,425

The directors intend to publish supplementary accounts based on the provisions contained in Statement of Standard Accounting Practice No. 16 entitled 'Current Cost Accounting'.

The following additional information is provided:

1. Sales, purchases and other expenses accrue evenly during the year.

2. The company purchases and sells all goods on an immediate cash basis.

3. The fixed assets were purchased on 1 January 1979 and are being depreciated on the straight line basis over a period of eight years assuming a nil residual value. The depreciation charge in the 1981 accounts was, accordingly, £125,000.

4. The following price indices are provided for the company's stock and fixed assets:

	Stock	Fixed Assets
1 January 1979	*	100
Average for December 1980	130	*
31 December 1980	132	120
Average for 1981	136	124
Average for December 1981	144	*
31 December 1981	145	132

*Indices not provided.

5. The company's stocks turn over, on average, once a month.

Required:

The current cost profit and loss account and balance sheet of Tisch plc for 1981, (1980 comparatives need not be given) in accordance, so far as the information permits, with the principles contained in Statement of Standard Accounting Practice No. 16. The profit and loss account should contain a depreciation adjustment, a cost of sales adjustment and a gearing adjustment. The balance sheet should contain a current cost reserve.

NOTES: The monetary working capital adjustment is not applicable to the affairs of Tisch plc.

All calculations to the nearest £000.

[30]

Solution

Workings (nearest £000):
Fixed assets and the depreciation adjustment:
  (i) Depreciation adjustment

$$\text{CC charge } 125 \times \frac{124}{100} \dots\dots\dots\dots\dots\dots\dots\dots\dots\dots\dots\dots\dots\dots\dots\dots \quad 155$$

    Less: HC charge   125

                                                                    30

(ii) Current cost at 31 December   *1980*   *1981*

$1,000 \times \dfrac{120}{100}$ 1,200

$1,000 \times \dfrac{132}{100}$ 1,320

(iii) Accumulated CC charge at 31 December

$1,200 \times \dfrac{2}{8}$ 300

$1,320 \times \dfrac{3}{8}$ 495

                                                                         ———   ———
                                                                         900   825

(iv) Backlog depreciation
    Accumulated CC charge   495
    Less: HC charge to date   375
    Depreciation adjustment for 1981   30   405

                                                                                  ———
                                                                                   90

Stock and COSA:
  (i) COSA
    Increase in book value (900 – 600)   300

    Restate closing stock $900 \times \dfrac{136}{144}$ 850

    Restate opening stock $600 \times \dfrac{136}{130}$ 628
                                                                                  ———
    Increase due to volume change   222

    Increase due to inflation   78

  (ii) Current cost of: opening stock $600 \times \dfrac{132}{130}$ 609
                                                                                  ———
    closing stock $900 \times \dfrac{145}{144}$ 906

Gearing adjustment:

                                                                         1980   *1981*
  (i) Average net borrowing
    15% debentures   400   400
    Corporation tax   100   150
    Cash ....   (30)   (50)

                                                                         ———   ———
                                                                         470   500
    Average $(470 + 500) \div 2 = 485$
  (ii) Average net operating assets
    Fixed assets   900   825
    Stocks   609   906

                                                                         ———   ———
                                                                         1,509   1,731

    Average $(1,509 + 1,731) \div 2 = 1,620$
  (iii) Gearing adjustment $= \dfrac{485}{1,620} \times 108$ (depreciation adjustment + COSA) $= 32$

Current cost reserve:

Current Cost Reserve Account

Backlog depreciation	90	Revaluation of plant (1,320 – 1,000)	320
Gearing adjustment	32	COSA	78
Closing balance	282	Revaluation of stock (906 – 900)	6
	404		404

Current Cost Profit and Loss Account, 1981

	£000	£000
Historical cost profit before interest charges and taxation		355
Less: Current cost operating adjustments:		
COSA	78	
Depreciation	30	108
Current cost operating profit		247
Less: Interest payable	60	
Deduct gearing adjustment	32	
		28
Current cost profit before tax		219
Less: Corporation tax		150
Current cost profit attributable to shareholders		69
Add: Retained profit at 1 January, 1981		180*
Retained profit at 31 December, 1981		249

*Not amended to take account of previous years' operating adjustments due to the absence of necessary information.

Current Cost Balance Sheet, 31 December, 1981

	£000	£000
Fixed assets at current cost		1,320
Less: Accumulated depreciation		495
		825
Current assets		
Stock	906	
Cash	50	
	956	
Less: Current liability		
Corporation tax payable	150	
Net Current Assets		806
		1,631

Financed by:	£000
Share capital (£1 ordinary shares)	700
Retained profits	249
Current Cost Reserve	282
	1,231
15% Debenture repayable 1990...	400
	1,631

Examiner's comments
Most common errors: Same basic comments as for example 6.9.
In addition, the gearing adjustment caused a great deal of difficulty.

Question 6.3

Tanley Ltd., is a trading company. The summarised accounts for 19X2, prepared on the historical cost basis, are as follows:

Profit and Loss Account for 19X2

	£000
Net profit...	1,052
Corporation tax.....................................	418
Retained profit for year	634
Retained profit at 1 January, 19X2.............	1,016
Retained profit at 31 December, 19X2.........	1,650

Balance Sheet at 31 December, 19X2

	£000	£000	£000
Fixed assets at cost			4,000
Less: Accumulated depreciation			1,200
			2,800
Current assets:			
Stock		1,402	
Debtors		1,210	
Cash		50	
		2,662	
Less: Current liabilities:			
Creditors	994		
Taxation due 30 September, 19X3.............................	418	1,412	
Net current assets	—	—	1,250
			4,050

Financed by:	£000
Share capital..	2,400
Retained profit..	1,650
	4,050

The directors have decided to prepare current cost accounts for 19X2 based on the provisions contained in SSAP16.

The following information is provided:
  (i) The company's fixed assets were purchased on 1 January, 19X0 and have been depreciated on the straight line basis assuming a ten year life and zero residual value at the end of that period. The cost of similar *new* fixed assets at 31 December, 19X2 has been estimated at £6,000,000.
 (ii) Sales, purchases and other expenses accrue evenly during the year.
(iii) The company allows *two* months credit to customers and receives similar terms from suppliers. Closing stock represents *three* months' purchases.

The following figures appeared in the historical cost balance sheet of Tanley Ltd. at 31 December, 19X1:

	£000
Stock	1,172
Debtors	818
Creditors.........	750

(iv) The directors have decided to calculate the cost of sales adjustment (COSA) and the monetary working capital adjustment (MWCA) using 'the averaging method'. The following index numbers are appropriate for each of these calculations:

Average index for:	October–December, 19X1............	104
	November–December, 19X1.........	106
	19X2.......................................	118
	October–December, 19X2............	126
	November–December, 19X2.........	127
Index at:	31 December, 19X1....................	107
	31 December, 19X2....................	128

For the purpose of calculating the MWCA, the monetary working capital should be considered to consist of Creditors and Debtors.

REQUIRED
A current cost profit and loss account for 19X2, and balance sheet at 31 December, 19X2, so far as the information permits, in accordance with the principles contained in SSAP16.

NOTES: 1. Ignore the gearing adjustment.
        2. Calculations to the nearest £000.

Solution

Workings (nearest £000):
Fixed assets and the depreciation adjustment:

(i) Depreciation adjustment

CC charge 6,000 × 10%..	600
Less: HC charge	400
	200

(ii) Current cost at 31 December... 6,000

(iii) Accumulated CC charge at 31 December
6,000 × 10% × 3 (years) 1,800

(iv) Backlog depreciation

Accumulated CC charge..		1,800
Less: HC charge to date......................................	1,200	
Depreciation adjustment for 19X2	200	1,400
		400

Stocks and COSA:

(i) COSA

	£000	£000
Increase in book value (1,402 − 1,172)......................................		230
Restate closing stock $1,402 \times \dfrac{118}{126}$..	1,313	
Restate opening stock $1,172 \times \dfrac{118}{104}$	1,330	
Decrease due to volume change		17
Increase due to inflation		247

(ii) Current cost of closing stock $1,402 \times \dfrac{128}{126}$.............. 1,424

MWCA:

Increase in book value (1210 − 994) − (818 − 750)		148
Restate closing MWC $216 \times \dfrac{118}{127}$..	201	
Restate opening MWC $68 \times \dfrac{118}{106}$..	76	
Increase due to volume change...		125
Increase due to inflation		23

Current cost reserve:

Current Cost Reserve Account

Backlog depreciation......	400	Revaluation of plant (6,000 − 4,000)		2,000
Closing balance	1,892	COSA		247
		Revaluation of stock (1,424 − 1,402)......		22
		MWCA.......................................		23
	2,292			2,292

Current Cost Profit and Loss Account 19X2

	£000	£000
Historical cost profit before taxation		1,052
Less: Current cost operating adjustments:		
COSA	247	
MWCA	23	
Total working capital adjustment	270	
Depreciation adjustment	200	
		470
Current cost operating profit		582
Less: Corporation tax		418
Current cost profit attributable to shareholders		164
Add: Retained profit at 1 January, 19X2		1,016*
Retained profit at 31 December, 19X2		1,180

*Not amended to take account of previous years' operating adjustments due to the absence of necessary information.

Current Cost Balance Sheet at 31 December, 19X2

	£000	£000	£000
Fixed assets at current cost			6,000
Less: Accumulated depreciation			1,800
			4,200
Current assets:			
Stock		1,424	
Trade debtors		1,210	
Cash		50	
		2,684	
Less: Current liabilities:			
Trade creditors	994		
Taxation due 30 September, 19X3	418	1,412	
Net current assets			1,272
			5,472
Financed by:			
Share capital			2,400
Current cost reserve			1,892
Retained profit			1,180
			5,472

CHAPTER 7

Share and Business Valuation

7.1 INTRODUCTION

The financial interest of ownership in a company is shown in the capital account, and is equal to the recorded value of the net assets, that is, the value of the assets less all liabilities. In the balance sheet, the capital is presented in a manner appropriate to the undertaking. The balance sheet of the sole trader contains a single capital account, while the capital contribution of each individual partner is shown for a partnership. Ownership interest in a limited company is represented by its share capital and reserves, and the fraction of share capital held determines the proportion of the entity owned by each member. In all cases the value shown as capital, that is, the amount invested in the entity by ownership, arises from the application of accounting concepts and conventions and is most unlikely to reflect the *current* value of the company. For example, fixed assets are shown at their historical cost *less* accumulated depreciation, but the historical cost of an asset does not represent its current value, and accumulated depreciation does not accurately reflect the value lost during the period of ownership.

The value of a business can be obtained by using any one of a number of techniques, but a true price can only be established when a buyer and seller agree to an actual transaction. These techniques are applicable to all business forms, sole traders, partnerships and limited companies, but this Chapter concentrates on the valuation of shares in limited companies. To a large extent each company is unique, with its own individual blend of such factors as management, assets, products and potential, and the theoretical approaches to valuation give only a guide to the value to be placed upon the entity. The circumstances where valuation is required are:

1. *Taxation* Capital Transfer Tax is levied when a chargeable transfer of assets takes place, that is, a transfer which conveys a gratuitous benefit such as a gift. It is charged on the open market value of shares at the date of transfer, and so, when shares for

which no market value exists are transferred, a theoretical valuation must be undertaken. The need for such valuations also arises when an individual dies, since capital transfer tax is levied on the value of his estate. For instance, if the estate includes unquoted shares, a market value is only established if they are sold: if they are bequeathed their value must be estimated.

A liability to Capital Gains Tax arises on the disposal of chargeable assets, and the gift of shares in an unquoted company is a chargeable disposal which again gives rise to the need for a theoretical market valuation.

2. *Private Sale of Existing Shares*   The owner of shares in a company may wish to sell all or part of his holding. In the absence of a ready market, the price must be determined by negotiation between the prospective buyer and seller, and in these circumstances the theoretical valuation of the shares provides a useful basis for the discussion which takes place. The price finally agreed is the outcome of the bargaining process, but this is aided by an indication of a reasonable range within which the price is likely to be located. A common misconception which may be noted at this stage is that the sale of shares already in issue provides additional funds for the company. This is wrong; the only entry needed in the company's books records the change of ownership in the traded shares.

3. *Private Issue of New Shares*   A company may decide to raise finance by the issue of additional shares, and, unless these are purchased by the existing members as a 'rights issue', the price must be set so as not to dilute the value of the existing shares.

Example 7.1   The Determination of Issue Price for Shares

The Newcash Company Ltd. wishes to raise £150,000 by the issue of shares with a nominal value of £1 each for cash. Prior to the issue, the balance sheet fairly reflects the current value of net assets.

Newcash Company Ltd. Balance Sheet Prior to Issue

	£000		£000
Ordinary Shares of £1 each	200	Net Assets	300
Profit and Loss Account	100		
	300		300

Although the nominal value of each share is £1, its asset value is $\dfrac{£300,000}{200,000} = £1.50$, and so the new shares should be issued at £1.50 each: £1 is the nominal value and 50 pence is the share premium.

Newcash Company Ltd. Balance Sheet after Issue

	£000		£000
Ordinary Shares of £1 each.........	300	Net Assets	300
Share Premium.......................	50	Cash................	150
Profit and Loss Account............	100		
	450		450

All shares, both original and newly issued, are worth $\dfrac{£450{,}000}{300{,}000} = £1.50$ each.
The issue would not be taken up if the price had exceeded £1.50, which is the underlying value per share, while to price shares at less than £1.50 effectively transfers value from the existing to the new members. For example, 150,000 shares would have been issued if they were priced at £1, and the value of the old and new shares would become $\dfrac{£450{,}000}{350{,}000} = £1.29$.

It is most unlikely that the balance sheet shows fair current values, which is assumed in example 7.1, and so in practice the issue price of the shares must be determined theoretically.

4. *Flotation of Shares on the Stock Market* A market on the Stock Exchange for the shares of a company may be created either by owners selling their existing shares, or by the company issuing new shares. In either instance the shares must not be over- or under-priced. In the former case the shares would not be purchased, while the latter would create excessive demand and result in the vendor losing potential receipts. The price at which the market is established must be set carefully, and again, valuation techniques give a guide to the appropriate level.

5. *Business Amalgamations* The need for valuation arises where one company wishes to take over or merge with another. In a takeover, the price offered for the shares of the company to be acquired must be decided: too low an offer will cause the bid to fail; too high an offer will result in over-payment. When two companies merge, valuation is required to determine the relative interest in the combined entity to be given to each set of shareholders.

6. *Security* Shares may be lodged with a bank as security for a loan, and the bank will wish to ensure that they represent adequate cover. Unless the shares are quoted on the stock market, and therefore have an ascertainable price, the valuation must be made on a theoretical basis.

7.2 MARKETS FOR BUYERS AND SELLERS
The ease with which an ownership interest can be sold depends on

the type of business involved. A sole trader is free to dispose of his business in any way, but a partner cannot sell his share of the partnership without the agreement of the other partners. The freedom to transfer shares in a private limited company is restricted by its Articles of Association; in all cases the number of shareholders is limited to a maximum of fifty and the public cannot be invited to subscribe for shares. A public limited company has no restriction on the number of shareholders, and can invite the public to subscribe for shares: its shares may also be listed, that is, traded on a recognised stock exchange. There also exists, with the approval of the Stock Exchange, an Unlisted Securities Market, on which are traded shares of companies which are not large enough to warrant listing in the main market; only a limited number of companies have their shares traded in this market.

Where markets exist they provide contact between prospective buyers and sellers of shares, and the price established for each share equates supply and demand. The price of a share rises when demand exceeds supply and stabilises when equilibrium is restored as the result of demand being depressed, more sellers offering their shares on the market, or a combination of both these factors. Conversely, prices fall when supply exceeds demand. The causes of a change in the price of a particular share may be related to the individual company, the market as a whole, or a combination of both. The prospects of a single company may be re-appraised in the light of new information, such as the announcement of profits that are better than expected, and the price of its shares will react accordingly. A share price index shows the state of the market as a whole and reflects the general demand for equity shares which can be affected by a single occurrence, such as a cut in interest rates or a fall in the rate of inflation. Therefore, the price of an individual share is determined both by the state of the market as a whole and the prospects of the company itself: nevertheless, the price of a share may fall while the market index is rising, for example, as the result of the company's own dismal prospects outweighing the beneficial effect of a fall in interest rates, or it may rise when there is a general fall in share prices.

The value of quoted shares is readily available in the financial press, but it must be appreciated that the prices quoted relate to the relatively small proportion of total share capital which is sold and purchased at a particular time. Therefore, although the capitalised market value of a company is often calculated by multiplying the number of shares in issue by the quoted price per share, this is not the amount it would cost to acquire all of the share capital. An attempt to buy all of the shares of a company represents an increase in demand, drives up the price, and thereby increases the capitalised market value. Therefore, a reliable estimate of the value of the whole company is more likely to be obtained by the use of theoretical valuation techniques than by simply using the quoted price which results from trading in a small proportion of the company's shares.

It is more difficult for prospective buyers and sellers to meet when a company's shares are not traded in the market. A buyer may identify the area of activity in which it is desired to invest, actively seek an appropriate company and then approach its owners with an offer. In this exercise the buyer often seeks guidance from financial advisers, possibly bankers, who may carry out the procedure on the purchaser's behalf. Sellers are also likely to seek advice from the same sources, and so a point of contact is created. Alternatively, contact may be established through advertising, personal acquaintance, or trade connections. The identification and bringing together of a buyer and seller is only the first requirement, and, if the transaction is to take place, must be followed by the negotiation of an acceptable price. Theoretical valuations of the company will provide a useful basis for negotiation, and the size of the stake to be acquired must be borne in mind; the price per share is higher where the purchase of the whole company is contemplated than if only a minority holding is to be acquired.

The various methods of valuation are examined in sections 7.3 and 7.4.

7.3 BREAK-UP VALUATION

This valuation technique looks on a business as a collection of assets which may be sold off piecemeal, with the owners receiving any residue left after all other contributors of finance have been reimbursed. (For the order of repayment on liquidation, see Chapter 4, section 6.2).

The steps used to calculate the break-up value of a business are:
1. Estimate the sales proceeds of the individual assets.
2. Estimate the liquidation costs and identify the liabilities.
3. Find the value of the business entity by deducting 2 from 1.

Example 7.2   Valuation on the Break-up Basis

The summarised balance sheet of Vend Ltd. at 31 December, 19X1 is as follows:

Vend Ltd. Balance Sheet at 31 December, 19X1

	£000	£000
Fixed Assets:		
Freehold Premises:		1,000
Plant and Machinery		750
		1,750
Current Assets:		
Stock	250	
Debtors	125	
Cash at bank	25	
	400	
Less: Current Liabilities	150	
Working Capital		250
		2,000
Financed by:		
Ordinary Shares of £1 each		600
Retained Profits: Brought forward	650	
For 19X1	250	
		900
		1,500
10% Debentures Repayable 19X9		500
		2,000

It is estimated that in a forced sale on liquidation the expenses would be £50,000 and the assets would realise:

	£000
Premises	1,350
Plant and Machinery	700
Stock	300
Debtors	125
	2,475

The break-up value of the owners' interest is:

		£000	£000
Step 1	Estimated proceeds from sale of assets......................		2,475
	Cash at bank..		25
			2,500
Step 2	*Less:* Liquidation Expenses	50	
	Debentures..	500	
	Current Liabilities	150	
		—	700
Step 3	Value of Total Equity		1,800

On liquidation *each share* would be worth $\dfrac{£1,800,000}{600,000} = £3.$

Liquidation values are based on the assumption of a forced sale of individual assets in the second-hand market. This approach ignores the possibility that the assets together may be worth more than the sum of their individual values because of the particular manner in which the company uses them. Furthermore, when applied to a going concern, the assumption that the company is to be liquidated is contrary to the facts. Many factors indicate that Vend Ltd., in example 7.2, is a viable company: it has a healthy working capital and liquidity position; the capital structure is balanced; there is no pressure from imminent debenture repayment; and enough profit was made in 19X1 to add substantially to reserves. Another weakness is that the values placed on the costs and assets are estimates. The values of items such as cash and debtors may be assumed with confidence, but the sale value of premises and plant and machinery can only be truly ascertained in an actual sale. When liquidation is considered, it is also necessary to take into account any consequential costs which result from that course of action, such as redundancy payments or liabilities for breach of contract.

The break-up value of a business does, however, have some relevance for prospective buyers and sellers. It represents, for the seller, the minimum value at which the transaction should take place, especially if pessimistic valuations are applied to the assets. This is illustrated if the position of the owner of 95% of the equity shares of Vend Ltd. is considered, as a holding of this size gives the owner power either to sell the business as a going concern or to liquidate it. The owners of the remaining 5% of the shares cannot on their own exercise such a choice. No offer to acquire *the company* at less than £3 per share is acceptable since it is estimated that at least this sum would be received on liquidation. The buyer has a bargain if the vendor is ignorant of the break-up value of the company and accepts less than £3 per share, a possibility exploited by 'asset strippers' who, after acquisition, sell off the assets to realise a profit.

It is possible for the shares of a company listed on the Stock Exchange to be traded at less than break-up value, but the volume of shares dealt in to determine this price would not give control and so the buyer could not enforce sales of assets. A bid to acquire full control has to be made under Stock Exchange rules and the directors are then likely to inform shareholders of the underlying asset value. Ignorance of the current value of the asset backing for their shares, on the part of shareholders, largely stemmed from the use of historical cost for reporting purposes. The inclusion of more up to date valuations in the Directors' Report and the publication of current cost accounts by some companies (see Chapter 6) now keeps members better informed.

The break-up value also gives ownership an indication of the minimum amount of capital which could be obtained from the business for investment elsewhere. For example, if the valuations are accurate, the majority shareholder in Vend Ltd. would receive in cash, on liquidation, $95\% \times 600,000 \times £3 = £1,710,000$, and it might be possible to place this in a safe fixed-interest investment to yield, say, a 7% return, that is, £119,700 per annum. This possible return can then be weighed against that expected to be received from the investment in Vend Ltd. in the form of dividends and capital growth. The majority shareholder would be expected to retain his shares only if they produced a sufficiently high return to compensate for the additional risk of an equity investment. As Vend Ltd. is profitable, sale as a going concern is likely to yield a greater sum for alternative investment than liquidation and would also protect the interests of other people dependent on the company, such as employees and suppliers.

7.4   GOING CONCERN VALUATION

The liquidation, or break-up, value of a business is of little relevance other than to indicate a minimum price when sale as a going concern is contemplated. A company is a collection of assets which has been brought together with the aim of producing a profit which accrues to ownership. It also provides a return for those who input other factors, such as employees and providers of debenture or overdraft finance, who are rewarded by earned income and interest respectively. To value an entity as a going concern assumes that it will continue to operate with substantially the same combination of assets, employees and management as previously. There are a number of approaches to going concern valuation, and these are examined in sections 4.1–4.6 of this Chapter.

7.4.1 Book Value The balance sheet of an entity contains categorised details of all assets and liabilities and is an obvious starting point for a valuation. In the case of limited companies the annual report, including a balance sheet, is readily obtainable from the Registrar of Companies, irrespective of the company's wishes, while the accounts of partnerships and sole traders are not available for public inspection, and the owners therefore have control over their distribution.

An undertaking's book value is calculated from its balance sheet, which contains the values held in the books of account. The entries in the books are normally made at historical cost, and so this technique values assets at their historical cost, less accumulated depreciation in the case of fixed assets other than freehold land.

Example 7.3   Calculation of Book Value

The summarised balance sheet of Hist Ltd., a trading company, at 31 December, 19X1 is as follows:

Hist Ltd. Balance Sheet at 31 December, 19X1

	£000	£000
Fixed Assets:		
Land and Buildings: at cost	500	
less depreciation	150	
	—	350
Vehicles: at cost	300	
less depreciation	75	
	—	225
		575
Current Assets:		
Stock	400	
Debtors	150	
	550	
Less: Current Liabilities:		
Trade Creditors	125	
Overdraft	50	
	175	
Working Capital		375
		950
Financed by:		
Ordinary Shares of £1 each		350
Share Premium		150
Retained Profits		200
		700
8% Preference Shares		100
10% Debentures Repayable 19X7		150
		950

The company belongs to the owners of the ordinary shares, and the book value of their investment is £700,000 in total, or £2 per share. The value is calculated either as the total of ordinary share capital plus reserves, or as fixed assets plus working capital *less* non-equity debts, that is, (£000) 575 + 375 − 150 − 100 = 700.

The argument for the popular use of book value calculations is that the figures are factual, as they are based on historical cost: they are also easily obtainable as they come from routinely produced reports. However, there are serious deficiencies in this technique. These must be appreciated whenever it is applied.

The historical cost of an asset is the amount paid for it at the time of acquisition, and this is not relevant to a current valuation. A company which has been established for a number of years has, in its books, assets which have been purchased at various times throughout its life and they are recorded at cost. The impact of inflation means that, in general, historical cost is not an accurate measure of current value, and becomes less accurate the longer an asset is held. The effects of inflation have called into question the relevance of accounts prepared on the historical cost basis (see Chapter 6), and so their use for valuation purposes must also be doubted. Even in the absence of price movements, the written-down value of fixed assets does not measure their current value. Accumulated depreciation is deducted from the historical cost of fixed assets, other than freehold land, in order to recognise their decline in value while in use by the business. The depreciation charge is an arbitrary apportionment of the cost of an asset over its estimated life and is not intended to reflect accurately the loss in value of the assets during an accounting period. It is common for firms to hold in their books fixed assets which are fully depreciated, but are still providing useful service, and so must have a value greater than zero.

It is not only fixed assets which are undervalued by the historical cost convention in times of inflation: the cost of stock shown in the books is also unlikely to reflect its current value, both because the cost figures are not current and because a market valuation will include an element of profit. However, the discrepancy is not so great, as stocks are held for a shorter period of time than fixed assets and the historical cost is more recent. On the other hand, the debtors figure in a properly prepared set of accounts will be acceptable as the amount to be received (it can be assumed that adequate provision has been made for bad debts). The values of non-equity liabilities in the balance sheet are shown at the amount of cash owed and so accurately reflect the indebtedness of the business.

A further criticism of the book value basis of valuation is that it ignores the possible existence of intangible assets such as goodwill. The manner in which a business combines the factors of production under its control may enable it to earn a profit in excess of that which is expected from the individual assets. Excess, or super, profit is earned because, for example, the firm has a good reputation, location or contacts which should be taken into account in a valuation. The ability to earn an annual super profit is therefore attributed to the possession of goodwill.

Example 7.4 The Identification of Goodwill

Washer, a sole trader, regularly makes an annual profit of £15,000. His summarised balance sheet, which fairly reflects the current value of the assets, is as follows:

Washer: Balance Sheet at 31 December, 19X1

	£	£
Freehold Premises		10,000
Stock	5,000	
Debtors	3,000	
Cash	1,500	
	9,500	
Less: Current Liabilities	2,500	
Working Capital		7,000
		17,000
Capital Account—Washer		
Balance at 1.1.19X1		17,000
Profit for 19X1		15,000
Drawings for 19X1		(15,000)
Balance at 31.12.19X1		17,000

Assume that Washer could cease to work as a sole trader and obtain employment at a salary of £8,000 per annum; that he could let the premises for £2,000 per annum; and that surplus cash could be invested at an annual rate of interest of 8%. These sums represent the opportunity cost to Washer of the inputs to his business, namely, his labour, the premises, and working capital. The excess return derived from his business each year is therefore:

	£	£
Profit..		15,000
Less: Foregone: Salary.....................	8,000	
Rent.......................	2,000	
Interest $(7,000^* \times 8\%)$.	560	
		10,560
Super profit...................................		4,440

*The approximate amount Washer would obtain by realising his investment in working capital.

Washer obtains an income from his business £4,440 greater than he would receive if the inputs used by it were put to their next most profitable use. In the event of Washer selling the firm as a going concern, he would require payment not only for the tangible assets, but also for the goodwill which enables the extra profit to be earned, provided that profitability can be maintained by the new owner and does not derive from a personal attribute of Washer which cannot be transferred to the purchaser.

Purchased goodwill usually appears in a company's balance sheet at historical cost less any amounts written off. (See Chapter 3, section 7 for the treatment of goodwill in the accounts of limited companies).

7.4.2 Replacement Cost   The valuation of a business at the book value of its assets has little relevance: the historical costs, on which book values are based, are usually out of date because of the impact of both general inflation and the specific price changes related to individual assets. To make an asset-based valuation in terms of current prices, the assets must be valued at their replacement cost. A person who considers buying an existing business has the option of assembling for himself an identical collection of assets: goodwill apart, he would accordingly be unwilling to pay more to obtain the assets through the purchase of an existing business. The maximum price the buyer will be willing to pay is therefore calculated by ascertaining, in physical terms, the assets owned by the company and then, possibly with expert advice from a professional valuer, estimating their replacement cost. In most cases the identification of assets can only be achieved with the co-operation of the company although sometimes the major assets may be clearly visible, such as the shops owned by a retailing company, which may even advertise a list of branches.

Example 7.5 Replacement Cost Valuation

The share capital of Shelf Ltd., a profitable company, is owned in equal proportions by four brothers who are also the company's directors. The brothers are nearing retirement age and wish to sell the company as a going concern. Two of the brothers consider that the values shown in the balance sheet should be used to calculate the price at which to offer to sell the company, while the other two feel that the replacement cost is appropriate. You are required to offer advice to the brothers on the basis of the following information:

(i)   *Shelf Ltd. Balance Sheet at 31 December, 19X1*

	£000	£000
Fixed Assets:		
Freehold Premises		100
Plant and Machinery at written down value		200
		300
Current Assets:		
Stock..	75	
Debtors	50	
Cash..	10	
	135	
Less: Current Liabilities	65	
Working Capital		70
		370
Financed by:		
Ordinary Shares of £1 each		100
Retained Profits...		170
		270
Secured Loan		100
		370

(ii) The replacement costs of the assets, based on expert advice are:

	£000
Freehold Premises	250
Plant and Machinery.........	500
Stock...........................	80

VALUATIONS
  (i) Book Value: £270,000 or £2.70 per share
  (ii) Replacement Cost

	£000	£000
Freehold Premises		250
Plant and Machinery		500
Stock		80
Debtors		50
Cash		10
		890
Less: Current Liabilities	65	
Secured Loan	100	
	—	165
		725

The total replacement cost of the company is £725,000 or £7.25 per share.

ADVICE
It is clear that the replacement cost value of £7.25 per share is far higher than that based on the book value, of £2.70. To sell the company for £270,000 charges the buyer the same amount, in cash terms, for the assets as was paid by the company, *less* depreciation on plant and machinery. It would cost a prospective purchaser £890,000 to acquire a similar set of assets, which would be reduced to an outlay of £725,000 if the same contribution is obtained from loans and current liabilities. In these circumstances, it is fair to expect a buyer to meet the replacement costs of the assets. However, earnings valuations (sections 4.3 to 4.6 of this Chapter) are even more relevant to a profitable company such as this.

The use of replacement cost, as above, provides a current valuation of the company's tangible assets, but does not recognise the possible existence of goodwill. A set of assets identical to those used by an existing profitable company could be assembled, but the owner would not necessarily make a similar profit. It may not be possible to attract a similar skilled work force, establish trading contacts, or obtain a management team with the same ability. Where a business earns a profit in excess of the opportunity cost of the inputs of ownership valued at replacement cost, it possesses goodwill: so the use of replacement cost of only the *tangible* assets results in under-valuation. However, even goodwill can be created, *at a cost*, for instance, by means of advertising and special offers to attract customers who must then be retained by providing an efficient service.

In different circumstances replacement cost may over-value a company (see Question 7.1). For instance, it is possible that a company fails to earn an adequate profit, but, because the investment in fixed assets represents a 'sunk' cost, it continues to trade. The trading conditions and expectations which existed when the firm was established may not have transpired, and yet the nature of the assets gives rise to a high current replacement cost. The acquisition of the present combination of business assets would not be repeated, however, because they could not be used to yield an adequate return. In these circumstances, the replacement cost of the assets over-values the company.

The introduction of the requirement to publish Current Cost Accounts for some companies (see Chapter 6) makes available information on the current replacement cost of assets, this being the valuation base required by SSAP 16. The current replacement cost of fixed assets shown in accounts prepared under SSAP 16 must, however, be interpreted with care when used for valuation purposes. The replacement cost is that of a new asset, not one which has been used for the same period of time as that owned by the company, and the annual depreciation charge is based on the asset's anticipated life. The written down replacement cost of the asset is therefore unlikely to reflect the actual replacement cost of an asset in the same condition as that owned by the company. A further limitation of these accounts for valuation purposes is the exclusion of goodwill which has been generated by the operations of the company. (The Companies Act 1981 allows goodwill to be shown only if it is acquired for valuable consideration.)

Valuations based on assets measure the resources possessed by companies, but the purpose of owning these is to produce income. When a company is bought, the purchaser acquires not just a collection of assets, but their earning potential, and, therefore, the techniques of valuation which follow are generally considered more relevant.

7.4.3 Earnings Yield Valuation Companies use assets in conjunction with other inputs, such as labour, to earn profits, and when a company is sold as a going concern the new owner acquires the right to the profits made after the date of purchase. The return made by a company can be expressed as the 'Earnings Yield' which relates the profit to the amount invested. For example, if a company has a value of £16 million and makes an annual profit of £2.4 million, its earnings yield is $\frac{2.4}{16} \times 100 = 15\%$. The value of a company on the earnings yield basis is the value of the stream of profit, or earnings, which the company is expected to generate. Calculation of an earnings yield value involves three steps:

1. Predict the future maintainable profits (annual earnings) of the company being valued.
2. Identify the required earnings yield by reference to the results of similar companies.
3. Apply the earnings yield to future profits using the formula:

$$\frac{\text{Annual Earnings (from step 1)}}{\text{Required Earnings Yield (from step 2)}}$$

Example 7.6 Earnings Yield Valuation

A company is expected to generate future profits of £24,000 per annum. What is its value based on its earnings yield if investments of this type are expected to give an annual return of 12%?

VALUATION

Step 1 Annual Earnings: £24,000.

Step 2 Required Earnings Yield: $12\% = \frac{12}{100} = 0.12$.

Step 3 Value: $\frac{£24,000}{0.12} = £200,000.$

The buyer could be expected to pay £200,000 to obtain the right to receive annual profits of £24,000, representing a return of 12%.

The profit made by a company is given in its profit and loss account. However, this figure relates to a past accounting period, whereas the earnings yield value of a company should be based on its ability to make profits in the future. To predict likely future earnings, information from past years is a useful starting point, but it must be adjusted to take account of any factors which cause distortions and any changes which are anticipated in the future.

Example 7.7 Profit Adjustment

The directors of Chair Ltd., who also own the company, have been approached in 19X4 by Table plc with a takeover offer. The directors of Table plc suggest that the price is the capitalised value of the expected future earnings of Chair Ltd. on the assumption that the takeover is completed. This is agreed by the directors of Chair Ltd. who consider that the average of the last three years' profits after adjustment is appropriate and produce the following information:

(i) Profit and Loss Account Extracts:

	19X1 £000	19X2 £000	19X3 £000
Net profit	300	281	261
Directors' remuneration	70	80	90
Overdraft interest	20	15	10
Depreciation	100	100	100

(ii) A provision was made in 19X0 against a single doubtful debt of £50,000, but this did not materialise and the provision was written back in 19X1.

(iii) Directors' remuneration has been increased to reduce tax liability; if it acquires the company, Table plc would reduce the cost to £60,000 per annum.

(iv) The equipment of Chair Ltd. is old and Table plc would soon have to replace it at an estimated cost of £2 million. The expected life of the new plant is ten years.

(v) Table plc is the holding company of a large group and would give Chair Ltd. access to group financial resources. This would enable the overdraft to be repaid, but an annual intra-group charge of £12,000 would be made for treasury services.

REQUIRED

(i) Calculate the average profit of Chair Ltd. for the past three years after making any adjustments considered necessary to reflect the company's likely future earnings if taken over by Table plc.

(ii) Capitalise the adjusted average profit at an earnings yield of 17% per annum.

Solution

(i) *Profit Adjustment*

	19X1 £000	19X2 £000	19X3 £000
Net profit before adjustment	300	281	261
Bad debt written back 19X1	(50)	—	—
Reduction in directors' remuneration	10	20	30
Increase in depreciation	(100)	(100)	(100)
Finance charge adjustment	8	3	(2)
Adjusted annual profit	168	204	189

$$\text{Summary:} \quad \begin{array}{ll} 19X1 & 168 \\ 19X2 & 204 \\ 19X3 & 189 \\ \hline & 561 \end{array}$$

Average profit: $\dfrac{561}{3} = £187,000$

(ii) *Earnings Yield Valuation*

$$\frac{\text{Earnings}}{\text{Yield}} = \frac{187,000}{0.17} = £1,100,000$$

Many of the details required for the earnings yield valuation, such as the imminence of plant replacement and consequent change in depreciation charge, are only accurately ascertainable with the help of the business being valued. Therefore, the ability of the valuer to prepare an accurate forecast will depend on access to relevant information, and this will be determined by the relationship between the valuer and the business. Co-operation exists where the valuation is undertaken at the instigation of the company itself, but no help would be given to a valuer working for a competitor who is preparing an unwelcome takeover bid. Even where full assistance is given, the forecast of future earnings is an estimate which is unlikely to prove accurate, and, the greater the uncertainty attached to achieving targets, then the greater is the risk associated with the investment. Results achieved in the past will not necessarily reflect the future earnings of a business: ideally the estimate of future earnings should be derived from budgets based on detailed forecasts of activity, costs and revenues (see Chapter 10), although these are still liable to error.

The value of the business bears an inverse relationship to the earnings yield used for capitalisation. For instance, an earnings stream of £10,000 per annum capitalised at 10% is worth £100,000; capitalised at 20% the value is £50,000. This places great importance on the determination of the appropriate yield, and, in general, the higher the risk attached to an income stream, the greater is the earnings yield required and hence the lower the capitalised value. The earnings yield of a listed company is calculated from its quoted market price and its most recently reported profit, and this may be used as the basis for an earnings yield valuation of an unlisted company. However, earnings yields vary between listed companies because they are of different sizes, do not undertake the same trade, have different locations or levels of efficiency, or possess dissimilar risk levels. The valuation of an unlisted company should therefore be based on the earnings yield of a listed company which approximates to it, so far as is possible, in terms of size, trade, and risk.

The market price of the listed company, or companies, used to calculate the earnings yield is influenced by general economic factors which affect the individual share, a sector of the market, or the market as a whole. Similarly, the profit figures used for the calculation may be distorted because of exceptional circumstances. To avoid the selection of an unrepresentative earnings yield, the average of a number of measurements taken at different times for a number of companies may be used. Alternatively, an anticipated earnings yield can be agreed on as part of overall discussions on valuation, although these are still likely to be based on yields observed in the market.

7.4.4 Price/Earnings (P/E) Ratio Valuation The P/E ratio is calculated for listed companies, and relates the market price of a company's share capital to its most recently reported earnings. It is calculated by using the formula:

$$P/E \ ratio = \frac{Market \ Price \ of \ One \ Share}{Earnings \ per \ Share}$$

The market price of a share is found in the list published after each day's trading on the stock market, and the value of earnings per share must be given in the published accounts of listed companies. For example, a company with five million issued shares and earnings of £1.2m. has an earnings per share of $\dfrac{£1.2m.}{5m.} = 24$ pence. If its market price per share is 180 pence, then it has a P/E ratio of $\dfrac{180}{24} = 7.5$, that is, the value of each share is 7.5 times the earnings related to that share. There is a direct link between the P/E ratio and the earnings yield of a company:

$$Earnings \ Yield = \frac{1}{P/E \ ratio} \times 100$$

This is illustrated by the use of the figures given above:

$$Earnings \ Yield = \frac{24}{180} \times 100 = 13.3\%; \ or \ \frac{1}{7.5} \times 100 = 13.3\%$$

The P/E ratio is therefore the inverse of the earnings yield, and they produce exactly the same company valuations. For example, the value of the company for which details are given above can be calculated in either of the following ways:

P/E Ratio: 7.5 (P/E Ratio) × £1.2m. (Earnings) = £9m.

Earnings Yield: $\dfrac{£1.2m. \ (Earnings)}{0.133 \ (Earnings \ Yield)} = £9m.$

An unlisted company can therefore be valued by multiplying its earnings by the P/E ratio of a similar, but listed, company. To give consistency, the earnings of both companies must be measured on the same basis: the listed company's earnings per share given in its accounts are calculated on earnings before tax and extraordinary items, and the same basis must be used for the unlisted company's profit. Distortions which arise from the use of a single company's result are avoided by the calculation of an average ratio for a number of similar companies over a number of years.

Example 7.8   Valuation by P/E Ratio

The directors of Door Ltd. in 19X4 wish to value the company on the basis of the P/E ratios of similar, listed, companies. The average annual earnings of Door Ltd. for the previous three years are £150,000 before tax and extraordinary items and after adjustments considered necessary by the directors. The P/E ratio of the listed companies to be used for the calculations are:

	19X1	19X2	19X3
Glass plc.............	6.4	7.1	6.9
Rock plc.............	5.5	5.8	6.1
Stone plc	6.9	6.6	7.2

As each of the three companies is considered to be equally comparable to Door Ltd. in terms of size, type of business etc., you are required to calculate the value of Door Ltd. on the basis of a single average P/E ratio.

Calculation

The P/E ratios of the three listed companies are averaged as follows:

	Average P/E Ratio 19X1—19X2—19X3
Glass plc.............	6.8
Rock plc.............	5.8
Stone plc	6.9
	___
	19.5
	___

The average P/E ratio is $\dfrac{19.5}{3} = 6.5$

The value of Door Ltd. is: $150,000 \times 6.5 = £975,000$.

The apparent precision of the P/E Ratio and Earnings Yield as a basis for company valuation must not be allowed to mask their limitations. A major matter to consider is the extent to which the listed companies used for valuation truly compare with the company to be valued. Listed companies offer significant advantages to their members as their shares are marketable and their large size gives them an element of stability: these advantages make their shares more desirable, and therefore more highly priced, than those of an unlisted company. The P/E ratio of an unlisted company is expected to be less than that for a corresponding listed company, and so the use of unadjusted quoted ratios can result in over-valuation.

Consideration must also be given to the size of the holding valued. The price of shares in a listed company is set to equate supply and demand, but in routine trading only a small proportion of a listed company's share capital changes hands. A bid to buy control of a listed company has to be well above the market price to attract those shareholders reluctant to sell at the current rate. The P/E ratio of a company increases with a rise in price, and so the ratio calculated with the day-to-day market price is less than would result from the use of the price needed to buy enough shares to give control. To value the whole of an unlisted company's share capital with a P/E ratio derived from transactions of non-controlling holdings gives rise to under-valuation.

It must also be remembered that the calculation of the P/E ratio uses the most recent figure for earnings and the current market price. Immediately prior to the publication of new information, the figures used for earnings are of considerable age, and, if trading conditions have changed, are of little relevance to current valuation. A final matter for consideration is the fact that the value of a business should be based on its future earnings whereas the P/E ratio, and earnings yield, utilise figures for profit made in the past. The accuracy of these earnings based valuations, therefore, relies on the extent to which the past results of a company reflect its future. The method of capitalisation assumes that the same level of earnings is achieved in every future year, and this is an unlikely occurrence even where past results are adjusted for anticipated changes. However, these limitations do not invalidate P/E ratio valuations as useful reference points in negotiations and discussions about value.

7.4.5 Dividend Yield Valuation Ownership of shares in a company entitles the holder to receive any dividends which are declared. For an individual member to be able to influence the size of a company's dividend, enough shares must be held to enable significant voting power to be wielded; the owner of less than fifty per cent of the equity shares can always be out-voted by the remainder, although significant influence may be exerted by the holder of a large, but non-controlling, block of shares when the remainder are spread over a large number of small investors (see 'Associated Companies' in Chapter 5). When valuing a small shareholding (which cannot influence the proportion of earnings to be distributed), the calculation should be based on the dividends, rather than earnings, per share.

The dividend yield of a listed company is expressed as a percentage, i.e.:

$$\frac{\text{Dividend for the year (pence per share)}}{\text{Quoted market price}} \times 100$$

The dividend for the year will include any interim dividend as well as the final dividend.

If a company pays an interim dividend of 5 pence per share, declares a final dividend of 10 pence and has a quoted share price of 130 pence, 'cum div', its dividend yield is:

$$\frac{10+5}{130-10} \times 100 = \frac{15}{120} \times 100 = 12.5\%$$

As long as the share price remains 'cum div', a buyer of the shares acquires the right to receive the final dividend. Once this dividend is paid the price falls to the share's underlying capital value, in this instance 120 pence. It is then termed 'ex dividend' and will be quoted 'ex div' or 'xd' in the financial press.

The use of the dividend yield to value shares in an unlisted company rests on the assumption that the relationship between value and dividend is the same as for the listed company, or companies, chosen for the calculation. Listed companies in the same area of trade are selected, and, to avoid the application of undue weight to a single observation, the average dividend yield may be calculated for a number of companies over a number of years. The dividend of the unlisted company is capitalised at the average yield of the listed companies to give a present value in a manner similar to that used for the earnings yield valuation, namely:

1. Identify the annual dividend of the company being valued.
2. Identify the required dividend yield.
3. Apply the dividend yield to the annual dividend using the formula:

$$\frac{\text{Annual dividend (from step 1)}}{\text{Required dividend yield (from step 2)}}$$

Example 7.9 Dividend Yield Valuation

Mill Ltd. has an issued share capital of 100,000 ordinary shares of 50 pence each, the ownership of which is concentrated in the hands of the directors, although some members of their families hold small numbers of shares. The company has regularly paid a total annual dividend of £25,000, and expects to maintain this level of distribution in the future.

You are required to calculate the value of 250 shares in Mill Ltd. on the dividend yield basis. The average dividend yield for listed companies in the same line of business is 11.2%.

Calculation

1. Dividend per share $= \dfrac{£25,000}{100,000} = 25$ pence.

2. Dividend Yield $= 11.2\%$.

3. Value of one share $= \dfrac{25}{0.112} = 223.2$ pence.

   Value of 250 shares $= 250 \times 223.2 = £558$.

The assumption that the dividend policies of listed and unlisted companies are the same is questionable. In practice the private company is likely to distribute a smaller proportion of its earnings, with the result that it is undervalued by this technique. This difference is compensated to some extent by the fact that more risk may be deemed to attach to the dividends of small companies and so they are expected to offer a higher yield on the shareholders' investments.

The disparity between the dividend policies of unlisted and listed companies is caused by a number of factors. The listed company tries to prevent falls in its share price which leave it vulnerable to a takeover bid and unable to attract additional investment; a generous dividend policy helps maintain a high share price. Unlisted companies, and especially private companies, find it more difficult to attract external funds, for example, because they are not so well known, and are reliant on retained earnings to finance development. The need to plough back into the business a large proportion of earnings leaves limited amounts available for distribution. In many cases the directors of private companies are also major shareholders and there are tax advantages if they take increased directors' remuneration in lieu of dividends. This reduces the company's corporation tax liability and, in the hands of the directors, their remuneration is treated as earned, instead of investment, income and thereby avoids an income tax surcharge.

One drawback of the dividend yield valuation of an unlisted share is that it is usually based on past dividends, and these may not be representative of future expectations, which should help determine the current price. A company may pay small current dividends, but still be able to justify a high share price if it is retaining a large proportion of its earnings to finance profitable developments leading to a higher level of future distributions.

It is unlikely that a company will pay the same dividend each year, and a successful company may be expected to increase its dividend annually. Where it is expected that a *listed* company's dividends in cash terms will grow on average by $G_1\%$ per annum, the dividend yield is calculated by the formula:

$$\text{Dividend Yield (Y)} = \frac{\text{Current Dividend per Share (D)}}{\text{Market Price per Share (P)}} + G_1$$

$$\left(\text{more briefly, } Y = \frac{D}{P} + G_1\right)$$

To find the value (V) of an *unlisted* company, on the assumptions that it has the same dividend yield (Y) as the listed company and its own dividends will grow by $G_u\%$ per year, the above formula is transformed to give:

$$V = \frac{D}{Y - G_u}$$

Example 7.10 Dividend Yield Valuation with Growth

Calculate the value of one share of Grass Ltd. on the basis of the following information:

	Grass Ltd.	Moss plc (a listed company)
Market price per share.............................	—	560 pence
Current dividend per share	25 pence	50 pence
Expected average annual growth of dividends	8%	5%

Calculation

Dividend Yield of Moss plc $= \dfrac{50}{560} + 0.05 = 13.9\%.$

Value of one share of Grass Ltd. $= \dfrac{25}{0.139 - 0.08} = 424$ pence.

Valuation on the basis of the dividend yield is particularly relevant for preference shares as they carry a fixed rate of dividend. The ownership of preference shares normally gives only the right to the stated dividend, although the risk exists that the dividend may not be paid because of the lack of distributable profits or the fact that the company does not have sufficient cash available.

Cumulative preference shares reduce risk, as the right to receive unpaid dividends is carried forward to future years. The current value of preference shares is the value placed on the dividend stream, which is capitalised to give a return commensurate with the amount of risk. As some risk exists with any corporate investment, the required return is higher than for relatively safe investments such as government securities. It is however lower than for equity shares; these carry greater risk as they do not receive any dividends until the claims of preference shareholders are satisfied.

Example 7.11 Preference Share Valuation

Lawn Ltd. has in issue 100,000 preference shares of £1 each which carry a dividend of 8%. The 6% preference shares of Seed plc with a nominal value of £1 each have a market price of 60 pence per share and carry the same risk as those of Lawn Ltd.

You are required to calculate the value of one preference share of Lawn Ltd.

Calculation

The dividend yield set by the market for Seed plc is $\frac{6}{60} \times 100 = 10\%$.

The ownership of 1 preference share of Lawn Ltd. gives 8 pence per year dividend;

8 pence per year capitalised at $10\% = \frac{8}{0.1} = 80$ pence.

The value of one preference share of Lawn Ltd. is 80 pence.

7.4.6 Valuation Based on Cash Flows

The most theoretically acceptable method of valuation is to examine the cash flows which result from the acquisition of the whole, or part of, a business. The valuation takes place as follows:

Step 1 Predict the prospective buyer's annual cash flow on the assumption that the acquisition *does not* take place.

Step 2 Predict the prospective buyer's annual cash flow on the assumption that the acquisition *does* take place.

Step 3 Calculate the difference between the cash flows found in Steps 1 and 2 and reduce it to a *present value* (see Chapter 11, section 5.3).

The complexity of Step 2 compared with Step 1 depends on the size of the holding acquired. A minority holding yields only dividends; total ownership gives access to the cash flow measured by earnings plus depreciation and adjusted for acquisitions and disposals of fixed assets, taxation and capital redemptions. In the latter case, the forecasts are very difficult to make with sufficient accuracy for an adequate number of years, especially if access to the company's records is denied. Also, in both cases, it is difficult to determine the rate at which to discount the cash flows to present values.

7.5 THE VALUATION OF MINORITY AND MAJORITY INTERESTS

The relevance of particular business valuation techniques to individual circumstances is determined, in part, by the extent of control given by the holding to be valued. There exists a number of classes of share capital, and not all of them carry voting rights. For example, there are specific non-voting ordinary shares, and preference shares usually bestow no say in how the business is run so long as dividends are paid. A majority holding of shares is defined, for the purpose of this section, as one which gives the owner over 50% of the votes, and hence control; a minority holding is less than 50%. Where a number of minority shareholders, who together own more than 50% of the votes, act in concert for valuation purposes, the considerations appropriate to a single majority shareholder apply.

Ownership of a majority shareholding gives control over the company, including its distribution policy and whether it is to be liquidated. The fact that the management of companies is the responsibility of the directors is irrelevant as the board can be changed by a majority shareholder with whose wishes it does not comply. A majority interest in a going concern is, therefore, properly valued on the basis of the earnings yield, or the P/E ratio, as the disposition of earnings between distribution and retention is at the owner's discretion. The liquidation basis of valuation is appropriate where it cannot be assumed that the business is a going concern, or the majority shareholder wishes to ascertain the minimum value of his investment. Dividend yield valuation is not relevant in circumstances where the level of dividend is effectively set by the majority shareholder, as such control gives access to the company's earnings and assets.

The owner of a minority interest is the passive recipient of dividends and is unable to influence their size without support from other members. Accordingly, the dividend yield approach to valuation is appropriate for small blocks of shares. Valuations based on earnings and assets are of little relevance to minority shareholders as they are not able to gain access to them for the purpose of enhanced distributions. However, for *listed* companies the market attaches great importance to underlying earnings, as evidenced by the popular use of the P/E ratio by investment analysts, and it can be argued that the value of a listed share based on long-term considerations reflects earnings rather than dividends. A listed company will normally distribute a larger proportion of its earnings because the continued maintenance of low dividends is likely to depress the share price and attract a takeover bid. If existing shareholders see no prospect of higher dividends, the acquisition of a majority interest in these circumstances gives the bidder access to the earnings at a relatively cheap price.

It is possible for the balance of voting power to alter over time, and so, when consideration is given to the valuation of majority and minority interests, it is necessary to examine whether the position is likely to change in the future. There are a number of ways in which additional voting power may be created:

1. Share Option Schemes The employees of a company, especially the directors, may, as an incentive, be given the option to purchase additional shares at a pre-determined price at some time in the future. A profit is made if, between the grant of the option and its exercise, the share value rises to a level above the agreed price, presumably as a result of the efforts of those holding the options.

2. Share Warrants These may be attached to, for example, the issue of loan stock to make it more attractive to investors. Warrants give the right to apply for a future issue of shares at a pre-determined price.

3. Convertible Securities The owners of convertible debentures and convertible preference shares have the option to convert them to ordinary shares at a set rate. The resulting alteration of the capital structure also changes the earnings available for equity shares.

Example 7.12 Convertible Securities

Tree Ltd. was established on 1 January, 19X1 and raised capital by the issue of:
- (a) 2 million £1 ordinary shares at a premium of 50 pence per share.
- (b) 1 million 7% convertible preference shares at their face value of £1 each. They may be converted to ordinary shares at the rate of 3 ordinary shares for every 4 preference shares.
- (c) A 10% convertible debenture for £1 million which is convertible to 500,000 ordinary shares.

In both 19X1 and 19X2 the earnings of the company before interest and tax were £850,000, corporation tax was 50%, and a 12% ordinary dividend was paid.

The holders of the preference shares and debenture exercised their options to convert on 1 January, 19X2.

You are required to:
1. Prepare the summarised balance sheets of Tree Ltd. on 31 December, 19X1 and 31 December, 19X2.
2. Calculate the value of one ordinary share at each balance sheet date if the required earnings yield, based on after tax profit available for ordinary shareholders, is 5%.

Solution

1.

Tree: Balance Sheet at 31 December

	19X1 £000	19X2 £000
Net assets	5,065	5,100
Financed by:		
Ordinary Shares of £1 each	2,000	3,250 (working 1)
Share Premium.................................	1,000	1,750 (working 2)
Profit and Loss Account......................	65 (working 3)	100 (working 4)
	3,065	5,100
7% Convertible Preference Shares of £1 each	1,000	—
10% Convertible Debentures	1,000	—
	5,065	5,100

Calculations (£000)

	Working 1 Ordinary Share Capital	Working 2 Share Premium
Shares issued 1 January, 19X1	2,000	1,000
Converted Preference Shares............	750	250
Converted Debenture......................	500	500
	3,250	1,750

	Working 3 Retained Profit 19X1	Working 4 Retained Profit 19X2
Earnings before interest and tax ..	850	850
Debenture Interest....................	100	—
	750	850
Taxation................................	375	425
	375	425
Preference Dividend..................	70	—
	305	425
Ordinary Dividend....................	240	390
	65	35
Profit brought forward.............	—	65
Profit carried forward..............	65	100

2.

	31 December, 19X1	31 December, 19X2
Annual Earnings	£305,000	£425,000
Required Earnings Yield	5% = 0.05	5% = 0.05
Value of Company..............	$\dfrac{£305,000}{0.05} = £6,100,000$	$\dfrac{£425,000}{0.05} = £8,500,000$
Value of One Share.............	$\dfrac{£6,100,000}{2,000,000} = £3.05$	$\dfrac{£8,500,000}{3,250,000} = £2.62$

4. Preference Shares The Articles of Association of a company may give voting rights to preference shareholders in certain circumstances, for example, when a dividend is not paid or when a resolution to wind up the company is proposed.

In all of these cases the balance of voting power is altered by the creation of additional votes. Sufficient new votes may arise to convert a majority into a minority interest, although to assess the full impact requires the study of the distribution of all the shareholdings.

7.6   NEGOTIATION AND PRICE FIXING

The application of the various techniques of valuation produces a range of values, and each is likely to be given different weight by the parties engaged in negotiations to decide a price. A seller wants to receive as much as possible, while the buyer wants to minimise the price, and so each favours the valuation which supports his position. In practice an owner may argue, at various dates, in favour of different valuations for the same shares: a low one for the calculation of capital transfer tax; a high one when a holding is sold. However, it is not up to the parties to negotiations to select the valuation they desire and insist on its acceptance. The essence of negotiation is that agreement should result from compromise on both sides. Where an offer to buy or sell is at a totally unacceptable price, and there is no chance of movement, there is nothing to be gained from negotiation and the sale does not take place.

A factor which may affect the negotiations is the availability of information and its interpretation. The owner of shares in an unlisted company, especially if they represent a majority holding or are significant enough to give a directorship, will (as vendor) often have a useful access to information, whereas the prospective buyer starts with only the data which is published (see Chapters 2 and 3). In the course of negotiations for a substantial holding, the gap in knowledge often narrows. The purchaser may request authority to carry out independent investigations within the company, and this request is usually granted, since refusal of access may well deter the buyer from proceeding.

Interpretation of information is important as it affects the view of the future. For example, both sides may agree on the number of units of output likely to be sold, but have different views on the price of each unit, or, where exports are concerned, on the rates of foreign currency exchange. A pessimistic seller faced with an optimistic buyer may agree a price less than the buyer would be willing to pay. The taxation effects of the transaction to the buyer and seller must also be considered.

The valuation procedures described in this chapter do not make it possible to predict the outcome of negotiations, but some indicators and boundaries can be set.

(a) A small minority holding has a price set by its expected dividends but different people may still value the shares at different amounts; views on the size of future dividends may vary; or a higher price may be achieved where the buyer needs the small holding to establish, together with shares already owned, a majority interest.

(b) For a majority shareholding, liquidation value sets the minimum selling price since the option of liquidation is available as an alternative to the sale of the shares. Replacement cost, including an allowance for goodwill, is the maximum a buyer would pay; the price is likely to be agreed somewhere in between.

7.7 QUESTIONS AND SOLUTIONS

The following questions examine the valuation techniques covered in this chapter and, where appropriate, an indication is given of areas of weakness disclosed by candidates' answers.

Question 7.1 Over-valuation by Replacement Cost

Down Ltd. is entirely financed by Ordinary Share Capital and owns only one asset, a building, for which it collects an annual rent of £14,000. The company's expenses are £2,000 per annum, and these would have to be met by any owner of this building or a similar one. The rent is lower than expected as a result of a general lack of economic activity.

The historical cost of the building is £100,000 and its current replacement cost is £200,000. Funds can be invested currently with a similar element of risk to give a return of 10%.

What is a reasonable value to place on the company if it is offered for sale?

Discussion

The value of the company is equal to the value of the building, its only asset. A net profit of £12,000 per annum is made, and this amount would be received by the owner of this, or a similar, building.

(i) The return on a newly constructed building is $\frac{12}{200} \times 100 = 6\%$. This compares with a return of 10% available for this class of investment and so a purchaser would not pay a sum equal to the replacement cost.

(ii) Based on historical cost the return is $\frac{12}{100} \times 100 = 12\%$, which exceeds 10% and so the seller would expect a sum higher than £100,000.

(iii) The investment required to give a return of £12,000 per annum at a 10% rate of interest is £120,000. At the given level of risk this is the value of the building, and hence the company, to both the buyer and seller.

Question 7.2 (Taken from the April, 1979 *Accountancy* paper)

Redlands owns 5,000 ordinary shares in Whitchurch Ltd., a private company. The shares were inherited by Redlands from his father, who died some years ago. Redlands has received an offer of £1·80 for each of his ordinary shares.

The following up to date information has been obtained concerning the affairs of Whitchurch Ltd.

Balance sheet at 31 March 1979

	£		£
Issued share capital (£1 shares)	100,000	Freehold property at cost	60,000
Reserves	50,000	Plant at cost less depreci- ation	40,000
Current liabilities	35,000	Stock at cost	42,000
		Debtors	39,000
		Cash	4,000
	£185,000		£185,000

The profits earned by the business have been consistently in the region of £20,000 per annum and a regular annual dividend of 12% on the nominal share capital is paid. A valuation of the freeholds was recently undertaken by a local firm of surveyors and this produced a figure of £120,000. The plant is thought to possess a second-hand value of no more than £15,000, whilst the net realisable value of stock is considered to be in the region of £49,000. Liquidation costs of £5,000 would be incurred if the company's assets were sold separately.

It is discovered that private companies in the locality are normally sold at prices which give an earnings yield of 12%. Quoted companies, engaged in a line of business similar to that of Whitchurch Ltd., currently pay dividends which represent a return of 6% on the market value of their shares.

Required:

(a) Valuations of Redlands' shares in Whitchurch Ltd., presented in the following manner:

Valuation of one £1
ordinary share

(i) Book value (net asset) basis
(ii) Liquidation (break up) basis
(iii) Earnings yield basis .. ..
(iv) Dividend yield basis ..

(b) Comment on the relevance to Redlands of each valuation.

NOTE: It is essential that candidates show how they arrive at the figures in the answer to this question. Ignore Taxation.

[20]

Solution

(a)

	Valuation £
1. Book value	1.50
2. Liquidation	1.87
3. Earnings yield.........	1.67
4. Dividend yield	2.00

Workings

1. Book value $\dfrac{150,000}{100,000} = £1.50$

2. Liquidation:

Freehold property	120,000
Plant	15,000
Stock	49,000
Net monetary assets........	8,000
	192,000
Liquidation costs...........	5,000
	$187,000 \div 100,000 = £1.87$

3. Earnings yield $\dfrac{£0.20 \text{ (earnings per share)}}{0.12 \text{ (required earnings yield)}} = £1.67$

4. Dividend yield $\dfrac{£0.12 \text{ (dividend per share)}}{0.06 \text{ (required dividend yield)}} = £2.00$

(b) The book value basis has no relevance since it fails to provide a guide to future cash flows in any circumstances.

The liquidation basis is relevant only where the offerree can in some way influence the continue/discontinue decision of management. This is unlikely to apply in the case of a minority shareholder.

Earnings yield is often considered to be the most valid measure, particularly when calculated on the basis of maintainable earnings. It should be borne in mind, however, that re-invested profits are likely to be efficiently reflected in the value of the shares only where there is a ready market. The dividend yield basis is relevant in the case of a minority shareholding provided, as is the case here, there are no erratic fluctuations in the level of dividend paid out. The relevance of this method stems from the fact that the minority shareholder is unable to influence the quantity of resources paid out or re-invested and so becomes a passive recipient of the annual distributions declared by the management.

The offer exceeds the valuation on the basis of earnings yield and compares well with the dividend yield basis if it is accepted that compensation is required for the additional risks associatiated with investment in a private company.

Examiner's Comments:

Areas of weakness: 1. Valuation based on Dividend Yield and Earnings Yield.
              2. The discussion in part (b).

Question 7.3   (Taken from the April, 1981 *Accountancy* paper)

The entire share capital of Tongue Ltd., an unlisted company, is held by the directors. They have decided to sell their shares and wish to discover their likely value prior to approaching a number of prospective purchasers. Should they fail to agree a price with a buyer the company will be liquidated and the assets sold off piecemeal. The following facts and information are provided:

(i) *Balance sheet of Tongue Ltd. at 31 December 1980*

	£000	£000
Fixed assets:		
Freehold properties at cost		260
Equipment at cost less depreciation		624
Current assets		
Stock	279	
Debtors	193	
Bank	26	
	498	
Less current liabilities	164	
Working capital		334
		1,218
Financed by:		
Ordinary shares (£1 each)		600
Reserves		618
		1,218

(ii) *Extracts from the published profit and loss accounts for the last three years:*

	1978 £000	1979 £000	1980 £000
Depreciation	90	90	90
Directors' remuneration	100	116	120
Net profit before deducting dividend	130	144	167
Dividend	90	90	90

It was discovered that stock was over-valued at the end of 1977 by £24,000.

The directors have increased directors' remuneration in order to minimise the aggregate tax liability; a realistic charge for services rendered would be £75,000 per annum. The equipment is old and in need of replacement; annual depreciation based on current replacement cost would be in the region of £120,000.

(iii) One of the directors, Alfred, expresses the view that it is most appropriate to value shares on the basis of the price/earnings ratio. For this purpose he argues that earnings should be defined as the average reported profits for the last three years, after making 'proper' charges for depreciation and directors' remuneration and correcting the stock error made in 1977.

(iv) Relevant data relating to two listed companies engaged in the same line of business as Tongue Ltd.

	Dividend yield	Price/earnings ratio
Company 1	9%	5·4
Company 2	11%	6·6

(v) Figures obtained from experts for items appearing in the balance sheet of Tongue Ltd. at 31 December 1980:

	Replacement values £000	Liquidation values £000
Freehold properties	600	600
Equipment	946	216
Stock	290	320

Required:

(a) A table completed in the following form, showing valuations for the entire share capital of Tongue Ltd:

Valuation

1. Price/earnings basis (with earnings computed on the basis proposed by Alfred)

2. Book value basis

3. Liquidation (break up) basis

4. Replacement cost basis

5. Dividend yield basis

(b) Comment on the significance of the above valuations in the light of the following comment made by Tongue Ltd.'s bank manager, when asked for his advice:

'None of these valuations is of much interest since the price depends on negotiation and expectations regarding likely future cash flows'.

Notes

1. **Assume you are making the valuations at 31 December 1980.**
2. **Ignore taxation and liquidation costs.**

|30|

Solution

(a) 1. *Price/Earnings Valuation*

Earnings:	19X2	19X3	19X4	Total
	£000	£000	£000	£000
Reported profit..............................	130	144	167	441
Stock adjustment	24	—	—	24
Directors' remuneration.....................	25	41	45	111
Additional depreciation	(30)	(30)	(30)	(90)
	149	155	182	486

Average adjusted earnings: $\dfrac{£486,000}{3} = £162,000$

Average P/E ratio for similar companies: $\dfrac{5.4 + 6.6}{2} = 6$

Value of company £162,000 × 6 = £972,000

2. *Book Value*

Total from Balance Sheet: £1,218,000

3. *Liquidation Basis*

	£000
Freeholds	600
Equipment	216
Stock	320
Debtors	193
Bank	26
Current Liabilities	(164)
Value of company	1,191

4. *Replacement Basis*

	£000
Freeholds	600
Equipment	946
Stock	290
Debtors	193
Bank	26
Current Liabilities	(164)
Value of company	1,891

5. *Dividend Yield Basis*

Average dividend yield of similar companies $\dfrac{9\% + 11\%}{2} = 10\%$

Dividend of Earth Ltd.: £50,000

Value of company: $\dfrac{£90,000}{0.1} = £900,000$

SUMMARY

Basis	Value
	£000
1. Price/Earnings	972
2. Book Value	1,218
3. Liquidation	1,191
4. Replacement	1,891
5. Dividend Yield	900

(b) *Points for Discussion*
1. Book value and dividend yield are of little relevance to the calculation of the selling price for the whole company.
2. The directors will not accept less than the liquidation value.
3. The price/earnings basis is often used to obtain a valuation. Its validity depends on the extent to which past results can be regarded as a fair indicator of likely future returns. Where those past results are adjusted to take account of changed circumstances, as has been done in the case of Tongue Ltd., one might expect the predictive ability of those earnings to be improved. A drawback is the fact that the P/E ratio used to obtain the valuation has been drawn from the accounts of two listed companies, whereas Tongue Ltd. is unlisted.
4. The fact that the equipment needs replacement commits a purchaser to obtain the necessary finance. The buyer will not pay the replacement value as this presupposes that the replacement has already been undertaken.

5. The bank manager is correct to assert that the price depends on negotiation. Cash flows are fundamental to valuation, but are very difficult to calculate.

Examiner's Comments:

Areas of Weakness: 1. Calculation of adjusted earnings, especially the over-valuation of stock.
2. The identification of an appropriate P/E ratio and dividend yield.

CHAPTER 8

Interpretation of Accounts: Ratio Analysis

8.1 PRINCIPLES OF RATIO ANALYSIS

8.1.1 Objective It is the purpose of accountancy to communicate useful information to a wide range of individuals who wish to assess the progress of a business. The banker is one important consumer of accounting information, but there are many others, including shareholders, suppliers, employees and management. The decisions which these user groups wish to take will quite naturally differ; for instance the bank manager will have to decide whether to make the loan requested from him, the shareholder may want to make up his mind whether to continue investing in the company, while the employee may be trying to assess the ability of the company to meet his union's demand for a pay increase. Despite these differences, there is a common need for financial information in order to help assess corporate achievement.

The accounts published annually by companies constitute an important source of information for external users, and their form and content are carefully regulated (see Chapters 2 and 3) to ensure that they are a helpful and reliable guide to corporate progress. The result is that the annual report is an extensive document containing a director's report, auditors' report and chairman's report (in the case of larger companies), as well as a profit and loss account and balance sheet which are in turn elaborated upon in often voluminous footnotes. The chairman's report is usually interesting to read, but it is the profit and loss account and balance sheet which together attract the bulk of the readers' attention, since these are factual statements of the financial results of past activity. Often the banker will not be restricted to published financial information as the basis for loan decisions, although the amount of additional data which companies are willing to provide does vary considerably. In general, large public companies are reluctant to provide detailed trading figures, though there are always useful indicators of what is happening in the chairman's report: in small private companies there are no such indicators, but the accounts submitted to the bank nearly always include a full breakdown of trading results.

The amount of useful information which can be gleaned from the profit and loss account and balance sheet, however, is severely limited, even when a detailed breakdown of trading results is provided. For example, the profit and loss account might show that purchases amount to £500m. and the balance sheet might disclose trade creditors totalling £21m. but, taken in isolation, it is impossible to assess whether these amounts are satisfactory or unreasonable. Ratio analysis has therefore been developed as a technique designed to help translate the information contained in the accounts into a form more helpful and readily understandable to users of financial reports. The ratios do not, however, appear in the accounts and the user must make the calculations himself or employ someone with the necessary skill to do the job. Due to the banker's particular relationship with his customer, that is, his ability to insist on the regular provision of up to date financial information for the duration of the advance, ratio analysis can be used to follow through the underlying commercial business, establish the reasons for unexpected variations in performance, and make a fair assessment of the degree of risk involved at periodic intervals. No other user of accounting reports, except management, is in a better position to make this analysis.

8.1.2 Calculation Accounting ratios are calculated by expressing one figure as a ratio or percentage of another with the objective of disclosing significant relationships and trends which are not immediately evident from the examination of individual balances appearing in the accounts. The ratio which results from a comparison of two figures will only possess real significance, however, if an identifiable commercial relationship exists between the numerator and the denominator. For example, one would expect there to be a positive relationship between net profit and the level of sales. Assuming that each item sold produces a profit, one would expect a higher sales figure to produce more profit. So mere observation of the fact that profit is £5 million, is not particularly illuminating. What is of greater interest is net profit expressed as a percentage of sales. If sales were found to be £25 million, the net profit percentage could be calculated as follows:

$$\text{Net profit percentage} = \frac{\text{Net profit}}{\text{Sales}} \times 100 = \frac{5}{25} \times 100 = 20\%$$

8.1.3 Interpretation The significance of an accounting ratio is enhanced by comparison with some yardstick of corporate performance. There are three options available, namely comparison with:

1. results achieved during a previous accounting period by the same company (trend analysis);
2. results achieved by other companies (inter-firm comparisons);
3. predetermined standards or budgets.

The advantage of making comparisons is that it enables users to classify a company's performance as good, average or poor in certain key areas.

Example 8.1

For 19X0 Bradford Ltd. reported net profit and sales figures respectively of £50,000 and £400,000. In 19X1 net profit increased to £90,000 and sales for the year amounted to £900,000. The net profit percentages are as follows:

$$\text{Net profit percentage} = \frac{\text{Net profit}}{\text{Sales}} \times 100$$

$$19X0 \quad \frac{50,000}{400,000} \times 100 = 12.5\%$$

$$19X1 \quad \frac{90,000}{900,000} \times 100 = 10\%$$

The company's accounts report a significant *increase* in net profit, but the accounting ratio shows that net profit expressed as a percentage of sales has *declined*. We cannot make a definitive assessment of Bradford's progress on the basis of a single accounting ratio, but it does point to the need for further investigation. (The net profit percentage is examined further in section 5.2 of this chapter).

There are certain attractions and limitations attached to each of the three bases for comparison listed above. Last year's results are readily available, but observed changes over time are not necessarily significant. A comparison may show that there is an improvement in the net profit percentage, but last year's results may have been disastrous. Problems with inter-firm comparisons include the difficulty of finding a company engaged in a similar range of business activities, while differences in accounting policies might detract from the significance of any findings. It is, however, important to discover how a company is faring in relation to its competitors since this should throw a great deal of light on the efficiency of management and the long-term prospects of the concern. A comparison of actual results with predetermined budgets should, in theory, be the best test of whether the work force has achieved a reasonable level of efficiency. There is, however, the problem and cost of establishing standards. Also, it will be little consolation to discover that work is being carried out efficiently if, due to the existence of a declining market, profits are falling. In practice management rarely publishes forecasts of future results and so external users of accounting reports will usually have to confine their attention to trend analysis and inter-firm comparisons.

8.2 CLASSIFICATION OF ACCOUNTING RATIOS

A meaningful accounting ratio is calculated by comparing balances between which there exists some identifiable economic relationship, but there are certain balances between which there exists no apparent link, e.g. accumulated depreciation and trade creditors. In many cases, however, a significant relationship does exist and the large number of financial totals appearing in the accounts produce numerous combinations which form the basis for the calculation of accounting ratios. Many of these ratios duplicate one another, whereas others are of limited significance and can probably be ignored without detracting from the value of the analysis. The authors believe that the following representative list of fourteen ratios is adequate for most purposes:

1. Working capital (current) ratio
2. Liquidity (quick) ratio
3. Proprietorship ratio
4. Interest cover
5. Rate of stock turnover
6. Rate of collection of debtors
7. Rate of payment of creditors
8. Fixed asset turnover
9. Total asset turnover
10. Gross profit margin
11. Net profit percentage
12. Rate of return on gross assets
13. Rate of return on shareholders' equity
14. Debt/equity ratio

The procedure followed, in sections 3 to 6 of this chapter, is to use the detailed final accounts of Ludlow Ltd., for 19X1 (see figure 8.1), to illustrate the calculation and significance of the above ratios. There is a legal requirement for published accounts to give corresponding figures for the previous year, and these will be used for comparative purposes to help develop the analysis. The aim is to build up a corporate profile describing Ludlow Ltd.'s performance during 19X1 as compared with a year earlier. It is unlikely that all the ratios will produce the same conclusions regarding the company's performance; we may find that in certain areas results have improved whereas elsewhere the performance is less satisfactory than in the previous year. This emphasises the importance of not attaching too much attention to individual accounting ratios, and the overall assessment of Ludlow Ltd.'s progress will require us to balance carefully the relative significance of the ratios which are calculated. The limitations of ratio analysis are examined more fully in section 7 of this chapter.

The balance sheet and profit and loss account of Ludlow Ltd., for 19X1, together with certain additional information, is given overleaf as figure 8.1:

Figure 8.1

Towards the end of 19X0 the directors of Ludlow Ltd., a firm of wholesale merchants, decided to raise additional capital in the form of a debenture of £800,000 to facilitate expansion of the business.

The annual accounts for the year ended 31 December, 19X1, together with corresponding figures for 19X0, are set out below:

Trading and Profit and Loss Account

	19X0		19X1	
	£	£	£	£
Sales: Credit		5,500,000		6,600,000
Cash		500,000		400,000
		6,000,000		7,000,000
Less: Opening stock	1,340,000		1,360,000	
Purchase (on credit)	4,700,000		5,670,000	
Closing stock	(1,360,000)		(1,500,000)	
Cost of sales		4,680,000		5,530,000
Gross Margin		1,320,000		1,470,000
Expenses: Administration	270,000		275,000	
Selling	395,000		400,000	
Warehouse and distribution..	280,000		325,000	
Depreciation	30,000		35,000	
		975,000		1,035,000
Operating profit		345,000		435,000
Less: Debenture Interest		—		80,000
Net profit		345,000		355,000
Corporation tax		172,500		177,500
Net profit after tax		172,500		177,500

Statement of Retained Earnings

	19X0	19X1
	£	£
Reserves at 1 January	655,000	750,000
Add: Net profit after tax	172,500	177,500
	827,500	927,500
Less: Dividends proposed	77,500	77,500
Reserves at 31 December	750,000	850,000

Balance Sheet

	19X0		19X1	
	£	£	£	£
Fixed Assets:				
Cost..		700,000		900,000
Accumulated depreciation		150,000		185,000
		550,000		715,000
Current Assets:				
Stock	1,360,000		1,500,000	
Trade debtors	960,000		1,560,000	
Cash at bank	20,000		120,000	
	2,340,000		3,180,000	
Less: Current liabilities				
Trade creditors	562,500		667,500	
Dividends payable	77,500		77,500	
	640,000		745,000	
Working capital		1,700,000		2,435,000
		2,250,000		3,150,000
Financed by:				
Share capital.....................................		1,500,000		1,500,000
Reserves		750,000		850,000
		2,250,000		2,350,000
Debentures.......................................		—		800,000
		2,250,000		3,150,000

The following additional information is provided:
1. At 1 January, 19X0 trade debtors amounted to £800,000, gross assets to £2,710,000 and shareholders' equity to £2,155,000.
2. The product range and buying prices were unchanged over the period 1 January, 19X0 to 31 December, 19X1.
3. The debenture loan was received on 1 January, 19X1 and additional warehouse facilities became available on that date at a cost of £200,000.
4. No fixed assets were purchased during 19X0.
5. Ignore advance corporation tax.

The fourteen accounting ratios listed previously are illustrated in the following sections of this chapter:
section 3 Ratios measuring solvency and financial strength
section 4 Asset turnover ratios (5–9)
section 5 Profit ratios (10–13)
section 6 Gearing ratio (14)

8.3 RATIOS MEASURING SOLVENCY AND FINANCIAL STRENGTH

The ratios illustrated in this section may be further classified into those which examine short-term solvency and those which investigate the longer term financial strength of the concern.

SHORT-TERM SOLVENCY

8.3.1 Working Capital (Current) Ratio Working capital is defined as the excess of current assets over current liabilities, and an adequate surplus is normally interpreted as a reliable indication of the fact that the company is solvent. The working capital *ratio* is calculated as follows:

$$\text{Working capital ratio} = \frac{\text{Current assets}}{\text{Current liabilities}} : 1$$

The purpose of the ratio is to shed further light on the short-term solvency of the company and, more specifically, on its ability to pay debts as they fall due by calculating the relationship between current assets and current liabilities. A question which students, and businessmen, often ask is—'What is a correct working capital ratio?' Textbooks often quote a ratio of 2:1 but, although this is often a useful guideline, it must be used with care. The analyst must familiarise himself with the rate at which current assets are converted into cash and how quickly current liabilities must be paid. This will, in turn, very much depend on what is normal practice within the industry. For example, a retailer who sells goods for cash, will normally operate with a much lower ratio than a manufacturer who sells goods on credit. In the case of the retailer, resources will be converted directly from stocks into cash, whereas in the manufacturing firm goods sold will probably be 'tied-up' as debts outstanding for six to eight weeks before cash becomes available. Then again, the period for which stocks are held will vary from one industry to another. A manufacturer of small value metal products is likely to convert raw materials into finished goods and sell them much more quickly than a construction company, and in the latter case stocks are likely to comprise a much higher proportion of current assets to reflect the relatively slower rate of stock turnover. For these, and other reasons (see section 7 of this chapter), readers should be on their guard against always accepting accounting ratios at face value, and should instead consider carefully what they really mean.

Ludlow Ltd. is a firm of wholesale merchants, and we can see from its accounts that most of its sales are made on credit and that the company also receives credit from its suppliers. The company will require a working capital ratio sufficiently in excess of 1:1 to accommodate the large quantity of resources tied up in stocks. This is because the company is *likely* to allow customers roughly the same amount of credit that it receives from suppliers, and so resources tied up in stocks will not be converted into cash in time to pay trade debts as they fall due. It is on the assumption that one half of all current assets are invested in stocks that a working capital ratio of 2:1 is often regarded as a reasonable 'rule of thumb'.

Calculations for Ludlow Ltd:

$$19X0 \quad \frac{2,340,000}{640,000} = 3.7:1$$

$$19X1 \quad \frac{3,180,000}{745,000} = 4.3:1$$

We do not know what type of wholesaler Ludlow Ltd. is, but a ratio of about 1.5:1 is quite common in that sector of the economy, and so the calculated figures suggest that the company is financially stable. The high ratio may, however, have unfavourable implications for the profitability of the firm, since resources unnecessarily tied up in stock, cash and debtors are not earning a return. In business there is often a conflict between profitability and financial stability, and managerial policies which place an excessive amount of emphasis on financial stability may cause profits to be unduly depressed.

8.3.2 Liquidity (Quick) Ratio The working capital ratio is widely used, but it is sometimes of dubious significance primarily because the numerator includes stocks which are often not converted into cash sufficiently quickly to help pay current liabilities as they fall due. The purpose of the liquidity ratio is again to examine solvency, but it concentrates attention more directly on the company's prospect of paying its debts as they fall due by excluding current assets which will not be converted into cash within the next couple of months. It is for this reason that the calculation is often colourfully described as the 'quick ratio' or 'acid-test of solvency'.

It is necessary to examine carefully current assets in order to decide which items should be included or omitted. Stocks sold on credit should be excluded, as should any trade debts not receivable within the next few months, e.g. because the sales price is payable on an instalment basis spread over a year. Marketable securities held as a temporary means of employing surplus funds should be included, whereas prepayments should technically be excluded though the amount involved is usually immaterial.

The normal approach is to include all current liabilities irrespective of the payments date. Trade creditors and proposed dividends will, of course, usually be payable within a relatively short time-span, but this is not necessarily the case with taxation payable. Companies formed after April 1965 pay tax nine months after the end of the accounting year, and so a strong case could be made for excluding this item from the calculation. It might also be argued that, for many companies, the bank overdraft is a revolving source of finance which is unlikely to be withdrawn without advance warning, though much may depend on the company's financial position and the general economic climate. It is probably because accountants are inclined to favour conservative measures of corporate progress that all current liabilities are usually included in the calculation of the liquidity ratio. We will comply with this convention, but bear in mind the limitation which this places on the significance of the ratio that results.

Calculations for Ludlow Ltd. (the fact that a small proportion of sales are for cash is ignored and all stocks are excluded):

$$19X0 \quad \frac{980,000}{640,000} = 1.5:1$$

$$19X1 \quad \frac{1,680,000}{745,000} = 2.3:1$$

A liquidity ratio of 1:1 is desirable: a ratio significantly below unity would cause a company to encounter great difficulty in meeting its debts as they fall due, while a ratio in excess of unity would indicate that the company is in possession of cash resources surplus to requirements. At the end of 19X0 Ludlow Ltd.'s ratio is more than adequate, and a year later it has 'improved' even further. While there is no doubt that the company is solvent, there must be some doubt whether it is making the best use of available resources.

The liquidity ratio is of major importance to the banker, particularly in times when the customer is in financial difficulty. For this reason the bank will normally request customers to provide the information on which the calculation is based, namely cash, debtor and creditor levels, on a regular basis from the management accounts.

LONGER-TERM FINANCIAL STRENGTH

8.3.3 Proprietorship Ratio The total assets belonging to a company are financed by a combination of resources provided by shareholders and creditors. The proportion of business assets financed by the shareholders is measured by the proprietorship ratio which is conventionally calculated by expressing the shareholders' investment, or equity, in the company as a percentage of total sources of finance.

$$\text{Proprietorship ratio} = \frac{\text{Shareholders' equity}}{\text{Total sources of finance}} \times 100$$

This ratio, conventionally expressed as a percentage, is a measure of financial stability, since the larger the proportion of business activity financed by shareholders the smaller will be the creditors' claims against the company. This produces two advantages:

1. Equity finance is normally repaid only when the company is wound up, and even then repayment will only occur if sufficient cash remains after all other providers of finance have been refunded the amounts due to them. Where an excessive proportion of total finance is provided by short-term creditors, management is likely to be under continuous pressures to finance repayments falling due. In these circumstances any withdrawal of, or reduction in, a source of finance will cause the company acute financial embarrassment.
2. Dividends are payable at the discretion of management whereas interest payable on loan capital is a legally enforceable debt. A company with a large proportion of equity finance is therefore more able to survive a lean period of trading than a highly geared company (see section 6 of this chapter) which is legally obliged to make interest payments irrespective of profit levels.

It is difficult to specify an appropriate percentage, as this will depend a great deal upon trading conditions within the industry. In general, a higher percentage would be expected in those industries where there are greater fluctuations in profitability since, in such circumstances, heavy reliance on external sources of finance is undesirable. In any event, one would normally expect shareholders to provide at least half the finance, and the implications of significant changes from one year to the next should receive careful investigation.

The proprietorship rato, viewed from the creditors' standpoint, provides a useful indication of the extent to which a company can stand a fall in the value of its assets before the creditors' position is prejudiced. Book values are not the same as current values, of course, but a proprietorship ratio of say 75% would indicate that there exists a significant cushion for creditors, and the resale value of assets would have to fall to less than one quarter of their book value before the creditors position on liquidation would be jeopardised.

Calculations for Ludlow Ltd.

$$19X0 \quad \frac{2,250,000}{2,250,000 + 640,000} \times 100 = 78\%$$

$$19X1 \quad \frac{2,350,000}{3,150,000 + 745,000} \times 100 = 60\%$$

Shareholders provide a healthy 78% of total finance at the end of 19X0, but there is a decline to 60% by the end of the following year. The main reason for this change is the debenture issue which had a significant effect on the financial structure of the company. Shareholders remain the dominant source of funds, but there is now a much greater reliance on external finance and a corresponding need to meet heavy annual interest payments.

8.3.4 Interest Cover   The fact that a company is legally obliged to meet its interest charges was referred to when examining the proprietorship ratio (section 3.3 of this chapter). There is no legal restriction on sources which may be employed by management to meet it's interest payments, and it may even make an additional share issue with the intention that part of the proceeds should be used for that purpose. Nevertheless, interest payments are a business expense and, in the long run, all such costs must be met out of sales revenue if the company is to remain viable. 'Interest cover' stresses the importance of a company meeting its interest charges out of revenue, and it does this by expressing net profit before interest charges (operating profits) as a multiple of the interest charged.

$$\text{Interest cover} = \frac{\text{Net profit before interest and tax}}{\text{Interest charged}}$$

The purpose of this calculation is to indicate the ease with which a company meets its fixed interest obligations out of profit. A low figure might indicate that interest payable is imposing a heavy burden on the company's finances and that the risk of insolvency is increasing. It should be recognised, however, that interest cover would be expected to fall immediately following a loan issue. For example, debentures are often raised with two/three years' capital requirements in mind, but a full utilisation of the additional resources made available is unlikely to be achieved straight away. In this situation, current earnings will have to bear the full weight of the additional charges but the extra revenue, which is expected to result from an expansion programme, will take longer to materialise.

Interest cover is a ratio which has, in recent years, received increased attention from analysts in general, and bankers in particular. This is because traditional measures of asset utilisation and asset cover for advances are of little relevance in *service based industries* where tangible assets are at a low level. In these circumstances, it is particularly important to measure the ability of companies to generate enough revenue to cover finance charges and leave a sufficient balance over for dividends and to finance eventual loan repayments. The ratio of earnings: finance charges helps a great deal in this direction.

Calculations for Ludlow Ltd.

19X0   No interest charged

19X1 $\dfrac{435,000}{80,000} = 5.4$ times

The interest cover for Ludlow Ltd. appears adequate.

8.4   ASSET TURNOVER RATIOS

The four ratios calculated in this section are designed to examine how fully management is utilising the resources placed at its disposal by shareholders and creditors. These ratios help to explain any improvement or decline in the solvency of a business: they also provide clues to the reasons underlying changes in profitability which are measured by the accounting ratios contained in section 5 of this chapter.

8.4.1 Rate of Stock Turnover The term 'ratio' is used loosely in accountancy to cover all the calculations which measure the relationship between two financial totals. We have already seen that net profit is conventionally expressed as a *percentage* of sales and that interest cover is presented as a simple multiple, i.e. 'N' times. The rate of stock turnover, which measures the speed with which a company turns over its stock, may also be expressed as a single figure. The calculation is made as follows:

$$\text{Rate of stock turnover} = \frac{\text{Cost of goods sold}}{\text{Average stock level}}$$

Example 8.2

The calculation may be illustrated by assuming figures for cost of goods sold and average stock levels of £240,000 and £20,000 respectively.

$$\text{Rate of stock turnover} = \frac{240,000}{20,000} = 12 \text{ times a year}$$

Regarding the above formula, two typical queries raised by students are as follows: why use cost of sales rather than sales, and why use average stock levels rather than closing stock? The reason is to ensure that both the numerator and denominator are computed on a comparable basis. Stocks, which make up the denominator, are valued at cost for accounting purposes, and the numerator must be computed on a similar basis. The sales figure *can* be used to produce a ratio which enables users to make helpful inter-period comparisons, when cost of sales figures are not available, but there is a risk that wrong conclusions will be drawn when there are changes in the gross profit margin from one accounting period to another.

Turning to the reason for using average stock levels; the numerator measures the cost of goods despatched to customers *during* an accounting period, and the denominator must therefore represent the investment in stocks *during* the same time period. In practice, stock levels are likely to fluctuate a great deal; they will often be built up during relatively quiet times and subsequently run down when the level of activity increases. For this reason, it is important to calculate the average investment in stocks rather than use the stock level at a particular point in time. The average is usually based on opening and closing stock figures; a more precise calculation would make use of stock levels at various dates during the year, perhaps at the end of each month (For similar reasons, average figures are used in a number of the ratios calculated below). Many analysts prefer to present this ratio in terms of the number of days which elapse between the date that goods are delivered by suppliers and despatched to customers, i.e. the stock holding period. This can be done by dividing the result of the calculation presented in example 2 into 365, or by modifying the formula so as to achieve the desired result in a single step.

$$\text{Rate of stock turnover, in days} = \frac{\text{Average stock}}{\text{Cost of goods sold}} \times 365$$

$$= \frac{20,000}{240,000} \times 365 = 30 \text{ days}$$

Companies strive to keep the stock holding period as low as possible in order to minimise associated business costs. If the above company held its stock for an average of 60 days, rather than 30, this would cause the investment in stocks to double to £40,000. Extra finance would then have to be raised, handling costs would increase, and the potential loss from stock damage and obsolescence would be much greater. Although management's aim will be to keep stocks to a minimum, it must nevertheless ensure that there are sufficient raw materials available to meet production requirements (in the case of a manufacturer) and enough finished goods available to meet consumer demand. It is therefore management's job to maintain a balance between conflicting objectives.

Calculations for Ludlow Ltd.:

$$19X0 \quad \frac{\frac{1}{2}\,(1,340,000 + 1,360,000)}{4,680,000} \times 365 = 105 \text{ days}$$

$$19X1 \quad \frac{\frac{1}{2}\,(1,360,000 + 1,500,000)}{5,530,000} \times 365 = 94 \text{ days}$$

There has been a significant reduction in the average period for which stocks are held, and this suggests that the management has streamlined the purchasing, selling and distributive functions. A comparison of the two balance sheets does reveal an increase in the figure for stocks, but this is to be expected as there has been a significant increase in the level of sales during the year. Indeed, a higher level of business activity normally calls for an equivalent increase in stocks in order to ensure that additional consumer requirements can be met without delay. It is because Ludlow's management has succeeded in increasing sales without a commensurate increase in stock levels that resources, which would otherwise be tied up in stock, remain available for use elsewhere in the business.

The above presentation of the rate of stock turnover produces a satisfactory measure for wholesalers and retailers, but only a rough approximation for manufacturing companies. This is because manufacturers have three different categories of stocks, namely raw materials, work-in-progress and finished goods. Ideally each of these should be accounted for separately in order to compute the total stock holding period. The calculations are demonstrated in Chapter 10, section 4 where the 'cash operating cycle' is examined.

8.4.2   Rate of Collection of Debtors   The period of credit taken by customers varies between industries but, as a general rule, companies extract the maximum amount of credit from suppliers since, in the absence of discounts for prompt payment, accounts unpaid represent a free source of finance. At the same time undue delays should be avoided as these will have a harmful long run effect on the company's credit standing. In practice it is quite usual for customers to take from six to eight weeks to pay their bills.

The rate of collection of debtors is calculated, in days, as follows:

$$\text{Rate of collection of debtors} = \frac{\text{Average trade debtors}}{\text{Credit sales}} \times 365$$

It will be noted that the denominator is confined to credit sales, since only these give rise to debts outstanding. Where the split between cash and credit sales is not given, the total sales figure may be used to calculate a ratio which gives useful comparative information provided there is no significant change in the proportion of total sales made for cash.

Calculations for Ludlow Ltd.:

$$19\text{X}0 \quad \frac{\frac{1}{2}(800,000 + 960,000)}{5,500,000} \times 365 = 58 \text{ days}$$

$$19\text{X}1 \quad \frac{\frac{1}{2}(960,000 + 1,560,000)}{6,600,000} \times 365 = 70 \text{ days}$$

It is taking Ludlow Ltd. on average nearly two weeks longer to collect its debts in 19X1. The result is that a disproportionate amount of money is tied up in trade debts: these resources are yielding no return and also losing value during a period of inflation. The reasons for the change should be investigated, e.g. it may be the result of a conscious policy decision to offer customers additional credit in order to make the company's products more attractive. This can be a sound business tactic, particularly when credit is tight, but management must make arrangements to finance the much higher level of trade debtors which result. An alternative explanation for the slower rate of debt collection may be slackness in the credit control department, whose functions include confirmation of a new customer's credit-worthiness before goods are supplied and the task of following up overdue accounts. Failure to discharge both these duties efficiently will result in an unduly large figure for trade debtors and a substantial increase in bad debts.

8.4.3 Rate of Payment of Creditors This ratio measures the average period of time taken by companies to pay their debts. The result must be interpreted with particular care since not all suppliers grant similar terms of credit, but provided there are no significant changes in the 'mix' of trade creditors the average payments period should remain stable.

$$\text{Rate of payment of suppliers} = \frac{\text{Average trade creditors}}{\text{Credit purchases}} \times 365$$

We are not given Ludlow's balance for trade creditors at the beginning of 19X0 and so we cannot make the above calculation for that year. We could make the calculation for 19X1 but, without a comparative figure for 19X0, this would be of little interpretive value. The answer is to base both years' calculations on the *closing* figure for trade creditors rather than the average figure for the year. This gives comparative figures for the approximate number of days' purchases represented by the closing balances of trade creditors. The result is open to criticism since purchases may not occur at a uniform rate throughout the year, but it must be remembered that too much weight ought not to be attached to an individual ratio which should be used only to help build up an overall corporate profile.

Calculations for Ludlow Ltd. based on closing trade creditor balances:

$$19X0 \quad \frac{562,500}{4,700,000} \times 365 = 44 \text{ days}$$

$$19X1 \quad \frac{667,500}{5,670,000} \times 365 = 43 \text{ days}$$

A change in the rate of payment of suppliers' invoices may well reflect an improvement or decline in a company's liquidity. For instance, if a company is short of cash it is likely that creditors will have to wait longer for the payment of amounts due to them. This may be an acceptable short-term strategy, particularly where suppliers are familiarised with their customer's 'temporary' predicament. Management should, however, take prompt steps to arrange for additional finance; otherwise supplies of goods will eventually be curtailed. The solvency ratios calculated in sections 3.1 and 3.2 of this chapter show that Ludlow Ltd. has no cash problems and, as might therefore be expected, the average period of credit taken from suppliers remains fairly stable at just over six weeks.

8.4.4 Fixed Asset Turnover A new company will need to arrange for the provision of accommodation and the installation of any necessary plant and equipment. It is unlikely that these facilities will immediately be used to their full capacity, but as business builds up the level of utilisation will increase. The ratio which measures the degree of fixed asset utilisation is computed as follows:

$$\text{Fixed asset turnover} = \frac{\text{Sales}}{\text{Average fixed assets}} : 1$$

The ratio may reveal excess capacity, from time to time during the life of a business, and it may be unavoidable. Reasons may include:
1. Temporary inconveniences such as a strike or a fire which destroys essential equipment.
2. The collapse in demand for a product line, unless steps are promptly taken to dispose of the equipment or transfer it to an alternative use.
3. The acquisition of additional fixed assets. The point will eventually be reached where existing fixed assets are used to their full capacity, and a further increase in business activity

will first require the acquisition of additional plant. It will be some while before demand increases sufficiently to absorb the extra capacity, however, and meanwhile fixed asset turnover will decline.

Example 8.3

During 19X0 Rhyl Ltd. operated at full capacity and 1,000 units of output were produced and sold for £50 each, using plant which cost £20,000. On 1 January, 19X1 management purchased for £20,000 additional plant with a capacity to produce a further 1,000 units. Output for the years 19X1–19X3 is as follows:

19X1	1,200 units
19X2	1,500 units
19X3	2,000 units

The selling price remained unchanged at £50 per unit.

Fixed asset turnover, ignoring depreciation, is:

$$19X0 \quad \frac{50,000}{20,000} = 2.5:1$$

$$19X1 \quad \frac{60,000}{40,000} = 1.5:1$$

$$19X2 \quad \frac{75,000}{40,000} = 1.875:1$$

$$19X3 \quad \frac{100,000}{40,000} = 2.5:1$$

The new plant is working at only 1/5th of its capacity during 19X1, and the result is that fixed asset turnover declines to 1.5:1. Only when both the new and old plant are working at full capacity, in 19X3, is the ratio restored to 2.5:1.

Calculations for Ludlow Ltd.:

$$19X0 \quad \frac{6,000,000}{\frac{1}{2}\,(580,000 + 550,000)} = 10.62:1$$

$$19X1 \quad \frac{7,000,000}{\frac{1}{2}\,(750,000^* + 715,000)} = 9.56:1$$

*The additional warehouse facilities become available on 1 January, 19X1 at a cost of £200,000.

The ratio has declined and this suggests that the additional warehouse facilities may not have been used to their full capacity during 19X1.

8.4.5 Total Asset Turnover Management should be striving to make the fullest use of available resources and only if this objective is achieved will profits be maximised. The stock turnover, fixed asset turnover and debt collection ratios are designed to measure management's ability to control the level of investment in certain selected areas, whereas 'total asset turnover' has the broader aim of assessing the extent to which management utilises *all* available resources. It is computed as follows:

$$\text{Total asset turnover} = \frac{\text{Sales}}{\text{Average total assets}} : 1$$

A high ratio indicates that management is using the assets effectively to generate sales; most probably the company is working at near full capacity. A decline in the ratio suggests that assets are being underutilised, and should either be used more fully or sold. One drawback of the calculation is that it benefits companies using older assets. This is partly the effect of inflation, but also because company accounts show fixed assets at net book value which declines each year.

Calculations for Ludlow Ltd.:

$$19X0 \quad \frac{6,000,000}{\frac{1}{2}\,(2,710,000 + 2,890,000)} = 2.14:1$$

$$19X1 \quad \frac{7,000,000}{\frac{1}{2}\,(3,690,000^* + 3,895,000)} = 1.85:1$$

*Assets at the end of 19X0 totalled £2,890,000, but a debenture issue of £800,000 was made on 1 January, 19X1 and this is included in the opening balance for the purpose of computing average total assets during 19X1.

The ratio may be expressed either in the above form or as an amount of sales per £1 invested, i.e. sales were £2.14 per £1 invested in 19X0 and £1.85 per £1 invested in 19X1. It is therefore apparent that a significant reduction in asset utilisation has occurred, and earlier calculations suggest that this is principally due to the much longer period of credit allowed to customers in 19X1.

8.5 PROFIT RATIOS
The purpose of profit ratios is to help assess the adequacy of profits earned by the company and also to discover whether profitability

is increasing or declining. A proper appreciation of the significance of the gross profit margin and the net profit percentage (examined in sections 5.1 and 5.2 below) is dependent upon a thorough understanding of the different ways in which business costs respond to changes in the levels of production and sales. It is for this reason that readers are referred to Chapter 10, sections 5.1 and 5.2 which contain a discussion of fixed and variable costs.

8.5.1   Gross Profit Margin   The calculation is made as follows:

$$\text{Gross profit margin} = \frac{\text{Gross profit}}{\text{Sales}} \times 100$$

The popular view that the gross profit margin should remain unchanged, irrespective of the level of production and sales, is based on the assumption that all costs deducted when computing gross profit are directly variable with sales.

Example 8.4

Chester is a trader who purchases 'frame' tents for £40 each and sells them, through a mail-order catalogue, at a price of £50. During 19X0 and 19X1 sales amounted to 1,000 tents and 2,000 tents respectively. Ignore opening and closing stocks.

Trading Account	19X0	19X1
	£	£
Sales	50,000	100,000
Less: Cost of goods sold.........	40,000	80,000
Gross profit.........................	10,000	20,000
Gross profit margin	20%	20%

Sales have doubled in 19X1 and, because costs debited to the trading account are directly variable with sales, the gross profit is also twice the 19X0 level. A gross profit of £10 *per unit* continues to be earned, however, and the gross profit margin therefore remains unchanged at 20%.

A stable gross profit margin would be quite usual for a trader, like Chester, and also for a retailer, but less likely for a manufacturer. This is because the cost of goods sold figure, for a manufacturing company, includes fixed costs such as factory rent and rates, and semi-variable costs such as factory lighting and heating. Except in highly capital-intensive industries, variable costs will nevertheless remain dominant and large fluctuations in the gross profit margin would be unexpected. A stable gross profit margin is therefore the 'norm' and variations which call for careful investigations may be caused by any of the following events:

1. Price Cuts. The company may need to reduce its selling price in order to achieve the desired increase in sales. For instance, assuming Chester had to reduce the selling price to £48 in order to sell 2,000 tents in 19X1, the revised trading account would be as follows:

Trading Account 19X1	£
Sales.................................	96,000
Less: Cost of goods sold.........	80,000
Gross profit.........................	16,000
Gross profit margin	16.7%

2. Cost increases. The price which a company pays its suppliers, during a period of inflation, is likely to rise, and this will reduce the gross profit margin unless an appropriate adjustment is made to the selling price. Assume Chester had to pay £44 for his tents in 19X1 and he keeps his selling price at £50.

Trading Account, 19X1	£
Sales...	100,000
Less: Cost of goods sold..............................	88,000
Gross profit...	12,000
Gross profit margin	12%

3. A change in the range or mix of products sold will cause the overall gross profit margin to vary, assuming individual product lines earn different gross profit percentages.

4. Under or over-valuation of stocks. If stocks are undervalued, cost of goods sold will be inflated and profit understated. An incorrect valuation may be the result of an error during stock-take or it may be due to fraud. For instance, a businessman might intentionally undervalue his stocks so as to reduce the amount of tax payable. It must, of course, be remembered that the closing stock of one period is the opening stock of the next, and so the effect of errors will cancel out unless repeated.

Calculations for Ludlow Ltd.:

$$19X0 \quad \frac{1,320,000}{6,000,000} \times 100 = 22\%$$

$$19X1 \quad \frac{1,470,000}{7,000,000} \times 100 = 21\%$$

The reduction from 22% to 21% appears small, but the effect is to reduce profit by 1% of £7,000,000, i.e. £70,000. The reason for the decline is implied by note 2 to the accounts which tells us that the product range and buying price were unchanged over the period 1 January, 19X0 to 31 December, 19X1. Assuming stock was properly valued, the lower margin may therefore be attributed to lower selling prices. Whether the policy of reducing prices, presumably to increase sales and profit, is successful, can be discovered by examining the further profit ratios calculated below.

8.5.2   Net Profit Percentage   The ratio is calculated as follows:

$$\text{Net Profit Percentage} = \frac{\text{Net profit before interest and tax}}{\text{Sales}} \times 100$$

The ratio is designed to focus attention of the profitability of business operations. In many banks the convention is to express profit after tax and interest as a percentage of sales. A drawback is that the percentage which results will vary depending on the sources employed to finance business activity. It is for this reason that net profit (i.e. earnings) before interest and tax (sometimes abbreviated to EBIT) is used in this chapter. Both ratios may of course be calculated, but a choice has been made to avoid unnecessary duplication, particularly in view of the fact that profit *after* interest is used for the purpose of calculating the rate of return on shareholders equity in section 5.5 of this chapter.

When examining the gross profit margin we saw that an increase in sales would be expected to produce an equivalent increase in gross profit, also that gross profit expressed as a percentage of sales would normally remain stable. Similarly net profit increases with sales but, in this case, the increase occurs also as a percentage of sales. The different response of the two profit balances to increases in sales is explained by the fact that, whereas most of the costs debited to the manufacturing and trading accounts are variable, the majority of the costs debited to the profit and loss account are fixed. The result is that an increase in sales causes cost per unit to decline because the fixed costs are spread more thinly over a larger volume of output (fixed costs and variable costs are examined in more detail in Chapter 10). It will often be useful to express each item of costs as a percentage of sales in order to help illustrate changes in their relative impact over time.

Example 8.5

Assume the same facts as for example 8.4. In addition Chester pays rent and rates of £3,000 each year while other overhead expenses, including the salary of a part-time employee, stationery and electricity, amount to £4,000 in 19X0 and £6,000 in 19X1.

Trading and Profit and Loss Account

	19X0		19X1	
	£	%	£	%
Sales...	50,000	100	100,000	100
Less: Cost of goods sold......................................	40,000	80	80,000	80
Gross profit.....................................	10,000	20	20,000	20
Less: Rent and rates..	3,000	6	3,000	3
Other overhead expenses	4,000	8	6,000	6
Net profit.......................................	3,000	6	11,000	11

The net profit percentage has risen from 6% to 11% because of the reduced impact of fixed costs as sales increase; the rent and rates have remained unchanged and therefore fallen from 6% to 3% of sales, while other overhead expenses have increased by just 50% and fallen from 8% to 6% of sales. The point will eventually be reached where output cannot be increased further without incurring a significant addition to fixed costs. For instance, if Chester's business grows further he may have to rent new premises thereby causing a large increase in overhead costs. This will cause an at least temporary reduction in the net profit percentage until full use can be made of the higher capacity.

Calculations for Ludlow Ltd.:

$$19X0 \quad \frac{345,000}{6,000,000} \times 100 = 5.75\%$$

$$19X1 \quad \frac{435,000}{7,000,000} \times 100 = 6.2\%$$

There has been a small increase in the net profit percentage, but rather less than might have been expected in view of the fact that sales were increased by 1/6th and expenses debited to the profit and loss account kept under tight control (this could be confirmed by expressing the expenses individually or in total as a percentage of sales). The main problem is the fall in the gross profit margin, since this caused net profit to be approximately £70,000 lower, (see section 5.1 of this chapter), than would have been the case if the 22% margin achieved in 19X0 had been repeated in 19X1.

8.5.3 Rate of Return on Gross Assets The rate of return on gross assets is often alternatively described as the rate of return on capital employed. The problem with the latter description is that the term capital employed is used, in accountancy, to signify three different financial totals:
1. Shareholders' equity.
2. Long-term capital employed (shareholders' equity plus long term loans).
3. Gross assets.

In order to avoid potential confusion, the term 'rate of return on capital employed' is not used in this text. Depending on the version of capital employed under investigation, we will use the term rate of return on shareholders' equity or rate of return on long term capital or rate of return on gross assets. The last of these is discussed in this section, and is calculated as follows:

$$\text{Rate of return on gross assets} = \frac{\text{Net profit before interest}}{\text{Average gross assets}} \times 100$$

It is management's job to ensure that the most effective use is made of available resources: the rate of return on gross assets measures the extent to which this objective has been achieved and, for this reason, is often described as the 'primary accounting ratio'.

Calculations for Ludlow Ltd.:

$$19X0 \quad \frac{345,000}{\frac{1}{2}\,(2,710,000 + 2,890,000)} \times 100 = 12.3\%$$

$$19X1 \quad \frac{435,000}{\frac{1}{2}\,(3,690,000 + 3,895,000)} \times 100 = 11.5\%$$

The reason for the decline in the ratio is examined in the following section.

8.5.4 Relationship between Accounting Ratios An analysis of corporate performance made by students, and even by trained accountants, is often unsatisfactory, and a common weakness is the failure to explore the relationship between the various ratios which have been calculated. The essence of the relationship is contained in the following formula:

SECONDARY RATIOS   PRIMARY RATIO

$$\frac{\text{Total asset}}{\text{turnover}} \times \frac{\text{Net profit}}{\text{percentage}} = \frac{\text{Rate of return on}}{\text{gross assets}}$$

Management will be endeavouring to maximise the return earned on gross assets, and it can accomplish this objective in two ways: it can increase the net profit percentage and/or it can achieve a higher rate of asset utilisation. It may well happen that greater asset utilisation, for instance more sales, can only be achieved by lowering prices, and management will have to judge whether the larger volume of activity will be sufficient to justify the lower gross and net margins which will result from implementing a policy of price reductions.

Example 8.6

Holly and Head run separate businesses in different geographical areas, manufacturing a similar product for which there exists a ready market. They meet at a conference and are interested to discover that, whereas Holly keeps prices low in order to keep his factory at full capacity, Head supplies goods only at 'normal margins for the industry'. They decide to compare their results and extract the following information from recently published accounts:

	Holly	Head
	£	£
Net profit before interest.........	50,000	100,000
Sales.....................................	600,000	750,000
Average gross assets...............	200,000	500,000

Applying the formula:

$$\frac{\text{Total asset}}{\text{turnover}} \times \frac{\text{Net profit}}{\text{percentage}} = \frac{\text{Rate of return}}{\text{on gross assets}}$$

$$Holly = \frac{600,000}{200,000} \times \left(\frac{50,000}{600,000} \times 100\right) = \frac{50,000}{200,000} \times 100$$

$$3 \times 8.3\% = 25\%$$

$$Head = \frac{750,000}{500,000} \times \left(\frac{100,000}{750,000} \times 100\right) = \frac{100,000}{500,000} \times 100$$

$$1.5 \times 13.3\% = 20\%$$

The above calculations show that Holly achieves the greater asset utilisation (£3 of sales per £1 invested as compared with the £1.50 achieved by Head) but his net profit percentage is lower (8.3% compared with Head's 13.3%). Overall Holly's policies seem to be more successful, i.e. the greater asset utilisation more than compensates for the lower margins, and he achieves a rate of return on gross assets of 25%.

The formula may also be used to shed further light on the performance of Ludlow Ltd. by extracting, from sections 4.5, 5.2 and 5.3, of this chapter, the following ratios previously calculated:

	SECONDARY RATIOS				PRIMARY
	Asset utilisation		Profit margin		RATIO
19X0	2.14	$\times$	5.75%	=	12.3%
19X1	1.85	$\times$	6.2%	=	11.5%

The asset utilisation is much lower in 19X1, and the explanation for this is that much of the money raised through issuing an £800,000 debenture has been absorbed by increasing the period of credit allowed to customers by nearly two weeks. The directors have, however, succeeded in increasing the net profit percentage. Sales have been increased and, although price cuts have reduced the gross margin by one point to 21%, overhead expenses have been kept under tight control and a small reduction in the total cost per unit has been achieved. The higher net profit margin does not sufficiently compensate for the lower asset utilisation, however, and the primary ratio suffers a significant decline.

8.5.5   Rate of Return on Shareholders' Equity   The factor which motivates shareholders to invest in a company is the expectation of an adequate rate of return on their funds, and they will want periodically to assess the rate of return earned in order to decide whether to continue with their investment. There are various ways of measuring the return earned including the earnings yield and dividend yield which are examined in Chapter 7. Another useful measure is the rate of return on the book value of shareholders equity which is calculated as follows:

$$\text{Rate of return on shareholders' equity} = \frac{\text{Earnings* for equity shareholders}}{\text{Average shareholders' equity}} \times 100$$

*The ratio may be computed on either a pre- or post-tax basis but, whichever basis is used, any preference dividends payable must be deducted since they reduce profits available for ordinary shareholders. An argument for using the pre-tax basis is that the resulting ratio can be related more meaningfully to the other calculations demonstrated in this chapter. On the other hand corporation tax must be deducted in order to arrive at the balance available for distribution to shareholders and the post-tax basis implies full recognition of the fact.

Calculations for Ludlow Ltd.

Pre-tax

$$19X0 \quad \frac{345,000}{\frac{1}{2}\,(2,155,000 + 2,250,000)} \times 100 = 15.7\%$$

$$19X1 \quad \frac{355,000}{\frac{1}{2}\,(2,250,000 + 2,350,000)} \times 100 = 15.4\%$$

Post-tax

$$19X0 \quad \frac{172,500}{\frac{1}{2}\,(2,155,000 + 2,250,000)} \times 100 = 7.8\%$$

$$19X1 \quad \frac{177,500}{\frac{1}{2}\,(2,250,000 + 2,350,000)} \times 100 = 7.7\%$$

There has been a modest decline in the return earned for shareholders, but rather less than might have been expected in view of the fairly sharp decline in the primary ratio from 12.3% to 11.5% (see section 5.3 of this chapter). The reason for this difference is that the return earned for shareholders is dependent on management's achievements in three key areas.

1. Profit margins.
2. Utilisation of assets.
3. Capital structure.

We saw, in section 5.4 of this chapter that the rate of return on gross assets is a function of profit margins and asset utilisation, but it takes no account of the company's capital structure. (This can be confirmed by observing the fact that the numerator comprises net profit *before* deducting any interest charges.) The significance for the equity shareholders of financing a part of a company's activities with loan capital is examined in section 6 of this chapter.

8.6   GEARING

Capital is derived from two sources: shares and loans. It is quite likely that only shares will be issued when the company is formed, but loans will invariably be raised at some later date. There are numerous reasons for issuing loan capital. For instance, the owners might want to increase their investment but avoid the risk which attaches to share capital, and they can do this by making a secured loan. Alternatively, management might require additional finance which the shareholders are unwilling to supply, and so a loan is raised instead. In either case, the effect is to introduce an element of gearing or leverage into the capital structure of the company. There are numerous ways of measuring gearing, but the debt/equity ratio is perhaps most commonly used. For the purpose of calculating this ratio, debt may be calculated in either of two ways:

(a) Debt defined as long-term loans.

$$\text{Debt/equity ratio} = \frac{\text{Long term loans*}}{\text{Shareholders' equity}} \times 100$$

*Where there are preference shares outstanding, these are included for the purpose of calculating this ratio.

(b) Debt defined as total borrowings.
The banker, when assessing risk, will want to examine *total* borrowing in relation to the equity base. For this reason he will often find it useful to extend the definition of debt, for the purpose of calculating the debt/equity ratio:

$$\text{Total debt/equity ratio} = \frac{\text{Total financial debt*}}{\text{Shareholders' equity}} \times 100$$

*includes loans from directors and bank overdrafts which, although technically for the short-term, are a permanent source of financing for many businessess.

The use of debt capital is likely to have direct implications for the profit accruing to the ordinary shareholders, and expansion is often financed in this manner with the objective of increasing, or 'gearing up', the shareholders' rate of return. This objective will only be achieved, however, if the rate of return earned on the additional funds raised exceeds that payable to the providers of the loan.

Example 8.7

The directors of Conway Ltd. are planning to undertake a new project which calls for a total investment of £1m in fixed assets and working capital. The directors plan to finance the investment with a long-term loan bearing interest at 12% per annum, and the financial controller forecasts an annual profit, before finance charges, of £150,000 from the new project. (Taxation ignored.)

	£
Additional profit contributed by new project	150,000
Less: Interest charge, 12% of £1m	120,000
Surplus	30,000

The existing shareholders will benefit from the project, to the extent of £30,000, because the new venture yields a return of 15% whereas providers of the required finance have contracted for interest at the lower rate of 12%. Profit may, of course, not come up to expectations, and if it is less than £120,000 the introduction of gearing will be detrimental to the ordinary shareholders whose rate of return will suffer.

Returning to the case of Ludlow Ltd., calculations of the debt/equity ratio are as follows:

$$19X0 \quad \text{Zero gearing (no loans)}$$

$$19X1 \quad \frac{800,000}{2,350,000} \times 100 = 34\%$$

A significant element of gearing was introduced in 19X1 by the issue of an £800,000 debenture to finance an expansion of operations. The policy was not entirely successful and the rate of return on total assets declined from 12.3% to 11.5%. The shareholders return suffered only a modest decline, however, (see section 5.5 of this chapter) and this suggests that, assuming 19X0's results would otherwise have been repeated, the additional activity produced a return only marginally below the 10% interest payable on the debenture.

The shareholders of a highly geared company will reap enormous benefits when there are increases in earnings before interest and tax. This is because interest payable on a large proportion of total finance will remain unchanged. The converse is also true, and a highly geared company is likely to find itself in severe financial difficulties if it suffers a succession of trading losses. It is not possible to specify an optimal level of gearing for companies but, as a general rule, gearing should be low in those industries where demand is volatile and profits are subject to fluctuation. The effect of profit fluctuations on the rates of return earned by companies with different levels of gearing is demonstrated in example 8.8.

Example 8.8

The following information is provided relating to the affairs of two companies engaged in similar trading activities:

	A Ltd.	B Ltd.
	£	£
Ordinary share capital.........	800,000	500,000
15% Debentures	200,000	500,000

Each company earned a trading profit before finance charges of £110,000 in year 1 and £190,000 in year 2.

Corporation tax is charged at 50% on the trading profits after finance charges have been deducted.

The company pays out as dividends its entire post-tax profits, (i.e. there are no reserves).

REQUIRED:
(a) Summary profit and loss accounts, dealing with the results of each of the two companies' activities during years 1 and 2, so far as the information given above permits.
(b) Calculations of profits before tax expressed as percentages of ordinary share capital for each company in respect of both years 1 and 2.
(c) A discussion of the returns earned for shareholders over the two year period.

Solution:

(a)

	A Ltd.		B Ltd.	
	Year 1	Year 2	Year 1	Year 2
	£	£	£	£
Profit before finance charges	110,000	190,000	110,000	190,000
Loan interest	30,000	30,000	75,000	75,000
Profit before tax	80,000	160,000	35,000	115,000
Corporation tax	40,000	80,000	17,500	57,500
Profit after tax..............................	40,000	80,000	17,500	57,500
Dividends....................................	40,000	80,000	17,500	57,500

(b)   10%   20%   7%   23%

(c) Changes in the relative performance of the companies over the two year period are explicable in terms of the financial effects of gearing. B. Ltd. is relatively high-geared and a disproportionately large slice of the company's earnings will be required to finance debt capital when profits are low. In year 1 the pre-tax return on long term capital is 11% (£110,000 on £1,000,000), but the interest rate payable on loans is 15% producing a pre-tax return of only 7% for the shareholders of B. Ltd. This may be contrasted with A Ltd. where the claims of the debenture holders are far less and so the ordinary shareholders get more, in this case 10%. The position alters as profits rise. Additional profits of £80,000 represent a return of 10% on the investment made by the shareholders of A Ltd. but 16% on the shareholders of B. Ltd.'s investment. Therefore, the return to the ordinary shareholders of A Ltd. increases at only a slightly faster rate than profits before finance charges, whereas the return earned for the shareholders of B Ltd. increases three times more quickly.

8.7 LIMITATIONS OF ACCOUNTING RATIOS

The various calculations illustrated in this chapter suffer from a number of limitations which should be borne in mind by anyone attempting to interpret their significance. The main limitations are as follows:

1. Accounting ratios can be used to assess whether performance is satisfactory, by means of inter-firm comparison, and also whether results have improved, worsened or remained stable, by comparing this year's results with those achieved last year. The ratios do not, however, provide *explanations*

for observed changes, and the external users' ability to obtain further information varies considerably. The shareholder may ask questions at the annual general meeting, while the lending banker may demand extra information when an advance is requested, but it is only management that has direct access to the information needed to provide the right answer.

2. A deterioration in an accounting ratio cannot necessarily be interpreted as poor management. For example, a decline in the rate of stock turnover might appear undesirable, but further investigation might reveal the accumulation of scarce raw materials which enable the plant to continue working when competitors are forced to suspend production.

3. Too much significance should not be attached to individual ratios, e.g. a rate of return on gross assets of 30% might indicate that all is well, but this conclusion would be unjustified if further analysis revealed a liquidity ratio of 0.4:1.

4. Changes in many ratios are closely associated with one another and produce similar conclusions, e.g. the ratio of total debt to total assets (not illustrated in this chapter) and the debt/equity ratio. Care should therefore be taken when selecting ratios to be used as the basis for the analysis: a representative selection should be made and duplication avoided.

5. Company financial statements are usually based on historical cost and, therefore, accounting ratios based on these figures would be expected to improve, irrespective of efficiency, during a period of rising prices, e.g. total asset turnover of £3 per £1 invested might be computed from historical cost accounts, whereas a figure of £1.80 per £1 invested might be obtained if assets were restated at current values.

6. Differences in accounting policies may detract from the value of inter-firm comparisons, e.g. the valuation of stock on the LIFO basis rather than the FIFO basis would probably produce a much lower working capital ratio.

7. Financial statements and accounting ratios can be distorted as the result of 'one off' large transactions such as the credit purchase of plant, which will significantly increase current liabilities until payment is made, or a profit on the sale of a fixed asset. Analysts should similarly be on their guard for

evidence of 'window dressing', perhaps designed to conceal a deteriorating financial position.

8. Where a company undertakes a mix of activities, it is important to calculate separate ratios for each section wherever possible.

9. Particular care must be taken when interpreting accounting ratios calculated for seasonal businesses. Where sales are high at a particular time during the year, e.g. at Christmas, stock might be expected to increase and cash to decline in the months leading up to the busy period. In these circumstances, deteriorations in both the liquidity ratio and the rate of stock turnover are not necessarily causes for concern.

10. Consideration must be given to variations in commercial trading patterns when assessing the significance of accounting ratios computed for particular companies. For example, a retail chain of supermarkets would be expected to have a much lower liquidity ratio and a much higher rate of stock turnover than a constructional engineering firm. In this context, accepted 'norms' such as a working capital ratio of 2 : 1 must be used with care.

8.8 QUESTIONS AND SOLUTIONS
The following two questions test students' ability to calculate and interpret the significance of accounting ratios.

Question 8.1 (Taken from the April, 1980 *Accountancy* examination).

The following are the summarised revenue accounts and balance sheets of Aix Limited.

Revenue Accounts for years ended 31 December

	1978		1979	
	£ thousands			
Sales		800		1,100
Less: Opening stock	110		130	
Costs of production	500		700	
Closing stock	(130)		(170)	
Cost of goods sold	480		660	
Running expenses (including interest charges)	260	740	362	1,022
Net profit		60		78
Proposed dividend		—		40
Retained profit		60		38

Balance Sheets as at 31 December

	1978	1979
		£ thousands
Ordinary share capital	200	200
Retained profit	100	138
12% debentures, issued 1 January 1979 ..	—	200
Bank overdraft..	10	—
Dividends	—	40
Creditors	110	120
	420	698
Fixed assets	170	338
Stock	130	170
Debtors	120	160
Bank	—	30
	420	698

No dividends were paid during either 1978 or 1979.

Required:

(a) A calculation of the following accounting ratios and percentages for 1978 and 1979 presented in the following tabular format:

	1978	1979
Liquid ratio		
Average rate of stock turnover		
Net profit as a percentage of sales		
Earnings as a percentage of long-term capital employed		
Net earnings for ordinary shareholders as a percentage of equity		
Ratio of sales to long-term capital employed		

For the purpose of your calculations equity and long-term capital employed are to be included at their estimated figures at 30 June in each year, assuming no seasonal variations in the level of business activity.

(b) Comments on the implications of the differences between the above ratios and percentages between the two years.

NOTE: Ignore taxation.

[20]

Solution

£ thousands

(a)

	1978	1979
Liquid ratio	$\dfrac{120}{120} = 1:1$	$\dfrac{190}{160} = 1.2:1$
Average rate of stock turnover	$\dfrac{480}{120} = 4$ (91 days)	$\dfrac{570}{150} = 3.8$ (96 days)
Net profit as a percentage of sales.	$\dfrac{60}{800} \times 100 = 7.5\%$	$\dfrac{78}{1,100} \times 100 = 7.1\%$
Earnings as a percentage of long-term capital employed	$\dfrac{60}{270*} \times 100 = 22.2\%$	$\dfrac{102}{539\dagger} \times 100 = 18.9\%$
Net earnings for ordinary shareholders as a percentage of equity	$\dfrac{60}{270*} \times 100 = 22.2\%$	$\dfrac{78}{339\ddagger} \times 100 = 23\%$
Ratio of sales to long-term capital.	$\dfrac{800}{270*} = 2.96:1$	$\dfrac{1,100}{539\dagger} = 2:1$

*240 (equity at 1 January, 1978) + ½ × 60 (net profit for 1978).
†300 (equity at 1 January, 1979) + 200 (debenture isued) + ½ × 78 (net profit for 1979).
‡300 (equity at 1 January, 1979) + ½ × 78 (net profit for 1979).

(b) Comments should include:
1. The liquidity ratio has increased from a satisfactory level in 1978 to a situation verging on excess solvency. This is perhaps because rather too much long-term finance was raised during 1979.
2. The rate of stock turnover is down, implying a marginal slackening of stock control procedures, or a policy decision change regarding stock holdings.
3. Net profit percentage has declined despite the fact that sales have increased by almost 30%. The gross profit margin is stable so the problem would seem to be with running expenses.
4. Return on long term capital employed has also declined, and this is mainly due to the lower level of asset utilisation during 1979.
5. Return on equity has nevertheless improved slightly due to the effect of gearing; only 12% was paid for funds while 18.9% was earned on long term capital.
6. Asset turnover is slower in 1979; not only has the rate of stock turnover declined but twice the investment in fixed assets has only resulted in a 40% increase in sales, implying the existance of idle capacity.

Examiner's comments:
Most common errors:
1. The working capital (current) ratio calculated instead of the liquid ratio.
2. Failure to add the interest charge back to profit for the purpose of computing earnings as a percentage of long-term capital employed.
3. Ratios 4–6 based on *year-end* figures for long-term capital employed and equity, rather than the figures at 30 June as instructed in the question.

Question 8.2 (This is taken from the September 1981 *Accountancy* examination with modifications).

Belvedere Ltd. is a medium sized engineering firm engaged in the manufacture of metal products. The following is a summary of its assets, capital, liabilities and provisions for the years to 30 June, 19X0 and 30 June, 19X1, prepared in accordance with the historical cost convention.

Assets:	19X0 £000s	19X1 £000s
Tangible fixed assets at cost	2,116	2,197
Less: Accumulated depreciation	1,016	1,186
	1,100	1,011
Goodwill at cost	32	32
Trade investments at cost (market value £75,000)	58	63
Stock and work in progress at cost	1,125	1,505
Trade and other debtors	1,221	1,006
	3,536	3,617

Capital, liabilities and provisions:		
Issued share capital	400	400
Reserves	1,057	1,219
Loans: 18% repayable on or before 31 December, 19X3	110	—
Other	116	116
Provisions for deferred taxation	247	218
Bank overdraft (secured)	490	420
Trade and other creditors	903	937
Proposed dividend	50	50
Taxation payable	163	257
	3,536	3,617

The profit and loss accounts are as follows:

Profit and Loss accounts to 30 June

	19X0 £000s	19X0 £000s	19X1 £000s	19X1 £000s
Turnover		5,249		5,416
Trading profit before charging depreciation		613		737
Less: Depreciation		190		170
Trading profit		423		567
Less: Interest paid, *less* interest received		122		103
Net profit		301		464
Taxation: Charge for year	163		257	
Transfer to (from) deferred tax account	36		(29)	
	—	199	—	228
Profit after taxation		102		236
Less: Dividends paid and proposed		74		74
Retained profit for the year		28		162

In 19X0, and previous years, the company valued stock and work in progress at prime cost. This treatment contravened Statement of Standard Accounting Practice 9, and as a result the auditors qualified their report to the shareholders. For the purposes of the 19X1 accounts, stock and work-in-progress at 30 June, 19X1 has been valued on the total cost basis, but no adjustment was made to the value of stock and work-in-progress at the beginning of the year. It has since been discovered that the total cost for stock at 30 June, 19X0 was £1,478,00, made up as follows:

	£000s
Direct material..................	700
Direct labour....................	425
Prime cost	1,125
Production overheads.........	353
Total cost	1,478

The company's overdraft facility is, at present, £500,000. The directors have requested an increase to £700,000.

REQUIRED:
A full discussion of the past progress, present financial position and future prospects of Belvedere Ltd. from the viewpoint of the company's bank. You should support your discussion with relevant accounting ratios.
   NOTES:
   1. Ignore advance corporation tax.
   2. You are not required to reach a decision regarding the request for an increased overdraft facility.

Solution:
The discussion should cover the following matters:
   1. Change of Accounting Policy.
      The company has changed its basis of stock valuation from prime to cost to total cost. This has implications for:
      (a) the reported profit for the year to 30 June, 19X1.
      (b) the comparability of the results achieved in each of the two years.
      Stocks should be valued on a consistent basis and total cost will be used for the purpose of (a) and (b). The effect is considered below.

   2. Solvency and Financial Strength.
      Valuing stock on the total cost basis produces the following calculations of working capital and relevant accounting ratios:

	19X0		19X1	
	£000s	£000s	£000s	£000s
Stock, etc. at total cost		1,478		1,505
Debtors...		1,221		1,006
		2,699		2,511
Less: Creditors...	903		937	
Proposed dividend	50		50	
Tax..	163		257	
Bank overdraft..................................	490		420	
	—	1,606	—	1,664
Working capital:..		1,093		847
Working capital ratio..................................		1.68:1		1.51:1
Liquidity ratio..		0.76:1		0.60:1
Proprietorship ratio†		46.5%		44.8%

†Re-stating stock at total cost on 30 June, 19X0:
— shareholders equity becomes £400,000 + £1,057,000 + £353,000 = £1,810,000
— total sources of finance become £3,536,000 + £353,000   = £3,889,000
The working capital ratio has declined to 1.51:1, but this is about average for a medium sized engineering firm. A company's liquidity ratio should normally be in the region of 1:1, and the figures for Belvedere appear very low, particularly at the end of 19X1. The company will be helped by the fact that taxation is not payable until the 30th September, but it clearly has to depend heavily on the bank to pay its bills as they fall due. The proprietorship ratio is a little low, but is fairly steady with shareholders providing approximately 45% of total finance.

3. Asset Turnover

	19X0	19X1
Rate of collection of debtors‡...........................	85 days	68 days
Total asset turnover‡	1.35:1	1.5:1

‡Using closing balances for debtors and total assets.
The company is making more effective use of its assets in 19X1. The much faster rate at which debts are being collected (nearly two and a half weeks quicker) has contributed significantly to the higher rate of total asset turnover.

4. Profit ratios
The reported profit for the year to 30 June 19X1 must first be recalculated using the total cost value for opening stock.

	£000s
Trading profit per the accounts	567
Less: Increase in opening value of stock	353
	214
Net profit percentage	4%
Rate of return on gross assets*...........................	5.9%
Pre-tax rate of return on shareholders' equity*......................................	6.9%

*Using closing balances for gross assets and shareholders' equity.

Directly corresponding figures for the year to 30 June 19X0 cannot be calculated as we are not given an opening stock balance valued on the total cost basis. Using the prime cost valuation, the net profit percentage comes out at 8.1% and the rate of return on gross asset at 12%. It is therefore nevertheless clear that, contrary to the impression given in the accounts, a significant decline in Belvedere's profitability has occurred. Consideration might therefore be given to amortising the balance for goodwill which remains at cost £32,000.

5. Gearing

	19X0	19X1
Debt/equity ratio.........	12.5%	7.2%

Gearing is low in both years, and has declined due to the repayment of the 18% loan.

6. Conclusion:

The financial performance of Belvedere Ltd. during the year to 30 June 19X1 is generally depressing, although this is not immediately clear from the draft accounts due to the changed method of stock valuation.

Examiners' comments:

Most common errors:

The majority of candidates failed to recognise the implications of the changed basis of stock valuation for (a) the calculation of reported profit for the year to 30 June, 19X1, and (b) the comparability of the two years' results. An appreciation of each of these matters was an essential requirement for a satisfactory answer, and consequently the question was poorly done.

CHAPTER 9

Interpretation of Accounts: Funds Flow Analysis

9.1 INTRODUCTION

British companies have been legally required to publish a balance sheet since 1900; the additional obligation to publish a profit and loss account was introduced in 1929, though in each case the quantity of information initially disclosed was much less than is the case today. It is perhaps a consequence of the historical importance of these two documents that introductory courses on accountancy traditionally start with a thorough examination of their form and content, and there is no doubt that they do contain a great deal of useful and important information. The balance sheet contains detailed lists of the assets owned by a company and the ways in which those assets have been financed. The profit and loss account sets out the effect, on profit, of transactions undertaken during the year, and also gives the allocation of profit between distribution and retention. Accounting ratios (see Chapter 8), calculated on the basis of information included in these two documents, may be utilised by management, and external users of accounting reports, to obtain further insights into the financial progress and position of the company.

The balance sheet and profit and loss account do not, however, contain a sufficiently wide range of information to enable users to make a full assessment of a company's performance. More specifically, an important gap is left because the profit and loss account provides financial information relating only to a *limited range* of financial transactions entered into during an accounting period, namely those which impinge on the calculation of reported profits, i.e. revenues and expenditures. Other transactions involving flows of resources, such as an issue of shares or debentures or the purchase of a fixed asset, are not reported in the profit and loss account since these are capital transactions as opposed to revenue transactions. Gradually the view developed that these transactions, which often involve large amounts of money, are of interest to investors and should be reported to them. The statement of funds was devised as a means of filling this gap, and, during the 1960s and early 1970s, an increasing number of companies began to publish the statement on a voluntary basis. SSAP10, entitled the Statement of Source and Application of Funds, was issued by the Accounting Standards Committee in 1975, and this makes publication a requirement for all companies with a turnover of £25,000 or over. The published statement must contain full details of the financial resources which have become available during an accounting period, and the ways in which those resources have been used up. It is therefore designed to supply answers to the following types of questions:

1. Why could the company not afford to pay an increased dividend in view of the higher profits?
2. How was the increase in working capital financed?
3. How much money was borrowed during the year?
4. Why was so much money borrowed during the year?
5. How did the company finance the acquisition of the new office block?
6. Why has the bank balance gone down when the accounts show a healthy profit?
7. How did the company manage to expand in the same year that it suffered an operating loss?
8. What happened to the proceeds from the rights issue of shares?

Before we examine how the statement of funds can be used to provide answers to questions of this kind, it is useful to examine the sources of finance available to a business and the various ways in which those resources may be employed.

9.2 SOURCES OF FINANCE
The finance available to a company may be conveniently classified into the following two basic sources: internal finance and external finance.

9.2.1 Internal Finance This may be obtained by a company either reducing its investment in business assets or generating finance from business operations.

1. *Reduce the investment in business assets.* A company may be able to raise cash by reducing the level of stocks or debtors where these are excessive in relation to business needs. Alternatively, a company may be in possession of fixed assets or investments, surplus to operating requirements, which can be sold. Where outright sale is not feasible, there are other schemes which may be used to release cash tied up in business assets. In this context, 'sale and leaseback' has become a fairly popular device in recent decades. The procedure followed is for the company to sell the freehold property which it occupies, perhaps to an insurance company, and then to lease the property back for an agreed number of years. The company benefits from a substantial injection of much needed cash, but drawbacks include the obligation to pay an annual rental, the loss of an asset which might have been expected to appreciate in value (and which could have been used as security for further loans), and perhaps also the need to move out and find new accommodation when the lease expires.

ExTRA ORDINARY ITEMS

'Debt factoring' is another scheme for releasing cash tied up in business assets. It can take a number of different forms: one version is for the company to invoice the customer in the usual way, while the 'factor' maintains accounts for each debtor and takes responsibility for collecting the cash. The factor will then make guaranteed payments to the company at specific intervals after the goods have been invoiced. Depending on the terms of the agreement, the company may obtain cash more quickly than if it had to wait for the customer to pay. The company also benefits from a more predictable cash flow, while the cost of operating a debt collecting department is avoided. The charges made by the factor are substantial, however, and must be compared with the cost of alternative sources of finance.

2. *Finance generated from business operations.* This is made up of the following main items:

Profit...	xxx
Add: Depreciation.............................	xxx
Finance generated from operations.........	xxx

The reason for including depreciation as part of the finance generated from operations requires further comment. During the course of trading activity a company generates revenue, principally in the form of sales proceeds, and incurs expenditure comprising a wide range of different outlays. These outlays can be divided into two categories for the purpose of this chapter: those which produce an outflow of resources in the accounting period under review and those which do not. Most outlays fall into the first category, e.g. the cost of materials consumed, wages, salaries and rent. There is, however, a small number of items (the most important of which is depreciation) which are charged against profit but do not result in an equivalent outflow of resources during the accounting period under review. The purpose of the depreciation charge is to reflect the fact that business has benefitted from using a fixed asset, acquired in a previous accounting period, to help provide goods or services. The asset will decline in value, as the result of business use, and this decline is recorded in the profit and loss account, but no corresponding cash outlay occurs. It is necessary, for this reason, to add back the depreciation charge to the reported profit figure in order to arrive at the total for finance generated from operations. The extent to which finance, represented by the depreciation charge, is available for investment purposes is examined in section 7.1 of this Chapter.

9.2.2 External Finance The ability of a company to raise finance from external sources depends upon a number of factors. These include:
1. The nature of the business. Whether it is a sole trader, a partnership or a registered company, e.g. only the last of these can issue shares.
2. The size of the business. For example, all public limited companies may issue shares to the general public, but the high fixed costs involved mean that this is only a feasible proposition for a *large* public company.
3. The personality of the directors. This may be a particularly important factor in the company's relationship with its bank.

The following is a list of the main types of external finance available to businesses:
   Trade credit from suppliers
   Taxation and dividends payable
   Bank overdraft
   Hire purchase
   Unsecured loans (long-term and short-term)
   Debentures
   Shares

Note: Sole traders and partnerships are unable to issue shares, and access to certain other sources of finance will often be difficult due to their inability to provide adequate security.

It is a part of management's job to make sure that the finance raised is appropriate for the intended purpose. As a general rule, long-term investments should be financed from long-term sources, while short-term sources and applications will often be linked together in a similar manner (the reasons for this are examined in section 7 of this Chapter). It is therefore necessary to consider the likely duration for which the above types of finance are normally made available, so that we can assess, in due course, whether outgoings have been properly financed.

The period of credit received from suppliers will depend on the normal practice for the trade; it will usually be somewhere between one and three months. Provisions for corporation tax and dividends are made out of profits, but they are not payable immediately and, meanwhile, they comprise a temporary source of finance. The final dividend recommended by the directors will be paid following its confirmation at the annual general meeting, normally held three or four months after the end of the accounting year. The date on which corporation tax is payable is given in the accounts though, in the case of companies formed since 5 April, 1965, it is always nine months after the end of the accounting period. For companies, who are required to charge Value Added Tax (VAT) on the goods or services they supply, the tax collected on behalf of the government is a substantial temporary source of finance until paid over to the Inland Revenue at three monthly intervals.

Bank overdrafts do not fit neatly into the legal classification of creditors into amounts falling due within one year and amounts falling due in more than one year. In practice, bank overdrafts are often outstanding for very long periods of time, but they are technically repayable on call or at short notice and are therefore placed in the former category. Hire purchase finance may consist of instalments which are payable over a number of accounting periods, but the payment dates will have been agreed and an allocation is made between creditors falling due within and beyond one year on the basis of this information. Unsecured loans can be raised for varying durations, while debentures and share capital are sources of long-term finance. Debentures will, however, normally be repayable at some future date, while share capital is redeemable in certain circumstances (see Chapter 4, section 4.1). As the redemption date for unsecured loans and debentures gets nearer, the relevant amounts must be viewed as medium-term finance and ultimately be classified as an amount falling due for repayment within one year. For creditors falling due for payment after one year, the Companies Act 1981 requires registered companies to disclose, by way of note, amounts repayable within five years. For the purpose of this Chapter, we will therefore regard amounts repayable between one and five years of the balance sheet date as medium-term finance.

9.3 APPLICATIONS OF FINANCE

The way in which cash raised from the types of finance available is employed reflects the priorities of management at a particular point in time. Basically there are three alternatives:

1. *Distribute.* A company will normally pay an annual dividend, both to ensure that the share price remains at an acceptable level, and to increase the likelihood of the company being able to raise further finance from shareholders when required. The dividend will normally be declared out of the current year's profit but, if this is insufficient, retained profits brought forward from previous years may be used. In the latter case, the cash payment cannot be financed out of the current year's profits, and the statement of funds will help to identify the source of finance which has been used instead. More often, profits exceed dividends, and the excess is available for either of the purposes identified under 2 and 3 below.

2. *Invest.* Each year a company is likely to purchase fixed assets in order to maintain its present level of business activity, and sometimes also to put into operation a programme of expansion. In the latter case, an additional investment in working capital will also be called for. Where management wishes to increase the scale of business operations by external growth (see Chapter 5, section 2), finance will be required for the purpose of acquiring either the assets of, or the shares in, another company.

3. *Reduce external finance.* The directors may choose to use available cash to repay the bank or providers of loan capital and, in certain circumstances (see Chapter 4, section 4), share capital. This course may be adopted because repayment is due, or because management takes the view that the company is excessively reliant on external finance, or because there are cash resources available which are not needed for any other purpose.

9.4 THE STATEMENT OF FUNDS

The statement of funds may be defined as an account which sets out, in an orderly manner, the sources of funds which have been raised during an accounting period, and the ways in which those funds have been applied. The purposes of the statement are to provide some insights into the financial policies pursued by management, and to indicate their effect on the financial position of the company.

9.4.1 Definition of Funds The form which the statement takes, and the information it contains, depends on how *funds* are defined. There are three main alternatives:

Definition of Funds	Content of Statement
Cash	Transactions which increase or decrease cash
Net monetary assets*	Transactions which increase or decrease net monetary assets
Working capital	Transactions which increase or decrease working capital

*debtors + cash + temporary investments − creditors

Many transactions will be accounted for in the same manner, in the statement of funds, whichever definition of funds is employed. For instance, an issue of 100,000 shares of £1 each, for cash, will cause an immediate increase in cash, net monetary assets and working capital of £100,000, while the cash purchase of goods, for £70,000 will immediately cause all three financial magnitudes to decrease by £70,000. Where goods or services are purchased or sold on credit, however, there will be significant differences between the content of the three statements depending on the definition used.

Example 9.1

Peter, a trader, deals in second-hand cars on a part-time basis. The following information is provided relating to 19X1:

Date	Transaction	£
7 January	Purchased a second-hand Fiat car, on credit, from T. Jones for	4,000
16 February	Sold the Fiat to K. Smith, on credit, for	6,000
27 March	Collected cash from K. Smith	6,000
4 April	Paid T. Jones	4,000

Assuming that statements of funds are prepared on a monthly basis, the effect of the above transactions on each of the three financial magnitudes is demonstrated in the following table:

Accounting Period	Transaction	Cash	Funds defined as: Net Monetary Assets	Working Capital
		£	£	£
January	Credit purchase of car	—	−4,000	*
February	Credit sale of car	—	+6,000	+6,000
				−4,000
March	Collection of cash	+6,000	—	—
April	Payment of cash	−4,000	—	—
		+2,000	+2,000	+2,000

*Stock + £4,000; creditors + £4,000; net effect, zero.

The final effect of the four transactions on each of the three financial magnitudes is exactly the same: they all increase by £2,000. Therefore, statements of funds covering the entire four month period, by which time the trading cycle is complete, will contain the same information whichever definition is used: that is, inflows of funds will be £6,000 and outflows will be £4,000. In practice, there will be credit transactions which are incomplete at the end of an accounting period, and the details contained in the above table demonstrate their effect. In the first accounting period, January, the second-hand car is purchased on credit. There is no cash flow, and neither is working capital affected as both creditors and stock increase by a similar amount. However, the acquisition does cause net monetary assets (debtors + cash + temporary investments − creditors) to decline by £4,000, and so the credit purchase appears as an outflow in the statement where funds are defined as net monetary assets. In February, the credit sale causes net monetary assets to increase by £6,000 (debtors + £6,000) and working capital to increase by £2,000 (debtors + £6,000, stock − £4,000); cash is unaffected. The collection of cash in March, affects neither net monetary assets nor working capital (cash + £6,000, debtors − £6,000), but an inflow of £6,000 is reported in the statement which defines funds as cash. In a similar manner, the payment of cash, in April, is again reported only in the statement which uses the cash definition of funds.

There is no doubt that cash, liquidity and working capital are each important indicators of the financial health and well-being of a company. However, it would be confusing to publish statements of funds prepared on *all three* bases, and this is not done. SSAP10 encourages companies to use a presentation which is best suited to their particular circumstances and, in practice, a great deal of diversity exists in the reporting procedures employed. The illustrations contained in the appendix to SSAP10 emphasise changes in working capital, and we will concentrate on statements prepared in accordance with this definition of funds. In section 10 of this

Chapter, however, we examine the adjustments which must be made to convert a working capital based statement into a cash based statement of funds.

9.4.2 Constructing a Statement of Funds The statement of funds should be prepared in two stages:

Stage 1: List the sources from which working capital has been derived during the accounting period, and the ways in which working capital has been used up, i.e. list the transactions which *cause* working capital to increase or decrease.

Stage 2: Analyse the net increase or decrease in working capital into changes in the constituent items, i.e. stock, debtors, creditors and cash.

The relationship between the two stages is shown in figure 9.1

Figure 9.1

Changes in Working Capital Explained and Analysed

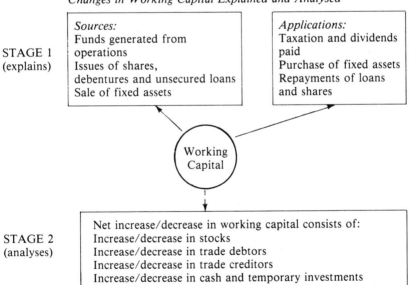

—▸indicates flow of working capital.
- ▸indicates composition of working capital.

Example 9.2 (To illustrate the construction of a Statement of Funds).

The following financial information is provided relating to the affairs of Langstone Ltd.

Balance Sheets, 31 December

	19X1	19X1	19X2	19X2
	£000	£000	£000	£000
Fixed Assets				
Plant and machinery at cost		147		226
Less: Accumulated depreciation		66		98
		81		128
Current Assets				
Stock	50		74	
Trade debtors	36		50	
Bank balance	12		30	
	98		154	
Less: Current Liabilities				
Trade creditors	48		50	
Working capital		50		104
		131		232
Financed by:				
Share capital (£1 shares)		100		120
Share premium account		—		5
Reserves		31		57
		131		182
15% Debentures repayable 19X9		—		40
Bank loan repayable 31 December, 19X4		—		10
		131		232

Extracts from Profit and Loss Account

	19X2
	£000
Net profit (after charging depreciation, £32,000)	38
Interim dividend paid, 30 June, 19X2	12
Retained profit for 19X2	26
Reserves, 1 January, 19X2	31
Reserves, 31 December, 19X2	57

On 2 January, 19X2, Langstone Ltd. issued for cash 20,000 ordinary shares of £1 each at a premium of 25p per share. Plant costing £79,000 was purchased during the year; there were no sales of fixed assets.

REQUIRED:
A statement of funds for 19X2.
Note: Ignore taxation.
Stage 1. The company has issued 20,000 shares at a premium of 25p per share. This has caused share capital to increase from £100,000 to £120,000, and has resulted in the creation of a share premium account, of £5,000, which is included in the balance sheet as at 31 December, 19X2. The company has therefore raised £25,000 from the share issue and this amount should appear as a source of funds. A comparison of the two balance sheets shows that the company has also issued debentures for £40,000 and raised a loan of £10,000 from its bank. Reserves have increased by £26,000 to £57,000, but reference must be made to the profit and loss account in order to build up the figure for funds generated from operations. The profit and loss account shows that funds generated internally amounted to £70,000, made up of net profit of £38,000 and a depreciation charge of £32,000. It should also be noted that, during 19X2, trade creditors increased from £48,000 to £50,000. However, this does not represent a source of net working capital, it merely reflects a change in the *composition* of working capital and is dealt with under stage 2.

During 19X2, the directors of Langstone Ltd. applied working capital in two ways: firstly, they paid a dividend of £12,000 and, secondly, they spent £79,000 on plant and machinery causing the balance sheet figure for plant at cost to increase from £147,000 to £226,000.

The sources and applications of working capital are presented below in accordance with the illustrations contained in SSAP10.

SOURCE OF FUNDS	£000	£000
Profit..		38
Adjustment for item not involving the movement of funds:		
Depreciation..		32
TOTAL GENERATED FROM OPERATIONS......................		70

FUNDS FROM OTHER SOURCES	£000	£000
Shares	25	
Debentures	40	
Bank loan	10	
	—	75
		145
APPLICATION OF FUNDS		
Purchase of plant and machinery	79	
Dividends paid	12	
	—	91
		54

Sources of funds, defined as working capital, exceed applications by £54,000. The fact that working capital has increased by £54,000 can be confirmed from the balance sheets of Langstone Ltd., at the end of 19X1 and 19X2, which respectively show figures for working capital of £50,000 and £104,000.

Stage 2. An analysis of the net increase in working capital into changes in the constituent items shows increases in stock of £24,000, trade debtors of £14,000, the bank balance of £18,000 and trade creditors of £2,000. SSAP10 presents these changes in the following manner:

INCREASE/DECREASE IN WORKING CAPITAL	£000
Increase in stocks	24
Increase in trade debtors	14
Increase in trade creditors	(2)
Movement in net liquid funds:	
Increase in bank balance	18
	54

Note the following points:

1. The increase in trade creditors is shown as a negative figure as it represents a decrease in working capital.

2. The movement in net liquid funds must be shown as a separate item. SSAP10 defines net liquid funds as 'cash at bank and in hand and cash equivalents (e.g. investments held as current assets) *less* bank overdrafts and other borrowings payable within one year of the accounting date.'

The Stage 1 and Stage 2 calculations are combined, for presentation purposes, as follows:

Statement of Source and Application of Funds, Langstone Ltd., 19X2

SOURCE OF FUNDS	£000	£000
Profit		38
Adjustment for item not involving the movement of funds:		
Depreciation		32
		—
TOTAL GENERATED FROM OPERATIONS		70
FUNDS FROM OTHER SOURCES		
Shares	25	
Debentures	40	
Bank loan	10	
	—	75
		—
		145
		—
APPLICATION OF FUNDS		
Purchase of plant and machinery	79	
Dividends paid	12	
	—	91
		—
		54
		—
INCREASE/DECREASE IN WORKING CAPITAL		
Increase in stocks	24	
Increase in trade debtors	14	
Increase in trade creditors	(2)	
Movement in net liquid funds:		
Increase in bank balance	18	54
	—	—

9.5 SSAP10: SOME PROBLEM AREAS

9.5.1 Non-Fund Items There are a number of accounting entries made by companies which neither use funds nor provide funds. In order to explain their significance for the statement of funds, it is useful to classify them on the basis of whether or not they affect the level of reported profit before tax.

1. *Non-fund items which affect pre-tax profit.* SSAP10 requires the disclosure of non-fund items which affect pre-tax profits. The most important item falling into this category is depreciation which, in example 9.2, is disclosed under the heading 'adjustment for item not involving the movement of funds'. A loss arising on the sale of a fixed asset is accounted for in the same way, since it is in the nature of an adjustment to previous depreciation charges. A non-extraordinary profit on the sale of a fixed asset, which has

been credited to the profit and loss account, must be deducted, since the entire sales proceeds are shown separately under the heading 'funds from other sources'.

2. *Non-fund items which do not affect pre-tax profit.* The most common adjustments are transfers to reserves, a transfer to the deferred tax account, a bonus issue of shares and the revaluation of fixed assets. Since these adjustments do not represent either sources or applications of working capital, and do not affect the resources available to the company, they should not be reported in the statement of funds.

9.5.2 Taxation and Dividends SSAP10 requires companies to disclose the figure for dividends *paid* as an application of funds, while the illustrations, attached to the statement, also show tax *paid* as an application of funds. Strict compliance with the working capital concept of funds would instead require companies to show dividends paid *and proposed* and the current year's *provision* for taxation as applications of funds, while differences between the previous and current years' figures for proposed dividends and taxation payable would appear as part of the analysis of the net increase or decrease in working capital. Treatment of taxation and dividends on the *cash* basis, rather than the *accruals* basis, therefore represents a significant departure from the working capital notion of funds.

9.5.3 Work Schedules Where examination questions require candidates to prepare a statement of funds, many of the figures can be obtained from a straightforward comparison of the balances appearing in successive balance sheets. This procedure is not acceptable, however, where a number of transactions have occurred, during the year, some increasing and others decreasing the opening balance. The inclusion of 'net' figures, in the statement of funds, does not provide a complete view of financial developments, and so 'gross' changes must be computed in order to comply with SSAP10. Students will often find it helpful to use either ledger accounts or a work schedule to build up the gross figures.

Example 9.3

The following information is provided in respect of Stanmore Ltd's plant and machinery:

Balances at 31 December	19X0	19X1
	£	£
Plant and machinery at cost...	206,500	317,800
Less: Accumulated depreciation	104,200	123,500
	102,300	194,300

During 19X1 the company sold plant, which cost £26,000 some years ago, for £7,000. Accumulated depreciation, at the date of sale, was £16,000.

Figures for 'additions to plant' and the 'depreciation charge' are not given, but they can be calculated, as the balancing items, using the following work schedule:

	Cost	Accumulated Depreciation
	£	£
Opening balances	206,500	104,200
Sale of plant..	(26,000)	(16,000)
Additions to plant (balancing item)........................	137,300	
Depreciation charge (balancing item)......................		35,300
Closing balances..	317,800	123,500

9.6 A MORE COMPLEX EXAMPLE

Example 9.4

The following information is provided relating to Stanfield Ltd., a manufacturing company:

Profit and Loss Account for 19X1

	£000	£000
Profit before tax		620
Corporation tax:		
Charge for the year...	350	
Transfer from deferred tax account......................	(30)	
	—	320
Profit after tax and before extraordinary item..........................		300
Profit on the sale of investment (net of tax, £90,000)................		210
		510
Less: Dividends paid and proposed.......................................		200
Retained profit for 19X1..		310

Balance Sheet as at 31 December, 19X1·

19X0 £000		£000	19X1 £000
2,089	Plant and equipment at cost		3,702
362	*Less:* Accumulated depreciation		509
1,727			3,193
360	Investments at cost		—
	Current Assets		
620	Stocks...	580	
375	Debtors	406	
204	Bank...	98	
1,199		1,084	
	Current Liabilities		
275	Creditors	307	
—	Short-term loans..	100	
291	Taxation due 30 September...............................	440	
100	Proposed dividends..	30	
666		877	
533	Net Current Assets...		207
2,620			3,400
	Financed by:		
1,000	Share capital (£1 ordinary shares)		1,500
1,150	Reserves		960
2,150			2,460
170	Deferred tax account......................................		140
300	15% Debentures repayable 19X6...........................		800
2,620			3,400

Notes:
  1. During 19X1, the company sold equipment, which cost £130,000 some years ago, for £47,000. A profit arising on disposal of £15,000 has been credited to the profit and loss account.
  2. On 1 January, 19X1, the company made a bonus issue of one ordinary share, fully paid, for every two shares held on that date.

REQUIRED:
A statement of source and application of funds for 19X1, prepared in compliance with the instructions contained in SSAP10.
Note: Ignore advance corporation tax.

Solution:

Work schedule:	Cost	Accumulated Depreciation
Plant and Equipment	*£000*	*£000*
Balances at 1 January	2,089	362
Sale of plant	(130)	(98) W1
Additions to plant (balancing item)	1,743	
Depreciation charge (balancing item)		245
Balance at 31 December	3,702	509
W1 Cost of plant sold		130
Less: Sales proceeds	47	
Profit on disposal	(15)	
Book value at date of disposal	—	32
Accumulated depreciation		98

Statement of Source and Application of Funds, Stanfield Ltd., 19X1

SOURCE OF FUNDS	£000	£000
Profit before tax		620
Adjustments for items not involving the movement of funds:		
Depreciation	245	
Profit on sale of plant	(15)	
	—	230
TOTAL GENERATED FROM OPERATIONS		850
FUNDS FROM OTHER SOURCES		
Debentures	500	
Sale of investments	660 W2	
Sale of plant	47	
	—	1,207
		2,057
APPLICATION OF FUNDS		
Purchase of plant and equipment	1,743	
Dividends paid	270 W3	
Tax paid	291	
	—	2,304
		(247)
INCREASE/DECREASE IN WORKING CAPITAL		
Decrease in stocks	(40)	
Increase in debtors	31	
Increase in creditors	(32)	
Movement in net liquid funds:		
Decrease in cash balance	(106)	
Increase in short-term loans	(100)	
	(206)	(247)

W2 £360,000 (book value) + £300,000 (profit on sale before tax).
W3 £100,000 (proposed final dividend for 19X0) + £170,000 (interim dividend for 19X1).

9.7 FINANCING BUSINESS INVESTMENT

Section 1 of this Chapter gives eight examples of questions that information contained in the statement of funds can help to answer. This list is not exhaustive and, without too much difficulty, many more questions could be added. However, when making an assessment of a particular company's financial developments, and of the financial policies pursued by management, it will normally be useful to start by considering whether investment has been financed correctly. The appropriate source for financing particular types of business investment must therefore be considered.

Companies invest in projects with widely different life spans; for example, a surveyor may decide to purchase a property in a dilapidated condition with the intention of renovation and resale. If events go according to plan, perhaps only six months will elapse between the dates when the initial investment is made and the property is resold. An investment may be made for an even shorter duration; a retail trader may be given the opportunity to purchase a considerable quantity of fire damaged stock at an extremely low price and, although this may be additional to his normal trading activity, he seizes the opportunity for a quick profit and resells the stock, within days, at a favourable price. Often, however, investment decisions tie up resources in a project for years rather than weeks or months. The purchase of a lathe and the construction and operation of an oil rig are examples of long-term investments, though there is a tremendous difference between the quantity of resources committed to each of these two projects.

The guiding factor, when making a decision concerning the type of finance to use, is the duration of the investment. It is perfectly reasonable to finance a short-term investment with equivalent finance. The surveyor may finance his project out of a bank over-draft, while the retailer may be able to resell the damaged stock before he is obliged to pay his supplier who therefore finances the whole transaction. Long-term investments, on the other hand, should normally be paid for out of long-term sources of finance, because the funds committed to them are recovered over a much longer time period.

Example 9.5

Complex Ltd. plans to invest in a new project. It is estimated that the project will require an initial investment of £100,000, and that funds generated from the project, before deducting finance charges, will amount to £25,000 for each of the next ten years.

Complex Ltd. is an established company with a wide range of other activities but, for illustrative purposes, we will first examine the financial implications of the new project in isolation. Assume that Complex Ltd. decides to finance the investment by way of a medium-term bank loan, repayable in 3 years time, and that the interest payable is 10% per annum throughout the three year period. In these circumstances, a problem will arise at the end of year 3, by which time the project will have generated £75,000 (3 × £25,000), of which £30,000 (3 × £10,000) will have been paid out as bank interest. There will be a surplus of £75,000 − £30,000 = £45,000, which is insufficient to repay the bank loan of £100,000. If the company is committed to repay the £100,000 at the end of year 3, acute financial embarrassment may result. Perhaps it will be possible to raise the shortfall of £55,000 from elsewhere, at that stage, but the risk will not necessarily be one which management will wish to take; at least *some* long-term finance should therefore be raised, by Complex Ltd., at the outset. An extreme course of action would be to finance the entire project out of a ten year loan, in which case the company would not be obliged to repay the finance until it had received the full benefit of resources generated from the project. Such a cautious option need not be followed; finance is generated throughout the life of the project and it would be perfectly feasible to employ a combination of medium-term and long-term finance.

If we relax the assumption that the project is being undertaken in isolation, account may be taken of the financial implications of the other activities of Complex Ltd. Although it will usually be prudent to finance long-term investments substantially out of long-term sources of finance, this is not an inviolable rule; for instance Complex Ltd., in anticipation of this new project, may have previously built up its cash resources over a period of months or years. If such a course had been followed, the balance sheet of Complex Ltd., immediately prior to the investment being undertaken, would probably include a large balance of working capital reflected in the existence of a working capital ratio significantly in excess of 2:1. It would be perfectly reasonable, in these circumstances, to finance at least some of the expansion out of working capital and, as a result, reduce the working capital ratio to a more conventional level. Furthermore, any finance which it is necessary to raise, at the outset, may be repaid not only out of cash generated by that particular investment but also out of cash generated from the other activities in which the company is engaged.

9.7.1 Depreciation as a Source of Finance

Funds generated from operations, during an accounting period, increase working capital by an equivalent amount. The two main components of funds generated from operations are profit and depreciation. The depreciation charge acknowledges the fact that the value of a fixed asset declines over its working life and earmarks, for retention within the company, a quantity of resources equal to the asset's original cost. Therefore, even if a company pays out its entire profit in the form of dividends, working capital will increase by the amount of the depreciation charged over the asset's useful life. The question arises whether these resources, as they arise, are available for investment purposes, or whether they should be set aside specifically to finance the replacement of the fixed asset when it is worn out.

In the past, management often took the precaution of setting aside, each year, a sum of money, equal to the amount of the depreciation charge, either in a separate bank account or invested in readily realisable securities. This procedure is no longer common and, instead, the resources are usually reinvested in operating assets. Even then, there are a number of alternative uses from which management may choose. The resources may be invested in current assets, for instance raw materials may be purchased in large quantities to obtain the benefit of discounts for bulk purchases. This will cause stock levels to rise but, when the date for replacing the fixed asset falls due, stocks can be restored to their former levels. Alternatively, the resources may be used to help finance a programme of expansion which involves the acquisition of additional fixed assets. If this is done, it will not be possible to release the resources when replacement falls due, and it will be necessary for management to arrange an alternative source of finance. Section 2 of this Chapter indicates the range of sources to which management may turn at this stage. For instance, it may well happen that replacements falling due in a particular accounting period will be partly or wholly financed out of funds earmarked for retention by the *total* depreciation charge made in respect of that accounting period.

Example 9.6

Goldcliffe Ltd. owns ten machines. Each machine cost £5,000 and has a five-year life and zero residual value at the end of that period. Replacement machines cost £5,000. Each year two machines wear out and are replaced.

Total depreciation charge each year on the straight line basis is:

$$\frac{£5,000}{5} \times 10 = £10,000$$

Replacements each year: Two machines at £5,000 = £10,000

Goldcliffe Ltd. is able to finance replacements entirely out of the current year's depreciation charge.

A final point which should be emphasised, in this section, is that a company which is suffering losses will still generate a positive flow of funds from operations, provided losses do not exceed depreciation (plus any other adjustments which do not involve an outflow of funds). For instance, a company which reports a loss of £1m, after charging depreciation of £4m, has generated funds from operations of £3m. This helps to explain how loss-making companies are able to carry on, at least in the short-run, despite the fact that they find it impossible to issue shares or raise loans in view of their poor performance (see also Chapter 4, section 5).

9.7.2 Working Capital Requirements A decision to increase the level of turnover will require an additional investment in fixed assets only if the planned increase will result in total output in excess of the presently available capacity. A company's working capital requirements are likely to increase, however, irrespective of whether or not expansion requires an additional investment in fixed assets. This is because levels of stocks, debtors and creditors are closely related to the level of business activity.

Example 9.7
As the result of an advertising campaign, Overton Ltd., a trading company, expects sales to increase significantly in 19X2. The following facts and estimates are provided.

	Facts 19X1 £	Estimates 19X2 £
Turnover..........................	600,000	800,000
Cost of goods sold..............	450,000	600,000
Stocks.............................	64,000	*
Trade debtors....................	80,000	*
Operating cash balance.........	6,000	*
Trade creditors..................	60,000	*
Working capital.................	90,000	*
Working capital ratio..........	2.5:1	*

*Management has not calculated its working capital requirements for 19X2, but expects that the stock-holding period and the periods of credit allowed to customers and obtained from suppliers will remain the same as in 19X1. The amount of cash required to finance operations is a function of the level of business activity.

REQUIRED:
A calculation of the *additional* working capital requirement of Overton Ltd. for 19X2.

Solution:
Turnover and cost of goods sold have each increased by one third. Stocks, debtors, cash and creditors are expected to increase by the same proportion, and so the estimated balances and additional working capital requirement are as follows:

	19X1 £	19X2 £
Stocks	$64,000 \times \frac{4}{3}$	85,333
Trade debtors	$80,000 \times \frac{4}{3}$	106,667
Operating cash balance	$6,000 \times \frac{4}{3}$	8,000
	150,000	200,000
Trade creditors	$(60,000) \times \frac{4}{3}$	(80,000)
Working capital	90,000	120,000
Less: Existing requirement		90,000
Additional requirement		30,000

Expansion is expected to result in additional investments in stocks, debtors and cash totalling £50,000 (£200,000 – £150,000), of which £20,000 is financed by creditors. The remaining £30,000 must be provided from medium or long-term sources in order for the working capital ratio to remain at 2.5:1 during 19X2. It therefore follows that it is not enough for an expanding company merely to arrange for an increase in its working capital; it must increase working capital by a sufficient amount to safeguard the existing ratio of stock + debtors + operating cash requirements: creditors. There are of course, exceptions to this general rule; for instance, it may be possible to reduce the average stockholding period by improved stock handling procedures, in which case working capital requirements will be correspondingly reduced. On the other hand, it may be necessary to offer customers more credit in order to increase sales, in which case there will be a more than proportionate increase in working capital requirements.

9.8 FUNDS FLOW ANALYSIS AND RATIO ANALYSIS

The statement of funds and accounting ratios are both tools for analysing the financial information contained in the profit and loss account and balance sheet. Their aim is to provide decision makers with the additional information they require to assess the past performance and financial position of the company, and also to help form an opinion concerning likely future progress. The way in which funds flow analysis and ratio analysis complement one another is illustrated in example 9.8

Example 9.8 (Taken from the September, 1982 *Accountancy* paper).

Maximon Ltd. is a well established company engaged in the manufacture and sale of metal products. The following information is obtained from the company's financial records.

BALANCE SHEET AT 30 JUNE

	1981		1982	
	£	£	£	£
Fixed Assets at cost		637,100		767,300
Less: Depreciation		297,500		321,400
		339,600		445,900
Trade investments at cost		106,000		106,000
Current Assets				
Stock and work-in-progress	230,200		260,100	
Trade debtors and prepayments	135,800		196,400	
Bank balance	—		9,300	
	366,000		465,800	
Less: Current Liabilities				
Trade creditors and accruals	96,800		101,700	
Taxation due: 31 March 1982	63,800		—	
31 March 1983	—		61,000	
Dividend payable	60,000		66,000	
Bank overdraft	71,000		—	
	291,600		228,700	
Net Current Assets		74,400		237,100
		£520,000		£789,000
Financed by:				
Ordinary share capital (ordinary				
shares of £1 each)		200,000		220,000
Share premium account		—		30,000
Reserves		320,000		339,000
		520,000		589,000
15% debenture		—		200,000
		£520,000		£789,000

PROFIT AND LOSS ACCOUNTS, YEAR ENDED 30 JUNE

	1981		1982	
	£	£	£	£
Operating profit		160,500		176,000
Less: finance charges—bank interest		9,200		—
—debenture interest		—		30,000
Net profit before taxation		151,300		146,000
Less: Taxation		63,800		61,000
Profit after taxation		87,500		85,000
Less: dividend proposed		60,000		66,000
Retained profit for the year		£27,500		£19,000

Notes

1. On 31 January 1982 a rights issue was made of one ordinary share for every ten ordinary shares currently held. For the purpose of this issue the ordinary shares were valued at £2.50 each.

2. The debenture is secured on the company's freehold property which is included amongst fixed assets in the balance sheet shown above.

3. During the year ended 30 June 1982, the company disposed of fixed assets which cost £65,200 some years ago for £17,900. A loss of £9,600 arising on disposal has been deducted in arriving at operating profit for the year.

Required:

(a) The statement of source and application of funds of Maximon Ltd., for the year ended 30 June 1982, in accordance with the provisions contained in Statement of Standard Accounting Practice No. 10 entitled 'Statements of Source and Application of Funds'.

[16]

(b) An examination of the respective financial positions of Maximon Ltd. at 30 June 1981 and 30 June 1982 and a discussion of the financial developments which have occurred during the intervening period. The financial statement prepared under (a) and relevant accounting ratios should be used to support your analysis.

[14]

NOTE: Ignore advance corporation tax.

[Total marks for question: 30]

Solution:

(a) *Work schedule:*

	Cost £	Depreciation £
Fixed assets		
Balance 30 June, 1981	637,100	297,500
Sales	(65,200)	(37,700) W1
Additions (balancing item)	195,400	
Charge (balancing item)		61,600
Balance 30 June, 1982	767,300	321,400

W1 £65,200 (cost) – £27,500 (book value)

Statement of Source and Application of Funds, Maximon Ltd., 1981/82

SOURCE OF FUNDS	£	£
Profit before tax		146,000
Adjustments for items not involving the movement of funds:		
Depreciation	61,600	
Loss on disposal of fixed assets	9,600	
		71,200
TOTAL GENERATED FROM OPERATIONS		217,200
FUNDS FROM OTHER SOURCES		
Shares	50,000	
Debenture	200,000	
Sale of fixed assets	17,900	
		267,900
		485,100
APPLICATION OF FUNDS		
Purchase of fixed assets	195,400	
Taxation paid	63,800	
Dividends paid	60,000	
		319,200
		165,900
INCREASE/DECREASE IN WORKING CAPITAL		
Increase in stocks	29,900	
Increase in debtors	60,600	
Increase in creditors	(4,900)	
Movement in net liquid funds:		
Increase in cash balance	80,300	
		165,900

(b) *Relevant Ratios:*

	1981	1982
Working capital ratio	1.3:1	2:1
Liquidity ratio	0.5:1	0.9:1
Proprietorship ratio	64%	58%
Rate of return on gross assets*	19.8%	17.3%
Rate of return on shareholders' equity†	16.8%	14.4%
Gearing (total borrowing‡ ÷ equity) × 100	14%	34%

*using profit before interest and tax
†using post-tax profit
‡bank overdraft + debenture

The solvency ratios show that the short-term financial position of Maximon Ltd., at 30 June, 1981, was unsatisfactory; both the working capital and liquidity ratios were significantly below the accepted 'norms' for a manufacturing company. The proprietors, however, provided nearly two thirds of the total finance required, and a healthy post-tax return of 16.8% was achieved on shareholders' funds.

The statement of funds sets out the financial developments which occurred during the year ended 30 June, 1982. The main changes were as follows: funds amounting to £217,200 were generated from operations; a debenture of £200,000 was raised and £195,400 was spent on fixed assets. Long-term sources of funds, both raised and generated during the year, significantly exceeded applications, with the result that working capital was increased by £165,900. The statement of funds reveals an improvement in the cash position of £80,300, and the balance sheets show that, over the twelve month period, a large overdraft was converted into a small bank balance.

Operating profits remained buoyant, but there were reductions in the rates of return on both gross assets and shareholders' equity. Possible reasons for this are the cost of the debentures, needed to strengthen the financial position of Maximon Ltd., and the heavy expenditure on fixed assets which may not have produced its full benefits during the year of acquisition.

At 30 June, 1982, the short term solvency ratios are satisfactory. The improvement in the company's financial position was partly brought about by introducing a larger element of gearing into the long term capital structure, but it remains at an acceptable level.

Examiner's comments:
Main student errors:
  1. Failure to calculate and record properly the loss arising on the disposal of fixed assets.
  2. Depreciation and purchase of fixed assets shown 'net' instead of 'gross'.

9.9   UNBALANCED FINANCIAL DEVELOPMENT

The successful development of corporate activity depends on the existence of a system of forward planning which examines the likely profitability and financial implications of investment proposals. Even the best laid plans may of course be thwarted and unforeseen events can render unprofitable a project which careful planning suggested would produce a highly satisfactory rate of return. Nevertheless planning is important, otherwise companies will embark upon projects which, even in the most favourable conditions, will yield an unacceptable return on the amount invested. Planning for the financial implications of an investment proposal is just as important.

When a new company is formed, it is management's job to ensure that sufficient long-term finance is raised to cover planned expenditure on fixed assets and make an adequate contribution towards the financing of current assets, with the balance provided by current liabilities, mainly in the form of trade credit and a bank overdraft. Throughout the life of the company, it remains management's job to maintain an appropriate balance between long-term, medium-term and short-term finance, and within the first category, an acceptable relationship must exist between share capital and loan capital (see Chapter 8, section 6). When expansion occurs, additional long-term finance will be needed to cover the cost of fixed assets and working capital requirements; while a reduction in the scale of a company's operations may permit the repayment of certain sources of finance. In practice, management often fails to achieve a balanced financial structure, either because it does not plan ahead or because unexpected events occur. It is possible to identify two main aspects of unbalanced financial development.

9.9.1 Over-capitalisation This occurs where management is unable to make full use of the capital available to it. For instance, it may not have proved possible to achieve the volume of activity anticipated at the outset, when the capital structure was decided upon. Alternatively, management may find itself in possession of surplus resources, for instance, as the result of selling a division of the company's activities. In these circumstances, it may be appropriate to return capital to the members by either purchasing shares or redeeming shares or reducing capital in accordance with the conditions contained in Chapter 4, sections 3 and 4.

9.9.2 Over-trading This occurs when the volume of business activity is excessive in relation to the finance provided by the shareholders, with the result that there is undue reliance on external finance in the form of loan capital, bank overdrafts and trade credit. The situation arises because of significant errors in the financial policy pursued by management; often it occurs because management has expanded the volume of business activity beyond the level justified by the resources available to the company. In essence, management has attempted to do 'too much too quickly', with the result that the company is left with insufficient resources to meet its currently maturing liabilities, that is, the company will be under severe financial pressure to pay wages due to employees, debts due to suppliers, tax payable to the government and money owing to the bank. The financial signs of over-trading, which should be looked for in a balance sheet, are a decline in the ratios of debtors/creditors and current assets/current liabilities, a low figure for working capital, perhaps even a deficit, a high ratio of fixed assets to working capital and a severe shortage of cash.

Over-trading is a common cause of business failure, and is therefore of considerable interest to bankers. The following case study sets out some of the possible causes of over-trading and the potential remedies which are available.

Over-trading: a case study. The following financial information and facts are provided relating to the affairs of Elford Ltd., a manufacturing company which carries on its activities from rented accommodation.

Extracts from Profit and Loss Accounts

19X1 £000		19X2 £000
1,600	Turnover.....................................	1,800
80	Operating profit............................	100
40	*Less:* Proposed dividend	40
40	Retained profit for the year..............	60
30	Retained profit at 1 January.............	70
70	Retained profit at 31 December.........	130

Balance Sheets at 31 December

19X1 £000		19X2 £000	£000
	Tangible Fixed Assets		
500	Plant and machinery at cost..............	800	
(220)	*Less:* Accumulated depreciation.........	296	
		—	504
20	Fixtures and fittings at cost..............	20	
(10) ·	*Less:* Accumulated depreciation.........	12	
		—	8
290	carried forward		512

£000		£000	£000
290	brought forward		512
	Current Assets		
100	Stocks	154	
90	Trade debtors...............................	130	
30	Cash at bank	—	
220		284	
	Less: Current liabilities		
80	Trade creditors.............................	200	
40	Proposed dividend	40	
—	Bank overdraft..............................	26	
120		266	
100	Net Current Assets...........................		18
390			530
	Financed by:		
320	Share capital £1 ordinary shares)...........		336
—	Share premium account......................		4
70	Retained profits..............................		130
390			470
—	Loan repayable 19X5........................		60
390			530

Notes:
1. The additional plant was acquired on 1 March, 19X2.
2. 16,000 shares were issued at a premium of 25p per share on 10 February, 19X2.
3. Taxation is ignored.

A casual examination of the above information indicates that 19X2 has been a year of rapid expansion. A particularly significant development was the additional investment of £300,000 in plant and machinery, implying an increase in productive capacity of approximately 60%. The information given also suggests that the expansion has been a success since turnover has increased by £200,000 and trading profit has increased from £80,000 to £100,000. Even larger increases in turnover and profit might have been expected in view of the significant increase in productive capacity, but it must be borne in mind that the additional plant and machinery was not acquired until 1 March, and the extra capacity it provided is unlikely to have been fully utilised immediately. The sources used to finance this investment must be examined, and the following statement of funds helps to clarify the financial developments which occurred at Elford during 19X2.

Preparation.

Statement of Source and Application of Funds, Elford Ltd., 19X2

SOURCE OF FUNDS	£000	£000
Profit		100
Adjustment for item not involving the movement of funds:		
Depreciation		78 W1
TOTAL GENERATED FROM OPERATIONS		178
FUNDS FROM OTHER SOURCES		
Shares	20	
Loan	60	
	—	80
		258
APPLICATION OF FUNDS		
Purchase of plant and machinery	300	
Dividend paid	40	
	—	340
		(82)
INCREASE/DECREASE IN WORKING CAPITAL		
Increase in stocks	54	
Increase in debtors	40	
Increase in creditors	(120)	
Movement in net liquid funds:		
Decrease in cash balance	(56)	(82)

W1 £76,000 (plant and machinery) + £2,000 (fixtures and fittings).

Interpretation. Students will generally find it useful to ask themselves the following two questions as the basis for interpreting the financial data contained in the statement of funds:

Question 1: Has expansion, if any, been financed from the right sources? Elford has used four sources to finance expansion: funds generated from operations; share capital; a loan and working capital. Of these, funds generated from operations and share capital are acceptable sources for financing long-term investment (see section 7 of this Chapter), but the propriety of a medium-term loan and working capital are more doubtful. A medium-term loan may be used to finance part, or even the whole, of a long-term investment provided profit margins are sufficient to generate, and enable the company to retain, enough cash to repay the loan on its due date. Alternatively, where margins are lower, it may be acceptable to finance part of an investment on a medium-term basis, provided the remaining finance is long-term. Neither of these conditions appear to be fulfilled at Elford: profit has increased in 19X2, but margins are not exceptionally high; moreover, a significant portion of the investment (£82,000) has been financed out of working capital.

Question 2: What has been the effect of financial developments, during 19X2, on Elford's working capital position?

Working capital has declined from £100,000, on 1 January, to £18,000 on 31 December. The short-term solvency ratios are as follows:

	19X1	19X2
Working capital ratio.........	1.8:1	1.1:1
Liquidity ratio..................	1:1	0.5:1

For a manufacturing company, these ratios are satisfactory at the beginning of the year; admittedly the working capital ratio is a little below the conventional norm, but the more important *liquidity* ratio shows that the company was capable of meeting its short-term obligations as they fell due for payment. The financial position appears far less acceptable at the end of 19X2. The working capital ratio is just 1.1 : 1 and more than half the current assets are tied up in stocks, while the liquidity ratio suggests that the company can pay only 50% of the current liabilities outstanding at the balance sheet date. Manufacturing capacity appears to have been increased by about 60%, judging from the increase in the balance sheet figure for plant and machinery, and the increases in stocks and debtors indicate that the company was operating at this level of activity by the end of the year. However, trade creditors at 31 December, 19X2, are two and a half times the corresponding figure a year earlier. This is a disproportionate increase and probably means that suppliers are being asked to wait a considerable period of time before their claims are met. They are unlikely to be satisfied with this state of affairs and will probably be pressing for payment.

Conclusion. The directors have not succeeded in arranging satisfactory sources of finance for the investment programme undertaken in 19X2. The directors have over-stretched the available resources and the totally inadequate solvency ratios prove that the company is in a critical financial position at the year end. Further unfavourable financial characteristics, which reveal evidence of *over-trading*, are the sharp increase in the ratio of fixed assets to working capital, the deterioration in the structure of the current assets which have become less liquid, and the decline in the ratio of debtors to creditors which has fallen from 1.1 : 1 to 0.65 : 1 during 19X2. It is important to realise that these financial difficulties have arisen despite the fact that the new project appears to have been a success judged in terms of profitability. For example, the rate of return on the shareholders' equity investment in the company has increased as follows:

Rate of return on shareholders' equity

$$19X1 \quad \frac{80,000}{390,000} \times 100 = 20.5\%$$

$$19X2 \quad \frac{100,000}{470,000} \times 100 = 21.3\%$$

An unbalanced financial position can of course produce disastrous consequences. The company is short of money and will find it difficult to pay its bills on their due dates. As a result, any goodwill built up in the past, between the company and its suppliers, will quickly disappear. Suppliers may refuse to deliver more goods until existing bills are paid and, if the bills continue to remain unpaid, it is probable that the creditors will take legal action to recover the amounts due to them. Failure, on the part of the company, to comply with the court's instruction to honour its obligations will result in its liquidation. This sequence of events need not necessarily occur; it is one of the purposes of financial information to draw the reader's attention to a declining financial position, and it is the job of management to heed the 'warning lights' and take the necessary steps to restore an acceptable measure of financial stability. This emphasises the need for management to obtain up to date information as the basis for performance assessment and resource allocation decisions and, for this reason, quarterly and even monthly management accounts are prepared in many companies. Even this type of information may be made available too late to avoid unnecessary financial loss, however, and the preparation of forecast accounts to provide management with advance notice of the need to take remedial action is discussed in Chapter 10.

Prospects of Recovery. The company finds itself in financial difficulties because the directors have undertaken a heavy investment programme without due regard to the financial implications of such an expansionist policy. Clearly further investment is out of the question at this stage; a period of consolidation is needed, and management should concentrate its attention on the various ways in which the finances of the company might be improved. There are a number of possible courses of action which should be considered.

1. *Raise additional external finance.* The directors should consider the feasibility of issuing shares or raising a loan. In some respects, a further share issue would seem to be the better prospect. The company undertook a substantial investment in 19X2, and the shareholders were called upon to inject only £20,000. There is the additional fact that the shareholders have most to lose if the company goes into liquidation. The company is profitable, producing a return of over 20% on the book value of the shareholders' investment and paying regular dividends; whereas on liquidation the shareholders might lose most of their investment. The company seems viable, apart from the cash difficulties, and, provided this short-term problem is overcome, there is no reason why it should not prosper. An offer of shares to existing members in proportion to their present holdings, i.e. a 'rights issue', should be carefully considered.

The ability of the directors to attract further loans must be more doubtful. Whether the directors attempt to obtain further finance from the bank or look elsewhere to raise a loan, they will be faced with a major stumbling block, namely the financial position displayed in the balance sheet at 31 December, 19X2. This document casts severe doubt on the financial capability of Elford's management; it shows clear evidence of a policy of expansion pursued without due consideration being given to its financial implications. Had management approached the bank at the outset, and produced budgeted financial information to support an application for a substantial loan, the prospects of success may well have been quite high, particularly as the project promised a good profit. An approach to the bank, early in 19X3, with a request for funds to help overcome the financial problems which have now emerged, is quite a different proposition. The banker may well take the view that the directors have made bad errors in the past and he may not be convinced that they will succeed in avoiding similar mistakes in the future. The absence of a satisfactory security for any loan request would be likely to reinforce this cautious attitude.

2. *Economise on working capital.* The directors should examine

the possibility of releasing funds by cutting down on its holding of stocks and reducing the period of credit allowed to customers. The feasibility of these courses of action will depend on whether or not the larger balances, at 31 December, 19X2, are reasonable in relation to the higher level of business activity now undertaken by Elford. The systems of stock control and credit control should be examined carefully; for example, if management wishes to increase sales, it may offer extended credit periods in order to make its products more attractive relative to those supplied by competitors. This is a sound business tactic in certain circumstances, but it can tie up large amounts of money with very little real benefit. The possibility that stock levels were increased, in anticipation of an increase in sales which did not fully materialise, should also be examined.

Where companies are under severe financial pressure, management may decide to cut back the level of activity so as to reduce the working capital requirement and perhaps also remove the need for certain fixed assets which can then be sold. This is not likely to be a popular solution to a company's financial problems, since it reduces the scale of business activity, and the level of funds generated from operations is therefore likely to diminish in the long run. It is, however, an option which remains available as the last resort, but it is unlikely to be called upon in the case of Elford Ltd.

3. *Utilise funds generated from operations.* The company is profitable and, provided it is able to continue in business, it is likely to generate funds which can be used to help correct the present financial imbalance. The financial changes which will then occur are demonstrated using the following facts and forecasts, for 19X3, prepared by Elford's management and checked by a firm of accountants.

 (i) The company will benefit from using the new plant throughout 19X3 and forecast profits are £120,000, after charging depreciation of £80,000 (plant £78,000, fixtures £2,000).

 (ii) Plant which cost £90,000, and is now fully depreciated, will be replaced during 19X3 at a cost of £110,000. The old plant has no disposal value.

 (iii) The dividend proposed for 19X2 will be paid, but no dividends will be paid in respect of 19X3.

 (iv) Trade creditors will be reduced to £155,000.

(v) The investment in stocks and debtors are reasonable in relation to the level of business activities, and will remain unchanged.

(vi) The bank has agreed to provide overdraft facilities of up to £30,000 for a period of 12 months.

Estimated Statement of Source and Application of Funds, Elford Ltd., 19X3

SOURCE OF FUNDS	£000	£000
Profit...		120
Adjustment for item not involving the movement of funds:		
Depreciation...		80
		—
TOTAL GENERATED FROM OPERATIONS.....................		200
APPLICATION OF FUNDS		
Purchase of plant and machinery.....................................	110	
Dividend paid...	40	
	—	150
		—
		50
		—
INCREASE/DECREASE IN WORKING CAPITAL		
Decrease in trade creditors...	45	
Movement in net liquid funds:		
Increase in cash balance..	5*	50
	—	—

*balancing item

Estimated Balance Sheet, Elford Ltd., 31 December, 19X3

	£000	£000
Tangible fixed assets		
Plant and machinery at cost (800 + 110 − 90)..........................	820	
Less: Accumulated depreciation (296 + 78 − 90).....................	284	
	—	536
Fixtures and fittings at cost	20	
Less: Accumulated depreciation	14	
	—	6
		542
Current Assets		
Stock	154	
Trade debtors	130	
	284	
Current Liabilities		
Trade creditors..	155	
Bank overdraft..	21	
	176	
Net Current Assets..		108
		650
Financed by:		
Share capital (£1 ordinary shares)		336
Share premium account		4
Retained profits		250
		590
Loan repayable 19X5		60
		650

The estimated balance sheet, at 31 December, 19X3, shows a significant improvement in the financial position of the company, compared with a year earlier, and this is reflected in the following solvency ratios:

	19X2 (actual)	19X3 (estimated)
Working capital..................	1.1:1	1.6:1
Liquidity..........................	0.5:1	0.7:1

However, the estimated ratios remain well below the 31 December, 19X1 levels and it will take more time to achieve those figures. The loan of £60,000 falls due for repayment in 19X5, and it will probably be the end of that year before the balance sheet appears as financially sound as it was at the end of 19X1. The recovery process is therefore gradual and depends on the achievement of forecast profit levels, further support from the bank and the continued tolerance of trade creditors. The balance due to creditors, at the end of 19X1, was £80,000. The 60% expansion, which we have assumed took place during 19X2, suggests that the balance outstanding to suppliers should not have increased beyond £130,000. At 31 December, 19X2, creditors were owed £200,000. The estimates for 19X3 include plans for a reduction to £155,000 by the year end, but it will be well into 19X4 before a balance of £130,000 is achieved. The sympathetic support of creditors is therefore a crucial element in the success of this plan. If the directors are unwilling to rely heavily on creditors, they must look to alternative sources. One possibility would be to raise a modest amount of external finance to tide the company over the next three years, by which time sufficient funds should have been generated from trading operations to complete the recovery process. Elford's prospects of recovery appear hopeful, but this is mainly because the company has been profitable and it has assumed, for the purpose of analysis, that this situation will continue in the future. If profit margins were narrower, the recovery period would be much more drawn out and the prospects of survival greatly reduced.

9.10 THE CASH APPROACH

The working capital definition of funds is most commonly used by companies for external reporting purposes. However, a statement which defines funds as cash is better suited to explain why cash has gone up or down, and answer such queries as 'How can I possibly have earned a profit when there is no cash in the bank?'

The adjustments needed to convert a working capital based statement of funds to a cash based statement of funds are straightforward. They involve restating, on a *cash* basis, total funds generated from operations, which appears in the statement of funds on an *accruals* basis. the cash approach is demonstrated using the statement of funds prepared for Stanfield (example 9.4), which is reproduced below for ease of reference.

Statement of Source and Application of Funds, Stanfield Ltd., 19X1

SOURCE OF FUNDS	£000	£000
Profit before tax		620
Adjustment for items not involving the movement of funds:		
Depreciation	245	
Profit on sale of plant	(15)	
		230
TOTAL GENERATED FROM OPERATIONS		850
FUNDS FROM OTHER SOURCES		
Debentures	500	
Sale of investments	660	
Sale of plant	47	
		1,207
		2,057
APPLICATION OF FUNDS		
Purchase of plant and equipment	1,743	
Dividends paid	270	
Tax paid	291	
		2,304
		(247)

INCREASE/DECREASE IN WORKING CAPITAL			
Decrease in stocks		(40)	
Increase in debtors		31	
Increase in creditors		(32)	
Movement in net liquid funds:			
Decrease in cash balance	(106)		
Increase in short-term loans	(100)	(206)	(247)

Schedule of Changes from the Accruals Basis to the Cash Basis

	£000
Total funds generated from operations	850
Add: Working capital changes providing cash or not requiring cash:	
Decrease in stocks	40
Increase in creditors	32
Increase in short-term loans	100
	1,022
Less: Working capital changes requiring cash or not providing cash:	
Increase in debtors	31
Total cash generated from operations	991

Statement of Source and Application of Cash, Stanfield Ltd., 19X1

SOURCE OF CASH	£000	£000
TOTAL GENERATED FROM OPERATIONS......................		991
CASH FROM OTHER SOURCES		
Debentures..	500	
Sale of investments	660	
Sale of plant..	47	
		1,207
		2,198
APPLICATION OF CASH		
Purchase of plant and equipment.....................................	1,743	
Dividends paid...	270	
Tax paid...	291	
		2,304
DECREASE IN CASH BALANCE...................................		(106)

9.11   QUESTIONS AND SOLUTIONS

Question 9.1 (Cohen Limited) tests the student's understanding of the relationship between the balance sheet and the statement of funds. The student is given an opening balance sheet and an estimated statement of funds for the forthcoming accounting period and, from this information, a forecast balance sheet, as at the end of the accounting period, must be prepared. Question 9.2 (Millbrook Engineering Ltd.) is a searching question which requires students to assess the progress, position and prospects of a company based on a wide range of financial information which is provided. A good analysis would include an historical and a forecast statement of funds, and also relevant accounting ratios. A question of this level of complexity would be more likely to appear in the *Practice of Banking 2* paper, but students will find it a useful basis for making an assessment of their understanding of the interpretive techniques examined in Chapters 8 and 9.

Question 9.1 (Taken from the September, 1980 *Accountancy* paper).

The following balance sheet has been prepared for Cohen Limited at 31 December 1979:

BALANCE SHEET AT 31 DECEMBER, 1979

	£	£		£	£
Ordinary share capital (£1 shares) ..		800,000	Freehold pro-perty at cost		400,000
10% redeemable preference share capital		300,000	Plant and mach-inery at cost.. *Less* deprecia-tion	1,446,600 617,900	
Reserves ..		625,500			828,700
		1,725,500	Investments at cost		230,000
12% deben-tures, 1990 ..		500,000	*Current Assets:*		
Current Liabilities:			Stock ..	1,063,700	
Trade creditors	476,200		Debtors ..	682,300	
Taxation due 30.9.1980 ..	196,000				1,746,000
Dividend ..	60,000				
Bank overdraft	247,000				
		979,200			
		£3,204,700			£3,204,700

The directors of Cohen Limited are concerned about the fact that the present overdraft is close to the facility allowed by the company's bank. The financial director has prepared the following estimated statement of funds for 1980:

ESTIMATED STATEMENT OF FUNDS FOR 1980

	£	£
Sources:		
Profit before taxation..		437,100
Add items not involving the outflow of funds—		
Loss on sale of plant (note 1)		3,500
Depreciation		247,600
Funds generated by trading activities		688,200
Funds from other sources:		
Sale of investments (note 2)		175,000
Sale of plant (note 1)		2,000
Ordinary share capital (note 3)		240,000
	carried forward	1,105,200

	£	£
brought forward		1,105,200

Applications:

	£	£
Dividend paid—ordinary shares	60,000	
preference shares	15,000	
Redemption of preference shares (note 4) ..	300,000	
Taxation paid	196,000	
Purchase of plant and machinery	206,500	
		777,500
		327,700

Changes in working capital items:

	£	£
(Increase) in trade creditors	(43,400)	
Increase in debtors	59,700	
Increase in stock	103,500	
Increase in net liquid funds	207,900	
		327,700

NOTES ON THE ABOVE ACCOUNTS

1. Plant which had cost the company £25,000 some years ago will be sold for £2,000.

2. This represents the proceeds arising from the sale of 20,000 shares which had cost the company £7.00 each in 1970.

3. As the result of the share issue the company's authorised and issued ordinary share capital will consist of one million ordinary shares of £1 each.

4. The preference share capital is to be redeemed, at par value, on 1 July 1980.

5. The freehold property is to be revalued during 1980. It is expected that a firm of professional valuers will place a figure of approximately £660,000 on the property, and this revised figure will be written into the books.

6. Tax payable on the estimated profits for 1980, including the capital gain on the sale of investments, will be £203,800, and the directors propose to pay a final dividend of 10p on each ordinary share.

Required:

The estimated balance sheet of Cohen Limited at 31 December, 1980, presented in vertical format and taking account of the above information. You should show clearly how the figure for reserves, appearing in the forecast balance sheet, has been calculated.

NOTE: Ignore Advance Corporation Tax.

[20]

Solution:

Estimated Balance Sheet at 31 December, 1980

Fixed Assets	£	£	£
Freehold property at professional valuation, 1980....................................			660,000
Plant at cost................................		1,628,100 W1	
Less: Accumulated depreciation		846,000 W1	782,100
			1,442,100
Investments at cost			90,000
Current Assets			
Stock		1,167,200	
Debtors		742,000	
		1,909,200	
Current Liabilities			
Trade creditors...........................	519,600		
Taxation due 30 September, 1981....	203,800		
Dividend..................................	100,000		
Bank overdraft...........................	39,100		
	862,500		
Net current assets			1,046,700
			2,578,800
Financed by:			
Ordinary share capital (£1 shares)			1,000,000
Share premium account			40,000
Capital redemption reserve			300,000
Revaluation reserve.................................			260,000
Other reserves.....................................			478,800 W2
			2,078,800
12% Debentures 1990..............................			500,000
			2,578,800

	Cost	Accumulated Depreciation
W1 Plant and machinery	£	£
Opening balance....................................	1,446,600	617,900
Sales...	(25,000)	(19,500)
Purchases..	206,500	
Depreciation charge		247,600
Closing balance....................................	1,628,100	846,000

	£	£
W2 Reserves at 1 January, 1980.....................		625,500
Add: Profit for 1980.............................		437,100
Surplus on sale of investments.................		35,000
		1,097,600
Less: Taxation......................................	203,800	
Dividends—preference....................	15,000	
—ordinary	100,000	
Transfer to capital redemption reserve*	300,000	
		618,800
Reserves at 31 December, 1980................		478,800

*Alternatively, if the redemption is met partly out of the proceeds of the planned issue of ordinary shares (£240,000), only £60,000 need be transferred to the capital redemption reserve.

Examiner's comments:
Main student errors: Most of the problems centred upon the calculation of the balance on reserves. This was expected and, accordingly, candidates were specifically asked to show clearly how this figure was arrived at. Many answers failed to comply with this instruction.

Question 9.2 (Taken from the September, 1979 *Accountancy* paper).

The profit and loss accounts of Millbrook Engineering Ltd. for 1978 and 1979 are set out below.

Profit and Loss Accounts

	1978 £	1978 £	1979 £	1979 £
Sales		1,577,000		1,807,000
Profit on sale of investments		—		90,000
		1,577,000		1,897,000
Less: Direct cost of sales	945,000		1,084,000	
General expenses	420,500		486,200	
Depreciation	22,100		38,100	
Directors' emoluments	46,000		55,000	
Debenture interest	15,000		15,000	
Overdraft interest	—		12,100	
		1,448,600		1,690,400
Net profit		128,400		206,600
Corporation tax	49,100		70,200	
Dividends paid	20,100		20,100	
		69,200		90,300
Retained profit		£59,200		£116,300

Balance Sheets

	1978 £	1979 £
Issued share capital	300,000	300,000
Reserves	168,300	284,600
10% debentures 1989	150,000	150,000
Current taxation due 31 March 1979	39,200	—
31 March 1980	—	60,300
Creditors	247,700	283,500
Bank overdraft	—	56,000
	£905,200	£1,134,400

	1978 £	1979 £
Goodwill	—	50,000
Freehold properties at cost	60,000	110,000
Plant & machinery at cost less depreciation	209,700	278,700
Quoted investments at cost	68,700	38,500
Stock at direct cost	300,100	366,200
Debtors	262,500	291,000
Bank	4,200	—
	£905,200	£1,134,400

In July 1978 Millbrook Engineering Ltd added to its existing business by taking over the fixed assets and stock of a private company trading with a turnover of £200,000 per annum. The purchase price of £140,000 was allocated as follows:

	£
Goodwill	50,000
Freehold premises	50,000
Plant & machinery	10,000
Stock	30,000

The company was granted an overdraft facility of £75,000 in July 1978, to provide part of the finance required for the acquisition.

The management of Millbrook Engineering Ltd have recently undertaken a thorough examination of the business acquired. In July 1979 they inform their bank:

'In our view there is considerable under-utilised capacity at the premises acquired last year. We think that output can be doubled if we install additional machinery costing £100,000 in the factory taken over; necessary modifications to the existing accommodation will cost a further £50,000. We expect that this work will be completed by the end of November 1979, and by January 1980 sales at twice the present level should be possible from the newly acquired factory. With remaining activities fairly stable, we expect an increased investment in stocks and debtors, net of additional finance obtained from creditors, of approximately £40,000.'

An agreed condition of the overdraft granted in July 1978 was that it should be reviewed at 30 June 1979. In connection with this review, the management report:

'We have done well to reduce the overdraft to £56,000, in view of the necessary increase in working capital caused by the expansion of activity. To help finance the planned modernisation, an increase in the overdraft facility to £100,000 for twelve months is requested. With stabilisation in the level of activity from the beginning of 1980 onwards, we expect any remaining overdraft to be repaid rapidly.'

The company's borrowing is secured as follows:

10% debentures, 1989. Secured on the freehold property belonging to Millbrook Engineering Ltd before the acquisition of the private company.

Bank overdraft. Secured in two ways—by a fixed charge on the freehold property taken over, and with a floating charge over the stock and debtor balances.

You are provided with the following calculations:

	1978 %	1979 %
Direct cost of sales .. .. ——————— Sales.	59·9	60·0
Net profit .. .. ——————— Sales.	8·1	11·4
Net profit .. .. ——————— Gross assets	14·2	18·2
Stock at direct cost .. .. ——————— Direct cost of sales	31·8	33·8
Debtors and bank .. .. ——————— Creditors and bank overdraft	107·7	85·7

Required:

A full discussion of the financial progress, position and proposals of Millbrook Engineering Ltd from the viewpoint of the company's bank. You should support the discussion with whatever accounting ratios and calculations you consider relevant.

NOTE: *Advance corporation tax has been accounted for at $\frac{33}{87}$ on the dividends paid. The market value of the quoted investments at 30 June 1979 was £63,600.*

[30]

Solution:

A. Past Progress and Present Financial Position

Relevant accounting ratios:	1978	1979
Rate of return on shareholders' equity (pre-tax)	27.4%	35.3%
General expenses as a percentage of sales	26.6%	26.9%
Total asset turnover	1.74	1.59
Rate of collection of debtors	61 days	59 days
Working capital ratio (including quoted investments)	2.2:1	1.74:1
Proprietorship ratio	51.7%	51.5%

Statement of Source and Application of Funds, 1978/9

SOURCE OF FUNDS	£	£
Operating profit before tax (£206,600 – £90,000)		116,600
Adjustment for item not involving the movement of funds:		
Depreciation		38,100
TOTAL GENERATED FROM OPERATIONS		154,700
FUNDS FROM OTHER SOURCES		
Sale of investments (£30,200 + £90,000)		120,200
		274,900
APPLICATION OF FUNDS		
Purchase of fixed assets (goodwill, property and plant)	207,100	
Taxation paid (£39,200 + £9,900)	49,100	
Dividends paid	20,100	
		276,300
		(1,400)
INCREASE/DECREASE IN WORKING CAPITAL		
Increase in stocks	66,100	
Increase in debtors	28,500	
Increase in creditors	(35,800)	
Movement in net liquid funds:		
Decrease in cash balance	(60,200)	(1,400)

Profitability

The most significant event that requires explanation is the effect of the sale of investments on the reported profitability of the company and on its financial position at the year end. The summarised profit and loss account shows a net profit of £206,600, but, after deducting the capital profit arising from disposal of the investments, profit from trading operations becomes £116,600. This was a lower profit than for 1978, despite the higher level of sales attributable almost entirely to the trading activities of the private company whose fixed assets and stock were acquired at the beginning of the year. Recalculation of the profit percentages for 1979, excluding the extraordinary item gives:

Net profit percentage	6.5%
Net profit ÷ gross assets × 100	10.3%
Rate of return on shareholders' equity	19.9%

The corrected net profit percentage reveals a decline in margins between the two years. Since direct costs are fairly stable, as a percentage of sales, the narrower margin must be explained in terms of the more than proportionate increase in the depreciation charge and the large figure for bank overdraft interest. The fact that general expenses (which should include a significant fixed element) have not declined as a percentage of sales, during a period of expansion, requires some explanation.

Solvency

An assessment of Millbrook Ltd's solvency position, based on working capital and liquidity ratios, shows marginal reductions at 30 June, 1979 as compared with a year earlier. The liquidity ratio has fallen below unity. The 1979 figure, 0.86:1, is not uncommon for this type of business, but the sharp downward trend should be a cause for concern. But for the sale of investments, the financial position would quite probably have been much worse. The statement of funds shows that the investments were sold for £120,000 (£30,200 reduction in book value + £90,000 profit), and this went a long way towards financing the expansion of activity which occurred during the year. The proprietorship ratio is stable, but fairly low at only just over 50%. However, the freehold property is probably undervalued as are the quoted investments which remain unsold.

Asset Utilisation

The rate of collection of debtors has marginally improved; the collection period being 59 days compared with 61. In both cases the collection is fairly speedy for this type of company. The rate of payment of creditors cannot be computed, but an increase in the figure outstanding of 15% is roughly in line with the apparent level of expansion.

Sales per pound invested in gross assets is down from £1.74 to £1.59, so the lower percentage return on gross assets (10.3%) is due to a combination of *both* a lower net profit margin and less effective use of available resources. These percentages underline the less favourable results achieved during 1979 and it may well be that this is at least partly attributable to the 'under-utilised' capacity at the premises acquired last year. Separate accounts for the private company acquired in July, 1978 would be helpful to this analysis.

B. Prospects

The directors have provided some estimates for the forthcoming twelve months and these should be examined, in the light of past results, as a basis for assessing the request for overdraft facilities. The following forecast statement of funds may be prepared on the basis of information provided and by making certain assumptions:

Forecast Statement of Source and Application of Funds, 1979/80

	£	£
SOURCE OF FUNDS		
TOTAL GENERATED FROM OPERATIONS........		154,700 (1)
APPLICATION OF FUNDS		
Purchase of fixed assets (machinery and accommodation)	150,000 (2)	
Taxation paid	60,300 (3)	
		210,300
		(55,600)
INCREASE IN WORKING CAPITAL...................		(40,000) (2)
DEFICIT		(95,600)

Notes:

(1) No forecasts are provided, and it is assumed that last year's results will be repeated.
(2) Management's forecasts.
(3) Payable 31 March, 1980.

There is a deficit of £95,600. The bank is being asked for an additional £44,000, and so a shortfall of £51,600 remains. Before granting the requested facility the bank should, 'inter alia':

(a) confirm that satisfactory arrangements are being made to finance the shortfall; and
(b) satisfy itself that management is capable of reversing the underlying downward trend in profitability and liquidity.

Examiner's comments:

Main student errors:

1. Failure to recognise the significance of the sale of quoted investments for:
   (a) Profitability. The 'unadjusted' figures show profit to have increased, whereas there was, in fact, a significant decline.
   (b) Liquidity. The financial position would have deteriorated significantly but for the proceeds from the sale of the investments which were almost as great as funds generated from operations.
2. Generally, the analyses lacked depth (which does not mean that answers were short), and high marks were rare.

CHAPTER 10

Internal Accounting Reports

10.1 INTRODUCTION

The scope, contents and format of the accounts which are prepared by companies for general publication are prescribed by statutory and other requirements (see Chapters 2 and 3), and are of limited value for internal management purposes. The published accounts relate to a past period of time, usually a year, and to the entity as a whole; they show very little analysis of the global figures which they contain. Management is responsible for all aspects of a company's activity and makes use of accounting reports produced for internal purposes. The contents of these reports is decided by management itself, and they may concentrate on just a small section or single aspect of activity, relate to time periods other than a year, and forecast likely future results. For example, the published accounts contain a single figure for 'trade debtors' but the internal reports may analyse this figure on various bases, such as, the age or size of each debt, the type of product to which it relates, or the salesperson who made the sale: also, the level of debtors expected at various times in the future can be forecast. The uses to which the internal reports are put are under managerial control, and they may be released to interested parties, such as the company's bank. However, there are no general regulations to enforce the publication of this information and it must be remembered that it is not audited. The detailed results contained in *post facto* evaluations carried out for internal use should be arranged so that they can be summarised to give the figures for external reports; this avoids the need for companies to maintain two separate information systems, one for internal and the other for external reports.

This chapter deals with the *general principles* underlying the preparation of internal accounting reports, since the range of possible reports is unlimited. In practice, and in examination questions, the starting point is to determine the purpose for which the information is required and then to devise an appropriate report.

For example, to enable stock levels to be controlled, details are needed which show how long particular items have been held, and the rate of turnover of individual product lines gives a good indication of this. As well as being relevant, the information must also be timely, that is, it must be given to management in readiness for decisions to be made and action taken. For example, the fact that a debtor has exceeded the allowed period of credit must be promptly reported so that steps can be taken to recover the money due, and also to minimise the potential loss by stopping further credit sales to the customer involved.

Where a bank is considering a financial commitment to a customer, such as an overdraft, it will want to see accounting reports which support the request. This Chapter examines the internal accounting reports which may be prepared by companies and be of interest to the banker.

10.2 FORECASTS

When management takes decisions, it is important that consideration is given to their likely effects, and this is achieved by the preparation of forecasts which set out the expected financial results of a proposed course of action. Even when there are no plans to implement fundamental changes, such as a major expansion project or a price cutting campaign, forecast accounts should still be prepared to indicate what is expected to transpire and to alert management to any possible problem areas. It is most valuable to have advance notice of likely results so that alternative plans of action designed to meet a range of eventualities can be formulated. In some cases advance notice may be vital, for example, if a cash deficit is foreseen, appropriate sources of finance can be arranged to meet it in good time. To leave the search for funds until the company has a liquidity crisis may cause it to fail or be forced to obtain finance on disadvantageous terms.

The relationship between banker and customer is made more productive if the company's plans are discussed and its requirements for financial assistance and other services from the bank known in advance. The amount of detail required by the banker is likely to be less than that needed by management, but must be sufficient for an opinion to be formed on the reliability of the forecasts. It is, of course, open to the banker to ask for further details, and the bank's response to a request for help may be influenced by the readiness and ability of management to comply.

For example, the banker may be satisfied by the information that a proposed expansion involves additional monthly expenditure on wages of £2,500, while management needs to know what gives rise to this figure in terms of employees and wage rates. The credibility of the whole forecast can be questioned if, in fact, the £2,500 transpires to be simply a rough guess and cannot be substantiated further.

There are the following important links between accounting reports which deal with past results and forecasts relating to the future:

1. The historical accounts can be used as a basis for preparing forecasts.
2. The careful comparison of forecasts with actual previous results should prevent the acceptance of plans which reflect wild hopes rather than realistic expectations. For example, forecasts may show substantial future profits, but to achieve these it may have been assumed that the gross profit percentage will be much higher than in the past; this assumption would have to be justified fully to any external accounts user who is expected to base a decision on it.
3. Actual results for a period of time can be compared with the forecasts for that period and deviations investigated. The results of this study should aid the understanding of current performance, indicate the reliability of the forecasts, and provide a useful input to the process of preparing further forecasts.

Comparisons are made easier if the formats of the forecast and the actual results are the same; to achieve this the data processing system of the company must be designed to produce information analysed in the appropriate way. For example, if sales are forecast for individual product lines or geographical areas, then the reports on actual sales should be prepared on the same basis and compared with the anticipated results.

Forecasts are prepared to predict cash movements, the profit and loss account and the balance sheet, and these are now dealt with in turn. (See Chapter 9, section 7.2 for the forecast of working capital requirements).

10.2.1   The Cash Forecast   This shows the cash flows which are likely to result from the adoption of a particular plan. There are regular trading flows, such as result from sales and purchases, and

irregular flows from, for example, the issue of shares or the purchase of plant. When a company is trading steadily at a profit the
cash balance increases smoothly, but the occurrence of large
irregular flows of cash cause distortions.

Before starting to prepare a cash forecast, a number of matters
must be ascertained:

1. The overall period of time to be covered. The end date may
   be specified, or it may depend on a certain condition being
   satisfied, such as the identification of the maximum overdraft.
2. The detail to be contained in the forecast. Whether the figures
   should relate to weeks, months or years, and the extent of
   analysis of receipts and payments.
3. The area of activity to be covered. The forecast may be for
   an existing company, a newly established company, a new
   area of activity, or an existing company together with a new
   area of activity.

The time periods and detail contained in the forecast depend on
the purpose for which it is prepared. Cash management needs
frequent and detailed knowledge of the likely cash position of the
company, and so it is usual to draw up forecasts on a monthly basis.
It may even be desirable to draw up budgets covering periods
shorter than a month where the cash position is of crucial importance. A year, without further analysis, is likely to be too long a
period of time to aid cash management as within a year the balance
can fluctuate significantly, although for purposes such as investment appraisal (see Chapter 11) annual forecasts are often adequate. The amount of detail contained in the forecast is largely
conditioned by the time period it covers; the further it reaches into
the future, the less detailed and accurate it can be. Management is
not restricted in the number of forecasts it prepares, and may draw
up details of expected weekly cash flows for, say, the next two
months, monthly forecasts for two years and annual forecasts for
ten years. As time passes, the longer-term forecasts are revised in
the light of current expectations, which may change as a result of
current knowledge.

Time can be saved when forecasts are prepared by using the
columnar format which shows cash flows on one side and time
periods on another. This layout is demonstrated in example 10.3
below. Once the columnar layout has been prepared, it is then fairly
straightforward to work through the information given in the ques-

tion and insert the expected cash flows in the appropriate location.
The main items which appear in cash forecasts are:

1. *Sales.* A sale is an economic event which produces a cash inflow immediately, if it is a cash sale, or after some time has elapsed in the case of a credit sale. The amount expected to be received from cash sales is entered in the cash forecast against the time period when the sales take place. In the case of credit sales it is necessary to determine the time lag between the sale and the cash inflow; if debtors take discounts, the sums receivable must be reduced correspondingly. At any time, the sums uncollected from individual customers give, in total, the value of debtors.

Example 10.1

The accountant of Ceiling Ltd., a trading company, is preparing the company's cash forecast for the first six months of 19X7. Credit sales in November and December of 19X6 were £24,000 and £27,000 respectively; it is expected that sales, all on credit, for each of the first three months of 19X7 will be £30,000 and will then rise to £36,000 per month for the rest of the year. The company's policy is to allow customers two months' credit, and these terms apply to all sales up to 31 December, 19X6.

REQUIRED:
I. Prepare a forecast of Ceiling Ltd.'s monthly cash receipts for the first six months of 19X7 on the following alternative assumptions:
  (a) There is no change in the company's credit terms.
  (b) The company extends the period of credit on all sales made after 1 January, 19X7 to three months.
  (c) A discount of 2% is offered for prompt payment if the debt is settled within one month; this is taken in respect of half the company's sales. If the discount is not taken, payment must be made within two months.
II. Calculate the value of trade debtors at 30 June, 19X7 under each of the three alternatives given above.
Assume that each month consists of four weeks.

Solution:

I.

19X7	Sales £000	(a) £000	(b) £000	(c) Not taking discount £000	(c) Taking discount £000	Total £000
January	30	24	24	24	—	24
February	30	27	27	27	14.7	41.7
March	30	30	—	15	14.7	29.7
April	36	30	30	15	14.7	29.7
May	36	30	30	15	17.64	32.64
June	36	36	30	18	17.64	35.64

The heading spans: Sales, and *Cash Received under assumption:* covering (a), (b), and (c).

Note: The different credit policies affect the rate of cash inflows. Option (b) causes no cash to be received in March, while (c), at the cost of the discount, accelerates receipts in February.

II. Credit Sales Uncollected at 30 June, 19X7:

Debtors
£000

(a) May and June: £36,000 × 2 = ...   72
(b) April, May and June: £36,000 × 3 = ...   108
(c) Half of May and all of June: £18,000 + £36,000, less discount on half of
      June of £360 ....   53.64

As a general rule, it is best to prepare the calculations relating to sales first as these determine the level of activity on which other costs, such as purchases and direct wages, may depend.

2. Purchases. The volume of purchases is set by the company's stock policy, which determines the extent to which stock is held in anticipation of sales or production. If sales are expected to rise, additional stock is likely to be acquired, while stocks will be run down if a decline in sales is forecast. The purchasing pattern required to achieve the desired increase in stock level is super-imposed on the regular purchases required to replace stock which has been sold. Once purchases have been calculated, they can be converted into cash outflows by allowing for any period of credit and prompt payment discounts given by suppliers. The value of trade creditors for purchases at any time is the amount of stock received but not paid for.

Example 10.2

It is the policy of Ceiling Ltd., the company whose sales forecast for the first half of 19X7 is given in Example 10.1 above, to calculate its selling price at cost plus 50%. On 1 December and 31 December, 19X6 the value of stock held was £38,000 and £40,000 respectively.

REQUIRED:
   I. Calculate the monthly cash outflow in respect of purchases for the first six months of 19X7 on the alternative assumptions:
      (a) The company purchases stock each month sufficient to ensure that, at the end of the month, the level of stock is equal to the anticipated sales of the following two months.
          Suppliers allow the company one month's credit.
      (b) The purchasing policy is as given in (a) above, but in both 19X6 and 19X7 the company takes advantage of a 3% prompt payment discount on half of its purchases by paying within one month; the remaining creditors are paid within two months.
  II. Calculate the value of creditors at 30 June, 19X7 under both of the alternatives given in I. above.

Solution:

I.

	Purchases £000	Cash £000	(b) No Discount Taken £000	(b) Discount Taken £000	Cash £000
19X6					
November	20 (1)				
December	20 (2)				
19X7					
January	20	20	10	9.7	19.7
February	24 (1)	20	10	9.7	19.7
March	24 (1)	24	10	11.64	21.64
April	24	24	12	11.64	23.64
May	24	24	12	11.64	23.64
June	24	24	12	11.64	23.64

Notes:
1. Includes £4,000 increase in stock.
2. Includes £2,000 increase in stock.

II. Purchases unpaid at 30 June 19X7:

	Creditors £000
(a) June	24
(b) Half of May plus June	36*

*On the grounds of prudence, no discount is anticipated.

3. Other Variable Costs. The cost of these may depend on the level of sales, for instance, commission paid to salesmen, or on the rate of production, for example, direct manufacturing wages. Once determined, they are entered in the cash forecast with allowance for any payment in advance or arrears.

4. Regular Fixed Costs. These are independent of the level of sales and are entered in the forecast in accordance with any details given about their pattern of incidence during the period under review. It is usually assumed that they accrue evenly over time and are paid in equal instalments. Care must be taken to ensure that there is no element of depreciation in the fixed costs to be entered in the cash forecast as depreciation is a non-cash expense (see Chaper 9, section 2.2).

5. Irregular Flows. Information may be given about cash flows in respect of such items as the issue or redemption of shares or debentures, sales and acquisitions of fixed assets, and dividend payments. In some cases the value of the flow may have to be calculated, and it is then entered in the appropriate time period in the forecast.

Example 10.3 (Taken from the April, 1982 *Accountancy* paper).

Regent, a trader, has been in business for a number of years. The summarised trading and profit and loss account for 1981 was as follows:

SUMMARISED TRADING AND PROFIT AND LOSS ACCOUNT, 1981

	£	£
Sales (all on credit)		240,000
Less: Variable costs: purchases	180,000	
Fixed costs: general expenses, etc.	42,000o	222,000
Net Profit		£18,000

*General expenses include depreciation of £12,000 on fixed assets.

Regent believes that profits can be improved by increasing the sales of his product for which there exists a strong demand. The following plans and estimates are made:

(1) In January 1982 Regent will issue a circular informing customers that the period of credit allowed will be increased from one to two months on all sales from 1 February.

(2) The more favourable credit terms will produce an increase in monthly sales, over 1981 levels, of 10% for February to June 1982, and 20% thereafter.

(3) The period of credit received from suppliers will remain unchanged at one month.

(4) It is Regent's policy to maintain stocks at a level equivalent to expected sales over the forthcoming two months. Stocks at 31 December 1981 were £30,000.

(5) General expenses accrue evenly during the year and, depreciation apart, are paid for on a monthly basis.

At 31 December 1981 Regent's bank balance stands at £3,000. Regent's bank has agreed to provide overdraft facilities up to a limit of £13,000 for the forthcoming twelve months.

Required:

(a) A cash budget showing the forecast bank balance or overdraft at the end of each month during 1982.   [16]

(b) Comments, in the light of your calculations under (a), on the bank's requirement that the overdraft should not exceed £13,000.   [4]

Notes.

(i) Assume that 1982 consists of twelve months of equal length.

(ii) Trading transactions occurred at an even rate during 1981

[Total marks for question—20]

Solution:

(a)

| | | | *Purchases* | | | |
Month	Opening balance £000	Sales £000	Replace- ments £000	Stock- piling £000	General expenses £000	Closing balance £000
January	3.0	20	15.0		2.5	5.5
February	5.5	20	15.0	3.0 (W1)	2.5	5.0
March	5.0	—	16.5		2.5	(14.0)
April	(14.0)	22	16.5		2.5	(11.0)
May	(11.0)	22	16.5		2.5	(8.0)
June	(8.0)	22	16.5	1.5 (W2)	2.5	(6.5)
July	(6.5)	22	16.5	1.5 (W3)	2.5	(5.0)
August	(5.0)	22	18.0		2.5	(3.5)
September	(3.5)	24	18.0		2.5	—
October	—	24	18.0		2.5	3.5
November	3.5	24	18.0		2.5	7.0
December	7.0	24	18.0		2.5	10.5

Workings

	£000
W1 Estimated cost of goods sold: February	16.5
March	16.5
Stock level required at 31 January	33.0
Stock level 1 January	30.0
Additional January purchases, paid February	3.0

W2, W3

	W2 £000	W3 £000
Estimated cost of goods sold: June	16.5	
July	18.0	18.0
August		18.0
Required stock level: 31 May	34.5	
30 June		36.0
Stock level at: 1 May	33.0	
1 June		34.5
Additional purchases: May, paid June	1.5	
June, paid July		1.5

(b) The maximum overdraft is exceeded only in March but, if the plans are fulfilled, there will be a healthy balance at the bank by the end of December. Regent could comply with the bank's requirement by delaying, for a couple of months, the build up of stocks to the extent of £1,000.

Examiner's Comments:

Area of weakness: 1. Failure to exclude depreciation from fixed costs.

2. Calculation of required stock increases.

3. Pattern of cash inflows from sales; the effect of the grant of an extra month's credit.

10.2.2   The Profit Forecast   A principal objective of business activity is to maximise the rate of return on capital employed. Therefore, management needs to know the likely profitability (and capital employed) of alternative courses of action so that the option which appears to produce the best rate of return on capital employed can be studied further; for instance, it will be necessary to prepare a cash forecast to see whether the most profitable alternative is also viable from the financial viewpoint. The period covered by the profit forecast must be considered carefully; the option which shows the greatest profit in the short term may appear less favourable in the longer term. As is the case with cash forecasts, the further into the future the forecast is projected, the less accurate it will be.

The main elements to be predicted in a profit forecast are:

1. Sales. The value of future sales depends on the number of units to be sold and their price. Once a sales forecast has been prepared, consideration can be given to whether the necessary production capacity is available. If sufficient units cannot be produced to meet expected demand, the sales price may be raised to restrict demand or, alternatively, extra capacity may be arranged; the importance of a sales forecast is that it enables plans to be formulated well in advance to overcome any forseeable problems. Subject to the limitations imposed by the forecast available capacity of a business, a variety of combinations of selling price and resultant sales volume can be tried in order to see which gives the greatest forecast profit. In examination questions, the value of future sales may be given or may have to be calculated.

2. Cost of Goods Manufactured. In the case of a manufacturing concern, the various elements of cost incurred in production must be totalled to find the cost of goods manufactured, which is then transferred to the trading account. The costs may be broadly classified as fixed or variable. Variable costs (see section 5.2 of this Chapter) depend on the level of production and may be calculated on the basis of cost per unit or as a percentage of the value of production; fixed costs (see section 5.1 of this Chapter) do not vary over a limited range of output, and care must be taken to calculate and include depreciation on any new fixed assets.

3. Cost of Goods Sold. The volume of sales is likely to differ from purchases, in the case of a trading company, or from production in the case of a manufacturer. In either case there is a change in the level of stock; if more is sold than is produced or bought, stock levels fall. If production or purchases exceed sales, then stocks increase. Where stock levels change, the cost of goods sold is found by the familiar formula:

$$\text{Cost of Goods Sold} = \text{Opening Stock} + \text{Cost of Goods} \left\{ \begin{array}{c} \text{Purchased} \\ \text{or} \\ \text{Manufactured} \end{array} \right\} - \text{Closing Stock}$$

To apply this formula requires the valuation of opening and closing stocks, which is dealt with in Chapter 3, section 3.

4. Other Costs. These cover a wide range and include such items as discounts, interest charges and administration and delivery costs. They may be fixed or variable and the information given must be studied carefully to enable their calculation.

Example 10.4 (Taken from the April, 1981 *Accountancy* paper).

Popplewell Ltd. is an engineering company and the directors have decided to extend the range of items manufactured by producing a special type of steel pallet suitable for the storage of cylinders of dangerous gases. The summarised accounts of Popplewell Ltd. for 1980 are as follows:

MANUFACTURING, TRADING AND PROFIT AND LOSS ACCOUNT FOR 1980

	£	£
Sales		1,160,000
Less: Raw materials consumed	305,200	
Manufacturing wages	246,500	
Factory overheads (depreciation £27,000)	238,300	
Cost of goods manufactured	790,000	
Opening stock of finished goods	167,000	
Closing stock of finished goods	(167,000)	
Cost of goods sold		790,000
Gross profit		370,000
Administration, selling and distribution costs (depreciation £10,000)		277,000
Net profit		£93,000

BALANCE SHEET AT 31 DECEMBER 1980

	£		£
Share capital	300,000	Fixed assets at cost *less*	
Reserves	223,000	depreciation	301,000
	———	Stocks of raw materials	
	523,000	and finished goods.....	187,000
Trade creditors	62,000	Debtors	73,000
		Bank	24,000
	———		———
	£585,000		£585,000

It is expected that existing activities will continue at a similar level during the forthcoming year, and for forecasting purposes it is to be assumed that the 1980 results will be exactly repeated. None of the existing plant will require replacement until 1985.

The following plans and forecasts are provided in connection with the plan to manufacture pallets.

(i) Plant and machinery costing £80,000 will be required and this will be purchased in March and paid for immediately. The plant is expected to have a five year life and a nil scrap value at the end of that period.

(ii) The raw materials needed to manufacture 150 pallets will be purchased in March and sufficient purchases will be made in each subsequent month to replace quantities consumed. The raw materials cost per pallet is estimated at £50 and one month's credit will be obtained from suppliers.

(iii) Production will commence on 1 April 1981 at the rate of 100 pallets each month and sales are expected to be made at a similar rate commencing 1 May 1981. The selling price of each pallet is to be £130 and one month's credit is to be allowed to customers. No bad debts are expected to arise.

(iv) Direct wages are expected to amount to £30 per pallet, and factory overhead expenses (other than depreciation) relating specifically to this project will commence in March and will be £1,900 per month. Both wages and overheads will be paid for during the month the service is provided. There will be no increase in administration, selling and distribution costs.

Required:

(a) A forecast of cash receipts and cash payments for the *new project* covering each of the ten months to 31 December, 1981.

(b) A forecast profit statement for the *new project* for 1981.

(c) A calculation of the bank balance of Popplewell Ltd. at 31 December 1981.

(d) A brief report, for the company's bank, on the profitability and financial implications of the new project, for which the bank has been asked to provide overdraft facilities if required.

Notes:

1. *It is the company's policy to value finished stock at prime cost, i.e. raw materials and direct labour only, in its management reports.*

2. *Ignore work in progress, taxation, dividends and any bank interest payable.*

[30]

Solution:

(a)
Cash Receipts and Payments

1981	Opening Balance £	Sales £	Plant £	Raw Materials £	Wages £	Overheads £	Closing Balance £
March			80,000			1,900	(81,900)
April	(81,900)			7,500	3,000	1,900	(94,300)
May	(94,300)			5,000	3,000	1,900	(104,200)
June	(104,200)	13,000		5,000	3,000	1,900	(101,100)
July	(101,100)	13,000		5,000	3,000	1,900	(98,000)
August	(98,000)	13,000		5,000	3,000	1,900	(94,900)
September	(94,900)	13,000		5,000	3,000	1,900	(91,800)
October	(91,800)	13,000		5,000	3,000	1,900	(88,700)
November	(88,700)	13,000		5,000	3,000	1,900	(85,600)
December	(85,600)	13,000		5,000	3,000	1,900	(82,500)

(b)
Forecast Profit Statement for 1981

	£	£
Sales		104,000
Less: Raw materials purchased	52,500	
Less: Closing stock	7,500	
	45,000	
Manufacturing wages	27,000	
Depreciation	12,000 (W1)	
Other factory overheads	19,000	
Cost of goods manufactured	103,000	
Less: Closing stock of finished goods	8,000 (W2)	
Cost of goods sold		95,000
Profit		9,000

Workings

W1 Compute depreciation on the straight line basis:
   £80,000 (depreciable amount) ÷ 5 (expected life) × ¾ (plant used for nine months in 1981) = £12,000.

W2 Value stock on the prime cost basis:

	£
Raw materials per unit	50
Direct labour per unit.........	30
	80 × 100 units = £8,000

(c)   *Forecast Bank Balance at 31 December, 1981*

	£	£
Opening cash balance..		24,000
Add: Funds flow from existing activities:		
Profit...	93,000	
Depreciation	37,000	
		130,000
		154,000
Less: Deficit on new project		82,500
Closing cash balance..		71,500

(d) The profit of £9,000 seems a small return on an investment in plant and working capital totalling £103,500. But in a full year the return from the new project should be significantly higher:

		£
Sales............................		156,000
Less: Materials	60,000	
Wages..................	36,000	
Overheads............	22,800	
Depreciation.........	16,000	
		134,800
Net Profit.....................		21,200

Funds generated from existing activities amounts to £130,000 per annum (profit + depreciation) or nearly £11,000 per month. It is clear that the company will require some financial support from the bank during the first few months of the project, but the facility should be liquidated well before the year end as the result of funds generated from existing and additional business activities.

Examiner's Comments:

Area of weakness: 1. Calculation under (b) of the total profit rather than that for the new project as instructed in the question.
   2. The valuation and treatment of closing stocks of raw materials and finished goods.
   3. The calculation of the forecast bank balance at 31 December, 1981.

Example 10.4 draws attention to the kind of distortion which can arise where the forecast covers a time period which is not typical; in this case it covers less than a year and includes heavy start-up costs.

A reconciliation of the results for a full year and those of the first eight months is:

£

Eight months' profit expressed as a proportion of a full year's predicted results, (see (d)), £21,200 × $\frac{8}{12}$ 14,133

Profit in 1981, (see (b)).. 9,000

Shortfall.. 5,133

Shortfall made up as follows:
Non-recurring start-up costs:
    March and April Factory Overheads: £1,900 × 2 3,800
    April Depreciation: $\frac{£12,000}{9}$ 1,333

5,133

The sales of the first eight months of the new project bear ten months' overheads and nine months' depreciation. In future years, twelve months' expenses will be matched by twelve months' sales.

10.2.3 The Forecast Balance Sheet It is necessary to prepare a forecast balance sheet to discover the effect of forecast profit and cash flows on the financial position of the company. The forecast balance sheet may be analysed in the same way as a factual statement which relates to the past, and the analysis may point to the need for action to avoid any shortcomings which are revealed.

The items contained in a balance sheet forecast are calculated as follows:

1. Fixed Assets. These are reported at cost, or revalued amount, less accumulated depreciation. The opening position must be established; forecast acquisitions are then added to the opening assets at cost, or revalued amount, and the forecast depreciation charge is added to the figure for accumulated depreciation to date. The cost and related depreciation of forecast disposals are subtracted from the opening position. Where revaluations take place, the surplus is added to equity and a higher depreciation charge may result.

2. Stocks. The basis of stock valuation must be established (see Chapter 3, section 3). Where the valuation has already been made for the purpose of preparing the forecast for the cost of goods sold (see example 10.4), this figure should also be used in the balance sheet.

3. Trade Debtors. These represent a number of weeks' or months' sales, and may be calculated on the basis of specific patterns of sales (see example 10.1 above). Their level depends on the value of sales, the company's credit policy, and the willingness of customers to pay on the due date; allowance must be made for anticipated bad debts.

4. Cash and Overdrafts. This balance may be calculated in a separate cash forecast (see section 2.1 of this Chapter) or may be the balancing figure in the balance sheet found after all the other values have been entered. Where it is a balancing figure, it shows the cash surplus or deficit arising from the adoption of particular plans after a period of time has elapsed, but major drawbacks are that it reveals neither the fluctuations which take place over the period of the forecast nor the maximum or minimum surplus or deficit which is likely to be encountered. A detailed cash forecast is needed to satisfy these requirements.

5. Equity. This consists of share capital and reserves. The value of share capital is adjusted for issues, redemptions, and the purchase by the company of its own shares during the period of the forecast. Reserves are of many types and may change in value as a result of, for example, a premium on the issue of shares, capitalisation by a bonus issue, or the revaluation of fixed assets. The most usual change is caused by the impact on revenue reserves of the forecast profit retained or loss suffered during the current accounting period.

6. Non-equity shares and debentures and other loans. The opening balance must be adjusted for any issues or redemptions which are to take place in the period of the forecast.

7. Trade Creditors. The value of trade creditors depends on purchases and the period of credit granted by suppliers (see example 10.2 above).

8. Accruals and Prepayments. At the date of the forecast balance sheet, adjustments may be needed to match anticipated revenues with their related costs. A prepayment arises where a sum of money has been paid which provides benefits after the balance sheet date; accruals occur when benefits have been enjoyed prior to the balance sheet date but have not been paid for. Care must be taken to include dividends and taxation due at the balance sheet date.

Example 10.5 (Taken from the September, 1981 *Accountancy* paper).

A new trading company called Fayet Ltd. is to be incorporated in December 1981, and the intention is to commence business activity on 1 January, 1982. The directors, who will also own all the shares in the new company, are considering how much to invest in their new enterprise.

The bank has agreed to provide any overdraft facilities required during the year, provided that the forecast liquidity ratio (i.e. the ratio of debtors to current liabilities) at 31 December, 1982 is not less than 1.2:1. Accordingly, the directors intend to introduce sufficient share capital on 1 January, 1982 to produce a liquidity ratio of 1.2:1 at 31 December, 1982.

Other forecasts and estimates are as follows:

1. Current liabilities at 31 December, 1982 are expected to amount to £50,000.
2. Sales will accrue evenly during the year and the debtors' balance at 31 December, 1982 will represent one-and-a-half months' sales.
3. The working capital ratio at 31 December, 1982 will be 2:1.
4. On 1 January, 1982, £100,000 will be spent on fixed assets which are expected to last for ten years and have no resale value at the end of that time.
5. Purchases of stock will occur evenly during the year and one month's credit will be received from suppliers.
6. The gross profit margin will be 33⅓% of sales.
7. Running expenses, other than depreciation, are estimated at £125,000.

Required:

The estimated trading and profit and loss account of Fayet Ltd. for 1982 and the estimated balance sheet at 31 December, 1982. The balance sheet should show clearly the share capital which would have to be raised at the outset in order to meet the bank's requirement.

NOTES: **1** *Assume that a year consists of twelve months of equal length.*

2 *At 31 December 1982 current assets will consist of stocks and trade debtors. Current liabilities will consist of trade creditors and the bank overdraft.*

3 *No dividends will be paid during 1982.*

4 *Ignore taxation.* [20]

Solution:

Estimated Trading and Profit and Loss Account

	£		£
Purchases (W6)	360,000	Sales (W4)	480,000
Less: Stock	40,000		
	———		
Cost of goods sold (W5)	320,000		
Gross profit	160,000		
	———		———
	480,000		480,000
	———		———
Running expenses	125,000	Gross profit	160,000
Depreciation (W9)	10,000		
Net profit	25,000		
	———		———
	160,000		160,000
	———		———

Estimated Balance Sheet

	£	£		£	£
Share capital					
(balancing figure)....		115,000	Fixed assets at cost..		100,000
Net profit		25,000	*Less:* Depreciation..		10,000
		———			———
Equity		140,000			90,000
Current Liabilities:			*Current Assets:*		
Creditors (W7)	30,000		Stock (W3)	40,000	
Overdraft (W8)	20,000		Debtors (W1)	60,000	
	———	50,000		———	100,000 (W2)
		———			———
		190,000			190,000
		———			———

Workings

	£
1. Trade debtors, $1.2 \times 50,000$	60,000
2. Current assets, $2 \times £50,000$	100,000
3. Stocks, £100,000 − £60,000	40,000
4. Sales, $\frac{12}{1.5} \times 60,000$	480,000
5. Cost of goods sold, $66\frac{2}{3}\%$ of sales	320,000
6. Purchases, £320,000 + £40,000	360,000
7. Creditors, $\frac{1}{12} \times £360,000$	30,000
8. Overdraft, £50,000 − £30,000	20,000
9. Depreciation, $£100,000 \times \frac{1}{10}$	10,000

Examiner's comments:
Area of weakness: 1. Calculation of depreciation and its inclusion in the balance sheet.
2. Calculation of the gross profit.
3. Failure to show net profit as a separate item in shareholder's equity.

The following example requires the preparation of a forecast cash statement, profit and loss account and balance sheet. Note how these inter-link; for example, the forecast cash balance is used in the balance sheet, the forecast profit is added to capital, and the value of drawings in the balance sheet agrees with that in the cash forecast.

Example 10.6 (Taken from the September, 1981 *Accountancy* paper).

The summarised final accounts of Michael, a trader, for the year ended 30 June, 1981, are as follows:

PROFIT AND LOSS ACCOUNT, YEAR ENDED 30 JUNE, 1981

	£	£
Sales		480,000
Less: Cost of goods sold		360,000
Gross profit		120,000
Less: Depreciation	10,000	
General expenses	96,000	106,000
Net profit		£14,000

BALANCE SHEET AS AT 30 JUNE, 1981

	£		£	£
Capital	97,000	Fixed assets at cost		100,000
		Less: Depreciation		30,000
Trade creditors	60,000			70,000
		Current assets		
		Stock-in-trade	45,000	
		Trade debtors	40,000	
		Bank	2,000	87,000
	£157,000			£157,000

Michael has approached your bank for a loan to finance the acquisition of additional freehold premises. The premises are situated next door to his existing premises and occupation could be obtained on 1 October, 1981. The premises would cost £50,000 and payment would be made during the month of October. There is a heavy demand for the goods which Michael sells and he is confident that from 1 October monthly sales can be increased by 20% if the additional premises are obtained. The gross profit percentage would remain unchanged and general expenses, inclusive of an allowance for bank interest at 15%, would increase by £1,200 per month from 1 September. Michael intends to employ two sources of finance for the planned expansion.

1. He will offer customers a discount of 2% for immediate payment on all sales made from 1 October, 1981 onwards. He expects half the customers to take advantage of this offer. The remaining customers will take the same period of credit as in the previous year.

2. He has asked for a bank overdraft facility of £20,000 for the next twelve months.

Michael expects creditors to increase in proportion to sales; the stock-in-trade balance will remain at £45,000. The depreciation charge on existing fixed assets will remain unchanged. The additional buildings will be depreciated on the straight line basis assuming a life of twenty years; for this purpose the buildings are considered to comprise £40,000 of the planned expenditure on premises referred to above. General expenses are paid monthly for cash; Michael draws £1,000 from the business bank account each month to cover personal expenditure.

Required

(a) Michael's estimated profit and loss account for the year ended 30 June, 1982 and estimated balance sheet at 30 June, 1982.

(b) Calculations of the estimated maximum overdraft Michael will require during the year to 30 June, 1982 and of his bank balance or overdraft at 30 June, 1982.

(c) An assessment of Michael's plans for expansion.

NOTES:

1. *There are no seasonal fluctuations in the level of activity in Michael's trade.*
2. *Purchases and sales take place evenly during the year.*
3. *Your calculations under (a) and (b) should be based on the assumption that the bank agrees to finance the planned expansion.*

[30]

Solution:

(a)   *Forecast Profit and Loss Account, Year to 30 June, 1982*

	£	£
Sales		552,000 (W1)
Less: Cost of Goods Sold		414,000 (W1)
Gross Profit		138,000
Depreciation	11,500 (W2)	
Discounts	4,320 (W3)	
General Expenses	108,000	
		123,820
Net Profit		14,180

Workings

W1. (£000)

		Sales	*Cost of Goods Sold*
July–September:	480 × ¼	120	
	360 × ¼		90
October–June:	480 × ¾	360	
	Add 360 × 20%	72	
		— 432	
	360 × ¾		270
	Add 270 × 20%		54
			— 324
		552	414

W2. Depreciation:

	£
Existing fixed assets..	10,000
Additional buildings, (£40,000 ÷ 20) × ¾	1,500
	11,500

W3. Discounts: 1% of £432,000 = £4,320

Forecast Balance Sheet 30 June, 1982

	£	£		£	£
Opening capital....		97,000	Fixed assets at cost..........		150,000
Add: Net profit ...	14,180		*Less:* Accumulated		
Less: Drawings	(12,000)	2,180	depreciation...........		41,500
		99,180			108,500
Current Liabilities:			*Current Assets:*		
Trade creditors.....	72,000		Stock in trade.................	45,000	
Bank overdraft.....	6,320		Debtors........................	24,000	
		78,320			69,000
		177,500			177,500

(b)

Cash Forecast

Month	Opening Balance £	Sales Cash £	Sales Credit £	Purchases £	General Expenses £	Drawings £	Premises £	Closing Balance £
July	2,000		40,000	30,000	8,000	1,000		3,000
Aug.	3,000		40,000	30,000	8,000	1,000		4,000
Sept.	4,000		40,000	30,000	9,200	1,000		3,800
Oct.	3,800	23,520	40,000	30,000	9,200	1,000	50,000	(22,880)
Nov.	(22,880)	23,520	24,000	30,000	9,200	1,000		(15,560)
Dec.	(15,560)	23,520	24,000	36,000	9,200	1,000		(14,240)

The overdraft then declines at the rate of £1,320 per month until June, 1982 i.e. 14,240 – (6 × 1,320) = £6,320.

(c) The forecast profit is only marginally higher than that achieved in the year to 30 June, 1981. However, the increased sales were achieved only in the last nine months of the year. In a full year:

	£	£
Sales		576,000
Less: Cost of goods sold		432,000
		144,000
Depreciation	12,000	
Discounts	5,760	
General Expenses	110,400	
		128,160
Net profit		15,840

In addition:
(1) The bank overdraft will be repaid by the end of 1982 and interest charges will then cease.
(2) Alternatively, if possible, the company should discontinue the practice of allowing discounts for prompt payments. Although the company collects the cash, on average, a month earlier, it pays 2% (approximately 24% per annum) for this privilege.

The company marginally exceeds the requested overdraft facility in October. The excess is only for one month and so the facility, if granted, should be in the region of £25,000. The new premises will provide one possible source of security for the overdraft.

Examiner's comments:

Area of weakness: 1. The calculation of discounts and the inclusion of their effect in the profit and cash forecasts.
2. The calculation of depreciation and its inclusion in the profit and loss account and balance sheet.
3. Appreciation of the impact of a full year's trading under the new conditions.

10.2.4 The Identification of Alternatives

The forecasts so far considered have been prepared on the basis of well formulated plans. In other circumstances, there may be a number of possible courses of action; the forecaster must clearly identify the alternatives, prepare forecasts of the likely results from each, and, if required, give advice based on these forecasts.

Example 10.7 (Taken from the April, 1979 *Accountancy* paper).

Rowan recently won a premium bond prize of £50,000. At present he is employed as a travelling salesman with an annual income of £4,000 and a company car which is worth £1,000 a year to him. His wife works as a receptionist and her salary is £2,000 per annum. He has been exploring two investment possibilities.

(i) To invest his money in a local company. The proposal is that, with the £50,000 available, he should acquire 20,000 shares, which the firm intends to issue in order to finance a plan for expansion. The firm's managing director informs him 'Our annual profits are at present in the region of £30,000, of which two-thirds are paid out in dividends. As a result of the expansion profits should increase by 25% all of which will be added to the current annual dividend.' At present the company's share capital consists of 80,000 shares with a nominal value of £1 each. Under this option Rowan would play no part in the management of the company.

(ii) To acquire a shop which has recently come on to the market. The cost would be £60,000 and this includes stocks to which a value of £15,000 is attached. Finance would be provided out of his winnings and by realising some investments currently yielding a 'safe' return of 10% per annum (gross). These investments can be added to or reduced without affecting the rate of return. The following estimates are provided concerning this business:

Average annual rate of stock turnover	10
Gross profit as a percentage of sales	25%
Overhead expenses	£33,000

If this option is pursued, Rowan can either run the business with the help of his wife, both working full-time, or engage a manager at an annual salary of £8,000. Management salaries are not included in the overhead expenses shown above.

Required:

(a) A numerical analysis of the options open to Rowan, presented in a manner which will help him to make comparisons. Confine your calculations to the information given.

(b) An indication of the alternative you would recommend on the basis of the information given.

NOTE: Ignore taxation.

[20]

Solution:

(a) Alternative:

	£	£
1. Continue in present employment and purchase additional investments.		
Present salary		4,000
Value of company car		1,000
Wife's earnings		2,000
£50,000 invested at 10%		5,000
		———
		12,000

2. Continue in present employment and purchase shares in a local firm.

Salary, car and wife's earning as above....................................		7,000
Present dividend paid by firm	20,000	
Estimated increase in profits: 25% of 30,000............................	7,500	
Share of future dividend... $\dfrac{20,000}{100,000} \times 27,500 =$		5,500
		———
		12,500

3. Acquire a shop to be managed by Rowan and his wife.

Cost of sales = 10 × 15,000..	150,000	
Sales $= \dfrac{100}{75} \times 150,000$...	200,000	
	———	
Gross profit...	50,000	
Less: Overheads..	33,000	
Profit..	———	17,000
Loss of investment income: 10% of £10,000............................		1,000
		———
		16,000

4. Acquire a shop and engage a manager.

Present salary, car and wife's earnings as in 1............................		7,000
Profit as in 3...	16,000	
Less: Manager's salary	8,000	
	———	8,000
		———
		15,000

(b) Investment in the shares of a local company may produce some appreciation in the capital value of Rowan's investment, as well as the forecast dividend. But there is considerable risk and alternative 1 seems better than alternative 2 despite the marginally lower expected return. Going into business seems attractive. There is likely to be risk in any business venture but perhaps a travelling salesman is not in the most secure employment. Provided Rowan and his wife appear likely to possess the necessary expertise, it is probably better for them to manage the shop themselves.

Examiner's Comments:
Areas of weakness: 1. Failure to identify clearly and evaluate the four options open to Rowan. 2. Failure to differentiate between the capital sum and the income it could be used to generate. 3. Calculation of the shop profit.

10.3   THE FINANCING DECISION

The cash forecast provides information on the expected cash position of the company, and, where a deficit is revealed, consideration must be given to the manner in which it is to be financed. Two important aspects are the size of the deficit and its expected duration. To avoid overtrading, a company should not normally use short-term sources of finance to acquire long-term assets, but the size of the investment must be judged relative to the scale of the company. A large company can make a relatively small capital investment by using short term funds and not seriously impair a satisfactory working capital position, while a small company, investing a similar sum of money, would seriously deplete its working capital if it used short-term finance. A cash deficit must be funded in an appropriate manner if a firm's financial development is to be balanced; this requires the matching of a long-term deficit with long-term funds, such as share capital or debentures, while a deficit expected to last only a short time can be matched with short-term funds, such as an overdraft. The position from which a company starts is also relevant, as one with a healthy working capital position can accept a short-term deterioration but the future of a firm with existing liquidity problems would be jeopardised by any worsening. (See Chapter 9, sections 7 and 9, for a detailed discussion of the financial development of companies).

The cash flow patterns which result from alternative courses of action can be entered in cash flow forecasts to see which best suits the company's requirements. However, when deciding how to obtain finance, there are other factors to be considered:

1. Security. The ability of a company to attract finance may depend on the assets it can offer as security and the extent to which these are already pledged.

2. Gearing. The capital structure of the company should be developed in a balanced manner. A company with little or no gearing has the capacity to raise fixed interest loans, while a highly geared company should give priority to expanding its equity capital base.

3. Ownership. The owners of a company may be unwilling to allow it to issue new shares which are taken up by new members and, therefore, reduce their control.

4. Cost. Investors expect a return on their investment. Debentures and loans carry interest charges and shareholders expect dividends and capital growth. Management must weigh the relative costs of the different forms of finance available to the company.

5. *Assistance*. Some assistance towards the cost of fixed assets may be available from the government. To qualify, the assets might have to be of a specified type or be used in a designated location.

Example 10.8 (Taken from the September, 1982 *Accountancy* paper).

Norman Berman is a trader whose draft balance sheet as at 30 June 1982 is as follows:

BALANCE SHEET AT 30 JUNE 1982.

Capital.	£000s		£000s	£000s
Balance at 1 July 1981	120	Fixed assets at cost		89
Add: Net profit	24	Less: Depreciation		31
Less: Drawings	(18)			—
	—			58
Balance at 30 June 1982	126	Current Assets		
		Stock-in-trade	64	
Current Liabilities		Trade debtors	35	
Trade creditors	32	Bank	1	100
	—		—	—
	158			158

There is a bouyant demand for Berman's products, and sales have increased steadily over the years. The following forecasts and estimates are made for the year ending 30 June 1983.

1. Forecast monthly sales are as follows:
   1982. July-December £40,000 per month
   1983. January-June £45,000 per month
   July-December £50,000 per month.

2. The gross profit margin will be 20% on sales.

3. It is Berman's policy to maintain stocks, at the end of each month, sufficient to cover the expected sales for the following *two* months.

4. The period of credit allowed to customers and obtained from suppliers is expected to remain the same as for the year ended 30 June 1982 i.e. one month.

5. Berman has sufficient accommodation for the planned increase in sales, but vehicles and equipment costing £20,000 will need to be purchased and paid for in December 1982.

6. Wages and general expenses (including an allowance for bank interest) are paid for in the month that they are incurred and will amount to £5,000 per month.

7. The depreciation charge for the year is to be £12,000.

8. Berman will withdraw £2,000 each month for personal use.

9. Berman's bank has agreed to provide any overdraft facilities required during the year ended 30 June 1983 and will charge interest at a rate of 18% per annum.

Required:

(a) A forecast cash statement, showing the bank balance or overdraft at the end of each month, for the year ending 30 June 1983.

[10]

(b) Berman's forecast profit and loss account for the year ending 30 June 1983.

[6]

(c) Berman's forecast balance sheet at 30 June 1983.

[8]

(d) A discussion of the respective merits of bank overdraft finance as compared with loan finance, in the light of Berman's requirements, assuming that he could alternatively finance the purchase of vehicles and equipment by raising a five year loan at a fixed interest rate of 15% per annum.

[6]

NOTES: Ignore taxation.
Assume for the purpose of the question that your calculations are being made on 1 July 1982 and that the year to 30 June 1983 consists of twelve months of equal length.

[Total marks for question: 30]

Solution:

(a)   *Forecast Cash Statement*

Month	Opening Balance £000	Sales £000	Purchases £000	Vehicles £000	Wages Etc. £000	Drawings £000	Closing Balance £000
July	1	35	32		5	2	(3)
Aug.	(3)	40	32		5	2	(2)
Sept.	(2)	40	32		5	2	(1)
Oct.	(1)	40	32		5	2	—
Nov.	—	40	32		5	2	1
Dec.	1	40	36*	20	5	2	(22)
Jan.	(22)	40	36*		5	2	(25)
Feb.	(25)	45	36		5	2	(23)
March	(23)	45	36		5	2	(21)
April	(21)	45	36		5	2	(19)
May	(19)	45	36		5	2	(17)
June	(17)	45	40*		5	2	(19)

*includes additional purchases of £4,000 required to keep the stock level equal to the next two months' sales.

(b)   *Forecast Profit and Loss Account*

	£000	£000
Sales		510 (W1)
Less: Cost of goods sold (80%)		408
		—
Gross profit		102
Less: Wages and general expenses	60	
Depreciation	12	
	—	72
		—
Net profit		30

W1: Sales (£40,000 × 6) + (£45,000 × 6) = £510,000

(c)   *Forecast Balance Sheet, 30 June, 1983*

	£000	£000		£000	£000
Capital					
Balance at 1 July, 1982	126		Fixed assets at cost		109
Add: Net profit	30		*Less:* Depreciation		43
Less: Drawings	(24)				—
	—				66
	132				
Current Liabilities			Current Assets		
Trade creditors	40		Stock-in-trade	80	
Bank overdraft	19		Trade debtors	45	
	—	59		—	125
		—			—
		191			191

(d) Berman's firm is expected to generate funds from operations totalling £42,000 (£30,000 profit + £12,000 depreciation) during the year. Of this, Berman will withdraw £24,000 and the remaining £18,000 will be used to finance an increase in working capital, defined as stock + debtors − creditors. In addition fixed assets costing £20,000 will be purchased and this expenditure converts a £1,000 bank balance, at the beginning of the year, into a £19,000 deficit at the year end. The result is that the firm is expected to rely heavily on the bank for financial support, though the forecast working capital ratio is a fairly healthy 2.1:1.

Whether Berman should seek longer term finance for the additional fixed assets, for example, a five year loan, depends a lot on whether there are plans for further expansion. If the rate of expansion slows down, but profit margins continue at present levels, then the bank overdraft will be reduced fairly quickly. For instance, in the early months of 1982, before the second phase of expansion, the overdraft is expected to fall at the rate of £2,000 per month. In such circumstances the decision to raise a five year loan might soon result in the firm being in possession of liquid resources surplus to requirements. Despite the apparently favourable rate of loan interest, the total interest payable would then significantly exceed that accruing to a declining bank overdraft. If, however, further expansion is anticipated over the next five years, it would probably be wise to raise medium term finance at this stage.

Examiner's Comments:

Area of weakness: 1. The calculation of the stock increases needed to meet additional sales, and their conversion into cash flows.

2. The calculation of stock, debtors, creditors, and fixed assets for inclusion in the balance sheet.

10.4 THE CASH OPERATING CYCLE

A period of time elapses between the payment for goods or raw materials received into stock and the collection of cash from customers in respect of their sale. The gap is known as the 'Cash Operating Cycle' and, during this period of time, the goods acquired, together with the value added in the case of a manufacturer, must be financed by the company. The shorter the length of time between the initial outlay and ultimate collection of cash, the smaller is the value of working capital to be financed. To estimate the length of the cash operating cycle it is necessary to:

1. Calculate the time which the product spends in each stage of its progression from acquisition to sale and subsequent cash receipt.
2. Deduct from the length of time found in step 1 the period of credit received from suppliers.

The various elements in the calculation are described below and illustrated in example 10.9. For a trading company which buys and sells goods without processing them, omit stages 1 (a) and 1 (b).

1. Stocks. Items are added to stocks, held for a period of time, and then withdrawn. The following methods for estimating the length of time for which items are held are based on the *withdrawals* which take place during the period under consideration. An acceptable estimate can also be obtained by basing the calculations on the *additions* to stock.

(a) Raw Materials. These are acquired, held in stock, and then

418 INTERNAL ACCOUNTING REPORTS

transferred to production. Stocks of raw materials are related to raw materials consumed to find the average length of time for which they are held.

(b) Work in Progress. Raw materials are taken from stock and processed, which involves additional manufacturing costs. The average production time is found by relating the stock of work in progress to the cost of goods manufactured.

(c) Finished Goods. When production is complete, the finished goods are transferred from the factory to the warehouse. (In the case of a trader, finished goods, stored in the warehouse, are purchased from outside.) The average length of time for which items are held is found by relating the stock of finished goods to the cost of goods sold during the accounting period.

2. Debtors. The average age of debts is found from the values of debtors and sales (see Chapter 8, section 4.2).

3. Creditors. These finance the production and selling cycle from the time raw materials or goods are received into stock until they are paid for. The period of credit is found from the values of creditors and purchases (see Chapter 8, section 4.3).

The length of the cash operating cycle is obtained by aggregating the periods of time calculated for each of the above items; note that item 3 is negative.

Example 10.9 (Taken from the April, 1981 *Accountancy* paper).

The cash balance of Wing Ltd. has declined significantly over the last twelve months. The following financial information is provided.

Year to 31 December	1979	1980
	£	£
Sales	573,000	643,000
Purchases of raw materials	215,000	264,000
Raw materials consumed	210,000	256,400
Cost of goods manufactured	435,000	515,000
Cost of goods sold	420,000	460,000

Balance at 31 December	1979	1980
	£	£
Debtors	97,100	121,500
Creditors	23,900	32,500
Stocks: Raw materials	22,400	30,000
Work in progress	29,000	34,300
Finished goods	70,000	125,000

All purchases and sales were made on credit.

Required:

(a) An analysis of the above information, which should include calculations of the cash operating cycle (i.e. the time lag between making payment to suppliers and collecting cash from customers) for 1979 and 1980.

(b) A brief report on the implications of the changes which have occurred between 1979 and 1980.

Note:

1. *Assume a 360 day year for the purpose of your calculations, and that all transactions take place at an even rate.*

2. *All calculations are to be made to the nearest day.*

[20]

Solution:

(a) *Cash Operating Cycle*

		1979 days		1980 days
Raw material stock	$\frac{22,400}{210,000} \times 360$	38	$\frac{30,000}{256,400} \times 360$	42
Credit from suppliers	$\frac{23,900}{215,000} \times 360$	(40)	$\frac{32,500}{264,000} \times 360$	(44)
		(2)		(2)
Production period	$\frac{29,000}{435,000} \times 360$	24	$\frac{34,300}{515,000} \times 360$	24
Finished goods stocks	$\frac{70,000}{420,000} \times 360$	60	$\frac{125,000}{460,000} \times 360$	98
Credit to customers	$\frac{97,100}{573,000} \times 360$	61	$\frac{121,500}{643,000} \times 360$	68
Cash operating cycle		143		188
Gross profit %		26.7		28.5

(b) The cash operating cycle has increased by 45 days or 31.5%. This is reflected in an increased investment in working capital, calculated as follows:

	£	£
Stocks	121,400	189,300
Debtors...................	97,100	121,500
Less: Creditors.........	(23,900)	(32,500)
	194,600	278,300

The increased period for which raw material stock is held has been balanced by an equivalent increase in the period of credit taken from suppliers. Furthermore, the production period has remained constant at 24 days suggesting no change in the efficiency with which resources are moved through the factory. The areas of concern are the significant increase in the period of credit taken by customers and the massive increase in the holding of finished stock which has grown from the equivalent of two months' sales at the end of 1979 to more than three months' sales at the end of 1980.

The company has achieved a significant growth in its gross profit percentage; more information is needed in order to discover whether any resulting increase in profit sufficiently compensates the likely cost of the increase in capital employed.

Examiner's Comments:
Areas of weakness: 1. Lack of knowledge of what the cash operating cycle is.
　　　　　　　　2. Failure to relate the various elements of stocks to an appropriate flow.

10.5   COST BEHAVIOUR AND ANALYSIS

Sales revenue is the product of the number of units sold and the price per unit, but the number of units sold is, in turn, influenced by price; if the unit price rises, less units are sold, if it falls, more are sold. It is management's job to select the unit price and, thereby, the quantity sold and total revenue, so as to maximise profit. To measure profit at any forecast level of output, the related costs must also be estimated. This requires a clear understanding of the fact that different costs behave in different ways when output changes. It is therefore useful to analyse costs into different categories, each of which contains costs which respond in a similar manner. The categorisation is unlikely to be completely accurate, but the impact of any error is reduced by the fact that the information is used to help predict future results, and this exercise must necessarily contain an element of uncertainty. One useful classification of costs is fixed and variable (see sections 5.1 and 5.2 of this Chapter); another is marginal cost and sunk cost (see section 5.4 of this Chapter).

10.5.1   Fixed Costs

Certain costs are incurred irrespective of an enterprise's rate of activity. For example, once the decision has been made to rent a factory, the full rent must be paid irrespective of whether the occupier uses all, or just a small proportion, of the available floor area. Such costs are known as 'fixed costs' because they remain fixed over a limited range of output. Up to a certain level of activity, a company can expand its output without the need to incur additional fixed costs. However, once full capacity is reached, any further expansion will require the company to incur an additional set of fixed costs. To continue the example of factory rent, it is possible for a manufacturer to use all available space for all of the time and obtain maximum utilisation; when this point is reached, any increase in activity requires the acquisition of further space, and perhaps an additional factory will be rented. Other examples of fixed costs are straight line depreciation, administrative salaries, and audit fees.

It is important for a company to make available capacity appropriate to its planned scale of operations. If it starts on too small a scale, it will not be able to satisfy the potential demand for its product, and to expand an established operation may introduce inefficiencies, for example, the use of one large factory is likely to be more efficient than two separate smaller ones each of half the size. If it starts on too large a scale, this will mean that spare capacity exists and each unit of output will bear an unnecessarily high element of fixed cost.

10.5.2 Variable Costs These vary with the rate of activity; the greater the output of a company, the higher are its total variable costs. For example, when a shop makes extra sales it has to purchase additional stock, and this is a variable cost. In manufacturing, examples of variable costs are the direct labour and direct material costs. It is usual to assume that the variable cost per unit is constant, that is, each extra unit of throughput causes the company to incur the same additional cost. This relationship may not hold in practice; the unit cost of labour may rise with an expansion of output, as overtime is worked, while the unit material cost may fall as the result of receiving increased discounts on bulk purchases.

(See Chapter 8, examples 4 and 5, for simple illustrations of the effect of changes in the level of activity on costs and, therefore, profit margins).

Example 10.10 (Taken from the September, 1982 *Accountancy* paper).

The summarised profit and loss account of Merrill Ltd., a company which manufactures a single product is as follows:

PROFIT AND LOSS ACCOUNT, YEAR ENDED 30 JUNE 1982.

	£	£
Sales (25,000 units)		1,000,000
Less: Manufacturing costs—variable	500,000	
—fixed	180,000	
Cost of goods sold		680,000
Gross profit		320,000
Less: Running costs		200,000
Net profit		£120,000

There is strong demand for the company's product, but there is also keen competition from other suppliers. The directors of Merrill Ltd. believe that if the sales price remains unchanged, at £40 per unit, turnover will amount to only 23,000 units in the year to 30 June 1983. Further estimates show that turnover of 25,000 units could again be achieved if the price were reduced to £39, while a reduction in sales price to £38 would cause turnover to increase to 35,000 units. Variable manufacturing costs per unit and fixed manufacturing costs per annum are expected to remain unchanged whichever of the three options are chosen by the company's directors. At 23,000 units, running costs will fall to £165,000 whereas at 35,000 units they will rise to £320,000.

Required:

(a) Forecast profit and loss accounts of Merrill Ltd. for the year ended 30 June 1983, under each of the alternatives indicated above. [9]

(b) Calculations of the net profit ratio (net profit as a percentage of sales) under each of these alternatives. [3]

(c) An indication of the alternative which you would favour. You should explain your choice and also refer to any further information which might help the decision making process. [8]

NOTE: Assume for the purpose of this question that your calculations are being made on 1 July 1982.

[Total marks for question: 20]

Solution:

(a)   *Forecast Profit and Loss Accounts*

	23,000 units		25,000 units		35,000 units	
	£000	*£000*	*£000*	*£000*	*£000*	*£000*
Sales..		920		975		1,330
Less: Manufacturing costs:						
Variable...............................	460		500		700	
Fixed.....................................	180		180		180	
Cost of goods sold		640		680		880
Gross profit......................................		280		295		450
Less: Running costs		165		200		320
Net profit...		115		95		130

(b) Net profit ratio............................   12.5%   9.7%   9.8%

(c) The choice between the three options depends on which measure of performance is considered more relevant for the purpose of the decision which must be made, net profit or the net profit ratio.

Applying the former criterion, it would seem that the sales price should be reduced to £38 in order to enable production and sales to increase to 35,000 units. This results in a profit of £130,000 which is significantly higher than the net returns arising under the other two alternatives.

The net profit ratio is highest where sales amount to 23,000 units. This is because the smaller gross margin accruing to the reduced output is substantially offset by lower running costs.

Each of the above measures provide helpful guidelines but should be used in conjunction with other information and estimates. The amount of additional investment required to enable output to be increased to 35,000 units should be established and, when this information is obtained, the return on capital employed can be calculated. An estimate of the likely demand pattern after the expiration of the forthcoming twelve months is also needed.

Examiner's Comments:

Areas of weakness: 1. The treatment of fixed and variable costs; many candidates treated the fixed manufacturing cost as variable.
2. The calculation of sales revenue.
3. The treatment of running cost at different levels of output.

10.5.3 Break-even Analysis

This examines the behaviour of costs in response to changes in the level of output; it compares the total cost, that is, fixed plus variable costs, with sales revenue to determine the profit or loss. The point at which the firm breaks even is when it makes neither profit nor loss as total costs are exactly equal to sales revenue. Break-even analysis is useful both to discover the level of output required to achieve various profit targets and also to compare the likely results of different techniques of production. It is often possible to interchange fixed and variable costs; for example a method of production can be capital intensive or labour intensive. An instance of this is the car industry where either 'robots' or employees can be used to perform tasks on the assembly line. The depreciation on the robot is a fixed cost to be met irrespective of the volume of production, while the cost of employees can be made to respond to changes in the level of activity, for instance, by the use of overtime or short-time working. Balanced against this is the fact that capital intensive methods may give rise to savings in associated variable costs by, for example, using less material or causing less waste and rejects.

The numerical approach to break-even analysis is based on a financial balance, called the 'Contribution', which may be defined as the excess of selling price over the variable cost. The first charge on the revenue from the sale of a unit is its variable cost; any surplus is the contribution which goes to meet fixed costs. Once enough units have been sold to recover all the fixed costs, a profit is made. The break-even point, in terms of units, may be found by the formula:

$$Q = \frac{F}{C}$$

Where: Q = units sold

F = fixed costs

C = contribution = S – V,

where: S = selling price per unit

V = variable cost per unit

Q × S gives the break-even point in terms of sales revenue.

If it is desired to find the level of sales necessary to achieve a given level of profit, the formula is:

$$Q = \frac{F + P}{C}$$

Where: P = the desired profit, and the other items are as given above.

Example 10.11

Bevan Ltd., is considering two alternative methods to manufacture a new product it intends to market. The two methods each have a maximum output of 50,000 units and produce identical items with a selling price of £25 each. The costs are:

	Method I (Labour intensive) £	Method II (Capital intensive) £
Variable cost per unit	15	10
Fixed costs	100,000	300,000

REQUIRED:
(a) Calculate the break-even point of each method in terms of both units and sales revenue.
(b) Calculate the level of sales, in terms of both units and revenue, required under each method to produce a profit of £30,000.
(c) Calculate the profit of each method at full capacity.

Solution:

(a) *Break-even point*

	Method I	Method II
	£	£
Selling price per unit..........	25	25
Variable cost per unit.........	15	10
Contribution	10	15
$\dfrac{\text{Fixed cost}}{\text{Contribution}} = $	$\dfrac{100,000}{10}$	$\dfrac{300,000}{10}$
	= *10,000 units*	= *20,000 units*
Sales revenue:....................	10,000 × £25	20,000 × £25
	= *£250,000*	= *£500,000*

(b) *Target Profit £30,000*

Method I

$$\frac{100,000\ (\text{fixed cost}) + 30,000\ (\text{target profit})}{10\ (\text{contribution})} = 13,000\ units$$

13,000 (units sold) × £25 (unit price) = *£325,000*

Method II

$$\frac{300,000\ (\text{fixed cost}) + 30,000\ (\text{target profit})}{15\ (\text{contribution})} = 22,000\ units$$

22,000 (units sold) × £25 (unit price) = *£550,000*

(c) *Profit at full capacity*

	Method I	Method II
Contribution...........................	50,000 × 10 = £500,000	50,000 × 15 = £750,000
Less: Fixed costs.....................	100,000	300,000
Profit....................................	£400,000	£450,000

The method of production appropriate for Bevan Ltd. depends on the expected level of sales. More units have to be sold to reach break-even point under method II, and it carries the risk of greater loss, which at zero output is equal to fixed costs. At low levels of output, method I is therefore preferred. Once fixed costs have been recovered, the profit grows more quickly with each additional unit sold under method II as its contribution is greater. At maximum output, method II produces the higher profit.

The two methods produce equal profits where their total costs are the same, and this point is found by the formula:

$$F_I + V_I Q = F_{II} + V_{II} Q$$

Where: F = fixed costs

V = variable cost per unit

Q = units sold

I and II signify different methods of production

For Bevan Ltd. (example 10.11), equal profits are earned when:

$$100,000 + 15Q = 300,000 + 10Q$$

$$5Q = 200,000$$

$$Q = 40,000 \text{ units}$$

The relationship between costs, profit and volume can be clearly demonstrated using a graph, see figure 10.1, based on the information given in example 10.11. The horizontal axis measures units of output, while the vertical axis measures the value of sales revenue and business costs. Revenues and costs relating to individual projects are represented by the following straight lines on the graph.

Sales: When no sales are made the revenue is zero. The revenue at maximum output is plotted, R, and these two points are joined, O–R.

Fixed Costs: These are the same at all levels of output up to maximum capacity, and so the line is horizontal. For method I, fixed costs are £100,000 and are represented by the line FCI.

Variable Costs: When no output is produced, these are zero. The variable cost at maximum output is plotted, VCI for method I, and the two points are joined, O–VCI.

Total Cost: This is the total of fixed and variable costs, represented by the line TCI for method I.

The break-even point is where the total cost line crosses the revenue line; the profit or loss at any point is represented by the gap between these lines. The rate at which the width of the gap changes shows how quickly profits and losses respond to changes in output.

Figure 10.1

The break-even graph for both Methods I and II using the information given in Example 10.11 above for Bevan Ltd. is:

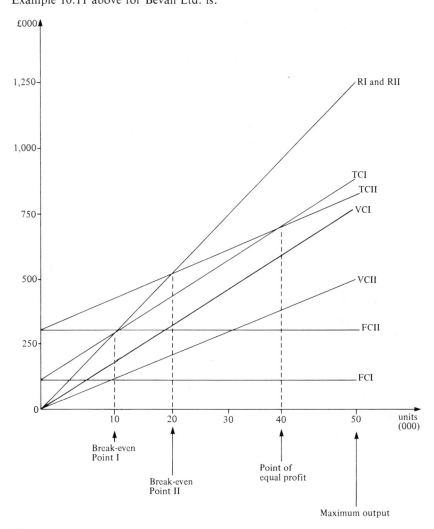

Notes:
1. For ease of interpretation the variable cost lines may be omitted.
2. Study the rate of growth of profit under each of the methods.

To emphasise the extent of vulnerability to changes in output, it is useful to calculate the 'Margin of Safety', which shows how far sales can fall before a loss is incurred. It is calculated, either in terms of units or value, by the formula:

$$\frac{\text{Anticipated Sales—Sales at Break-even Point}}{\text{Anticipated Sales}}$$

For example, if Bevan Ltd. (example 10.11) anticipated sales of 30,000 units, the margin of safety for each method is:

	Method I	*Method II*
Units:	$\dfrac{30,000-10,000}{30,000} = \dfrac{2}{3} = 67\%$	$\dfrac{30,000-20,000}{30,000} = \dfrac{1}{3} = 33\%$

OR

	Method I	*Method II*
Value:	$\dfrac{750,000-250,000}{750,000} = \dfrac{2}{3} = 67\%$	$\dfrac{750,000-500,000}{750,000} = \dfrac{1}{3} = 33\%$

These calculations show that under method I sales can fall by 67%, from forecast levels, before a loss is made, while under method II a loss occurs after a fall of only 33%. Therefore, method I has the greater margin of safety.

A great virtue of break-even analysis is its simplicity, but to achieve this simplicity a number of assumptions must be made, and these bring limitations and weaknesses. The main assumptions, and hence weaknesses, are that profit varies only in response to changes in output, and that each unit sold gives the same contribution. In practice, profit changes in response to many factors other than output, such as, the efficiency of production, the introduction of new techniques, the state of the market, and the unit cost of materials, and yet these are held constant in break-even analysis. Two further weaknesses are that it only deals with one product in isolation and so is not applicable to businesses which sell a variety of products; also, it concentrates on profit and therefore ignores other possible objectives of the company. However, break-even analysis is a useful managerial tool provided that its limitations are appreciated and its results interpreted accordingly.

Example 10.12 (Taken from the April, 1980 *Accountancy* paper).

The research department of Cavalaire Limited has recently developed a new product which can be manufactured using either of two methods. The costs involved under each of these methods are as follows:

Method I—Plant with an estimated useful life of five years and nil scrap value would be acquired for £200,000. Fixed expenses (other than depreciation) would amount to £60,000 per annum and variable costs per unit would be £35.

Method II—Plant with an estimated useful life of five years and nil scrap value would be acquired for £80,000. Fixed expenses (other than depreciation) would amount to £29,000 per annum and variable costs per unit would be £45.

The product is to be marketed at £60 per unit irrespective of the level of sales achieved. The maximum feasible production capacity under either method is 10,000 units. Working capital requirements are £40,000 under either method of production and the company depreciates plant on the straight line basis.

Required:

(a) Calculations of the number of units which must be produced and sold under either method each year in order to break even.

(b) Calculations of the number of units which must be produced and sold under either method each year in order to achieve a target return of 20 per cent on capital invested.

(c) A full discussion of the two alternative production methods, using the calculations made under (a) and (b) above and any other figures and/or diagrams you consider relevant.

NOTE: Ignore taxation.

[20]

Solution:

(a)

	Method I		Method II	
Fixed costs per annum:	£		£	
Depreciation	40,000		16,000	
Other fixed expenses	60,000		29,000	
	100,000		45,000	
Contribution per unit	£25		£15	
Break even point, in units	$\frac{100,000}{25}$	= 4,000 units	$\frac{45,000}{15}$	= 3,000 units

(b)

Capital invested:	£	£
Fixed assets	200,000	80,000
Working capital	40,000	40,000
	240,000	120,000
Target return 20%	48,000	24,000

Sales, in units, to achieve target profit $\dfrac{148,000}{25} = 5,920$ units $\dfrac{69,000}{15} = 4,600$ units

(c) Additional calculations include:

	Method I	Method II
(i) Profit at maximum feasible capacity, 10,000 units	£	£
Contribution	250,000	150,000
Fixed expenses	100,000	45,000
	150,000	105,000

(ii) Profit equality between I and II, $F_I + V_I Q = F_{II} + V_{II} Q$

$$100,000 + 35Q = 45,000 + 45Q$$

$$55,000 = 10Q$$

$$Q = 5,500 \ units$$

Relevant comments include:
1. Method I is relatively more capital intensive than Method II.
2. Method II achieves break-even and target profit at lower levels of sales than Method I. This is the effect of much lower capital investment requirements.
3. The total profit arising under either method is similar at 5,500 units of output. It is not until another 420 units have been produced and sold under Method I that the target return is reached; under Method II the target return is reached at 4,600 units.
4. Sales at the maximum feasible production levels makes Method I the more favourable.

Examiner's Comments:
Areas of weakness: 1. Omission of depreciation from fixed costs.
2. Omission of working capital from the capital invested.
3. Very few additional calculations were given in answer to part (c).

10.5.4 Marginal Costs and Sunk Costs

Marginal cost is the increase in costs caused by an increase in activity of one unit; for analytical purposes the unit may be, for example, a single article, a batch, an order, or a whole department. In the context of break-even analysis the marginal cost of producing one extra unit is its variable cost, but the approach has wider applications as it may be applied to, for example, an increase in productive capacity which also involves additional fixed costs. Unlike break-even analysis, marginal costing does not assume that each additional unit imposes the same extra variable cost; each marginal unit is considered separately. To aid decision-making, the marginal cost is compared with marginal revenue and, if there is an excess of revenue over cost, the activity is undertaken as it adds to the aggregate profit.

Sunk costs are those resources which have already been invested in a particular project, and they are ignored when the marginal cost approach is used to aid a decision between alternative courses of action, such as, whether to replace an existing machine or retain it in use. For example, a company which has a machine, still in working order, with a book value of £1m and a scrap value of zero will disregard its written down value if offered a new, technically improved machine at an annual hire charge of £200,000. If the new machine can produce savings in excess of £200,000 per annum it will be hired and the old machine scrapped; the £1m at which the old machine is held in the books is a sunk cost and no outflow of resources will occur if it is replaced by the new machine, then scrapped, and the balance written off. (See Chapter 11, example 16).

Consideration of marginal cost is particularly relevant when prices are determined by the market, especially where separate markets can be differentiated or bids have to be made to obtain work. The marginal cost is the minimum that can be accepted as a selling price, since below this the activity does not recover even its out of pocket expenses. Provided that a sale is made at above marginal cost, some contribution is made to fixed costs and profit. The alternative is to use a full cost approach which attempts to recover in each sale its full share of overhead costs, but this approach might result in orders being lost which would be beneficial to the company.

Example 10.13

Home Ltd. has a maximum productive capacity of 60,000 units but can only sell 50,000 units per year in the home market at a price of £10 each. The variable cost per unit is £6 and the company's annual fixed costs are £150,000. The company has been approached by an exporter who wishes to place an order of 15,000 units a year at a price of £8 each.

REQUIRED:
Prepare a financial statement on which the management of Home Ltd. can base a decision on whether, from the point of view of profitability, the export order should be accepted. No increase in productive capacity is to be made.

Solution:

	Without Export Order £000	With Export Order £000	£000
Variable Cost	50,000 × £6 = 300	60,000 × £6 =	360
Fixed Cost	150		150
Total Cost	450		510
Revenue	50,000 × £10 = 500	45,000 × £10 = 450	
		15,000 × £8 = 120	
			570
Profit	50		60
Average Total Cost	$\frac{450,000}{50,000} = £9$	$\frac{510,000}{60,000} =$	£8.5

In both cases the average total cost per unit is *greater* than the export price. However, acceptance of the export order increases overall profit as its marginal cost (£6 per unit) is less then its marginal revenue (£8 per unit).

10.6 QUESTIONS AND SOLUTIONS

Question 10.1 (Taken from the September, 1980 *Accountancy* paper).

Wrenbury, who has maintained an account with your bank for a number of years, plans to undertake a business venture for which finance is required.

At present, your client is a sales representative and he receives an annual salary of £8,000. He has recently been approached by an official of a company based overseas who offers to supply Wrenbury with a range of goods similar to those he sells on behalf of his present employer. The official claims that the goods he offers are of a higher quality than those currently being marketed in the United Kingdom and, after examining samples, Wrenbury fully agrees with this assessment.

During the course of discussions Wrenbury makes the following comments:

'I will need to maintain stocks of goods costing approximately £4,000. These will have to be delivered during December 1980 if I am to start business in the new year.'

'I have spoken to a number of contacts who have promised me orders amounting to £9,000 and £12,000 respectively for the quarterly periods January/March 1981 and April/June 1981. From July 1981 onwards I expect sales to be steady at a rate of £60,000 per annum.'

'The goods which I will be selling produce, on average, a gross profit of 20 per cent on selling price.'

'I intend to conduct most of my business from home, but I will need additional premises in which to keep the stocks of goods. I have found a small warehouse which I have been told I can use for the period 1 December 1980—31 May 1982 for £540, payable in January 1981. There should be no problem in finding alternative premises if the owner is unwilling to renew these arrangements in 1982. My telephone bill which is at present £50 per quarter, and which amount I will continue to pay privately, will probably rise to £200 per quarter as the result of running the business from my home. I estimate other incidental business expenses at £200 per quarter payable in cash.'

'I will arrange for monthly supplies of goods sufficient to replace items sold. The overseas company is willing to allow two months credit for all supplies, including the initial stocks to be delivered in December, and I will have to offer similar terms to my customers.'

'I will need a van to transport the goods. I can get one delivered in December 1980 for £7,000 provided I pay cash at once. I expect it will last five years and be worth about £2,500 at the end of that time.'

You discover that Wrenbury owns some investments which he purchased recently for £3,200; their present market value is only £2,600. Wrenbury will require the bank to meet all his other cash needs if the project is to be undertaken.

Required:

    (*a*) A cash budget for each of the four quarters of 1981, showing the cash surplus or deficit at the end of each quarter.

    (*b*) An estimated profit statement for 1981.

    (*c*) A reconciliation of the forecast change in the cash position over the next twelve months with the estimated profit figure.

    (*d*) Your reasoned assessment of Wrenbury's proposals.

NOTES:

1. *Ignore taxation.*

2. *Sales and purchases will occur at an even rate during each quarter of 1981.*

3. *Ignore interest on any forecast cash deficit.*

[30]

Solution:

(a)
Cash Budget for 1981

	Jan.–Mar.	April–June	July–Sept.	Oct.–Dec.
	£	£	£	£
Opening deficit	(4,400)	(8,690)	(7,040)	(4,790)
Receipts from sales	3,000	10,000	13,000	15,000
	(1,400)	1,310	5,960	10,210
Payments to suppliers	2,400	8,000	10,400	12,000
	4,000			
Rent	540			
Telephone	150	150	150	150
Other expenses	200	200	200	200
Closing deficit	(8,690)	(7,040)	(4,790)	(2,140)

Opening deficit is £2,600 – £7,000 = £(4,400)

(b)
Profit Statement for 1981

	£	£
Sales		51,000
Less: Opening stock	4,000	
Purchases	40,800	
Less: Closing stock	(4,000)	
Cost of goods sold		40,800
Gross profit (20% of sales)		10,200
Rent	390	
Telephone	600	
Other expenses	800	
Depreciation	900	
		2,690
Net profit		7,510

(c)   *Cash and Profit Reconciliation*

	£	£
Opening cash deficit...		(4,400)
Closing deficit..		(2,140)
Net improvement in cash..		2,260
Add: Investment in: stock		4,000
debtors		10,000
Prepaid rent		150
		16,410
Less: Credit from suppliers	8,000	
Depreciation..	900	
		8,900
Profit..		7,510

(d) Points to be covered include:
  (i) There is a forecast deficit at the year end of £2,140, but this takes no account of:
    (a) interest payable.
    (b) withdrawals for living expenses.
  (ii) The reported profit is £7,510 which is less than his salary. As the reconciliation shows, none of this profit is in the form of cash.
  (iii) In a full year's trading:

	£
Gross profit of 20% of £60,000	12,000
Less: Running expenses..	2,690
Net profit..	9,310

Examiner's Comments:
Area of weakness: 1. The inclusion of private telephone costs.
                      2. The inability to prepare a satisfactory reconciliation in requirement (c).

Question 10.2 (Taken from the April, 1979 *Accountancy* paper).

Canton Ltd. was recently incorporated and plans to commence trading on 1 June 1979. During May the company will issue 200,000 ordinary shares of £1 each at par and the cash will be subscribed at once. During the same month £130,000 will be spent on plant and £50,000 will be invested in stock, resulting in a cash balance on 1 June of £20,000.

Plans for the twelve months commencing 1 June 1979 are as follows:

1. Stock costing £40,000 will be sold each month at a mark-up of 25%. Customers are expected to pay in the second month following the sale.

2. Month-end stock levels will be maintained at £50,000 and purchases will be paid for in the month following delivery.

3. Wages and other expenses will amount to £6,000 per month, payable in the month during which the costs are incurred.

4. Bad debts are expected to be incurred at the rate of 2% of sales.

5. Plant will have a ten-year life and no scrap value. Depreciation is to be charged on the straight line basis.

6. No provision is to be made for corporation tax in view of the capital allowances which are to be claimed in respect of the new plant.

Required:

(*a*) A cash budget for Canton Ltd. which will be sufficient to reveal the maximum overdraft requirement on the basis of the information available. Do not continue the cash budget for more months than necessary.

(*b*) The company's estimated trading and profit and loss account for the year ending 31 May 1980 and estimated balance sheet at 31 May 1980.

(*c*) A calculation of the *additional* sales which would be needed in order to produce *additional* profits sufficient to cover a dividend of 6% on the issued share capital. For this purpose you may regard depreciation and 75% of wages and other expenses as fixed costs and the remainder as directly variable with output.

NOTE: The company's bank has agreed to provide the necessary overdraft facilities

[30]

Solution:

(a)

Cash budget £000

Month	Opening Balance	Sales	Purchases	Wages etc.	Closing Balance
June	20	—	—	6	14
July	14	—	40	6	(32)
August	(32)	49	40	6	(29)

	£
Overdraft at end of August	29,000
Net inflow September–May, 9 × £3,000........	27,000
Overdraft at 31 May, 1980	2,000

(b)   *Estimated Trading and Profit and Loss Account to 31 May, 1980*

	£000
Sales	600
Cost of sales	480
Gross profit (20% of sales)	120

Wages etc.	72	
Depreciation	13	
Bad debts	12	
	—	97

Net profit	23

Estimated Balance Sheet at 31 May, 1980

	£000
Share capital	200
Profit and loss account	23
	223
Creditors	40
Bank overdraft	2
	265

Plant at cost	130
Less: Accumulated depreciation	13
	117
Stock	50
Debtors	98
	265

(c)   *Calculation of Additional Sales Requirement*

	£	£
For additional sales		1.00
Related additional costs: Stock	0.80	
Wages, etc.	0.03	
Bad debts	0.02	
	—	0.85
Contribution		0.15

Sales required to cover a dividend of £12,000: $\dfrac{£12,000}{0.15} = £80,000$

Examiner's Comments:
Area of weakness: 1. Calculation of monthly payments for purchases.
2. Treatment of bad debts.
3. The calculation of the contribution and increased sales in part (c).

Question 10.3 (Taken from the September, 1979 *Accountancy* paper).

The summarised profit and loss account of Orchard Ltd for the year to 30 June 1979 and the summarised balance sheet at that date are as follows:

PROFIT AND LOSS ACCOUNT

	£	£
Sales		200,000
Less variable cost of goods sold:		
Materials consumed	100,000	
Wages & expenses	40,000	140,000
Contribution towards fixed costs:		60,000
Less fixed costs:		
Depreciation	6,000	
Other expenses	50,000	56,000
Net profit		£4,000

BALANCE SHEET

	£		£
Share capital	70,000	Fixed assets at cost ..	160,000
Reserves	46,000	*Less* depreciation	57,000
	116,000		103,000
Creditors for materials ..	30,000	Stock valued at variable	
		cost	35,000
Bank overdraft	32,000	Debtors	40,000
	£178,000		£178,000

The company manufactures a single product and has an available capacity capable of producing up to £300,000 of goods each year, valued at selling price. Any increase in the level of business activity would produce proportionate increases in the level of stocks, debtors and creditors.

The directors of Orchard Ltd are disappointed with the results achieved during the year to 30 June 1979, which represent a return of less than 4% on the equity investment at the beginning of the year. The company is also under strong pressure from its bank to reduce the bank overdraft to £16,000. The directors discover that a demand exists for the product manufactured, significantly in excess of present output.

Required:

Separate calculations to show:

(*a*) the level of sales required during the year to 30 June 1980 in order to produce a net profit of £13,000; and

(*b*) the level of sales required during the year to 30 June 1980 in order to reduce the bank overdraft to £16,000 by that date.

NOTE: *Ignore taxation. No dividends are to be paid during any of the relevant years*

[20]

Solution:

(a)

Target profit	13,000
Fixed costs	56,000
	69,000

Variable costs as a % of sales.................. 70%
Percentage for fixed costs and profit......... 30%

Sales required to produce profit £130,000

$$£69,000 \times \frac{100}{30} = £230,000$$

The above calculation could alternatively have been made using a diagram.

(b) Net funds generated during the year to 30 June, 1980 will be £10,000 (profit and depreciation) if the previous years' results are repeated. In this situation working capital requirements will be unchanged and the overdraft will be reduced to £22,000. A further reduction in the overdraft to £16,000 will require additional sales which will increase the working capital requirements.

	£	£
For every additional £1,000 of sales:		
Funds generated are 30% of £1,000 = ...		300
Additional working capital requirements will be:		
Stock: $1/200 \times 35,000$ = ...	175	
Debtors: $1/200 \times 40,000$ = ...	200	
	375	
Less: Creditors: $1/200 \times 30,000$ = ...	150	
		225
Surplus cash arising from each additional £1,000 of sales is therefore...		75

To reduce the overdraft by £6,000, additional sales must be:

$$\frac{£6,000}{75} \times £1,000 = £80,000.$$

Therefore, the total sales required are £280,000.

Examiner's Comments:

Area of weakness: 1. The calculation of the required cash flow in part (b).
2. The calculation of the contribution to cash flow from additional sales.

CHAPTER 11

Investment Project Appraisal

11.1 INTRODUCTION

Corporate management has funds at its disposal which should be invested to give the maximum possible return. This investment usually involves the outlay of substantial sums of money to acquire productive capacity or maintain existing capacity in working condition. The aim is that the investment will generate an inflow of cash sufficient both to repay the capital invested and to give a satisfactory surplus of profit. Management has to decide which investment projects to undertake, and the manner in which they are to be carried out. Examples of the types of project which may be considered are:

1. *Expansion.* This involves the acquisition of additional fixed assets and the associated working capital. The intention is to generate extra profit from a greater volume of sales, possibly involving the introduction of a new product.

2. *Modernisation.* Modern equipment is acquired with the aim of generating additional profit from the same volume of sales by reducing unit costs; this may in turn allow demand to be stimulated by enabling prices to be cut. The adoption of modern equipment and techniques will also involve reorganisation costs, such as redundancy payments, but may give rise to an offsetting reduction in working capital requirements.

3. *Production Technique.* Management has to decide how to meet an identified demand when there are alternative possibilities, for example, whether to adopt labour or capital intensive production techniques.

4. *Repair or replace.* When a vital machine is in need of repair, management should compare the cost of repair with that of replacing the asset, possibly with a more efficient modern equivalent.

5. *Lease, buy or hire purchase.* There are a number of ways in which the acquisition of fixed assets can be financed, the main alternatives being to buy them outright, to acquire them under a hire purchase agreement, or to lease them. Immediate purchase involves the outlay of the full purchase price, while leasing and hire purchase commit the company to a number of smaller payments spread over a period of time. All three methods of finance secure the services of the fixed assets for the company, and management has to decide which involves the least overall cost.

6. *Capital Repayment.* Companies have to pay interest on loans and dividends on share capital. The most profitable use of funds may be to repay loans or redeem capital so as to avoid the outflows of cash caused by the payment of interest and dividends.

Faced with a number of alternative investments, management has to decide which projects to select, and this decision should be based on the criterion: which best fulfil the firm's objective of maximising profit? It is important that the correct investment decisions are made as, once the investment has been undertaken, the funds are a sunk cost which must be recovered from the profitable use of the assets acquired. An unsuccessful investment will produce undesirable consequences of variable effect depending on the extent of the failure. Where the investment shows little or no return, it will not generate the internal funds required to support a policy of expansion. Moreover, the poor results reported will make it difficult to attract external funds as an alternative source for financing planned further developments. Finally, a project which produces heavy losses will erode the company's capital base and perhaps even cause it to be liquidated.

The selection of poor investment projects has implications not only for the individual company, but also for the economy as a whole. The total of funds available in the economy for investment is limited, and so the selection of one project precludes the adoption of another. If a project which is a commercial failure is undertaken, while one which would have been a success is rejected, the economy receives no stimulus from the creation of additional resources to provide funds for further developments.

This chapter examines a number of techniques which have been developed to help management choose the most appropriate projects, but it must be noted that these techniques are an aid to the decision-making process and do not provide the sole basis of selection. The decisions are based on assumptions about the future which are most unlikely to prove accurate, and managerial skill must be exercised to decide what weight to give to alternative possible outcomes and appraisal techniques. The level of risk must also be included in the evaluation, as, the greater the risk involved, then the greater the return that is required as compensation.

11.2   FORECASTS: SOME FURTHER COMPLICATIONS

Financial forecasts must be prepared to show the likely results of each investment project and, on the basis of these forecasts, management will select the most profitable projects and decide how they are to be implemented. The preparation of forecasts has been dealt with in Chapter 10, but there are two additional factors to consider which are particularly relevant in the case of investment project appraisal, namely, taxation and working capital.

11.2.1   Taxation   The manner in which the acquisition of plant and machinery is financed affects the company's corporation tax liability:

1. When plant and equipment are purchased by a company they attract a 100% first year allowance, that is, their full cost can be written off against profits for tax purposes. (Note that this does not apply to buildings.)
2. When assets are rented or leased, tax relief is obtained by the deduction from each year's taxable profit of the rental or leasing charge for that year.
3. When assets are acquired under a hire purchase agreement, a first year allowance equal to the *cash* price of the assets can be charged as soon as they are brought into use in the business. Tax relief is also received in respect of the interest element of each of the instalments (see example 11.1, option 2).

The effect of tax allowances is to reduce the tax payable by an amount equal to the allowance times the rate of tax. For example, if a company has taxable profits of £6m and the rate of tax is 50%, then the tax payable is £6m × 0.5 = £3m. The acquisition of a machine for £2m, which attracts a 100% first year allowance, reduces the taxable profit to £4m and the tax payable to £4m × 0.5 = £2m. Thus, additional allowances of £2m result in a reduction in the tax bill, and hence in the cash outflow, of £1m. Another way of interpreting the effect of taxation is that the net cost of the machine to the company is £2m (cost) – £1m (tax reduction) = £1m.

When a company sells a fixed asset on which a 100% first year allowance has been claimed (i.e. the asset has been fully written off for tax purposes) the sum received is added to taxable profit and therefore increases the amount of tax payable. For example, if in 19X6 a company sells for £60,000 an asset which cost £1m in 19X1 and on which a 100% first year allowance was received, the taxable profit of 19X6 is increased by £60,000 and, assuming a tax rate of 50%, £30,000 will be added to the tax payable for 19X6.

Care must be taken to allocate the cash effect of the tax saved or charged to the correct time period, as the payment of tax will not necessarily occur in the same year as the underlying transactions. Also taxable profits must be available against which to offset the allowances, for example, if the company is paying no tax, because it has incurred losses, further allowances cannot reduce the non-existent liability. When questions include the taxation aspects of projects, sufficient details will be given (such as, the time lag between transactions and their tax effect, the rate of tax, and the ability of the company to take full advantage of available allowances) to enable conclusions to be reached about the impact of taxation.

Example 11.1

On 30 June 19X3 a machine vital to the production process of Engine Ltd. broke down and was beyond repair. The company has to acquire a replacement machine, which can be obtained in one of the following ways:
1. By cash purchase of £120,000 on 1 July, 19X3.
2. Under a hire purchase agreement which requires a deposit of £40,000 to be paid on 1 July, 19X3 followed by four annual instalments of £30,000 payable on 1 July, 19X4, 19X5, 19X6 and 19X7. Each annual instalment includes an interest payment of £10,000.
3. Under a rental agreement which involves five rental payments of £36,000 on 1 September of each year from 19X3 to 19X7 inclusive.

The following information is relevant:
  (a) Under each alternative the machinery would be installed on 10 July, 19X3 and is expected to remain in use until 1 November, 19X7 when it is intended to re-equip the factory.
  (b) The estimated scrap value of the machine, which will be subject to corporation tax, on 1 November, 19X7 is £6,000.
  (c) The company can claim a 100% first year allowance under options 1 and 2.
  (d) Engine Ltd. is subject to Corporation Tax at the rate of 50% and has enough taxable profits to take full advantage of any allowances at the earliest possible opportunity.

(e) There is a one year time lag between transactions and their effect on tax payable, for example, expenditure in 19X3 reduces the tax payable in 19X4.

REQUIRED

Cash forecasts for each of the years 19X3 to 19X8 inclusive to show the annual net cash effect of each of the three alternative methods of acquisition.

Note: Ignore the time value of money.

Solution *(£000)*

Method 1

	Cash Price	Scrap	Tax	Net
19X3............	(120)	—	—	(120)
19X4............	—	—	60	60
19X5............	—	—	—	—
19X6............	—	—	—	—
19X7............	—	6	—	6
19X8............	—	—	(3)	(3)

Method 2

	Deposit	Instalments	Scrap	Tax	Net
19X3............	(40)	—	—	—	(40)
19X4............	—	(30)	—	60	30
19X5............	—	(30)	—	5 (1)	(25)
19X6............	—	(30)	—	5	(25)
19X7............	—	(30)	6	5	(19)
19X8............	—	—	—	2 (2)	2

Method 3 *(3)*

	Rental	Tax	Net
19X3............	(36)	—	(36)
19X4............	(36)	18	(18)
19X5............	(36)	18	(18)
19X6............	(36)	18	(18)
19X7............	(36)	18	(18)
19X8............	—	18	18

Notes:

1. Computed as follows: tax relief in respect of interest element of each instalment, $10 \times 50\% = 5$.
2. Computed as follows: 5 (tax saved on interest payment) − 3 (tax charged on scrapping of asset) = 2.
3. Under the rental agreement the company does not own the asset and is not entitled to receive its scrap value.

11.2.2 Working Capital Investment projects often involve changes in working capital requirements for stock, debtors and creditors, and these changes have an impact on cash flows (see Chapter 9, section 7.2). The initial investment in working capital causes a cash outflow, while, at the end of the project's life, the cash tied up in working capital is recovered as stocks are run down, amounts due from debtors are collected and creditors are paid. It is normal, and consistent with the idea of prudence, to assume that only a proportion of working capital will be recovered as bad debts and unusable stocks may materialise. In examination questions, full recovery of working capital can be assumed and tax effects of the recovery ignored, unless information to the contrary is given. Where changes in working capital requirements take place during the life of a project, the cash effect must be shown in the forecast.

Example 11.2

The directors of Tin Ltd., a trading company, are considering an investment project which will last for seven years and requires, on 1 January 19X1, the following initial investment in working capital:

	£000
Stock	70
Debtors (net of profit element*).............	100
	170
less: Creditors....................................	60
	110

*In terms of cash flow, the investment consists of the *cost* of the goods supplied to customers.

It is forecast that the price of stock purchased will rise by 10% in June 19X4. In the final year of the project's life it is expected to recover 90% of the value of stock and 95% of the value of debtors.

The cash flows which result from the movements in working capital are:

	Stock £000	Debtors £000	Creditors £000	Net Cash Flows £000
19X1.............	(70)	(100)	60	(110)
19X2.............	—	—	—	—
19X3.............	—	—	—	—
19X4.............	(7)	(10)‡	6‡	(11)
19X5.............	—	—	—	—
19X6.............	—	—	—	—
19X7.............	69.3	104.5	(66)	107.8

‡If the cost of stock rises by 10%, then so will the investment in debtors and the value of creditors unless the credit periods are varied.

11.3 PAYBACK

There are three main methods of investment appraisal: payback, accounting rate of return, and discounted cash flow. This section deals with payback, while accounting rate of return and discounted cash flow are covered in sections 4 and 5 of this Chapter respectively.

The payback technique of investment appraisal is based on the length of time taken by a project to recover its initial investment. It can be operated in two ways: either a company may specify that any project which recovers its capital investment within a given period of time should be accepted, or, when a choice has to be made between projects, the one which has the shortest payback period is selected.

The steps necessary to carry out an appraisal by means of payback are as follows:

1. Calculate the cash flows of each project.
2. Find the length of time for which each project has to operate to recover its initial investment.
3. Select those projects which pay back the initial investment within the specified time, unless there is some restriction in choice, in which case the project with the shortest payback period is selected.

Example 11.3

The directors of Tape Ltd. are considering the following three investment projects:

	Project 1 £000	Project 2 £000	Project 3 £000
Initial Capital Outlay	1,000	1,800	2,000
Cash Inflows, Year: 1	100	400	1,000
2	200	400	1,000
3	300	1,200	—
4	400	600	—
5	500	—	—
6	500	—	—
Total......................	2,000	2,600	2,000

REQUIRED:
(a) Calculate the payback period for each project.
(b) Which projects would be selected if the company specifies that payback must be completed within three years?
(c) Which project would be selected if only one of the three can be undertaken?
Note: Assume cash inflows occur at a uniform rate each year

Solution *(£000)*

  (a) Project 1: 4 years $(100 + 200 + 300 + 400 = 1,000)$.
      Project 2: 2 years 10 months (In year 3 the monthly inflow is 100, hence the payback
         is $400 + 400 + (10 \times 100) = 1,800$).
      Project 3: 2 years $(1,000 + 1,000 = 2,000)$.
  (b) Projects 2 and 3 are undertaken as they recover their costs within three years.
  (c) Project 3 as it has the shortest payback period.

The advantages claimed for payback are:

1. It involves simple calculations and is easy to understand.
2. The projects selected, because they are chosen to recover their costs rapidly, leave the company at risk for the shortest period of time. The initial capital investment reduces the company's cash resources, and so the selection of projects with short payback periods ensures a prompt restoration of liquidity, which may be of critical importance to a company with liquidity problems.
3. The technique implicitly acknowledges that the further into the future predictions are made, the less reliable they are.

The criticisms of payback are:

1. It ignores receipts expected to arise after the end of the payback period, for instance, in example 11.3 above, project 1 eventually creates a total cash inflow equal to 200% of the investment and is rejected, while project 3 is accepted although it only recovers its cost.
2. No account is taken of the timing of receipts, yet, the further into the future cash is expected to arise, the lower is its current value (see section 5.2 of this chapter).
3. The selection of the time period within which an acceptable project must recover its cost is arbitrary.
4. The technique does not take profitability into consideration. In example 11.3, project 3, on the basis of payback, is chosen, even though it gives no surplus.
5. Payback cannot be used to reach decisions where there are no cash inflows, for example, when deciding whether to lease or buy an asset.

In conclusion, the payback technique emphasises the need for projects to recover their costs in a reasonable period of time, but it is not satisfactory if used as the sole criterion. Its results should be assessed in conjunction with the findings from other, more acceptable, methods of investment appraisal.

11.4   ACCOUNTING RATE OF RETURN

The ratio 'Return on Capital Employed' has been discussed previously (see Chapter 8, section 5.3 'Rate of Return on Gross Assets' and Chapter 8, section 5.5 'Rate of Return on Shareholders' Equity'). A similar measure, the 'Accounting Rate of Return' can be used for investment project appraisal. This ratio relates the return, or profit, expected from a project to the amount of capital it employs, and, although there are a number of possible measures, the usual formula for its calculation is:

$$\frac{\text{Average Annual Return}}{\text{Average Capital Invested}} \times 100$$

The average annual return is found by dividing the project's total expected profits by the number of years over which they accrue. The average capital invested is the value of working capital plus half the cost of the initial investment in fixed assets. This is because the investment in working capital has to be maintained throughout the life of the project, while the value of fixed assets is depreciated and reduced to zero by the end of the project; the cash flow represented by depreciation is not required by the project and so is available for alternative investment. Where the split of the initial investment between working capital and fixed assets is not given, it is usual to take half of the value of the whole investment.

Projects are chosen which have an accounting rate of return in excess of a pre-determined level, or, where a choice has to be made between projects, the one with the highest accounting rate of return is preferred.

The steps to carry out the appraisal of an investment project by means of the Accounting Rate of Return are as follows:

1. Calculate the average capital invested in the project.
2. Determine the profits generated by the project.
3. Find the average annual profit of the project.
4. Express the average annual profit (from step 3) as a percentage of the average capital invested (from step 1).
5. Accept projects which have a rate of return in excess of the required level, or, where choice is restricted, select the project with the highest rate of return.

Example 11.4

The following information relates to two investment projects which are under consideration by the directors of Case Ltd.:

	Project A £000	Project B £000
Investment in: Working Capital............................	500	400
Fixed Assets...................................	1,000	1,600
Anticipated Profit: Year 1	540	200
Year 2..	440	300
Year 3..	330	400
Year 4..	130	600
Year 5..	—	600
Total..	1,440	2,100

REQUIRED:
   (a) A calculation of the accounting rate of return for each project.
   (b) Which of the projects would be accepted if the required accounting rate of return is 30%?
   (c) Which project would be accepted if they are mutually exclusive, that is, only one of them can be undertaken?

Solution *(£000)*

(a)	Project A	Project B
Working capital investment	500	400
Fixed asset investment × ½	500	800
Average capital invested (Step 1)	1,000	1,200
Total profit (Step 2).......................	1,440	2,100

Average annual profit (Step 3) .... $\dfrac{1,440}{4} = 360$ $\dfrac{2,100}{5} = 420$

Accounting rate of return (Step 4) ..... $\dfrac{360}{1,000} \times 100 = 36\%$ $\dfrac{420}{1,200} \times 100 = 35\%$

   (b) Both projects, A and B, would be undertaken as their accounting rates of return exceed the required minimum.
   (c) Project A would be undertaken as it has the higher accounting rate of return.

The advantages of the accounting rate of return as a technique of investment project appraisal are:
   1. It brings into consideration the profits earned over the whole life of the project.
   2. It allows the comparison of projects which require different amounts of initial capital investment.
   3. The idea of return on capital employed is generally understood, and this aids the comprehension of the accounting rate of return.

4. The minimum required rate of return can be set with reference to the cost of the finance used by the company plus the additional return it requires for its own profit.

The main disadvantage of this appraisal technique is that the timing of profit arising from alternative projects is ignored; for instance, in example 11.4 the technique is indifferent to the fact that project A has high early profits which reduce over the life of the project whereas project B earns the majority of its profit towards the end of its life.

11.5 DISCOUNTED CASH FLOW (DCF)

Disadvantages of the payback and accounting rate of return methods of investment appraisal include the facts that payback ignores cash flows arising after the payback period, while the accounting rate of return takes no account of the timing of cash flows. DCF techniques provide a means of overcoming these problems by expressing all cash flows in terms of a common point in time. To carry out a DCF appraisal, it is necessary to:

1. Prepare an annual cash forecast for each project under consideration. (The techniques involved in this have been covered in Chapter 10 and section 2 of this chapter.)
2. Develop a means of expressing monetary flows, which take place over a period time, on a common basis; this is done by calculating the time value of money, which is considered in section 5.1 of this chapter.

11.5.1 The Time Value of Money

A person who invests money in a bank deposit account expects to receive interest; for example, if £100 is deposited for one year at 10% interest, at the end of the year £110 is available to be withdrawn; the additional £10 is compensation for parting with £100 for one year. To the person willing to make this investment, £100 today is worth £110 in one year's time; this shows that money has a time value. Moreover, the longer the investor has to wait to withdraw the deposit, then the greater the compensation required. The rate of interest will also vary with the amount of risk attached to the investment; the greater the risk, then the greater the return required.

As well as calculating the amount to which a present sum will grow in the future, as a result of interest being added, it is possible to express sums receivable in the future in terms of their present value. This can provide useful information for all kinds of decisions. For example, an individual might want to know how much to set aside now in order to produce £1,000 which he intends to give to his daughter on her eighteenth birthday in one year's time. If he can invest money at 12%, he must set aside $\dfrac{£1,000}{112} \times 100 = £893$.

In one year's time he will receive back his £893 plus interest of £893 × 12% = £107 to give the required total of £1,000.

The examples given so far have only dealt with time periods of one year; to accommodate periods of two years or more it is necessary to use compound interest which, each year, adds interest to the initial sum deposited plus accumulated interest at the beginning of the year. For example, at 10% interest a sum of £100 will grow to £133.1 after three years:

	£
Initial deposit: 1.1.19X1	100
Interest: 19X1	10
Accumulated sum: 31.12.19X1	110
Interest: 19X2	11
Accumulated sum: 31.12.19X2	121
Interest: 19X3	12.1
Accumulated sum: 31.12.19X3	133.1

Alternatively, the present value of £133.1 receivable in three years' time, at 10% interest, is £100.

The computation of a present value, given a sum of money receivable some years in the future and a rate of interest, is a complicated process, and so discount tables have been developed which show the present value of £1 receivable at various times in the future and at different rates of interest. An example of such a table is given in figure 11.1. (There are also tables available which ease the calculation of future values, although this is a rather more straightforward, albeit time-consuming, process, for example, the above calculation of the value of £100 invested for three years at 10%.)

Figure 11.1

Table of Factors for the Present Value of £1

Years	10%	11%	12%	13%	14%	15%	16%	17%	18%	19%	20%	21%	22%
1	0.909	0.900	0.893	0.885	0.877	0.870	0.862	0.855	0.847	0.840	0.833	0.826	0.820
2	0.826	0.812	0.797	0.783	0.769	0.756	0.743	0.731	0.718	0.706	0.694	0.683	0.671
3	0.751	0.731	0.712	0.693	0.675	0.658	0.641	0.624	0.609	0.593	0.579	0.564	0.551
4	0.683	0.659	0.636	0.613	0.592	0.572	0.552	0.534	0.516	0.499	0.482	0.467	0.451
5	0.620	0.594	0.567	0.543	0.519	0.497	0.476	0.456	0.437	0.419	0.402	0.386	0.370

The discount table is used to calculate the present value of sums receivable or payable in the future, by identifying the appropriate 'interest rate' column and then finding the factor relating to the future date on which the money is to be received. Continuing the example of £133.1 receivable in three year's time at 10% interest, the relevant factor is 0.751 and the present value of £133.1 is £133.1 × 0.751 = £100. In this way the present value of any future sum can be determined, provided that the required rate of interest is known.

11.5.2   The Cost of Capital   The rate of interest applicable to a company's investment projects has to be decided upon to enable the use of discounting techniques. The appropriate interest rate is the cost of the finance provided to the company by shareholders and other investors, as investment projects have to earn a return at least sufficient to pay the interest on the funds they utilise. The main sources of finance and their costs to the company are:

1. Ordinary Shares. Shareholders receive a return on their investment in the form of dividends, and so the cost of equity finance is found by the formula:

$$\frac{\text{Dividends for the year (interim plus final)}}{\text{Shareholders' equity}} \times 100$$

2. Preference Shares. These carry a fixed rate of dividend, and this is their cost.

3. Debenture and Other Loans. The rate of interest on these is fixed, but, unlike dividends, the interest charge is an allowed expense for corporation tax purposes. Therefore, the net cost to the company is the rate of interest paid less tax relief, and is calculated by the formula:

$$\text{Rate of Interest} \times (1 - \text{Tax Rate})$$

For example, if a company has debentures which carry interest at the rate of 13% and pays corporation tax at 52%, the cost after tax is $13\% \times (1 - 0.52) = 6.24\%$.

4. Overdrafts. The interest payable fluctuates, but is allowed as an expense against taxable profit and so is reduced to find the after tax cost in the same way as debenture interest.

It is unusual for a company to rely on a single type of finance for each investment project, and so it is necessary to find the average cost of the capital used, which is known as the Weighted Average Cost of Capital (WACC) and is calculated as follows:

Step:
1. Calculate the after tax cost of each type of capital used by the company.
2. Ascertain the proportion of the total sources of finance represented by each type.
3. Multiply the cost of each type of capital (from step 1) by its proportion or weight (from step 2).
4. Add together the weighted costs (from step 3); the total is the WACC.

Example 11.5

The long term capital structure shown in the balance sheet of Duck Ltd. at 31 December, 19X1 is:

	£,000
Ordinary shares of £1 each............	1,000
Reserves...................................	500
7% Preference shares...................	250
10% Debentures	600
	2,350

The company regularly declares, per share, an interim dividend of 8 pence and a final dividend of 9 pence and pays corporation tax at a rate of 52%.

The WACC is calculated as follows:

Type of Finance	Value £,000	(A) After Tax Cost (Step 1)	(B) Weight (Step 2)	(A × B) WACC (Steps 3 and 4)
Equity	1,500	$\dfrac{8+9}{100} \times 100 = 17\%$	$\dfrac{1,500}{2,350} = 0.64$	10.88
Preference Shares...	250	7%	$\dfrac{250}{2,350} = 0.11$	0.77
Debentures	600	$10 \times (1 - 0.52) = 4.8\%$	$\dfrac{600}{2,350} = 0.25$	1.20
	2,350		1.00	12.85

The company's WACC is 12.85 but, as discount tables give factors only for whole numbers, it is usual to round the WACC to the nearest whole number, in this case 13%.

In example 11.5, the cost of the different types of capital and their weights is based on the balance sheet of the company, which relates to the past, whereas new projects will have to meet the cost of their finance in the future. The use of past costs and weights is acceptable when the company intends to maintain the same capital structure and can raise capital at the same cost as its existing funds. If the company intends to finance a project by raising capital in different proportions than in the past, or the costs of capital are different, then the weights and costs applicable to the new capital should be used.

Example 11.6

The directors of Goose Ltd. are considering whether to undertake an investment project at a cost of £½m. It is intended to finance the project as follows:

	£000	Pre Tax Cost %
Equity...................	200	17
Debentures............	200	13
Overdraft	100	15
	500	

Assume a corporation tax rate of 52%.

The WACC for the project is:

Type of Finance	After Tax Cost (%)	Weight	WACC
Equity..	17	0.40	6.80
Debentures.....................................	$13 \times (1 - 0.52) = 6.24$	0.40	2.50
Overdraft..	$15 \times (1 - 0.52) = 7.20$	0.20	1.44
		1.00	10.74

The project's WACC is 11% (to the nearest whole number), and this figure should be used for its appraisal.

11.5.3 Net Present Value (NPV)

This technique of investment project appraisal takes the cash flows which are expected to result from the adoption of a proposal and expresses them in terms of present value by the application of discount factors based on the company's required rate of return. For this purpose, the initial investment, assuming it takes place immediately, is already expressed in terms of its present value and does not need to be discounted. Future cash flows are discounted by applying factors which assume they arise at the end of the year in which they take place. This is an artificial assumption, but, it must be remembered, the calculations are intended only to provide a guide for decision-making and do not claim to be precise. The sum of the present values, including the initial investment which is a negative figure, is the NPV of the project.

The steps to carry out the appraisal of an investment project by means of NPV are as follows:

1. Determine the rate at which the project's cash flows are to be discounted. This may involve the computation of the company's WACC.
2. Identify the cash flows relevant to the project.
3. Select the appropriate discount factors from the table provided with the examination question.
4. Discount the cash flows (from step 2) using the appropriate discount factors (from step 3).
5. The project is accepted if it has a positive NPV, unless choice is restricted, in which case the project with the highest NPV is chosen (see below).

Example 11.7

An investment project involves an initial investment of £0.9m and produces an annual inflow of £0.5m for three years. The appropriate discount rate is 10%.

It is convenient to present the calculation of an NPV in the following tabular format:

Step 1: The discount rate is given as 10%.

Year	Step 2 Cash Flow (£000)	Step 3 Discount Factor (from figure 11.1)	Step 4 (Step 2 × Step 3) NPV (£000)
0	(900)	1.000	(900)
1	500	0.909	455
2	500	0.826	413
3	500	0.751	375
			343

Step 5: The project has a positive NPV of £0.343m and is accepted.

Note: An element of rounding of figures is acceptable in DCF techniques as it is based on a number of assumptions and forecasts. To work to the nearest pound or fraction of a pound suggests an accuracy which does not exist.

The significance of a positive NPV is that it shows the project is expected to generate a surplus, expressed in terms of present value, after all of its costs, including interest and the amount invested, have been recovered.

Where a choice has to be made between alternative projects which involve similar investments, the one with the greatest positive NPV is selected. However, if the projects involve different capital outlays, then it is useful to calculate the 'Profitability Index' as a guide to reaching an investment decision. This index shows, for each project, the present value generated by each £1 invested, and is calculated using the formula:

$$\text{Profitability Index} = \frac{\text{Present Value of Cash Inflows}}{\text{Capital Invested}}$$

Example 11.8

A company, with a cost of capital of 13%, is considering three projects which have the following cash flows (£m):

Project	A	B	C
Initial Investment	2.0	2.0	3.0
Cash Inflows: Year 1	0.6	1.0	1.3
Year 2	0.7	0.9	1.8
Year 3	0.8	0.9	1.6

REQUIRED:
Calculations to indicate which project the company should undertake if it is only able to adopt one of them.

Solution (£m)

Year	Discount Factor (Figure 1)	Project A Cash Flow	Project A Present Value	Project B Cash Flow	Project B Present Value	Project C Cash Flow	Project C Present Value
1	0.885	0.6	0.531	1.0	0.885	1.3	1.151
2	0.783	0.7	0.548	0.9	0.705	1.8	1.409
3	0.693	0.8	0.554	0.9	0.624	1.6	1.109
			1.633		2.214		3.669
Initial Investment			2.000		2.000		3.000
NPV			(0.367)		0.214		0.669
Appraisal on basis of NPV			Reject		Accept		Accept
Profitability index			—		$\frac{2.214}{2} = 1.11$		$\frac{3.669}{3} = 1.22$

Project C is accepted as it has the higher profitability index as well as the higher NPV.

The NPV technique can also be used where a company is faced with alternative ways of achieving the same objective, for example, whether to rent or buy a piece of equipment. Since this type of decision gives rise to cash outflows, but not cash inflows, the procedure is to reduce the cash outflows to their present values, and the option with the *smallest* total present value is chosen.

Example 11.9 (Taken from the September, 1982 *Accountancy* paper).

Sorter Ltd. requires some new equipment to help to manufacture a product for a period of four years, commencing 1 January 1983. The accounts of Sorter Ltd. are prepared on the calendar year basis. At the end of four years, demand for the product will collapse and the company will be unable to make any further use of the equipment.

The equipment required by Sorter Ltd. can be obtained in any one of three ways.

(i) The equipment could be purchased for cash on 1 January 1983.

(ii) The equipment could be acquired under a hire purchase contract which requires a deposit to be paid on 1 January 1983, and three further instalments at annual intervals following the date of the initial deposit.

(iii) The equipment could be rented, commencing 1 January 1983.

You are given the following financial information and facts relevant to an assessment of the three alternatives:

1. The cash price of the equipment is £50,000.

2. The equipment will have no resale value at the end of the four year period.

3. The deposit required under the hire purchase contract is £26,000.

4. The annual instalments payable under the hire purchase contract are £13,000, and each payment includes an interest element of £5,000.

5. The annual rental of the equipment, payable in arrears each year, is £20,000.

6. You may assume that Sorter Ltd. is subject to corporation tax at the rate of 50% and that the tax is payable one year following the end of the accounting period to which the assessment relates.

7. The company will be entitled to claim a 100% first year allowance on the cash price of the equipment under options (i) and (ii), and it is the company's policy to claim maximum capital allowances as soon as they become available.

8. Sorter Ltd's estimated cost of capital over the four year period is 15 per cent per annum.

Required:

(a) Calculations showing the best method of acquisition on the basis of the available information.

[16]

(b) A brief discussion of any further matters which might be taken into consideration when making a decision.

[4]

FACTORS FOR THE PRESENT VALUE OF £1 APPLYING A DISCOUNT RATE OF 15%

Year	15%
1	0.870
2	0.756
3	0.658
4	0.572
5	0.497

[Total marks for question: 20]

Solution

(a)   (i) *Cash Purchase*

Years	Purchase price £	Tax saving £	Net cash flow £	Discount factor £	Present value £
0	(50,000)		(50,000)	1,000	(50,000)
2		25,000 (W1)	25,000	0.756	18,900
					(31,100)

(ii) *Hire Purchase*

Years	Payments £	Tax saving £	Net cash flow £	Discount factor £	Present value £
0	(26,000)		(26,000)	1,000	(26,000)
1	(13,000)		(13,000)	0.870	(11,310)
2	(13,000)	25,000 (W1)	12,000	0.756	9,072
3	(13,000)	2,500 (W2)	(10,500)	0.658	(6,909)
4		2,500	2,500	0.572	1,430
5		2,500	2,500	0.497	1,242
					(32,475)

(iii) *Rent*

Years	Rentals £	Tax saving £	Net cash flow £	Discount factor £	Present value £
1	(20,000)		(20,000)	0.870	(17,400)
2	(20,000)	10,000 (W3)	(10,000)	0.756	(7,560)
3	(20,000)	10,000	(10,000)	0.658	(6,580)
4	(20,000)	10,000	(10,000)	0.572	(5,720)
5		10,000	10,000	0.497	4,970
					(32,290)

Workings
W1. First year allowance of 100% reduces the corporation tax liability by
£50,000 × 50% = £25,000.
W2. Interest element of £5,000 allowable for tax at 50%.
W3. Rental, £20,000, allowable for tax at 50%.
On the basis of the above analysis, the cash purchase option would be selected as its
associated cash flows have the lowest NPV.

(b) Points for consideration:
   1. Availability of cash. Option (i) has the lowest present value but requires an
      immediate outlay of £50,000.
   2. Costs of maintaining and repairing the equipment. If these are borne by the
      lessor, option (iii) may be relatively more attractive.
   3. Certainty of demand for the product continuing over the four year period
      Renting may give the option of returning the equipment if demand does not come
      up to expectations.

Examiner's Comments:

Areas of weakness:
1. The calculation of the tax effects of the alternatives and their impact on cash flows.
2. In many cases the separate elements of cash flow were discounted and the resulting present values summed to find the present value. Time is saved, and there is less chance of error, if the net cash flow is calculated prior to discounting.
3. The interpretation of the results was weak, with failure to specify the criterion for selection.
4. In part (b) there was a failure to appreciate that the results of the calculations were only one of a number of matters to consider when reaching a decision.

Where the cash flows arising from a project are the same each year, it is not necessary to discount them separately. The present value factors for the years in which the cash flows occur are added together, and the annual cash flow is multiplied by the aggregate factor which results. Tables exist which provide the cumulative values of various factors; an example is given in figure 11.2, column B.

Figure 11.2 *Cumulative Discount Factors (12%)*

Years	A Present value of £1 $(1+r)^{-n}$	B Present value of £1 received per year $\dfrac{1-(1+r)^{-n}}{r}$
1	0.893	0.893
2	0.797	1.690
3	0.712	2.402
4	0.636	3.038
5	0.567	3.605
6	0.507	4.112
7	0.452	4.564
8	0.404	4.968
9	0.361	5.329
10	0.322	5.651

Column B can be derived from column A, for example, the column B factor for three years, 2.404, is the sum of the first three factors in column A ($0.893 + 0.797 + 0.712 = 2.402$).

For example:
(a) If a project is to be appraised at 12% and produces an annual cash inflow of £0.5m for five years, the present value of the inflow is £0.5m × 3.605 = £1.8m.
(b) If a project with a life of six years is to be appraised at 12% and produces an annual cash inflow of £0.75m for the first three years of its life and £0.45m for the last three years, the present value of the inflow is: (£0.75m × 2.402) + (£0.45m × (4.112 − 2.402)) = £2.57m

11.5.4 DCF Yield or Internal Rate of Return (IRR) The IRR of a project is the rate of return at which its cash flows must be discounted to give an NPV of zero. Again, it is assumed that the cash flows, other than the initial investment, take place at the end of the year in which they arise. Projects are accepted if their IRR is greater than the company's cost of capital, or, where the number of projects to be undertaken is restricted, the projects with the greatest IRR are chosen. The IRR can be found by trial and error using a variety of different interest rates. This is a laborious process, and a reasonable estimate can be obtained if the results for two rates of interest are available, one of which gives a negative and the other a positive NPV.

The steps to appraise a project by the IRR method are:
1. Find the project's cash flows.
2. Calculate the project's NPV at two discount rates, one of which gives a positive and the other a negative result.
3. Compute the discount rate which gives an NPV of zero.
4. Accept the project if its IRR is in excess of the company's cost of capital. Where choice is restricted, the project with the highest IRR is selected.

Example 11.10

The expected cash flows of an investment project which requires an initial investment of £2.8m are:

Year	£m
1	0.7
2	0.8
3	0.9
4	0.8
5	0.7

The IRR is calculated as follows:

Steps 1 and 2:

Year	Cash Flow (£m)	10% Discount Factor	NPV (£m)	15% Discount Factor	NPV (£m)
1	0.7	0.909	0.636	0.870	0.609
2	0.8	0.826	0.661	0.756	0.605
3	0.9	0.751	0.676	0.658	0.592
4	0.8	0.683	0.546	0.572	0.458
5	0.7	0.620	0.434	0.497	0.348
			2.953		2.612
Initial Investment......................			(2.800)		(2.800)
NPV			0.153		(0.188)

Step 3:

The information found from the above can be represented diagrammatically:

%	15	IRR	10
NPV.........	(0.188)	0	0.153

The IRR of this project lies between 10% and 15%, at a discount rate which produces a zero NPV. The two discount rates used as reference points produce NPVs that differ, in total, by £0.341m (0.153 + 0.188). Since a 10% discount rate gives a positive NPV of £0.153m, the IRR is above 10% and is computed as follows:

$$\text{IRR} = 10\% + \left(\frac{0.153}{0.341} \times 5\%\right) = 12.24\% \text{ (12\% to the nearest whole number)}$$

Step 4:

If the project's cash flow forecast is discounted at 12%, it is found to have an NPV of zero, and so the project is accepted if the company's cost of capital is 12% or less.

Often examination questions requiring the calculation of the IRR also require candidates to compute the NPV. In these circumstances, the NPV should be the first calculated, and the IRR can then be found by using these results together with one other NPV based on a different discount rate.

Example 11.11 (Taken from the April, 1981 *Accountancy* paper).

The directors of Carter Ltd. have decided to undertake a programme of expansion. They have under consideration two mutually exclusive five year projects and intend to invest in the project which offers the greater financial gain. Project I requires an initial capital investment of £140,000 and Project II an initial capital investment of £280,000. The annual net cash flows which are expected to arise from the project are as follows:

Year	Project I	Project II
1	£30,000	£100,000
2	£60,000	£90,000
3	£60,000	£90,000
4	£60,000	£90,000
5	£24,155	£53,706

Required:

   (a) Calculations of the net present value of each of the two projects, assuming a 12 per cent cost of capital.

   (b) Calculations of the discounted cash flow yield (internal rate of return) of each of the two projects.

   (c) Compare and comment on the results of your calculations under (a) and (b). You should support your analysis with relevant numerical calculations.

Notes:
   1. The capital investment will be undertaken immediately and the annual cash flows may be assumed to arise at the year end.
   2. Ignore taxation.

Table of Factors for the Present Value of £1.

Years	12%	13%	14%	15%	16%	17%	18%	19%	20%	21%	22%
1	0.893	0.885	0.877	0.870	0.862	0.855	0.847	0.840	0.833	0.826	0.820
2	0.797	0.783	0.769	0.756	0.743	0.731	0.718	0.706	0.694	0.683	0.671
3	0.712	0.693	0.675	0.658	0.641	0.624	0.609	0.593	0.579	0.564	0.551
4	0.636	0.613	0.592	0.572	0.552	0.534	0.516	0.499	0.482	0.467	0.451
5	0.567	0.543	0.519	0.497	0.476	0.456	0.437	0.419	0.402	0.386	0.370

[30]

Solution

(a) *Net Present Value*

		Project I			Project II	
Year	Cash Flow £	Discount Factor 12%	Present Value £	Cash Flow £	Discount Factor 12%	Present Value £
0	(140,000)	1.000	(140,000)	(280,000)	1.000	(280.000)
1	30,000	0.893	26,790	100,000	0.893	89,300
2	60,000	0.797	47,820	90,000	0.797	71,730
3	60,000	0.712	42,720	90,000	0.712	64,080
4	60,000	0.636	38,160	90,000	0.636	57,240
5	24,155	0.567	13,696	53,706	0.567	30,451
			29,186			32,801

(b) Internal Rate of Return

	Project I			Project II		
Year	Cash Flow	Discount Factor 21%	Present Value	Cash Flow	Discount Factor 21%	Present Value
	£		£	£		£
0	(140,000)	1.000	(140,000)	(280,000)	1.000	(280,000)
1	30,000	0.826	24,780	100,000	0.826	82,600
2	60,000	0.683	40,980	90,000	0.683	61,470
3	60,000	0.564	33,840	90,000	0.564	50,760
4	60,000	0.467	28,020	90,000	0.467	42,030
5	24,155	0.386	9,324	53,706	0.386	20,731
NPV			(3,056)			(22,409)

Project I	Project II
IRR: $12\% + \left(\dfrac{29,186}{3,056+29,186} \times 9\%\right)$	$12\% + \left(\dfrac{32,801}{22,409+32,801} \times 9\%\right)$
$= 20\%*$	$= 17\%*$

*To the nearest whole percent.

Check:

	Project I			Project II		
Year	Cash Flow	Discount Factor 20%	Present Value	Cash Flow	Discount Factor 17%	Present Value
	£		£	£		£
0	(140,000)	1.000	(140,000)	(280,000)	1.000	(280,000)
1	30,000	0.833	24,990	100,000	0.855	85,500
2	60,000	0.694	41,640	90,000	0.731	65,790
3	60,000	0.579	34,740	90,000	0.624	56,160
4	60,000	0.482	28,920	90,000	0.534	48,060
5	24,155	0.402	9,710	53,706	0.456	24,490
			—			—

(c) At first sight the above calculations would seem to be of little help to the directors of Carter Ltd. in reaching an investment decision. Calculations under (a) show that Project II possesses the higher NPV and, on that basis, it is the superior investment. Project I however, gives the higher IRR and has a profitability index of 1.21 compared with that for Project II of 1.12; on these bases Project I is the superior investment (see also discussion after examiner's comments).

Examiner's Comments

Areas of Weakness:
1. The initial investment was frequently not deducted when calculating the NPV.
2. Very few students were able to calculate the IRR.
3. Part (c) was answered poorly, probably because of an inability to produce answers to both parts (a) and (b).

When the two DCF techniques, NPV and IRR, produce different results, a further calculation may be made to help reach a decision where the project requiring a lower investment produces a higher IRR. In these circumstances, it is necessary to calculate the incremental return earned on the additional investment required by the larger project and compare this with alternative investment opportunities. This calculation for Carter Ltd., which could be shown in answer to section (c) of example 11.11, is:

Year	Cash Flow Project I £	Cash Flow Project II £	Cash Flow Project II–I £	Discount Factor 13%*	NPV £
0	(140,000)	(280,000)	(140,000)	1.000	(140,000)
1	30,000	100,000	70,000	0.885	61,950
2	60,000	90,000	30,000	0.783	23,490
3	60,000	90,000	30,000	0.693	20,790
4	60,000	90,000	30,000	0.613	18,390
5	24,155	53,706	29,551	0.543	16,046
					666

*Found by the IRR technique or by trial and error.

The additional cash flows which arise under Project II represent a return of approximately 13% on the additional initial investment. This shows that Project II produces the same return as Project I (20%) on an equivalent amount of funds and a return of 13% on the remainder, which is in excess of the cost of capital. Therefore, Project II would be undertaken if no other investment was available which yields a return in excess of 13%.

11.5.5   The Impact of Inflation   Where the relevant information is given in the question, inflation should be taken into account when appraising capital projects. The rate of return which a company has to pay to its investors, the 'money cost', comprises two elements: it gives them compensation for parting with their cash for a period of time, which is known as the 'real cost of capital', and also recompenses them for the erosion in value which the money they invest undergoes as a result of inflation. If, with inflation, selling prices rise at least as fast as costs, the future cash inflows available to meet the capital and interest commitments of the company, which were established at the start of the project, also increase. In order to calculate the present value of a project, it is therefore necessary to ensure that both the discount rate and the cash flows are computed on the same basis. That is, they must either both be computed on a 'real' basis, or on a 'money' basis. These two approaches are now described.

1. *Use the Real Cost of Capital*

The cash flows of the project must be forecast at current prices, that is, on the assumption that there is to be no inflation. These amounts are then discounted at the real cost of capital, which is calculated by the formula:

$$\text{Real Cost of Capital} = \frac{m - i}{1 + i}$$

Where: m = money cost of capital

i = the rate of inflation

Example 11.12

A company has a money cost of capital of 19% and the expected annual inflation rate is 7%. It is considering an investment project which has a life of 5 years, costs £1m and generates an annual cash inflow of £0.3m at year 1 prices.

The company's real cost of capital is $\dfrac{0.19 - 0.07}{1 + 0.07} = 11\%*$

*To the nearest whole percent.

The NPV of the project is £ – 1m + (0.3 × 3.696†) = £0.11m, and so the project is accepted.

Note: If the project is discounted at 19%, the NPV is £ – 1m + (0.3 × 3.057†) = £ – 0.8m. The project would be rejected when, in fact, its cash flows will probably increase over the years because of inflation and so it will generate a surplus.

†The cumulative discount factor is derived from figure 11.1.

2. *Prepare the Cash Forecast in Monetary Terms*

The cash flows which are actually expected to take place are forecast, and these are discounted using the money cost of capital.

Example 11.13

A company is considering an investment project which costs £2.3m and produces an annual cash inflow, at current prices, of £0.8m for 4 years. The company's money cost of capital is 15%, and the expected rate of inflation is 6%.

The project's cash flows, in monetary terms, are:

Year	Cash Flow* £m	Present Value Factor 15% (figure 11.1)	Net Present Value £m
0	(2.300)	1.000	(2.300)
1	0.848	0.870	0.738
2	0.899	0.756	0.680
3	0.953	0.658	0.627
4	1.010	0.572	0.578
			———
			0.323
			———

*Adjusted assuming an annual inflation rate of 6%.

The NPV is positive and the project is accepted.
Note: If the cash flows are not adjusted, the NPV is £ − 2.3m + (0.8 × 2.856) = £ − 0.015m and a potentially profitable project is rejected.

Remember that care must be taken to match either the real cost of capital with cash flows which have not been adjusted for inflation, or the money cost of capital with monetary flows, that is, ones which are inflation adjusted.

Example 11.14 (taken from the April, 1983 *Accountancy* Paper).

Stamford Ltd. specialises in the production of plastic sports equipment. The company has recently developed a new machine for automatically producing plastic cricket bats. The machine cost £150,000 to develop and install, and production is to commence at the beginning of next week. It is planned to depreciate the £150,000 cost evenly over four years after which time production of plastic cricket bats will cease. Production and sales will amount to 30,000 bats each year. Annual revenues and operating costs, at April 1983 prices, are estimated as follows:

	£
Sales (£9·60 each)	288,000
Variable manufacturing costs	200,000

This morning a salesman has called and described to the directors of Stamford Ltd. a new machine ideally suited to the production of plastic cricket bats. This item of equipment is distinctly superior to Stamford's own machine, reducing variable costs by 30% and producing an identical product. The cost of the machine, which is also capable of producing 30,000 cricket bats per annum, is £190,000.

Assume the following:

1. Annual revenues and operating costs arise at the year end.
2. The general rate of inflation is 10% per annum.
3. The company's *money* cost of capital is 21%.
4. The existing machine could be sold immediately for £12,000.
5. If purchased, the new machine could be installed immediately.
6. Either machine would possess a zero residual value at the end of four years.

Required:

(a) Calculations of the net present value of the two options open to management using the *real* cost of capital. [22]

(b) Advice to the management as to which course should be followed, and an explanation of the significance of your calculations under (a). [8]

NOTE: Ignore taxation.

[Total marks for question—30]

Table of factors for n=4 years

Interest rate (per cent)	Present value of £1	Present value of £1 received per year
r	$(1+r)^{-n}$	$\dfrac{1-(1+r)^{-n}}{r}$
10	0·68	3·17
11	0·66	3·10
12	0·64	3·04
13	0·61	2·97
14	0·59	2·91
15	0·57	2·85
16	0·55	2·80
17	0·53	2·74
18	0·52	2·69
19	0·50	2·64
20	0·48	2·59
21	0·47	2·54
22	0·45	2·49

Solution

(a) (i) *'Real cost of capital'* $= \dfrac{m-i}{1+i} = \dfrac{0.21-0.10}{1+0.10} = 10\%$

where m = money cost of capital
i = inflation rate

(ii) *Annual contribution*

	Present machine £	New machine £
Sales	288,000	288,000
Variable costs	200,000	140,000
Contribution	88,000	148,000

(iii) *Present values:*

	£
Present machine:	
Annual contribution, £88,000 × 3.17	278,960
New machine:	
Annual contribution, £148,000 × 3.17	469,160
Scrap value of present machine	12,000
	481,160
Less: Cost	190,000
	291,160

(b) *Comments*

(i) The sales revenues and operating cash flows are expressed in real terms, rather than the actual amounts expected to be received, and so the cost of capital should be computed on a similar basis. A money rate of 21% is equivalent to a real rate of 10%, assuming general inflation is running at 10% per annum.

(ii) The new machine produces the higher return and seems to be the better choice. The main problem is that this option calls for an immediate outlay of £190,000, (less any sale proceeds from the present machine), whereas the present machine has been installed and no further capital outlay is called for. The differential between the present values is relatively small and, unless management is extremely confident that its estimates of sales revenue and operating costs will be fulfilled, it would probably be advisable to retain the present machine.

Examiner's Comments

Areas of weakness:
1. Many students did not appreciate the need to adjust for inflation.
2. The calulation of the annual contributions is simple, but was not done very well.
3. The majority of students failed to treat the cost of the existing machine as a sunk cost.
4. Depreciation was often included, wrongly, as part of the annual cost of the new machine.
5. The comments in section (b) relied too heavily on repeating the results of the appraisal and failed to explain them, as was requested.

11.5.6   Conclusion   The various applications of DCF discussed above show that, compared with other methods of investment appraisal, DCF has the advantage of bringing into consideration all of the cash flows associated with a project and also takes account of the timing of the cash flows. Against these advantages must be weighed the complexity of the technique which makes it difficult

to comprehend. There is a danger that, with their possible lack of understanding, managers will place too much reliance on its results. Like all investment appraisal techniques, it is based on estimates which are converted into numerical forecasts and are subject to error. The results of DCF analysis should be used by management as a guide, but should not be the sole criteria. Other, over-riding, factors which may have to be taken into account are:

1. The availability of cash. If a company is short of cash, it may have to lease an asset rather than purchase it, even if the latter is shown to be the better option on the basis of a DCF calculation.
2. Corporate policy may favour acquiring assets from a particular supplier or country.
3. Government policy may favour the acquisition of 'home' produced assets, and may even favour a particular supplier.
4. The ready supply of spare parts may be assured for one machine while not for another. The former may be chosen for that reason, even if it is not the one indicated by DCF appraisal techniques.
5. Some options which are acceptable on a DCF basis may not be acceptable to employees on, for example, the grounds of health and safety.
6. When the replacement of individual machines is considered, it may be desirable to maintain compatability with existing machines.

11.6 ERRORS IN FORECASTS

Management must recognise that the forecasts, on the basis of which investment appraisal is undertaken, will not be achieved precisely if the project is accepted. All aspects of the forecast are subject to error, for example:

1. *Errors in capital estimates:*
   (a) The investment in fixed assets and/or working capital may be greater or smaller than expected.
   (b) The period of time needed to acquire the fixed assets may be forecast inaccurately. Any delay in the start of revenue inflows reduces their present values.
   (c) The life of the fixed assets may be misjudged.

2. *Errors in trading estimates*
   (a) The forecast volume of sales may not materialise.

(b) The expected selling price per unit may not be achieved.
(c) Costs may differ from forecasts.
(d) Cash flows may arise earlier or later than expected.
(e) The total life of the project may be misjudged.

3. *Government Policy*
   (a) A change in tax rates, structure or capital allowances can have a significant impact on a project's cash flows and their timing.
   (b) Governments may impose restrictions which affect the company's exports.

Prior to undertaking a project, the significance of likely errors can be investigated. Appraisal may be undertaken on the alternative assumptions that the best likely or worst likely results are achieved, or the technique of 'Sensitivity Analysis' may be used. This technique involves the calculation of how far each element, taken individually, of the forecast can differ from expectations before the project becomes unacceptable. As the effect of variation in each separate element is examined, the other variables are held constant. The amount of error which is acceptable before a project is rejected can be weighed against the expected accuracy of the forecasts, and sensitivity analysis shows the areas in which a project is particularly vulnerable.

Example 11.15

The directors of Shovel Ltd. are considering the following investment project:

Capital Investment..............	£1.25m
Annual Cash Inflow............	£0.45m
Life of Project...................	5 years

The directors are positive that the company's cost of capital is 12%, but are concerned that, in the past, forecasts have proved inaccurate. They wish you to calculate the extent to which each variable can differ from the forecast before the project is rejected on the basis of an NPV appraisal.

Solution

The NPV of the project, based on the above forecasts is:

$$£ - 1.25m + (0.45m \times 3.605*) = £0.372m$$

*From figure 11.2.

The project will be rejected if the NPV is less than 0, so the amount of acceptable variation can be computed as follows:

1. *Capital Investment (CI)*
   The project remains acceptable provided that the capital investment does not rise above the level where CI + (£0.45m × 3.605) = 0.

   This occurs when capital investment is a negative figure which equals £0.45m × 3.605 = £1.622m.

   Therefore, the amount of acceptable upward variation in the capital investment is:

$$\frac{1.622 - 1.25}{1.25} = 30\%$$

2. *Annual Cash Flow (CF)*
   The project remains acceptable provided that cash flow does not fall below the level where £ − 1.25m + (CF × 3.605) = 0.

   This occurs when $CF = \left(\frac{£1.25m}{3.605}\right) = £0.347m$

   Therefore, the amount of acceptable downward variation in the annual cash flow is:

$$\frac{0.45 - 0.347}{0.45} = 23\%$$

3. *Life of Project*
   The project remains acceptable provided that CDF (representing the 12% cumulative discount factor) does not fall below the level where £ − 1.25m + (0.45 × CDF) = 0.

   This occurs when $CDF = \left(\frac{1.25}{0.45}\right) = 2.778$

   From the discount table in figure 11.2, it can be found that the cumulative discount factor for three years at 12% is 2.402, and that for four years is 3.038.

   The shortest acceptable life is $4 - \frac{3.038 - 2.778}{3.038 - 2.402} - 3.6$ years

   Therefore, the amount of acceptable downward variation in the life of project is:

$$\frac{5 - 3.6}{5} = 28\%$$

Once a project is undertaken, it is important that management establishes accounting systems to monitor its results. The resource flows which actually take place should be recorded under the same headings as were used for the project's appraisal so that their amount and timing can be compared with the forecast. This comparison will highlight deviations from the forecast, which enables management to take possible remedial action and also provides a useful contribution to current investment appraisals by indicating areas which have proved difficult to forecast accurately.

11.7 QUESTIONS AND SOLUTIONS
The various types of investment decisions faced by management are described in section 1 of this chapter, and the following two questions examine the use of DCF techniques to help achieve the most

effective use of available resources. Hartford Ltd. involves a decision between two alternative methods of producing a greater output, whereas the directors of Mercury Ltd. have to decide whether to keep existing equipment, or whether to replace it by purchasing or leasing a new machine. In both questions the basic steps are the same, namely, to identify the alternatives, to ascertain their related cash flows, and to reduce the cash flows to their present value.

Question 11.1 (Taken from the April, 1980 *Accountancy* paper).

Hartford Limited has for many years supplied a product designated Louton to various parts of the United Kingdom. The following budgeted profit statement for Louton covering the forthcoming twelve month period has recently been prepared for the directors.

Budgeted Profit Statement

	£	£
Sales (300,000 units at £3 per unit)		900,000
Less: *Variable costs:*		
Materials (300,000 units at £1 per unit) ..	300,000	
Labour (300,000 units at £0·60 per unit) ..	180,000	
Fixed costs:		
Depreciation	100,000	
Administration expenses etc.	260,000	840,000
Net profit		60,000

The demand for Louton is stable and the long-range planning department had forecast that these results would be achieved for each of the next ten years. Since the budget was prepared, however, Hartford's major competitor has been taken over by a large international company which has decided that the manufacture of Louton should be discontinued. Rather than attempt to limit demand to currently available supplies by raising the price of Louton the directors of Hartford Limited have decided to expand their scale of operations. Two possible ways of satisfying the excess demand, estimated at 100,000 units per annum for each of the next ten years, have been identified:

(1) *Evening shift*

Existing plant is operating at full capacity during the day shift, but an increase in output could be obtained by working an evening shift. This would involve paying employees at a rate equal to one-and-a-half times the amount paid for day work. Material costs per unit would be the same as is budgeted for existing output; total 'administration expenses etc.' for the production of Louton would increase by £40,000.

(2) *Construct new plant*

The company could construct additional plant with a capacity to produce 100,000 units of Louton per annum. It would take two years to build the plant and construction costs would be incurred as follows:

Year 1 ..   ..   .. £80,000

Year 2 ..   ..   .. £86,000

The company would use the new plant to produce the additional output from the beginning of year 3. Material costs and labour costs per unit would be the same as is budgeted for the existing output. Total 'administration expenses etc.' for the production of Louton would increase by £20,000. The new plant would be depreciated at the rate of £20,000 per annum in order to reduce it to an expected scrap value of £6,000 at the end of its useful life. If this option is chosen the company will, nevertheless, work the evening shift during the construction period.

Under either alternative additional working capital requirements will amount to £100,000.

Assume that:

(i)   The cost of capital to Hartford Limited in all relevant years is 15 per cent per year.

(ii) The investment in working capital would be made immediately; all other payments and receipts would be made at the end of the appropriate years.

(iii) One hundred per cent first year allowances could be obtained for the construction costs in year 1 and year 2 if it is decided to construct new plant. The company has sufficient profits from other activities against which to offset these capital allowances for taxation purposes. Tax liabilities are paid twelve months after the accounting period in respect of which they accrue. The tax rate is 50 per cent.

Required:

(a) A numerical analysis of the financial implications of

(i)   working an evening shift; and

(ii) constructing new plant in order to satisfy the excess demand.

(b) A brief discussion of the relative merits of the two alternatives based on your calculations under (a).

NOTE: Ignore taxation except in relation to the first year allowances, as indicated above.

[30]

Table of factors for r = 15 per cent.

Years	Future value of £1	Present value of £1	Present value of £1 received per year	Annual value of £1 received now
n	$(1 + r)^n$	$(1 + r)^{-n}$	$\dfrac{1-(1 + r)^{-n}}{r}$	$\dfrac{r}{1 - (1 + r)^{-n}}$
1	1·150	0·870	0·870	1·150
2	1·322	0·756	1·626	0·615
3	1·521	0·657	2·283	0·438
4	1·749	0·572	2·855	0·350
5	2·011	0·497	3·352	0·298
6	2·313	0·433	3·785	0·264
7	2·660	0·375	4·160	0·240
8	3·059	0·327	4·487	0·223
9	3·518	0·285	4·772	0·210
10	4·046	0·247	5·019	0·199

Solution

(a) (i) *Evening shift*

	£	£
Annual net cash flow:		
Sales, 100,000 × £3		300,000
Less costs: Materials and labour 100,000 × £1.90	190,000	
Additional overheads	40,000	
		230,000
		70,000

Present value of cash flows expected to arise over the next ten years:

		£
Annual net cash inflow, £70,000 × 5.019		351,330
Working capital disinvested at the end of year 10, £100,000 × 0.247		24,700
		376,030
Less: Working capital investment at outset		100,000
		276,030

(ii) *Construct New Plant*

	£	£
Annual net cash flow, years 3–10:		
Sales...		300,000
Less costs: Materials and labour 100,000 × £1.60	160,000	
Additional overheads....................................	20,000	
		180,000
		120,000

Present value of net cash flows expected to arise over the next ten years:

Annual net cash inflows:		
Years 1 and 2 £70,000 × 1.626		113,820
Years 3–10 £120,000 × (5.019 – 1.626)............................		407,160
Tax savings:		
Year 2 £80,000 × 0.756 × 50%		30,240
3 £86,000 × 0.657 × 50%		28,251
Working capital disinvested at the end of year 10 plus disposal value of		
plant, £106,000 × 0.247		26,182
		605,653
Less: Working capital investment	100,000	
Investment in plant: Year 1, £80,000 × 0.870..............	69,600	
Year 2, £86,000 × 0.756..............	65,016	
		234,616
		371,037

(b) The net present value of the second alternative is much higher but it would appear to involve greater risk. The company would have to spend an estimated £166,000 on the construction of new plant over the next two years. If there is significant doubt regarding the reliability of the estimated surplus demand, working an evening shift would appear to be the safer option.

Examiner's Comments

Areas of weakness:
1. Many students discounted each item of cash flow separately.
2. The treatment of the impact of tax allowances was weak.
3. In a number of cases, no attempt was made to discount the cash flows.

Question 11.2 (Taken from the September, 1978 *Accountancy* paper).

The directors of Mercury Ltd. are considering whether to replace the company's equipment for the manufacture of pobbles.

Pobbles are currently made on equipment which cost £20,000 14 years ago. The equipment's remaining useful life is estimated at six years and the net receipts from manufacturing pobbles can be assumed to continue at £12,000 per year for that period. The net receipts comprise sales minus costs of production, but no deductions have been made for depreciation or tax.

A leading company has approached Mercury Ltd. with an offer of new equipment. The equipment would be leased to Mercury Ltd. for £9,000 per year, payable at the *beginning* of each year in which the equipment is leased. The leasing contract would be effective for six years. The directors of Mercury Ltd. estimate that the equipment would produce £21,000 per year in net receipts (defined as above, but before lease payments).

The manager of Mercury's pobble-making department has discovered that new equipment identical to that offered by the leasing company can be purchased for £40,000. The purchased equipment would have a useful life of six years. Annual net receipts would be the same as if the equipment were leased, except that £1,000 per year would have to be spent on maintenance—which in the leasing arrangement would be covered by the actual leasing charge.

If either leasing or purchase were undertaken the old equipment would be sold for £2,000. No tax would be payable on that receipt.

Assume the following:

(1) In any sale or purchase of equipment the appropriate payment would be received or made immediately, and annual amounts would occur at the end of the appropriate years except where specifically stated to the contrary.

(2) Working capital is provided by creditors, and can therefore be ignored in the options open to the company.

(3) Mercury Ltd. will be subject to 50 per cent. corporation tax and will pay tax on taxable profits one year after those profits are earned. Taxable profits will be the company's net receipts after deduction of leasing charges or maintenance costs where appropriate. If the new equipment is purchased the company will get a 100 per cent. capital allowance on the purchase price to set against taxable profits. The company's profits from other sources would be sufficient to ensure that relief is received in full for the year in which the equipment is acquired (i.e. the tax relief can be treated as a receipt at the end of the second year).

(4) Mercury's cost of capital after tax in all relevant years is 12 per cent. per year.

Required:

(a) A numerical analysis of the options available to Mercury Ltd.

(b) Brief comments on the implications of your results, including reservations where necessary.

[30]

Table of factors for r = 12 per cent.

Years n	Future value of £1 $(1 + r)^n$	Present value of £1 $(1 + r)^{-n}$	Present value of £1 received per year $\dfrac{1 - (1 + r)^{-n}}{r}$	Annual value of £1 received now $\dfrac{r}{1 - (1 + r)^{-n}}$
1	1·120	0·893	0·893	1·120
2	1·254	0·797	1·690	0·592
3	1·405	0·712	2·402	0·416
4	1·574	0·636	3·037	0·329
5	1·762	0·567	3·605	0·277
6	1·974	0·507	4·111	0·243
7	2·211	0·452	4·564	0·219
8	2·476	0·404	4·968	0·201
9	2·773	0·361	5·328	0·188
10	3·106	0·322	5·650	0·177

Solution:

(a) *(£000)*

Keep Present Machine

Year	Net Cash Inflow	Tax	Net Cash Flow	Discount Factor	NPV
1	12		12	0.893	10.716
2	12	(6)	6		
3	12	(6)	6		
4	12	(6)	6	3.218*	19.308
5	12	(6)	6		
6	12	(6)	6		
7		(6)	(6)	0.452	(2.712)
					27.312

*Cumulative discount factor for years 2 to 6 (0.797 + 0.712 + 0.636 + 0.567 + 0.507) or (4.111 − 0.893).

Lease New Machine

Year	Lease Payments	Net Receipts	Tax	Sale of Present Machine	Net Cash Flow	Discount Factor	NPV
0	(9)			2	(7)	1.000	(7.000)
1	(9)	21			12	0.893	10.716
2	(9)	21	(6)		6		
3	(9)	21	(6)		6		
4	(9)	21	(6)		6	2.712*	16.272
5	(9)	21	(6)		6		
6		21	(6)		15	0.507	7.605
7			(6)		(6)	0.452	(2.712)
							24,881

*3.605 – 0.893.

Buy New Machine

Year	Purchase Price	Net Receipts	Tax	Sale of Present Machine	Net Cash Flow	Discount Factor	NPV
0	(40)			2	(38)	1.000	(38.00)
1		20			20	0.893	17.86
2		20	10		30	0.797	23.91
3		20	(10)		10		
4		20	(10)		10		
5		20	(10)		10	2.421*	24.22
6		20	(10)		10		
7			(10)		(10)	0.452	(4.52)
							23.47

*4.111 – 1.690.

(b) An appraisal of the alternatives on the basis of NPV suggests that the existing machine should be kept as this produces the highest NPV. However, by the end of the period under review it will be 20 years old, and so its reliability can be questioned, especially as new machines designed to perform the same job have an expected useful life of only 6 years.

 The choice between leasing and buying a new machine, if this course of action is selected, marginally favours leasing. The directors may decide to acquire the new machine, in which case the difference between the NPVs is so small that the choice may be decided by other factors, such as, whether the company has the cash available for outright purchase.

 Reservations can be expressed about all aspects of the forecasts as they are all subject to uncertainty.

Examiner's Comments

Areas of weakness:
1. Many students did not realise that to keep the existing machine is an available alternative.
2. Some time was wasted by failure to use cumulative discount factors for periods of constant annual cash flow.
3. The treatment of the impact of tax caused problems.
4. Depreciation was often, wrongly, included as a cash outflow.

APPENDIX

PREPARING FOR THE EXAMINATION AND EXAMINATION TECHNIQUE

Preparing for the Examination
Some Advice:
1. Work steadily throughout the preparation period. Accountancy is not a subject that you can 'mug up' in the last month or two. It requires serious application throughout the entire period of study leading to the examination.
2. Revise as you go along. This is important for two reasons. First, many of the topics are inter-related, e.g. ratio analysis and funds flow analysis, and it is therefore important to check that you have a thorough understanding of one topic before you proceed to the next. Secondly, it re-inforces the learning process and helps to ensure that you have not forgotten, by the time of the examination, aspects of accountancy studied some months previously.
3. Study past examination papers. The format of the examination is fairly standardised and so students should familiarise themselves with the normal method of presentation employed.
4. Work a past paper under examination conditions a week before the examination. This will prove a very useful experience in preparation for the 'real thing'.

Examination Technique
The pass mark is 51%. Very many candidates obtain marks around this figure; either just above or just below. None of the matters listed below are going to help the poor candidate to pass, but they can produce the few extra marks which make the difference between pass and fail for the student who has completed a period of serious study.
1. Take care when deciding which questions to attempt. Fifteen minutes reading time is allowed at the start of the examination. Read through the questions and make sure that you understand exactly what the examiner expects you to do. Students often find it useful to read the requirements first, and then to read through the question. Only when you are

fully familiar with each problem is it possible to make a rational choice between them. Many candidates fail because they choose a wrong question, and then waste time before rejecting it and switching to an alternative.

2. Read the whole of each question carefully; failure to do so can result in an unnecessary loss of marks, for example, requirement (iii) of question 4 in the April 1982 paper required candidates to calculate the 'percentage return on gross assets'. There are a number of possible interpretations of capital employed, but a note to the question defined it as 'gross assets', which was shown as a separate item in the balance sheet. Nevertheless, many candidates used different figures for capital employed, including the totally unacceptable 'issued share capital'.

3. Make sure that you attempt four questions; if you attempt only three questions, you are significantly increasing the standard which you must achieve on each of these in order to obtain a pass. The reason why students often attempt only three questions is because they believe they can do those well, but could only make a 'stab' at the fourth question and so do not bother. This is a mistake for two reasons. Firstly, a student sitting an examination is not in the best position to judge how well he or she can do a question. We know, from our own experience, that an examinee can be surprised how many marks were obtained on particular questions, and also disappointed with results on others. Secondly, even a 'stab' at the fourth question can produce the marks needed to turn a marginal fail into a pass.

4. Leave yourself time to make a reasonable attempt at each question. As a general guide:

$$
\begin{array}{llr}
\text{30 mark questions:} & \text{50 minutes each} = & 100 \\
\text{20 mark questions:} & \text{35 minutes each} = & 70 \\
\text{'Cushion'} & & 10 \\
\hline
& & 180 \\
\hline
\end{array}
$$

Often, students attempt first the question they think they can do best. This is quite acceptable, but do not get carried away and devote an excessive amount of time in the attempt to produce the perfect answer. If you become stuck on a question, leave it incomplete and move on to the next. If a reasonable amount of time and effort has already been allocated to the question, much further valuable time can be wasted struggling to get the extra few marks which will probably remain elusive anyway. You can of course always go back to the unfinished question later if you have time.

5. Presentation. Take a little time to consider the best method of presenting the data before writing it down. For example, question 5 of the April 1982 paper, reproduced as example 10.3 in this book, required candidates to prepare a monthly cash budget for Regent, a trader. The solution to this question is best presented using a matrix format with receipts and payments along one axis and the months of the year along the other. This format produces at least three advantages: it

(a) saves time which is often wasted writing out a separate ledger account for each month.

(b) reduces the likelihood of error. For instance there should be an entry each month, for some items, and the matrix will clearly reveal any errors of omission.

(c) improves comparability. For instance, the maximum and minimum overdraft can be identified at a glance.

For similar reasons, the columnar format should, wherever possible, be used where candidates are required to present accounting statements for a number of consecutive periods, see question 3.1 (Warmington Ltd) taken from the September 1980 *Accountancy* examination paper.

6. Show workings. Often a figure appearing in an answer is the product of a series of calculations and, unless workings are shown, it is impossible for the examiner to assess how many marks should be awarded. For example, the calculation of goodwill arising on consolidation in question 1 of the April 1982 paper, reproduced as question 5.2 in this book, is as shown overleaf:

Calculation of Goodwill:

	£000	£000
Price paid		600*
Less: Dividend received		45*
		555

Less: Value of business acquired:

Share capital	400*	
Reserves	120*	
Revaluation surplus	140*	

Proportion of shares acquired ¾* × 660 = 495

Goodwill.. 60

Six marks were awarded for the calculation; one for each item marked with a *. Where an error was made, it was possible to award a fair portion of the marks allocated only where workings were submitted showing clearly how the figure for goodwill had been computed.

7. Don't worry if it doesn't balance. As demonstrated above, marks are awarded for the calculations which are made as a preliminary step before preparing accounting statements. Marks are also awarded for the form and content of the statements, but none are awarded simply because the accounts balance, and time should not be wasted striving to achieve equality.

8. The analysis and discussion of financial information should be clear and to the point. No marks are awarded for irrelevant material, and valuable time will be wasted presenting it.

9. Write legibly. Remember that the examiner has to be able to read your answers in order to assess them. Presentation is therefore important, but don't waste time writing out answers a second time if the original version is clearly legible, even if a little untidy. Also, do not waste time applying correcting fluid, simply rule through the offending entry and clearly insert the replacement entry in a convenient location.

10. In the examination, DON'T BE PUT OFF BECAUSE IT SEEMS A DIFFICULT PAPER. Remember, everyone is 'in the same boat' and the well prepared candidate, who perseveres, will pass.

Index